RESPONDING TO IMPERFECTION

RESPONDING TO IMPERFECTION

THE THEORY AND PRACTICE
OF CONSTITUTIONAL AMENDMENT

Sanford Levinson, Editor

PRINCETON UNIVERSITY PRESS   PRINCETON, NEW JERSEY

Copyright © 1995 by Princeton University Press
Published by Princeton University Press, 41 William Street,
Princeton, New Jersey 08540
In the United Kingdom: Princeton University Press,
Chichester, West Sussex
All Rights Reserved

Library of Congress Cataloging-in-Publication Data

Responding to imperfection : the theory and practice of
constitutional amendment / Sanford Levinson, editor.
p.   cm.
Includes index.
ISBN 0-691-08657-5 (cl. : acid-free paper)
ISBN 0-691-02570-3 (pa. : acid-free paper)
1. United States—Constitutional law—Amendments.
2. Constitutional amendments.   I. Levinson, Sanford, 1941– .
KF4555.A75R47   1995
342.73′03—dc20
[347.3023]   94-27766   CIP

This book has been composed in Galliard

"Crude Foyer" from *Collected Poems* by Wallace Stevens,
copyright 1947 by Wallace Stevens, is reprinted
by permission of Alfred A. Knopf, Inc.

Princeton University Press books are printed
on acid-free paper and meet the guidelines
for permanence and durability of the Committee
on Production Guidelines for Book Longevity
of the Council on Library Resources

Printed in the United States of America

10 9 8 7 6 5 4 3 2 1

10 9 8 7 6 5 4 3 2 1
(Pbk.)

TO THE MEMORY OF

Judith Shklar _____

WHO FEARLESSLY ANALYZED
THE MEANING OF LEGALISM
IN THE LATE TWENTIETH CENTURY

Contents

Acknowledgments   ix

One
Introduction: Imperfection and Amendability
Sanford Levinson   3

Two
How Many Times Has the United States Constitution Been
Amended? (A) < 26; (B) 26; (C) 27; (D) > 27: Accounting for
Constitutional Change
Sanford Levinson   13

Three
Constitutionalism in the United States: From Theory to Politics
Stephen M. Griffin   37

Four
Higher Lawmaking
Bruce Ackerman   63

Five
Popular Sovereignty and Constitutional Amendment
Akhil Reed Amar   89

Six
The Plain Meaning of Article V
David R. Dow   117

Seven
Amending the Presuppositions of a Constitution
Frederick Schauer   145

Eight
Merlin's Memory: The Past and Future Imperfect of the
Once and Future Polity
Walter F. Murphy   163

Nine
The Case against Implicit Limits on the Constitutional
Amending Process
John R. Vile   191

Ten
The "Original" Thirteenth Amendment and the Limits to
Formal Constitutional Change
  Mark E. Brandon   215

Eleven
Toward a Theory of Constitutional Amendment
  Donald S. Lutz   237

Twelve
The Politics of Constitutional Revision in Eastern Europe
  Stephen Holmes and Cass R. Sunstein   275

Thirteen
Midrash: Amendment through the Molding of Meaning
  Noam J. Zohar   307

Appendix: Amending Provisions of Selected
New Constitutions in Eastern Europe   319

Contributors   325

Index   327

Acknowledgments

I AM GRATEFUL to various program chairs of the American Political Science Association, who allowed me to organize panels over a four-year period that explored various aspects of the issues surrounding constitutional change and the notion of "amendment." Several of the papers in this volume were first presented in that venue, and others were suggested by the discussions that ensued. A key participant in two of those panels was Will Harris, of the University of Pennsylvania. Unfortunately, circumstances made it impossible for him to contribute to this volume, but no one should doubt the immense impact—reflected explicitly in several of the essays—that he has had on those who study the theory of constitutional amendment. Chapter Four of his book *The Interpretable Constitution* is essential reading for anyone who shares these interests (as is, indeed, the entire book).

As always, the University of Texas Law School was supportive in every way, not least by giving me the opportunity to teach a seminar on the metatheory of constitutional amendment. My secretary, Cheryl Harris, is unending in her conscientiousness and good cheer, which made preparation of the final manuscript much easier.

I am also grateful to Malcolm DeBevoise of Princeton University Press for his consistent encouragement of this project, and for his toleration of the inevitable delays attached to edited collections. I appreciate as well Lois Krieger's thoughtful copy editing. Most of all, though, I must thank the contributors themselves, who participated in this project with unfailing cooperation.

RESPONDING TO IMPERFECTION

One

Introduction: Imperfection and Amendability

SANFORD LEVINSON

ON JUNE 11, 1787, George Mason of Virginia opened the discussion of constitutional amendment at the constitutional convention in Philadelphia with a forthright statement that "the plan now to be formed will certainly be defective, as the Confederation has been found on trial to be. Amendments therefore will be necessary, and it will be better to provide for them, in an easy, regular and Constitutional way than to trust to chance and violence."[1] Almost exactly five months later, as the new constitution drafted in Philadelphia was beginning to wend its uncertain path through the ratification conventions of the thirteen states, George Washington expressed importantly similar sentiments in a letter to his nephew, Bushrod Washington (who would be appointed by John Adams to the U.S. Supreme Court). "The warmest friends and the best supporters the Constitution has," admitted the president of the Philadelphia convention, whose stature was responsible for much of the legitimacy that both it and its handiwork enjoyed, "do not contend that it is free from imperfections; but they found them unavoidable and are sensible if evil is likely to arise there from, the remedy must come hereafter." Fortunately, "there is a Constitutional door open" to such remedies. "The People (for it is with them to Judge) can, as they will have the advantage of experience on their Side, decide with as much propriety on the alterations and amendment which are necessary." Indeed, wrote our national paterfamilias, "I do not think we are more inspired, have more wisdom, or possess more virtue, than those who will come after us."[2]

The title of this collection, *Responding to Imperfection*, is a recognition of Washington's and Mason's wisdom. One should not minimize the importance of their acknowledgment of imperfection. Surely more than a few founders of political orders have been tempted to adopt John Locke's conceit, when he drafted the 1669 Fundamental Constitutions

[1] Max Farrand, *The Records of the Federal Convention of 1787* (New Haven: Yale University Press, 1937), 1:202–3.

[2] Letter of George Washington to Bushrod Washington, November 10, 1787, in Michael Kammen, ed., *The Origins of the American Constitution: A Documentary History* (New York: Penguin Books, 1986), p. 83.

of Carolinas, that "these fundamental constitutions shall be and remain the sacred and unalterable form and rule of government . . . forever."[3] It was a fundamental breakthrough in American constitutional theory, manifested originally in the drafting of state constitutions, that the "rules of government" would be decidedly "alterable" through a stipulated legal process.[4] Indeed, Gordon Wood has described the very notion of an amendment process as the "institutionaliz[ation] and legitim[ation of] revolution."[5]

This truly radical implication of the notion of amendment is more than a little frightening, and James Madison can perhaps be viewed as trying to return to a more Lockean emphasis on inalterability when he emphasizes in *The Federalist*, No. 49 the need for "a reverence for the laws" that should, consequently, lead us to reject any frequent recourse to popular appeals that "would carry an implication of some defect in the government."[6] As Stephen Griffin argues in his essay in this book, the success in achieving Madison's sacralization of the Constitution may well have been purchased at a price of discouraging recognition of its all-too-present imperfections and/or blinding us to the ways that we have in fact responded to those imperfections by significantly, if sometimes stealthily, modifying our constitutional principles.

In any event, perhaps the basic questions within any jurisprudential system will be, first, the *substantive* criteria by which one in fact defines imperfection and, then, the *procedural* means by which one responds to any such recognitions.[7] How does (or should) presumptively necessary change take place within a given legal order? These are, obviously, analytically separable questions—one is descriptive, the other normative. Both are, however, central to this book.

[3] *The Fundamental Constitutions of Carolinas* § *120*, in Benjamin P. Poore, ed., *The Federal and State Constitutions, Colonial Charters, and Other Organic Laws of the United States*, 2d ed. (1878), p. 1408, quoted in Russell L. Caplan, *Constitutional Brinkmanship: Amending the National Convention* (New York: Oxford Univerity Press, 1988), p. 14.

[4] See Willi Paul Adams, *The First American Constitutions: Republican Ideology and the Making of the State Constitutions in the Revolutionary Era* (Chapel Hill: University of North Carolina Press, 1980), pp. 139–44.

[5] Gordon Wood, *The Creation of the American Republic, 1776–1787* (Chapel Hill: University of North Carolina Press, 1969), p. 614.

[6] *The Federalist*, No. 49, in Clinton Rossiter, ed., *The Federalist Papers* (New York: Mentor, 1961), pp. 314–15. See Sanford Levinson, "'Veneration' and Constitutional Change: James Madison Confronts the Possibility of Constitutional Amendment," *Texas Tech Law Review* 21 (1990): 2443, for a fuller elaboration of the arguments made in this paragraph.

[7] I am well aware that this distinction between substance and procedure can easily (and often properly) be "deconstructed." It is, however, a distinction that we in fact cannot do without, as a pragmatic matter, which is how it is used in the text above.

As Washington noted, the framers of the Constitution themselves indirectly acknowledged the possibility of imperfection by including within it Article V, which provides a procedure of amendment. Given the frequency with which Article V will be cited in the articles below, it is probably most efficient to set it out in full here (and, concomitantly, to ask the reader to return here when necessary in order to consult the specific text of Article V):

Article V

The Congress, whenever two thirds of both Houses shall deem it necessary, shall propose Amendments to this Constitution, or, on the Application of the Legislatures of two thirds of the several States, shall call a Convention for proposing Amendments, which, in either Case, shall be valid to all Intents and Purposes, as part of this Constitution, when ratified by the Legislatures of three fourths of the several States, or by Conventions in three fourths thereof, as the one or the other Mode of Ratification may be proposed by the Congress; Provided that no Amendment which may be made prior to the Year One thousand eight hundred and eight shall in any Manner affect the first and fourth Clauses in the Ninth Section of the first Article; and that no State, without its Consent, shall be deprived of its equal Suffrage in the Senate.

Article V raises a host of important questions. Consider only the following:

1. Can an individual state, prior to the collective ratification by three-quarters of the states, rescind its ratification, thus negating whatever prior approval it might have given to a proposed amendment? This is not at all an abstract hypothetical, for, of course, several of the states that ratified the Equal Rights Amendment (ERA) in the 1970s attempted to rescind their ratification. However, because the constitutionally re-quired number of thirty-eight states was never reached, under *any* defi-nition, before the time period for ratification expired, the country was not called upon definitively to resolve the issue.

2. How much control does Congress possess over the process of rati-fication? After all, Congress *extended* the time for ratification of the ERA for an additional three years beyond the initially promulgated seven years. Many scholars attacked the constitutionality of the extension, though, again, the ultimate failure of the ERA to gain ratification mooted the question as a practical matter.

3. How long do states have to ratify amendments, assuming that Congress does not specify a time limit? This question was made decid-edly nonhypothetical in regard to what was originally the second of the twelve amendments proposed by Congress in 1789, which required an intervening election before a congressional pay raise could take effect.

Only the initial third through twelfth amendments were ratified by 1791, and they, of course, are now known as the Bill of Rights. Nonetheless, states sporadically ratified the original second amendment, and in 1992 Michigan became the thirty-eighth state to ratify it. Given a union of fifty states, that meant that three-quarters of these states, in a process extending from 1789 to 1992, had ratified it. Several commentators, supported by dictum in a significant case decided in 1921 by the U.S. Supreme Court, suggested that the original second amendment had "died" at some point between 1789 and 1992 because of a constitutionally unspecified, but nonetheless inferrable, requirement of "contemporaneous ratification."[8]

4. Should one wish answers to questions about rescission, extension, and time limits for ratification, who should give them? The courts? Congress? (To name only two candidates.)

5. What if the states do in fact coordinately call for a new constitutional convention? Could its agenda be limited to any given topics mentioned by the states, or would the convention have *plenary* power, free in effect to be as wide-ranging in defining imperfection and proposing potential solutions as was the Philadelphia convention, which went far beyond its ostensible mandate simply to "revise" the Articles of Confederation? And who would set the rules by which the convention operated (e.g., majority vote of states or majority vote of delegates, to name only one issue)?

All of these questions are of vital importance and have spawned a significant scholarly literature.[9] It is important to state at the outset, though, that this book will only tangentially touch on them. To treat them with the depth they deserve would require a volume at least as long again as the one you now hold in your hands, and this, for better or worse, seemed inadvisable. This book, then, is not principally about what might be termed the "internal" structure of Article V, that is, the

[8] See Dillon v. Gloss, 256 U.S. 358, 374–75 (1921). I discuss the issue further in Sanford Levinson, "Authorizing Constitutional Text: On the Purported Twenty-Seventh Amendment," *Constitutional Commentary* 11 (1994): 101.

[9] I offer some exemplary citations, but no one should believe that these exhaust the field: Caplan, *Constitutional Brinkmanship*; Walter Dellinger, "The Recurring Question of the 'Limited' Constitutional Convention," *Yale Law Journal* 88 (1979): 1623, and "The Legitimacy of Constitutional Change: Rethinking the Constitutional Amendment Process," *Harvard Law Review* 97 (1983): 386; Ruth Bader Ginsburg, "Ratification of the Equal Rights Amendment: A Question of Time," *Texas Law Review* 57 (1979): 919; Grover Rees III, "Throwing Away the Key: The Unconstitutionality of the Equal Rights Amendment Extension," *Texas Law Review* 58 (1980): 875; Laurence Tribe, "A Constitution We Are Amending: In Defense of a Restrained Judicial Role," *Harvard Law Review* 97 (1983): 433.

basically procedural questions raised by recourse to the Article as a mode of constitutional amendment.

Instead, the focus of this volume involves somewhat different questions, even if most of the essays necessarily make reference at various points to Article V. For example, a central focus of several of these essays concerns the *exclusivity* of Article V as a method of bringing about amendment. Everyone concedes that Article V sets out *a* way by which the Constitution can be changed. Is it also *the* way? Or are there alternative means of achieving fundamental change within the American constitutional system? As a descriptive matter, can one possibly understand the changes that have undoubtedly occurred within that system by reference only to the mechanisms of Article V?

This last question is answered with a vigorous no by both Bruce Ackerman and Stephen Griffin. Both point to the presence of truly fundamental changes within the American political system that have taken place outside of the channels provided by Article V. If one agrees with them, at least descriptively, then the next question is whether these changes can be embedded within a legal-historical narrative that allows us to accept them as legitimate, with a legal integrity equal to those (other) amendments that have followed the route set out by Article V. Ackerman especially is insistent that such a narrative is available, and he sketches its outlines in his essay.

We should be aware, though, that one need not address the conundrums posed by Griffin or, especially, Ackerman unless we first recognize that a particular kind of change has occurred within the constitutional system. What kind of change that might be is the central topic of the essays by myself and by Noam Zohar. I am particularly interested in the distinction between what might be termed "ordinary" change within a legal system that is the result of standard-form interpretation of the relevant materials within that system and a special kind of change that we call "amendment." The latter, I believe, is generally thought to be presumptively unavailable through standard-form interpretation; it requires, therefore, some special kind of procedure for legitimation. Thus I ask the reader to submit to a multiple-choice question regarding the number of amendments to the U.S. Constitution, and I go on to argue that one cannot, or at least *should* not, answer this question by simple—and, I believe, simpleminded and atheoretical—reference to the numbered textual additions found following the text of the Constitution as ratified in 1788.

If one agrees, as do Ackerman and Griffin, that there *are* additional amendments beyond these numbered textual additions—consider, for example, "Congress may pass any regulation it believes conducive to the national health, safety, or welfare so long as the conduct regulated has any link whatsoever with 'interstate commerce'" (as distinguished from the present Article I, section 8, clause 3, which, properly interpreted, might allow only regulation that Congress can reasonably believe contributes to the facilitation of a smoothly flowing and flourishing national economy); or "the President may declare limited war on relatively insignificant foreign countries without formally consulting Congress"—then it is obviously necessary to account for their presence as part of our operative, legitimated constitutional understanding. This is only one reason, among many, that I think that the questions raised (and provoked) by Ackerman and Griffin are among the deepest in all constitutional theory.

Zohar writes from a quite different perspective, that of the scholar of Jewish law, or Halakha. Few deny that changes have occurred within this more than two-thousand-year-old legal system, but many would indeed deny that any of these changes should be termed "amendments." This underscores the importance of developing a theory of "amendment" per se, a point that is central, of course, to my own essay. Zohar's essay is also one of the several in the book that attempts to place the theory of constitutional amendment within a comparative perspective. Most of the comparisons, such as those discussed particularly in the essays by Donald Lutz and by Stephen Holmes and Cass Sunstein, deal with secular constitutions, whether those of the American states or of foreign countries. Zohar, of course, deals with an explicitly sacred legal system, where it may be especially difficult even to concede the presence of genuine "amendment" (in contrast to more incremental "change" legitimated by reference back to enduring foundational materials). If, as Madison exemplifies, it is sometimes difficult even for secular systems to grant center stage to recognition of their own imperfections, it is all the more difficult for a system that claims divine inspiration to do so. How can one declare that God's own artifacts are nevertheless flawed and in potential need of the particular kind of change we call "amendment"? Although Zohar obviously concentrates on only one particular religio-legal system, I hope that the questions he raises will resonate with readers from some other religious traditions as well.

Why, the reader might wonder, does this book contain a chapter on changes within Jewish law but not, for example, a chapter on changes within the British constitutional system? No doubt an interesting essay could be written on the latter; the reason I did not solicit one, though, is that Great Britain, like six other states,[10] has chosen to forego reliance

---

[10] My enumeration of the seven countries—Israel, New Zealand, Oman, Qatar, Saudi Arabia, United Arab Emirates, and the United Kingdom—is taken from Martin Edelman, *Courts, Politics, and Culture in Israel* (Charlottesville, Va.: University of Virginia Press,

on a canonical written text as the foundation of its legal system in favor of an *unwritten* constitution. This book focuses *not* on the general problem of change within structures of thought, a fascinating and clearly important topic in its own right, whether one is talking about constitutional orders like Great Britain's, moral conventions, or, indeed, science,[11] but, rather, on the particular problem of explaining change within practices that are derived, in terms of their own self-presentation, from certain specifiable foundational texts.

From a somewhat different perspective, less concerned with the actual history of post-1787 amendment than with constitutional possibility, Akhil Reed Amar also presses the case that Article V is by no means exclusive. Instead, he argues, the very meaning of popular sovereignty—captured by the first three words of the Constitution's preamble, "We the People"—entails the possibility that a popular majority can amend the Constitution through a national referendum. David Dow, on the other hand, just as vigorously contests the kinds of arguments made by Ackerman and Amar and makes the case for the exclusivity of Article V. Frederick Schauer, in turn, argues that it is a fundamental category error to look to the Constitution (or *any* constitution) to provide criteria for its own grounding. Constitutional amendment, from this perspective, is much more a question of empirical fact—does a relevant society in fact *recognize* certain changes and structure its behavior accordingly?—than one of constitutional interpretation as such. Formal interpretation begins *after* the recognition of something *as* the Constitution.

Another set of essays—those by Mark Brandon, Walter Murphy, and John Vile—cluster around the issue of *substantive limits* to constitutional amendments, including, of course, those proposed and ratified

---

1994), p. 133, n.1. Edelman offers an extensive discussion of Israel's struggle over a written constitution at pages 6–30, as does Gary Jeffrey Jacobsohn in *Apples of Gold: Constitutionalism in Israel and the United States* (Princeton: Princeton University Press, 1993), pp. 124–35.

It is arguable that the United Kingdom is gaining a de facto written constitution as the result of its submission to the European Court of Human Rights in Strasbourg and that Israel, too, is taking on the trappings of a written constitution as the result of certain "basic laws" passed by the Knesset. On Great Britain, see Vernon Bogdanor, "Britain: The Political Constitution," and Roger Morgan, "The European Community: The Constitution of a 'Would-Be Polity' (1957)," in Vernon Bogdanor, ed., *Constitutions in Democratic Politics* (Aldershot, Eng.: Gower Publishing Co., 1988), pp. 53–72, 367–74.

[11] It is surely significant that one of the most influential books of the past thirty years has been Thomas S. Kuhn, *The Structure of Scientific Revolutions* (Chicago: University of Chicago Press, 1970). There are, no doubt, important similarities between structures of scientific thought and American constitutionalism, but I think there are also important differences, one of which is the purported predication of the latter, unlike the community of nuclear physicists (or, for that matter, the United Kingdom) on a single foundational text.

through Article V. Does Article V set out only procedural hurdles that (at least some) amendments must run, or does it contain, albeit implicitly, substantive limits on what can legitimately be viewed as part of the American constitutional system? It was the very possibility that Article V was reducible to only its procedural requirements that apparently led the famous mathematical logician Kurt Gödel to refuse to become a citizen of the United States inasmuch as a predicate for naturalization is the new citizen's taking an oath of fidelity to the Constitution. Gödel, a refugee from Nazi Germany, was unwilling to commit himself to a constitution that might tolerate adoption of Nazi-like policies, as long as the procedural niceties of Article V were followed. Was Gödel correct, or can substantive limits on constitutional change be teased out of other parts of the Constitution or out of the basic notion of "constitutionalism" itself?

Walter Murphy presents the case for inherent limitation, drawing in part on the constitutional experience of Germany and India in regard to similar questions. Mark Brandon presents a case study of the "original" Thirteenth Amendment, in fact proposed by Congress but never ratified by three-quarters of the states, which would in effect have entrenched chattel slavery at least in those states that had already adopted that terrible system as of 1861. John Vile presents the case for a wholly procedural Article V and attacks theories such as Murphy's that would deny recognition to certain changes that had otherwise run the gauntlet established on the surface of that text.

Finally, as already suggested, two essays, by Donald Lutz and by Stephen Holmes and Cass Sunstein, offer comparative material on the question of constitutional amendment. Lutz presents a fascinating survey of the procedures for formal amendment as found in the constitutions of the fifty American states and in a number of foreign countries. He uses this data to construct an "Index of Difficulty" in regard to formal change and then suggests that those systems that are "too difficult" to change formally, most definitely including the U.S. Constitution, will develop alternatives, including amendment by purported interpretation. Not the least importance of Lutz's essay, in addition, is its recognition that one alternative to amendment is outright replacement by formally new constitutional structures. He notes that for the states making up the United States, it has definitely been the exception, rather than the rule, to have been governed by a single constitution since the state's founding.

Lutz's interest in structures of constitutional change comes in part from his experience in advising many foreign governments as to what would be apt constitutions, though his essay does not refer overtly to his experiences in this regard. Holmes and Sunstein, on the other hand, explicitly draw on their recent experience in advising several Eastern European countries about what kinds of constitutional structures to adopt in their transition from communism to some version (one hopes) of liberal democracy. Awareness of potential imperfection is at the heart of their own argument about the inadvisability of making constitutional amendment too difficult.

These essays are certainly not intended to serve as the last word on the extraordinarily important issues that they raise. My hope is that they will be viewed as helpful goads to a long overdue theoretical exploration that will take us to the very heart of the enterprise of constitutionalism.

Two

How Many Times Has the United States Constitution Been Amended? (A) < 26; (B) 26; (C) 27; (D) > 27: Accounting for Constitutional Change

SANFORD LEVINSON

THE NOTION of a living Constitution—especially when coupled with developmental or evolutionary notions—is one of the central metaphors, not to say clichés, of American constitutionalism. It is hard to find anyone who is truly willing to reject it, given that the alternative seems to be a *dead* Constitution, an option that has few, if any, public supporters. Still, as Justice Rehnquist once said, "The phrase 'living Constitution' has about it a teasing impression that makes it a coat of many colors,"[1] not all of them, it may be presumed, equally pleasing to the eye (or to the analytical temperament). Still, even Rehnquist was willing to quote, with apparent endorsement, Justice Holmes's famous 1920 statement that the framers of the Constitution had performed "a constituent act," "call[ing] into life a being the development of which could not have been foreseen completely by the most gifted of its begetters."[2]

The "organism" that was conceived in Philadelphia thus took on a life of its own; like most children, it grew up in ways that might well surprise (or, indeed, shock) its parents. Not for Holmes is a sterile form of "originalism" that would limit constitutional meaning to the first-order "intentions" of the Framers, their specific hopes and dreams as to how their progeny might develop. Instead there is due recognition of those later developments that in turn require more expansive and generous interpretation of the Fathers' handiwork than would ever have been imag-

Earlier versions of this essay were published in *Constitutional Commentary* 8 (1991): 409, and in Michael Brint and William Weaver, eds., *Pragmatism in Law and Society* (Boulder, Colo.: Westview Press, 1991), pp. 295–310. I gratefully acknowledge helpful criticism from Akhil Reed Amar, Jack Balkin, Scot Powe, Fred Schauer, and Jeffrey Tulis.

[1] William Rehnquist, "The Notion of a Living Constitution," *Texas Law Review* 54 (1970): 693.

[2] Missouri v. Holland, 252 U.S. 416, 433 (1920).

ined (or tolerated) at the time of 1787 conception or birth via the state ratifications of 1787–88. Interestingly enough, as perhaps is suggested by the very reference to Rehnquist, it is hard to find someone who *does* reject this version of the Holmesian insight. The most noted proponent of "the jurisprudence of original understanding," Robert Bork, most certainly does not, as witnessed by his insistent, and presumably heart-felt, argument before the Senate Judiciary Committee that *Brown v. Board of Education*,[3] however surprising it might have been to the actual proponents of the Fourteenth Amendment, was perfectly consistent with what he has termed the "only" legitimate approach to constitutional interpretation.[4]

What Bork and other "originalists" object to is not the fact of organic development as such, including the surprises sometimes presented by the fragile child who turns out to be a strapping mountain climber. Rather, what they oppose is the de facto creation—or substitution—of a *new* organism on the basis that the earlier one turns out to suffer from congenital defects. Similarly, even one willing to use developmental metaphors might nonetheless profess to be able to distinguish between, on the one hand, development that, however unexpected (and thus un-foreseen), can be shown to have been generated in substantial part by the organism's internal structure and, on the other hand, outright muta-tion generated by exogenous causes. It is not the case, of course, that such changes cannot occur, but the argument is that, precisely because they are genuine transformations—and not simply the product of what was truly immanent within the Constitution—they must be the product of a distinctive birth process of their own. One label we might apply to these transformations is "amendment"; concomitantly, we might focus on the specific procedures necessary to legitimate them.

Interpretation and Amendment

Acquaintance with the ordinary operations of the American legal system makes us aware of the crucial contrast typically offered between ordinary development by "interpretation" and extraordinary development by

---

[3] 347 U.S. 483 (1954).

[4] See Robert Bork, *The Tempting of America: The Political Seduction of the Law* (New York: Free Press, 1990), p. 143. Bork testified as follows to the Senate:

> Passing that historical evidence, which I think casts some doubt on the flat assumption that the 14th amendment really meant separate but equal, let me say this. [The framers] wrote a clause that does not say anything about separation. They wrote a clause that says "equal protection of the laws."
>
> I think it may well be true . . . that they had an assumption which they did not enact,

"amendment."[5] The former is, almost by definition, unexceptional; the latter signifies something out of the ordinary, something truly *new*.[6] Thus the Supreme Court, through Felix Frankfurter, insisted that "nothing new can be put into the Constitution except through the amendatory process. Nothing old can be taken out without the same process."[7] "New," in this context, is clearly a term of art, since presumably no one, most certainly including Frankfurter or, for that matter, Robert Bork, would deny that law could quite dramatically, and legitimately, change and in that sense be "new"—different at time $T+1$ from what was the case at time T. So it is not change per se that is at the heart of Frankfurter's assertion. The contrast between interpretation and amendment, rather, is akin to that between organic development and the *invention* of entirely new solutions to old problems. From this perspective "interpretations" are linked in specifiable ways to analyses of the text or at least to the body of materials conventionally regarded as within the ambit of the committed constitutionalist.[8] "Amendments," however, are something else.

---

but they had an assumption that equality could be achieved with separation. Over the years it became clear that this assumption would not be borne out in reality ever. Separation would never produce equality. I think when the background assumption proved false, it was entirely proper for the court to say "we will carry out the rule they wrote" and if they would have been a little surprised that it worked out this way, that is too bad. That is the rule they wrote and they assumed something that is not true.

. . . You could suppose they had written a clause that said "we want equality and that can be achieved by separation and we want that too."

By 1954 it was perfectly apparent that you could not have both equality and separation. Now the court has to violate one aspect or the other of that clause, as I have termed it hypothetically. It seems to me that the way the actual amendment was written, it was natural to choose the equality segment, and the court did so. I think it was proper constitutional law, and I think we are all better off for it.

U.S. Congress, Senate Committee on the Judiciary, *Nomination of Robert H. Bork to be Associate Justice of the Supreme Court of the United States: Hearings before the Senate Judiciary Committee*, pt. 1, 100th Cong., 1st sess., 1987, p. 286.

[5] This is also at the heart of the common contrast that is drawn between acceptable judicial "interpretation" and forbidden judicial "legislation." See, for example, the opening statement of Utah Senator Orrin G. Hatch in the hearing on Ruth Bader Ginsburg's nomination to the U.S. Supreme Court, where he noted that "under our system, a Supreme Court justice should interpret the law, and not legislate his or her own policy preferences from the bench." "Excerpts from Senate Hearings on the Ginsburg Nomination," *New York Times*, July 21, 1993, C26 (national ed.).

[6] *New*, in this context, should not be confused with *transformative*. The former is a question of interpretive theory; the latter, one of evaluating the significance of any given change.

[7] Ullmann v. United States, 350 U.S. 422, 428 (1956). See Peter Suber, *The Paradox of Self-Amendment* (New York: Peter Lang Pub., 1990), p. 163.

[8] See Philip Bobbitt, *Constitutional Fate* (New York: Oxford University Press, 1982),

Perhaps the simplest way of conceptualizing what we mean by an amendment is to describe it as a legal invention not derivable from the existing body of accepted legal materials. As Will Harris writes, "The persistent possibility of amendment inescapably implies precisely the boundedness of the constitutional order at any time." The Constitution "could contain what it does not,"[9] or, concomitantly, could have taken away from it what it now contains; presumably, though, either the adding or the taking away would require amendment. Consider in this context James Madison's plaintive argument to the First Congress, while attacking the legitimacy of chartering the first Bank of the United States, that the Constitution must be interpreted within an ideological framework that accepts as "the essential characteristic of the Government" its composition only from "limited and enumerated powers." By way of exemplifying his view that "no power, therefore, not enumerated could be inferred from the general nature of Government," he stated that "had the power of making treaties . . . been omitted, however necessary it might have been, the defect could only have been lamented, or supplied by an amendment of the constitution."[10]

If one needs additional proof of Madison's sincerity about distinguishing between what is constitutionally authorized and what would require amendment, it is surely provided by his 1817 veto of a bill providing for internal improvements. He readily acknowledged "the great importance of roads and canals" and the "signal advantage to the general prosperity" of their improvement. Yet he saw the bill as going beyond the enumerated powers, even as he confessed to "cherishing the hope that its beneficial objects may be attained by a resort for the necessary powers" to the procedures "providently marked out in the instrument itself [as] a safe and practicable mode of improving it as experience might suggest."[11] Madison thus had no principled political objection to federally financed internal improvements; he simply believed that Congress was without power to call them into being until the American people, operating through accepted procedures of amendment, fabricated new powers for the national government.

and *Constitutional Interpretation* (Cambridge, Mass.: Basil Blackwell, 1991), for elucidations of six "modalities" of constitutional interpretation, all of which are joined *as* "interpretations."

[9] William Harris, *The Interpretable Constitution* (Baltimore: Johns Hopkins University Press, 1993), p. 165.

[10] Madison's speech to the House of Representatives is reprinted in Paul Brest and Sanford Levinson, *Processes of Constitutional Decisionmaking*, 3d ed. (Boston: Little, Brown, 1992), pp. 11–13. The quoted passage is at page 13.

[11] The veto message is reprinted in Richard B. Morris and Jeffrey B. Morris, eds., *Great Presidential Decisions* (New York: Richardson, Steirman & Black, 1988), p. 81.

Such notions of what Judge Cooley called "constitutional limitations" are, of course, not confined to the United States. Thus German Chancellor Helmut Kohl justified the refusal of his country to send troops to the Persian Gulf by reference to the prohibition by the German Constitution of deployment of German troops outside the territory of the North Atlantic Treaty Organization. Kohl ostensibly regretted this situation and, according to one journalist, "advocate[d] a constitutional amendment specifically allowing German troops to join international alliances."[12]

In many contexts, therefore, to describe something as an amendment is at the same time to proclaim its status as a legal invention and its putative illegitimacy as an interpretation of the preexisting legal materials. To designate something as an interpretation, on the other hand, even if one is ultimately not persuaded by it, is to accord it a certain legal dignity that is absent if one rejects the very possibility of its having been offered as a "good faith" exercise in interpretation. If one doubts the presence of good faith, or equally if one accepts interpretive sincerity but finds the actual effort to be manifestly incompetent, then one will be tempted to describe what is being offered as a surreptitious attempt to "amend" the Constitution without going through the approved procedures by which inventions are accepted into the constitutional fabric.[13] This may be what Madison meant to suggest when he stated that "it was not possible to discover in [the Constitution] the power to incorporate a Bank,"[14] which is somewhat different from saying simply that he was not persuaded by Alexander Hamilton's ultimately successful defenses of congressional power. A pervasive problem in analyzing legal rhetoric, of course, is knowing when statements should be read as mere hyperbole—consider a recent comment by a dissenting Supreme Court justice that the majority's position "makes no sense"[15]—or as something presumably far more serious, challenging either the professional

[12] John Tagliabue, "A Threat to Kohl," *New York Times*, April 23, 1991, A1, A8 (late ed.).

[13] Though see Peter Suber's discussion of "amendment by interpretation" in *The Paradox of Self-Amendment*, pp. 197–206, and his comment that "since the New Deal era the fact of judicial amendment has become commonplace" (p. 415, n. 3). See also the essay by Donald Lutz in this volume, where he argues, altogether plausibly, that a constitutional structure that makes formal amendment too difficult will inevitably develop alternative routes toward achieving necessary transformations, including latitudinarian conceptions of permissible "interpretation." As Suber notes, though, "the debate has shifted from [the] occurrence [of amendment by interpretation] to its desireability and legitimacy" (ibid.), which suggests, among other things, that there is still more than a little resistance to accepting this "commonplace" practice.

[14] Brest and Levinson, *Processes of Constitutional Decisionmaking*, p. 11.

[15] See Justice White's denunciation of the majority opinion in *Shaw v. Reno*, 113 S.Ct. 2816, 2840 (1993).

competence or moral integrity of those who reject one's own proffered interpretations.

Anyone interested in constitutional hermeneutics can profit from asking what sorts of changes in our political system could, on the one hand, be authorized through ordinary legislation or judicial interpretation (or, for that matter, activity by the executive branch in the absence of explicit statutory authorization) and what sorts, on the other hand, would require the inventiveness of "amendment." For example, given the language of Article II, section 1 that "no person except a natural born Citizen . . . shall be eligible to the Office of President; neither shall any Person be eligible to that Office who shall not have attained to the Age of thirty five Years," could Congress simply authorize by legislation, or the Court otherwise legitimize through judicial decision, the election as president of a foreign-born twenty-three-year old? Most analysts, I dare say, would believe this to be impossible, suggesting that this is a paradigm instance where "amendment" would be necessary and plausible "interpretation" unavailable. Although this may in fact be open to dispute, as Anthony D'Amato has cleverly argued,[16] the point is not what can logically be done with language, or even the quite remarkable changes over time in what will be accepted as an interpretation of a given text. Instead, as participants in a practice of legal discourse, we are necessarily concerned with what most persons at any specific time within a given interpretive community will, on the one hand, accept as "legitimately assertible"[17] or, on the other, reject as "off the wall" and indicative of an inability to understand the working conventions of our constitutional system.[18] One of these conventions, I believe, is the distinction between interpretation and amendment and the entailed position that not *everything* can legitimately be inferred at any given moment from preexisting legal materials, at least if one wishes to retain membership in any existing "community" of interpreters.

Though I am primarily interested in raising our consciousness about how we construct in our constitutional discourse the boundaries between interpretation and amendment, I should note that the latter is a gross category that can itself be subjected to further refinement. Several of the essays in this collection, for example, discuss Walter Murphy's

---

[16] See Anthony D'Amato, "Aspects of Deconstruction: The 'Easy Case' of the Under-Aged President," *Northwestern University Law Review* 84 (1989): 250.

[17] See Saul A. Kripke, *Wittgenstein on Rules and Private Language* (Cambridge: Harvard University Press, 1982), p. 78.

[18] The notions both of an interpretive community and of "off-the-wall" argumentation are taken from Stanley Fish. See *Is There a Text in This Class? The Authority of Interpretive Communities* (Cambridge, Mass.: Harvard University Press, 1980), pp. 322, 357; *Doing What Comes Naturally: Change, Rhetoric, and the Practice of Theory in Literary and Legal Studies* (Durham, N.C.: Duke University Press, 1989), pp. 141ff.

argument, adopted from West German (now presumably German) constitutional law, that a true "amendment" does not "materially change" the preexisting structure of government, but merely "supplements" or otherwise perfects the structure.[19] Murphy's argument, albeit unusual in the contemporary context, is not original.

As early as 1865, during congressional consideration of what became the Thirteenth Amendment, which abolished slavery, opponents leveled attacks on the constitutional propriety of any such amendment. Representative C. A. White, for example, presented "the very term 'amendment' [as] itself a word of limitation," disallowing a "plenary, omnipotent, unlimited power over every subject of legislation."[20] Representative White therefore condemned the proposed amendment for invading the entrenched powers of the state to control property and domestic institutions. Interestingly, White's colleague Representative Boutwell, a warm supporter of the amendment, agreed with White's theoretical proposition that the amendment power was not unlimited. Thus he suggested that Article V did not authorize amendments that would "establish slavery, or . . . invite the King of Dahomey to rule over the country" insofar as this would contravene the purposes of the Constitution as laid out in the Preamble.[21] As John Vile elaborates in his essay in this volume, similar arguments were made earlier in this century by William Marbury and Selden Bacon before being revived more recently by Murphy and a group of contemporary scholars.

Our difficulties are not over, though, even if, by conceding that a particular change does not constitute a revolutionary transformation, we can finesse the question of inherent limits on constitutional amendment. Consider the fact that a number of states in the western United States, which include the popular initiative as a process of constitutional amendment, distinguish in the texts of their constitutions between "amendment" and "revision," the former amenable to the initiative process, the latter, presumably more fundamental, not so.[22] This distinction was at

[19] Walter F. Murphy, "An Ordering of Constitutional Values," *Southern California Law Review* 53 (1980): 703, 754–57. See Sotirios A. Barber, *On What the Constitutional Means* (Baltimore: Johns Hopkins University Press, 1984), p. 43: "In our everyday discourse we distinguish amendment from fundamental changes because the word *amendment* ordinarily signifies incremental improvements or corrections of a larger whole." See also the essays in this volume by Walter Murphy and Mark Brandon.

[20] See Daniel A. Farber and Suzanna Sherry, *A History of the American Constitution* (St. Paul, Minn.: West Publishing Co., 1990), p. 282, as well as the other speeches collected at pages 278–89 canvassing the issue.

[21] Ibid., pp. 285–86. I assume, incidentally, that Boutwell was not being racist in his reference to "the King of Dahomey" and that he would have been just as upset had an amendment been proposed to invite Queen Victoria or the Emperor Franz Josef to rule.

[22] See Gene Nichol, "Constitutional Judgment," *Michigan Law Review* 91 (1993):

the heart of *Raven v. Deukmejian*,[23] a 1990 decision of the California Supreme Court that concerned the legitimacy of Proposition 115, passed by popular referendum, which required multiple changes in California's criminal code in both its substantive and procedural aspects.

Among the challenges mounted against Proposition 115, the most important, for present purposes, was predicated on Article 18 of the California Constitution, which, while allowing California's "electors" to "amend the Constitution by initiative," goes on to require that a "revision" of the Constitution first be proposed either by a constitutional convention or by the legislature prior to popular ratification. The court pronounced one section of the proposition just such a "revision"—presumably substantially more transformative than a mere "amendment"—and therefore invalidated it, given its origin simply through popular initiative. As a "comprehensive change," it required "more formality, discussion and deliberation than is available through the initiative process."[24]

So we now have, at the very least, the following spectrum of possibilities in regard to describing any given legal development:[25]

1. It is, especially if the result of a judicial decision, simply a recognition, called "interpretation," of what was already immanent within the existing body of legal materials;

2. it is, whether a statute passed by a legislature, an executive order, or an administrative regulation, a change not disallowed by the constraints established by the Constitution and thus what might be termed a permissible "interpretation" of the powers allowed governmental actors by the Constitution;

1107, 118 (review of Philip Bobbitt, *Constitutional Interpretation*). The Colorado Constitution permits "legislation and amendments to the constitution" to be adopted by the initiative process (Art. V, sec. 1), while constitutional conventions may be employed to seek "revisions, alterations [and] amendments" (Art. XIX, sec. 1).

[23] 52 Cal. 3d 336, 801 P.2d 1077, 276 Cal. Rptr. 326 (1990).

[24] 52 Cal. 3d at 342.

[25] Although the principal focus of this chapter, and of most of the essays in this book, is the American legal system, it should be clear that "any given legal development" is intended to refer to any and all legal systems. Consider, for example, the insistence by Rabbi Barry Freundel that the rabbinic judge, like adjudicators in "all law-based-societies, harmonizes . . . and papers over historical differences. Texts are not deconstructed but are plumbed for old values applicable to new circumstances." Indeed, argues Freundel, "Judaism's principle of faith rests on the implicit claim, based on the Torah's divine origins, that the revealed word contains within it so much depth, such profound eternal values, that every new situation at every point in history can be dealt with . . . appropriately . . . *on the basis of the existing text and the values contained therein*." Barry Freundel, "Midrash & Deconstruction" (letter to the editor), *Commentary*, August 1993, pp. 12–13 (emphasis added, ellipses in original). See the essay by Noam Zohar in this volume for a somewhat different analysis of change within the Jewish legal tradition.

3. it represents a genuine change not immanent within the preexisting materials or allowable simply by the use of the powers granted (or tolerated) by the Constitution, although the change, being relatively marginal, is unproblematically described as an "amendment";

4. it represents a genuine change of such dimension as to be described as a "revision"—i.e., a special kind of amendment—but that change, nonetheless, is congruent with the immanent values of the constitutional order and is therefore otherwise unproblematic, assuming compliance with whatever constitutional procedures are established in regard to such "revisions"; and

5. it represents a change of such fundamental dimension, sufficiently alien from any conception of the immanent preexisting order, as to be best described as "revolutionary" and thus taken out of the language of amendment and legitimated, if at all, by some extraconstitutional set of events.

Lest we think that this full range is found only in state constitutions such as those of Colorado or California, I note that William Harris has argued that the multiple paths to constitutional amendment set out in Article V of the U.S. Constitution—including the possibilities of proposal by national constitutional convention and ratification by state conventions, in addition to proposal by Congress and ratification by state legislatures—are not in fact all equal. Those amendments that are truly transformative of the established political order, Harris argues, should require, in order to be legitimate, running the gauntlet of either a national convention or state conventions.[26]

All of these distinctions merit more discussion. What follows, however, will concentrate only on the difference between the clarification of what is immanent that we call "interpretation" and the addition to, or at least limited transformation of, what is immanent through amendatory change. We come now to the implication of the term *amendatory change*, consideration of which will benefit from a return to the controversy about the United States Bank already evoked by reference to James Madison.

Perhaps the most majestic single opinion of the U.S. Supreme Court in its two-century history is John Marshall's opinion upholding the constitutionality of the Second Bank of the United States in *McCulloch v. Maryland*.[27] Although it concerned only the second Bank—the first Bank had expired in 1811—I think it is fair to describe *McCulloch* as an advisory opinion that the first Bank was perfectly constitutional as well, thus joining the First Congress in rejecting Madison's heartfelt advice that it was not permitted by the new frame of government. Just as important, of course, is the host of congressional legislation that could

---

[26] Harris, *The Interpretable Constitution*, pp. 174–201.
[27] 17 U.S. (4 Wheat.) 316 (1819).

now be passed under the broad reading of national powers articulated by Marshall, who took the occasion to spell out an overarching theory of national power that can be read as assigning basically plenary authority to Congress. Surely one of the most famous quotations, not only in *McCulloch* but in our entire corpus of judicial writings, is Marshall's emphasis that he is expounding "a constitution intended to endure for ages to come, and consequently, to be adapted to the various *crises* of human affairs."[28] Interestingly, the word Marshall emphasizes is *crises*. I prefer, on the other hand, to put a bit more stress on the word *adapted*.

The theory, even if not the particular result, of *McCulloch* concerned, indeed appalled, many eminent Americans of the time, including James Madison himself. Although he had acquiesced in the constitutional legitimacy of the bill establishing the second Bank, which he had signed as president, he had never formally repudiated his opposition, on constitutional grounds, to the first Bank, and he was clearly disturbed by the breadth of Marshall's opinion, especially the key avowal that "all means which are appropriate [to any constitutionally authorized end], which are plainly adapted to that end, which are not prohibited, but consistent with the letter and spirit of the constitution, are constitutional."[29] Writing the great Virginia Justice Spencer Roane following *McCulloch*, Madison wondered what might have happened some three decades earlier had the supporters of the new Constitution frankly articulated "a rule of construction . . . as broad and pliant as what has occurred." He could not "easily be persuaded that the avowal of such a rule [at the state ratifying conventions] would not have prevented its ratification."[30]

Consider in this context, then, James Boyd White's somewhat laconic comment that Marshall's opinion in *McCulloch* "seems to be *less an interpretation of the Constitution than an amendment to it*, the overruling of which is unimaginable."[31] The "amendment" presumably involves not the legality of the bank per se, for there are a number of routes by which that could have been upheld,[32] but rather the doctrine by which

28 17 U.S. at 415.

29 Ibid., p. 421.

30 Letter of September 2, 1819, in Max Farrand, ed., *Records of the Federal Convention of 1787* (New Haven: Yale University Press, 1911), 3:435.

31 James Boyd White, *When Words Lose Their Meaning* (Chicago: University of Chicago Press, 1984). p. 263 (emphasis added). White is certainly not the first person to view Marshall as something other than the mere applier, through interpretation, of constitutional commands. Thus Peter Suber quotes from an 1890 report of the New York State Bar Association: "It is almost incorrect to say that throughout this period [1804–65] the Constitution was unamended, for it was so expanded by the decisions of Marshall that they amounted to virtual amendments to its text." Suber, *The Paradox of Self-Amendment*, p. 199.

32 Marshall could have, for example, stated that the necessary and proper clause required

Marshall justified it, which operated to give Congress (and the national government) far more power than would have a more limited reading of the Constitution.

It is crucial that White, who is unusually careful in his use of language, does not appear to be leveling a criticism against either the opinion or Marshall, even as he offers a kind of support to Madison's skepticism about the provenance of Marshall's analysis. White, that is, comes truly to praise Marshall rather than to criticize, let alone bury, him. But if we agree with White—if we share *both* his perception of *McCulloch* as a de facto amendment *and* his willingness to commend Marshall's performance in that case—then we need to integrate that understanding into the contemporary debate about constitutional interpretation.

This debate in substantial measure concerns the limits on the authority of constitutional interpreters, whether judges or others. It was Marshall, of course, who in *Marbury v. Madison* had defined the importance of a written constitution—the "greatest improvement on political institutions" put forth by the new American nation—as consisting in the specification of powers (and limits) of the government.[33] The problem, of course, is how we decide disputes about what the "writing" actually means. Is *McCulloch* an example of remembrance or forgetting? And does Marshall exhibit a mastery of judicial craft or a much more ominously Nietzschean—or Humpty-Dumptyish—mastery of text and language?[34] In any case, we must decide on our own appellation for Marshall's exercise in constitutional argument in *McCulloch*. Marshall's own

---

a determination by Congress that the bank was extremely important (and not merely convenient) and that Congress had done so, or he might have engaged in an independent determination of the "compelling interest" (to use a thoroughly anachronistic term) behind the bank and found that there was indeed such an interest. The fundamental doctrinal importance of *McCulloch*, of course, is that he did neither. The case is a not-very-removed ancestor of the contemporary "minimum rationality" approach to judicial review of legislative action, which, as many have noted, is minimal indeed and operates primarily to enhance governmental power.

[33] 5 U.S. (1 Cranch) 137, 178 (1803).

[34] Even Robert Bork is hesitant to condemn Marshall, whom Bork describes as "an activist judge" even as he goes on to assert that "his activism consisted mainly in distorting statutes in order to create occasions for constitutional rulings that preserved the structure of the United States. Although he may have deliberately misread the statutes, he did not misread the Constitution. His constitutional rulings, often argued brilliantly, are faithful to the document." Bork, *The Tempting of America*, p. 21. Bork would presumably vigorously disagree with White's analysis of *McCulloch*, not to mention Madison's criticisms as expressed in Spencer Roane. It is obvious, of course, that this raises significant problems for anyone who is, like Bork, committed to so-called "original intent" as the authoritative guide to constitutional meaning. One can hardly resist asking why Marshall is a more authoritative guide to constitutional meaning than is James Madison, sometimes given the appellation of "father of the Constitution."

word, presumably, would be (permitted, perhaps even compelled) *adaptation*; White's is *amendment*. Thomas Jefferson, always more plain-spoken, might well have chosen *usurpation*,[35] especially given his description in 1820 of the federal judiciary as a "subtle core of sappers and miners constantly working under ground to undermine the foundations of our confederated republic."[36]

The problem posed by Marshall and *McCulloch* is, of course, repeated in many other cases. Consider, as only one example, another foundational case of our constitutional order, the 1934 decision in *Home Building & Loan Association v. Blaisdell*,[37] which interpreted the constitutional text stating that "no State shall . . . pass any . . . Law impairing the Obligation of Contract" in effect as meaning that states were prohibited only from passing laws *unreasonably* impairing such obligations, but that impairments deemed necessary to important state ends were legitimate. Though the opinion by Chief Justice Hughes is suffused with reference to the "emergency" facing the nation, he blandly insisted that "emergency does not create power" but provides only the "conditions" for exercising otherwise legitimate power.[38] Among other things, this meant, in spite of Justice Sutherland's demonstration that the categorical textual language was the product of the Framers' strong desire to forestall debtor relief legislation by the states precisely in economic downturns such as the Great Depression, that no formal amendment was necessary in order for the Minnesota legislature to be able to meet the threat to economic stability posed by the Great Depression; ordinary interpretation sufficed to supply the needed authority. It should be obvious, though, that one could describe the result in *Blaisdell*, and its justification by Hughes, in the terms White applied to Marshall's opinion in *McCulloch*.

So how do we—*should* we—describe the opinions in *McCulloch* and *Blaisdell* if given the forced choices of "interpretation" and "amendment"? Are there formal criteria, teachable by constitutional adepts, to be learned by students of the Constitution, that will allow us to agree, as a presumed "factual" matter, on what constitute "interpretations" and "amendments"? (We could still disagree, of course, on the "value" attached to any particular proffered example.) What might the answers to these questions, in turn, tell us about our overarching topic—the implications for constitutional theory of grappling with the issue of constitutional amendment?

[35] See Letter to Spencer Roane (September 6, 1819), in Merrill D. Peterson, *The Portable Thomas Jefferson* (New York: Viking Press, 1975), p. 562.
[36] Letter to Thomas Ritchie (December 25, 1820), in Dumas Malone, *Jefferson and His Time* (Boston: Little, Brown, 1981), 6:356.
[37] 290 U.S. 398 (1934).
[38] Ibid., pp. 415, 426.

Identifying Amendment

I thus finally arrive at an explanation of the title of this essay and its request that the reader pronounce a view as to the number of amendments to the U.S. Constitution. If White is correct and the doctrine enunciated—indeed, the constitutional reality brought into being—by *McCulloch* is "in fact" an amendment to the Constitution, then it would seem to follow that the answer to my multiple choice question *cannot* be either "(b)" or "(c)," that is, "26" or "27," depending on the stance one takes toward the so-called Twenty-seventh Amendment,[39] however common (or ostensibly "commonsensical") those answers might be. Or, more precisely, it might be said that the answer would be "26" or "27" only if by some sheer coincidence one of them turned out to be the final number after applying a sophisticated theory of constitutional amendment, whose elucidation is the central purpose of this essay. In my multiple choice test, "26" and "27" refer simply—and, I want to argue, *merely*—to what are best termed the number of *explicit textual additions* to the canonical 1787 text of the Constitution.[40]

What I argue, then, is that it is almost literally thoughtless to believe that the best answer to my conundrum is either "26" or "27," at least if one means to be engaging in a genuinely interesting theoretical discussion. The only question to which one can be confident that either would be the best answer is "how many explicitly numbered textual additions to the Constitution have occurred since 1787?" Perhaps it is part of a kind of "cultural literacy" to know that the answer to *that* question is

[39] As noted in the introduction, the so-called Twenty-seventh Amendment is a professorial godsend for the questions it raises about the operation of Article V as a vehicle for amendment. As I explain there, this volume is not centrally concerned with what might be termed the "internal" questions posed by the Article V process, including the length of time that a proposed amendment remains on the table for state ratification, the issue presented by the purported Twenty-seventh Amendment.

[40] Even this way of putting it is not without its ambiguities, given the multiple topics of several of the amendments. That is, there is no particular rationale for the inclusion in the Fifth Amendment of both the right to a grand jury before indictment together with the right to compensation for a taking of private property. As Akhil Reed Amar has suggested, there may be a good political reason: the "bundling" of the compensation clause, which apparently only James Madison thought particularly important, with other provisions much more popular by definition meant that the chances of passing the former were raised significantly as compared with its prospects if considered entirely alone. See Amar, "The Bill of Rights as a Constitution," *Yale Law Journal* 100 (1991): 1131, 1181. The takings clause might therefore, at least as a theoretical proposition, have been given its own separate number. Similarly, it would not have violated any sense of organic integrity to join what we call the Fourth and Sixth Amendments, together with the grand jury and self-incrimination sections of the Fifth, into a single amendment dealing with criminal procedure. Nor would it have been jarring if the Fourteenth Amendment had been broken down into several separately numbered amendments.

either "26" or "27." (I have little doubt that most persons would in fact say the latter, given the acquiescence of both the executive and the Congress to the legitimacy of the Twenty-seventh Amendment.) But that answer, without more, demonstrates a theoretical impoverishment of imagination that is far more alarming than would be the failure to remember several of the numbered textual additions. Knowing the "correct" number of the latter demonstrates no more comprehension of American constitutionalism than does the knowledge of precisely how many different individuals have served as vice-president (knowledge that I happily admit I do not have). Central to understanding the practice of American constitutionalism, whether as lawyer, political scientist, or historian, is recognition, and concomitant theoretical assimilation, of the extent to which the Constitution has indeed been amended—been the subject of political inventiveness—by means other than the addition of explicit text.[41]

The reader could certainly be excused for believing, on the basis of my harsh criticism of offering "26" or "27" as the answers, that the answer at least cannot be "(a) fewer than 26." This would seem to follow from the proposition that there have been at least twenty-six numbered textual additions plus *at least one more* (e.g., Marshall's opinion in *McCulloch*), which suggests that the best answer is therefore "(d) more than 27," assuming that one accepts the legitimacy of the Twenty-seventh Amendment. Alas, I do not think that "(a)" can be rejected as the best answer quite so easily.

How can this be, given the existence of (at least) twenty-six numbered textual additions? The answer lies in determining if all of them genuinely differed from what was already immanent in the preexisting understandings of the Constitution. Some of them, that is, might simply have "declared" or "recognized" what was already there and what would readily be grasped by anyone with interpretive insight into the Constitution. There is no reason, I am arguing, to call a numbered textual addition a genuine "amendment" unless it truly changes the preexisting legal reality.

One might argue, though, that the very existence of the numbered textual additions is presumptive evidence that they were indeed thought to be required and that interpretation would be unavailing to bring the particular legal reality about. Phrased this way, the proposition is basically a historical one, making a claim about the likely views of the text's authors as to its "necessity." But it seems quite clear that even supporters of several of the textual additions believed that they in fact added nothing to the meaning of the Constitution, if correctly understood.

---

[41] This is obviously the crux of Bruce Ackerman's extraordinary work, though, as shall be indicated below, I believe that he has failed to confront the importance of the interpretation-amendment distinction for his own enterprise.

Consider in this context the great debate about the "necessity" of adding a "Bill of Rights" to the 1787 Constitution. Supporters of the Philadelphia handiwork insisted that no such additions were required to achieve the ends articulated by anti-Federalists, for the national Constitution, unlike its state counterparts, was ostensibly adopted under a theory of "assigned power." That is, the national government was not presumptively plenary, lacking only that power specifically excluded by the foundation document; instead, its power was limited only to what was plausibly granted by the constitutional text. Thus Hamilton, attacking those who criticized the Constitution for lacking a bill of rights, argued in *The Federalist*, No. 84, that no one could seriously believe that Congress *could* have the power to regulate the press, given that it was nowhere assigned any such power. "The constitution ought not to be charged with the absurdity of providing against the abuse of an authority, which was not given."[42] A similar argument was offered by James Wilson, who played a far more important role than Hamilton at the Philadelphia convention and who became one of the first members of the Supreme Court. Wilson, responding to Philadelphia citizens who demanded the addition of specific protection of freedom of the press, stated that "the proposed system possesses no influence whatever upon the press; and it would have been merely nugatory, to have introduced a formal declaration upon the subject."[43]

Indeed, to call it "nugatory" might be to compliment the First Amendment. James Iredell, who would join Wilson on the Supreme Court, told his fellow ratifiers in North Carolina that it would be "not only useless, but *dangerous*, to enumerate a number of rights which are not intended to be given up; because it would be implying, in the strongest manner, that every right not included in the exception might be impaired by the government without usurpation."[44] From this perspective, the addition of what we know as the First Amendment does indeed drastically change the constitutional understanding, though *not* by prohibiting Congress from regulation of speech or the press, which it lacked power to do in any case. Rather, the transformation comes by implicitly adding to Congress's powers the ability to regulate everything that is not specifically named in the Bill of Rights.[45]

[42] *The Federalist*, No. 84 (Hamilton), in Jacob E. Cooke, ed., *The Federalist Papers* (Middletown, Conn.: Wesleyan University Press, 1961), p. 575.

[43] James Wilson, "An Address to a Meeting of the Citizens of Philadelphia" (1787), quoted in Lucas A. Powe, *The Fourth Estate and the Constitution* (Berkeley: University of California Press, 1991), p. 44.

[44] Speech of July 29, 1788, before the North Carolina ratifying convention, quoted in Farber and Sherry, *A History of the American Constitution*, p. 224 (emphasis added).

[45] Indeed, the Ninth Amendment was added specifically to forestall such an interpretation. See Suzanna Sherry, "The Founders' Unwritten Constitution," *University of Chicago Law Review* 54 (1987): 1127, 1162–64. Even with the recent "rediscovery" of the Ninth

If one accepts the more moderate version of the Hamilton-Wilson argument, though,[46] then the First Amendment is rendered wholly "unnecessary" and adds nothing whatsoever to the 1787 Constitution.[47] Proper interpretation of the 1787 document would preclude conscientious members of Congress from passing, the president from signing, or the judiciary from enforcing a bill abridging speech, establishing a national church, or whatever, inasmuch as such power was not specifically assigned the Congress in Article I. It may be jarring to suggest that the First Amendment contributes nothing, strictly speaking, to the legal protection of fundamental liberties, but this may be evidence only of the distance we have traveled from the original understanding of the Constitution as creating only a limited government of assigned powers. In any event, there is no reason to believe that even all of the representatives who voted for the First Amendment did so in the belief that it was "required" in order to preserve the liberties enunciated. They might just as likely have believed that it was required as a political gesture to anti-Federalists who might, if not appeased, use the very procedures of Article V to bring into being a new constitutional convention that would reconsider the Philadelphia document narrowly ratified by the state conventions.[48]

Amendment, though, I think it is fair to say that Iredell's worries have been vindicated, as demonstrated by the burden of proof, if not opprobrium, placed upon those who argue on behalf of "unenumerated rights" as part of the constitutional understanding.

[46] One problem with their analysis, of course, was the existence of Article I, section 9, which specifically prevents the Congress from, among other things, passing bills of attainder or creating titles of nobility. Indeed, Hamilton specifically emphasizes the importance of section 9 as providing basic protection; he does not, however, address the point that if section 9 is in fact "necessary" in order to prevent such legislation, then the Wilson-Hamilton argument fails. Many opponents of the Constitution were quick to draw such an inference from the existence of section 9.

[47] Fred Schauer has suggested that the real importance of the First Amendment may be the product of its incorporation into the Fourteenth Amendment as a limitation on the states. If one predicate of eighteenth-century constitutional theory was the limitation of the national government only to its assigned powers, another was the basically plenary powers of the states, which indeed made it crucial to establish bills of rights in state constitutions against the power of the otherwise unconstrained state. Without the textual presence of the First Amendment, it might have been considerably harder to impose its norms on states. Perhaps, but surely one could have reached many of the same results through interpretation either of the "privileges or immunities" clause of the Fourteenth Amendment or of the "republican form of government" clause in Article IV. It is undeniable that the existence of the textual First Amendment provided a powerful rhetorical resource (once members of the Court in the mid-twentieth century became interested in protecting unpopular speech), but this is quite different from arguing that its presence was "necessary" to attaining the ends sought.

[48] See Paul Finkelman, "James Madison and the Bill of Rights: A Reluctant Paternity,"

It may be a nice thing to have a clear specification of the inability of Congress to regulate the press or establish a religion, but that is a stylistic, more than a legal, insight; nothing legally would be lost, according to the Hamiltonian argument, by the absence of the amendment. From this perspective, as a matter of law the amendment may be little more than a "guide to the dimwitted" who need the aid of textual specification even though the rest of us would arrive at precisely the same destination through the use of acceptable techniques of constitutional interpretation.

There is one other, more generous, explanation that might be offered, though even it scarcely supports the "necessity" of the amendment. Akhil Reed Amar has noted the importance that James Madison placed on the inclusion of "fundamental maxims of free government" within the constitutional text as a means of popular education.[49] Hamilton rather acerbically dismissed such didactic "aphorisms which make the principal figure in several of our State bills of rights," deeming them more suited to "a treatise of ethics than . . . a constitution of government."[50] Perhaps one finds Madison a better guide to constitution writing than Hamilton, and this would make the addition of the First Amendment to the Constitution of some genuine *political* significance in terms of the socialization of the citizenry, surely no small point for those concerned with maintaining, as well as "founding," a constitutional republic. But the rigorous lawyer would presumably find this of relatively little importance when trying to decide its *legal* significance.

One may resist the view that the *First* Amendment adds nothing of legal importance to the Constitution. But surely it is difficult to disagree with Madison's own concession that the *Tenth* Amendment "may be considered as superfluous."[51] Consider in this context the careful statement by Justice Rehnquist that "an express *declaration*" of federalistic limits on congressional power "is *found* in the Tenth Amendment," rather than, say, "*granted*" or "*established*" by that amendment.[52] Amar notes that "the congressional resolution accompanying the Bill [of Rights] explicitly described it as containing 'declaratory' as well as 're-

---

Supreme Court Review (1990): 301, 328–47, which offers just such a "political" interpretation of Madison's support for the Bill of Rights and thus rejects the oft-argued view that Jefferson had persuaded his fellow Virginian that such amendments were even necessarily desirable, let alone "necessary," on the merits.

[49] See Amar, "The Bill of Rights as a Constitution," pp. 1208–9. The quoted phrase comes from an October 17, 1788, letter of Madison to Thomas Jefferson.

[50] Ibid., p. 1208, n. 344, quoting *The Federalist*, No. 84.

[51] Ibid., p. 1154, n. 10, quoting Madison's speech to the House of Representatives on June 8, 1789.

[52] National League of Cities v. Usery, 426 U.S. 833, 842 (1976) (emphasis added).

strictive' provisions,"[53] which seems logically to imply that whatever the function of the former, it is not to change the preexisting legal reality.

Imagine, then, asking supporters of a textual addition to indicate precisely why they thought it was required. It is far different to say, on the one hand, "because the Constitution cannot legitimately be interpreted to allow X, and the new text will authorize X," or, on the other, "because even though the Constitution, correctly interpreted, already contains X within it, we nonetheless should add a patch of text either to control the stupid or politically malevolent adjudicator or to educate the citizenry who look to the Constitution for memorizable maxims of government." To take an easy example, I presume that many more supporters of the ultimately ill-fated Equal Rights Amendment believed that it was desirable for one of these second group of reasons rather than for the first.[54]

It should now be clear that one simply cannot assert with any confidence that all of the textual additions were viewed as legally necessary even by their supporters. There is, therefore, no guarantee that even Madison would have identified the number of amendments, as of 1791, as ten, at least once one accepts the difference between "amendment" and "numbered textual addition." The problem becomes far more complex when we address certain of the textual additions from our own, contemporary, perspectives as well-trained (or at least well-socialized) lawyers.

Take, for example, the Thirteenth Amendment, which abolished slavery. Surely those who believed, with Frederick Douglass, that the Constitution never allowed slavery in the first place could scarcely have be-

---

[53] Ibid., quoting *Documentary History of the Constitution* (Department of State, 1894), 2:321.

[54] Consider in this context the reasons given by Justice Ginsburg, during her confirmation hearings before the Senate Judiciary Committee, for endorsing the Equal Rights Amendment:

> I remain an advocate of the equal rights amendment, I will tell you, for this reason: because I have a daughter and a grand-daughter, and I would like the legislature of this country and of all the states to stand up and say, "we know what that history [of denying rights to women] was in the 19th century, and we want to make a clarion call that women and men are equal before the law, just as every modern human rights document does since 1970." I'd like to see that statement made just that way in the United States constitution.

"Excerpts from Senate Hearing on the Ginsburg Nomination," *New York Times*, July 22, 1993, A10 (national ed.).

Note well that, in advocating a "clarion call," Justice Ginsburg did *not* say that the ERA would in fact have granted women any legal rights that they do not now enjoy under a properly interpreted Fourteenth Amendment. She did *not* suggest that she would be forced, as a member of the Supreme Court, to decide cases differently because the present Constitution is different in meaning from one including the ERA.

lieved that an amendment was necessary to abolish it.[55] Still, Douglass undoubtedly represented only a minority position, and most partisans of the Thirteenth Amendment, including Abraham Lincoln, believed that it *was* legally necessary in order to abolish slavery, for example, in the slave states—Maryland, Delaware, Kentucky, and Missouri—that had remained loyal to the Union. But we in 1994 certainly need *not* believe, as a legal proposition, that without the Thirteenth Amendment slavery would have been protected against nationally imposed abolition.[56] To hold such a view would require, for starters, rejection of the propriety of practically every important commerce clause decision since 1937. Can it conceivably be the case, for example, that a Congress authorized to tell the Darby Lumber Company that it must pay a minimum wage to its laborers is without the power to transform chattel slavery?[57] If we accept the legitimacy of decisions such as *Darby, NLRB v. Friedman-Harry Marks Clothing Co.*[58] (the fascinating companion case to the far more famous *Jones & Laughlin* decision),[59] and *Wickard v. Filburn*,[60] all upholding what had previously been viewed as unacceptable federal regulation of "local" concerns, then we simply cannot believe that the Thirteenth Amendment is the only barrier, at least theoretically, to the reinstitution of slavery in a state.[61]

I am even more confident that few contemporary lawyers believe that the Fifteenth and Nineteenth Amendments are "necessary," given contemporary interpretations of the Fourteenth Amendment in regard to racial and gender classifications concerning such a fundamental interest as voting. And if the Supreme Court was correct in *Harper v. Virginia*

[55] For Douglass's argument (which was not original with him), see "The Constitution of the United States: Is It Pro-Slavery or Anti-Slavery?" in Philip Foner, ed., *The Life and Writings of Frederick Douglass* (New York: International Publishers, 1950), 2:467–80, discussed in Sanford Levinson, *Constitutional Faith* (Princeton: Princeton University Press, 1988), pp. 31, 76–77.

[56] No one denied that a state could voluntarily choose to abolish slavery within its jurisdiction.

[57] See United States v. Darby, 312 U.S. 100 (1941).

[58] 301 U.S. 58 (1937).

[59] National Labor Relations Board v. Jones & Laughlin Steel Corp., 301 U.S. 1 (1937)

[60] 317 U.S. 111 (1942).

[61] Both Fred Schauer and Akhil Reed Amar have pointed out that I am overlooking one important legal consequence of the Thirteenth Amendment, even given the modern recognition of Congress's extensive regulatory power under the commerce clause: The Thirteenth Amendment *entrenches* the abolition of slavery, thus removing from Congress the power it also has under the commerce clause to acquiesce to the use of slave labor in the states. Ordinary legislation, by definition, can be overridden by a subsequent legislature. Thus the Thirteenth Amendment is not a genuine parallel to the Equal Rights Amendment unless one adopts Douglass's view that the unamended Constitution, correctly read, was as hostile to slavery as the unamended Constitution, correctly read, is supportive of gender equality.

Board of Elections,[62] which held that Virginia's poll tax for state elections violated the Constitution, then surely the Twenty-fourth Amendment, which two years before barred a poll tax in federal elections, was a wholly gratuitous addition to the text. Only if one agrees with Justice Harlan's considerably less generous reading of the Fourteenth Amendment would it be the case that we would lose something legally significant were the Fifteenth, Nineteenth, and Twenty-fourth Amendments suddenly to disappear from the text of the Constitution.

Indeed, it is a fitting irony that some supporters of the *Fourteenth* Amendment argued that *it* was not at all necessary inasmuch as it simply spelled out what a correct interpretation of the Constitution already required.[63] I quickly concede that an accurate historical portrayal of the background of all of the amendments that I have been discussing would take into account the perception of some of the best constitutional analysts of the day that they were indeed "necessary." But this is only to highlight one of the central mysteries of our operative constitutional practice, which is the radical transformation through time of central legal doctrines, such as the power of Congress under the commerce clause, without formal amendment—the addition of text through the use of Article V mechanisms—ever being deemed necessary.

Returning to the initial conundrum, we can now see that someone who disagrees with James Boyd White's designation of *McCulloch* as an amendment—and disagrees as well with the description of any other decisions as de facto amendments—might well have an interpretive theory sufficiently generous to view many of the explicit textual additions as unnecessary and spelling out what was already "in" the Constitution to be teased out through legitimate interpretation. Once this move is taken, then "(a) fewer than 26" is clearly the best answer, certainly far more sophisticated theoretically than either "(b)" or "(c)." But, after all, the central premise of my argument is that practically *any* other answer is more sophisticated, as a theoretical matter, than a hapless counting up of the numbered additions.

[62] 383 U.S. 663 (1966).

[63] See Howard Jay Graham, "Our 'Declaratory' Fourteenth Amendment," *Stanford Law Review* 7 (1954): 3. Graham begins his article by noting that a " 'declaratory constitutional amendment' is today almost as baffling and incongruous a concept as an 'unconstitutional constitution.' " For contemporary readers, "to *amend* [the Constitution] is to revise it and change it, not to discover or 'declare' an antecedent meaning, much less to define or redefine some pre-existent natural right or rights." He immediately goes on to argue, however, that "it often was squarely otherwise with our ancestors" and that we must recapture the understanding, however alien to current sensibility, if we are to understand the theory underlying the Fourteenth Amendment on the part of at least some of its most important supporters. For a more recent statement of the "declaratory" thesis, see Michael Kent Curtis, *No State Shall Abridge: The Fourteenth Amendment and the Bill of Rights* (Durham, N.C.: Duke University Press, 1986), pp. 90–91.

Beyond Article V

I have proffered a distinction—a structural opposition—between interpretation and amendment even as I cheerfully concede serious doubt
that anyone can supply formal criteria by which to distinguish the two.
Indeed, I strongly suspect that clever analysts can repeatedly show that
what are thought to be "interpretations" are better viewed as "amendments" and, of course, just the opposite—that what were thought to be
great constitutional innovations, such as women's suffrage, were in fact
not necessary at all because they were already immanent in the properly
interpreted existing constitutional regime. Thus it may well be that the
opposition I am insisting on is what my colleague Jack Balkin has termed
a "nested opposition,"[64] by which he refers to basic notions that structure our thought even as they are constantly subject to conceptual revision and "deconstructive" analysis. The philosophy from which such an
approach is drawn is what has come to be called nonfoundational pragmatism. That is, regardless of our inability to provide an allegedly firm,
and formalistic, conceptual grounding of our terms, we nonetheless find
that we make our way through the world—or more accurately, through
the forms of life that make up our worlds—by recurrence to basic notions that we simply seem unable to leave behind.

I believe that the distinction between interpretation and amendment
is one of those notions. Our constitutional discourse would be far different if, for example, opponents of a particular decision by the Supreme
Court could no longer denounce it as a usurping "amendment" rather
than plausible "interpretation" or if senators could no longer
confidently assert (and receive a nominee's ready agreement) that a
judge's task is "to interpret" rather than "to amend" the materials by
illicit "legislation." Those who denounce decisions as unacceptable
"amendments" obviously do not mean that the Court has suddenly
placed a numbered textual addition in the canonical text that is placed in
our casebooks or distributed to school children by the government.
What they mean, of course, is that the Court's decision does not follow
from any authorized mode of interpretation and is merely a "pretext"
for judicially imposed transformation.

Nor is it only the critic of courts or presidents who depends on maintaining the rhetorical force of "amendment" as a distinction from ordinary interpretation. One cannot make the slightest sense of Bruce Ackerman's enterprise in constitutional transformation, summarized in his
contribution to this volume, without accepting the reality, and almost
overwhelming importance, of the distinction between "interpretation"

[64] J. M. Balkin, "Nested Oppositions," *Yale Law Journal* 99 (1990): 1669.

and "amendment." I do not know if Ackerman accepts White's description of *McCulloch* as an amendment (signifying a "constitutional moment," in Ackerman's language). But he surely must believe this to be true in regard to such cases as *West Coast Hotel v. Parrish*[65] and *Darby Lumber Co.*, even if he would argue that these decisions must be placed within the context of a supple and complex process of amendment of which they were simply the final step recognizing the completion of that process.[66]

Ackerman rejects in toto the earlier New Deal historiography by which the decisions of 1937 were simply restorations of the initial (and presumptively legitimate) Marshallian vision as spelled out in *McCulloch* and *Gibbons v. Ogden*. Were they merely restorations, or even genuinely new developments nonetheless legitimized by their accordance with generally accepted principles of constitutional interpretation, then there would be no need for him to construct his marvelously complex accounts of Publian politics and constitutional moments that provide an alternative rendering of the American constitutional process. Ackerman therefore could not possibly agree with the comment by Stephen Holmes and Cass Sunstein, in their own contribution to this volume, that, in contrast to Ackerman's view of "the New Deal as a structural amendment to the Constitution . . . [,] we think it is more accurate to see the New Deal as a product of reasonable interpretive practices."[67] Ackerman has committed himself to the view that, *because* the New Deal is better conceptualized as an amendment than as an interpretation, it becomes necessary to discern the heretofore hidden alternative to Article V that fully legitimates it. Not only have Americans been inventive in their use of Article V; more significant, their inventiveness has been manifested in the very process of invention itself. What we mean by constitutional governance has been transformed in the process of actually governing ourselves over the past two centuries. It is our ignorance about the methods and procedures that we have actually used to provide—and transform—our frameworks of constitutional governance that so disturbs Ackerman and drives his project. Our ignorance is not merely an academic affront; according to Ackerman, it leads to a fundamentally stunted view of political possibility and of our own capacities as potentially Publian citizens who can engage not only in constitutional

---

[65] 300 U.S. 379 (1937).

[66] I should note, however, that I think a glaring absence in Ackerman's work up to this point is a full-scale explication of his theory of interpretation by which he recognizes certain views of the Constitution as *not* in fact immanent within the preexisting materials and therefore in need of the special mode of justification that he gives through his theory of "structural amendment."

[67] Stephen Holmes and Cass R. Sunstein, "The Politics of Constitutional Revision," chap. 12 of this volume.

"interpretation," but also, more important, constitutional fabrication and innovation when thought necessary, even if done outside the specific forms provided by Article V.

But it is not only someone who accepts Ackerman's distinctive reading of our constitutional history who must think more deeply about the patterns and practices of constitutional transformation and, therefore, take seriously the multiple choice question that structures this essay. The best example of this point is provided by Robert Bork's critique of Ackerman's thesis in *The Tempting of America: The Political Seduction of the Law.* Bork devotes two pages to attacking his former colleague's theory of "structural [non-Article V] amendment." Though he agrees with Ackerman that "the Constitution's interpretation has undergone radical shifts in the past that cannot be accounted for by classical or lawyerly reasoning," including, one presumes, "the constitutional revolution worked by the New Deal Court," he refuses to "concede its legitimacy."[68] One might think, then, that Bork, were he on the Supreme Court, would refuse to recognize those putatively unconstitutional developments and, in order to return to the proper understanding of the Constitution, overrule them. This is, however, incorrect.

Repeating some of the argument he made before the Senate, Bork emphasizes in his book that the "it is too late to overrule . . . those decisions validating certain New Deal and Great Society programs pursuant to the congressional powers over commerce, taxation, and spending. To overturn these would be to overturn most of modern government and plunge us into chaos."[69] Similarly, although Bork denounced the Supreme Court's decision in *Bolling v. Sharpe,*[70] invalidating as a violation of the due process clause of the Fifth Amendment school segregation in the District of Columbia, as "lawless" and "a clear rewriting of the Constitution by the Supreme Court,"[71] he had, when testifying before the Senate, assured his interrogators that he would not, even if given the chance, overrule it. Unless we reduce Bork's argument to the rankest kind of prudentialism[72] (or, in the case of his testimony to the Senate, opportunism), it *must* be the case that he accepts, whatever his strong desires to do otherwise, the fundaments of Ackerman's theory. These are (1) that there indeed have been constitutional amendments besides those comprising the numbered textual additions and (2) that there is a set of political practices, perhaps including sheer reliance, that can legit-

[68] Bork, *The Tempting of America*, p. 215.

[69] Ibid., p. 158.

[70] 347 U.S. 497 (1954).

[71] Bork, *The Tempting of America*, pp. 83–84.

[72] See Bobbitt, *Constitutional Interpretation*, chap. 4 ("The Nomination of Robert Bork"), for a very interesting argument that Bork is indeed best viewed as a prudentialist, in contrast to his own self-presentation as a principled originalist.

imate these non-Article V amendments in the very specific sense that judges sworn to uphold the Constitution can (and should), without compunction, feel bound by them and refuse to overrule them. I would, therefore, be astonished if Bork gave "(b)" or "(c)" as his answer to the question posed by this chapter.

Conclusion

It is, I hope, now clear why anyone whose interest in normative constitutional law—i.e., identifying those constitutional norms that are obligatory for anyone who has promised "to obey" the Constitution of the United States—must view constitutional amendment as a major theoretical problem. But perhaps there are still some political scientists who would respond that the purported distinction between interpretation and amendment is of no interest to them, that they are interested only in the hard stuff of political behavior. Many (perhaps most) of us by now have been persuaded that this is an implausible account of how one in fact does political science, that one can scarcely ignore a culture's own self-understanding if one wishes to understand its behavior. But one need not resolve this theoretical debate in order to believe that the distinction between amendment and interpretation is of import even to the most tough-minded political scientist faced, for example, with the task of introducing "American government" to students. Almost undoubtedly students will be assigned textbooks purporting to explain basic constitutional practices, including how amendments are added to the Constitution. To the extent that such discussions focus exclusively on Article V, they are simply wrong, and students are terribly misled if they rely on them. The necessary expansion of discussion beyond Article V demands, however, structured analysis that rapidly leads into just the kinds of distinctions suggested in this essay (and throughout this volume).

Three

Constitutionalism in the United States: From Theory to Politics

STEPHEN M. GRIFFIN

> Cast a cold eye
> On life, on death.
> (*W. B. Yeats*)

PAST anniversaries of the signing and ratification of the U.S. Constitution were marked by awed self-congratulation and public indifference, and the bicentennial was no exception.[1] The Constitution—presented as a document establishing a framework for government in the late eighteenth century, which survives today essentially unchanged—was once again proclaimed an unqualified success.[2] The rhetoric of the bicentennial confirmed the judgment of Sanford Levinson and others that an essential element of the American civil religion is reverence and veneration of the Constitution.[3]

While I think the bicentennial assertions of the Constitution's success are extremely questionable, I do not propose to argue with them. Claims that the U.S. Constitution is a magnificent document that "embodies the American spirit, the American Dream,"[4] are not really open to rational debate. They are expressions of quasi-religious faith and patriotic sentiment and are not advanced on the basis of argument. It is questionable whether such assertions even have the Constitution as their subject—they seem to use the Constitution as a symbol for the nation as

The author gratefully acknowledges the helpful comments made on an earlier draft of this article by Cass Sunstein.

[1] See generally Michael Kammen, *A Machine That Would Go Of Itself: The Constitution in American Culture* (New York: Alfred A. Knopf, 1986); Richard B. Bernstein, "Charting the Bicentennial," *Columbia Law Review*, 87 (1987): 1565.

[2] See, e.g., William Bradford Reynolds, "Another View: Our Magnificent Constitution," *Vanderbilt Law Review*, 40 (1987): 1343.

[3] See Sanford Levinson, *Constitutional Faith* (Princeton: Princeton University Press, 1988), pp. 10–15; Gordon S. Wood, "The Fundamentalists and the Constitution," *New York Review of Books*, February 18, 1988, p. 33.

[4] Reynolds, "Another View," p. 1351.

a whole. As revered as the Constitution may be, it is primarily a political institution and deserves to be evaluated as we evaluate other fallible human projects.

More sober judgments are available concerning the Constitution's success. The 1980s saw the formation of the Committee on the Constitutional System, a group composed of members of Congress and former government officials who are concerned that constitutional deficiencies have at least partially contributed to the policy difficulties of the past two decades.[5] On the other hand, distinguished groups of lawyers, judges, and academics gathered by the American Academy of Political and Social Science in 1976 and the American Assembly in 1987 concluded that, despite the vast changes of the twentieth century and the numerous problems of governance facing the United States, no changes in the Constitution were necessary or wise.[6] Unfortunately, the debate over the Constitution's adequacy is often so abstract that it is hard to tell whether the two sides are discussing the same issue. Proponents of success often cite the document's longevity and the absence of significant amendments,[7] while critics argue that any success is due to the adjustments made by the generations that followed the Framers.[8] So far neither side has developed clear criteria that could be used to improve our understanding of the question at issue.

Evaluations of the Constitution's performance seem to turn on views about how constitutional change has occurred. If change primarily occurs through the formal amendment process set out in Article V, then the case for the Constitution's success is strengthened because not many significant amendments have been made. But if most significant constitutional change occurs through non-Article V means, then any claim of the Constitution's success becomes far more problematic. In this chapter, I propose a theory of how constitutional change has occurred in the United States and attempt to debunk claims of the Constitution's success. I contend that change has occurred primarily through non-Article V means and that the original purpose of constitutionalism has been undermined as the political branches have assumed a greater role in deter-

---

[5] See Donald L. Robinson, ed., *Reforming American Government: The Bicentennial Papers of the Committee on the Constitutional System* (Boulder, Col.: Westview Press, 1985).

[6] See Herbert Wechsler, "Reflections on the Conference," in *The Revolution, The Constitution, and America's Third Century: The Bicentennial Conference on the United States Constitution, Conference Discussions* (Philadelphia: University of Pennsylvania Press, 1980), pp. 451, 458; "Final Report of the Seventy-third American Assembly," in Burke Marshall, ed., *A Workable Government? The Constitution After 200 Years* (New York: Norton, 1987), pp. 235–36.

[7] See, e.g., William Van Alstyne, "Notes on a Bicentennial Constitution: Part I, Processes of Change," *University of Illinois Law Review* (1984): 941.

[8] See, e.g., Thurgood Marshall, "Reflections on the Bicentennial of the United States Constitution," *Harvard Law Review* 101 (1987): 5.

mining the meaning of the Constitution. My perspective assumes both that no human institution is fault-free, least of all political institutions, and that all political institutions are affected by the general tides of social, political, and economic history and are unlikely to survive without significant change for more than a generation. Moreover, I view the text of the Constitution and its settled interpretations as part of a larger constitutional-political system that influences the meaning of the text; the Constitution thus is a "text-based institutional practice."[9]

Part I of this chapter provides some necessary background on the concept of constitutionalism and introduces the key problems and tensions inherent in the U.S. constitutional-political system. Parts II and III develop the theory of constitutional change by reviewing the most significant constitutional developments of the nineteenth and twentieth centuries. Part IV considers the implications of this historical experience for the Constitution's third century.

I. Constitutionalism in Theory

A number of different definitions have been given for the concept of constitutionalism, but one essential element of any definition is the idea of constitutionalism as government limited by the rule of law. "In all its successive phases, constitutionalism has one essential quality: it is a legal limitation on government; it is the antithesis of arbitrary rule; its opposite is despotic government, the government of will instead of law."[10]

Controlling the power of the sovereign or the state was one of the most important ambitions of eighteenth-century constitutionalists. The American colonists criticized the rule of King and Parliament as arbitrary, and their experience with colonial charters and revolutionary state constitutions suggested that the national government could be controlled through a constitution that had the status of law.[11] A distinctive American method of constitution making evolved rapidly under the pressures of war and an unsettled peace. Constitutions were to be written by a special assembly of citizens and then submitted to the people for approval.[12] They generally contained a plan for the framework of the government and a list of fundamental rights guaranteed to the people.

[9] Stephen R. Munzer and James W. Nickel, "Does the Constitution Mean What It Always Meant?" *Columbia Law Review* 77 (1977): 1045.

[10] Charles Howard McIlwain, *Constitutionalism Ancient and Modern* (Ithaca: Cornell University Press, 1940), p. 24. See also Rune Slagstad, "Liberal Constitutionalism and Its Critics: Carl Schmitt and Max Weber," in *Constitutionalism and Democracy*, ed. Jon Elster and Rune Slagstad (New York: Cambridge University Press, 1988), pp. 108–9.

[11] See R. R. Palmer, *The Age of the Democratic Revolution: The Challenge* (Princeton: Princeton University Press, 1959), 1:234.

[12] Ibid., pp. 215, 224.

Further, constitutions were expected to be literally perpetual—legal checks that would last forever as protections against tyranny.[13] The Constitution of 1787 became famous for its brevity and its use of general rules and normative standards to guide the government through the centuries.

It is helpful to specify how the various kinds of provisions constitutions typically contain affect policy. Policy-structuring or *constitutive*[14] provisions are usually phrased in general terms and have the potential to influence a wide variety of policy outcomes.[15] Policy-determining or *regulative* provisions are generally indistinguishable in form from the rules contained in ordinary legislation and affect only a limited set of policy outcomes.[16] On these terms, the distinctive point of constitutionalism is to use constitutive provisions that have the force of law to influence how the government acts with regard to a wide range of specific policies.

Once we define constitutionalism as the attempt to control the state through the use of constitutive rules having the force of law and contrast this with the idea of controlling individual behavior through, say, the regulative rules of the criminal law, it becomes apparent that it is not at all certain whether constitutionalism can work in the manner intended. While eighteenth-century lawyers presumably had a good grasp of how the criminal law could control individual behavior, no similar body of experience existed for controlling a national government through an unchanging fundamental "law." Americans were attempting to do something that had never been done before, and the success of their experiment was by no means assured.

The main problem is that it is not clear that constitutive rules can function to control behavior in the same manner as ordinary legal rules.

---

[13] See Cecelia M. Kenyon, "Constitutionalism in Revolutionary America," in *Constitutionalism: Nomos XX*, ed. J. Roland Pennock and John W. Chapman (New York: New York University Press, 1979), pp. 84, 114–15. See generally Philip A. Hamburger, "The Constitution's Accommodation of Social Change," *Michigan Law Review* 88 (1989): 239–327.

[14] I take the terms *constitutive* and *regulative* from Stephen Holmes, who uses them for a somewhat different purpose. Stephen Holmes, "Precommitment and the Paradox of Democracy," in Elster and Slagstad, *Constitutionalism and Democracy*, pp. 195, 227.

[15] Most of the provisions of the Constitution have some constitutive effect. Examples of parts of the Constitution that mainly function as constitutive provisions include those providing for the manner of representation and election to the House of Representatives and the Senate in Art. I, secs. 2–3; the enumeration of the powers of Congress in Art. I, sec. 8; the powers of the president in Art. II, secs. 1–2; the privileges and immunities clause in Art. IV, sec. 2; and most of the Bill of Rights, including the First, Fifth, and Eighth Amendments.

[16] Examples of parts of the U.S. Constitution that mainly function as regulative provisions include the clause respecting titles of nobility in Art. I, sec. 9, clause 8; the specification of treason in Art. III, sec. 3; the fugitive slave provision in Art. IV, sec. 2, clause 3; and the Third Amendment.

To control the state over many generations, they must be phrased in a general way and so take the form of broad normative principles. They concern the most fundamental political issues and can influence any specific policy decision. General principles require interpretation before they can be applied, and legal interpretation inescapably involves making normative judgments about the purpose and point of the text.[17] It is likely that our judgments about what the constitutive rules of the constitution mean will not be independent of our judgments of the wisdom of specific policies because both sets of judgments will be influenced by the same values. Disagreements over the correct interpretation of the constitution will track party-political disagreements generally. It appears that a constitution's constitutive rules cannot function in a strong sense as an independent check on government because there is no basis to assess government action independent of reigning political values.

Constitutive rules thus exist in the uncertain boundary territory between law and politics. The experience of the new nation under the Constitution confirmed that important political disagreements would be expressed in constitutional terms as the founding generation began arguing about the meaning of the document almost immediately after it was ratified.[18] Noah Webster objected to the whole idea of constitutionalism on this basis, arguing that government "takes its form and structure from the genius and habits of the people; and if on paper a form is not accommodated to those habits, it will assume a new form, in spite of all the formal sanctions of the supreme authority of a State."[19] This phenomenon was the subject of Tocqueville's famous comment that "there is hardly a political question in the United States which does not sooner or later turn into a judicial one."[20] It is not often noted that this observation has two implications: American constitutionalism not only tended to judicialize politics; it also politicized the law. The consequence is a system of constitutional law that tangles political and legal considerations that are kept separate in other Western nations.[21]

Understanding constitutionalism as an instance of the interpenetration of law and politics helps to frame my inquiry into how constitutional change has occurred. As much as constitutionalism inevitably intertwines law and politics, much of American constitutional history can

[17] See, e.g., Ronald Dworkin, *Law's Empire* (Cambridge: Harvard University Press, 1986), pp. 65–68.

[18] See H. Jefferson Powell, "How Does the Constitution Structure Government?" in Marshall, *A Workable Government?*, pp. 13, 16–17.

[19] Quoted in Gordon S. Wood, *The Creation of the American Republic, 1776–1787* (Chapel Hill: University of North Carolina, 1969), p. 377.

[20] Alexis de Tocqueville, *Democracy in America*, trans. George Lawrence (New York: Doubleday, 1969), p. 270.

[21] See, e.g., Mirjan R. Damaska, *The Faces of Justice and State Authority: A Comparative Approach to the Legal Process* (New Haven: Yale University Press, 1986), pp. 46, 68.

be seen as a struggle to keep them separate and to preserve the unique status of the Constitution as supreme law. American constitutionalists faced two specific challenges: (1) how to keep constitutional law relatively separate from ordinary political struggles over time, especially as the original Federalist consensus on the nature of the constitutional-political order disintegrated in the nineteenth century; and (2) how to ensure that appropriate constitutional change occurred as the government was required to assume fundamentally new powers and responsibilities.

It will be helpful to briefly explore one answer to these challenges, that of "rule-of-law constitutionalism." The objective of rule-of-law constitutionalism is to preserve a clear separation between constitutional law and everyday politics by making sure that everyone has the same understanding of what the Constitution means. If everyone shares the same interpretation of the Constitution, the fractious nature of everyday politics will not be reproduced in constitutional debate. To achieve this unanimity in constitutional interpretation, rule-of-law constitutionalism applies the standards governing change in ordinary legislation to the constitutional sphere. Thus rule-of-law constitutionalism insists that every important change in constitutional practice be explicitly marked by an amendment, just as every important change in statutory law is ostensibly marked by new legislation. Resort to amendment ensures that significant changes in constitutional practice are clearly recognized and openly debated. Thomas Jefferson held this view in the debate over the constitutionality of the Louisiana Purchase in 1803.[22]

The attractiveness of rule-of-law constitutionalism lies in its use of the familiar standards governing statutory change. When a significant departure from the status quo is required, the rules of law must be formally changed. But it is not a feasible method of constitutional change and the reasons why it is not illustrate the differences between ordinary legislation and the unique mixture of law and politics that characterizes constitutionalism. Since amending the Constitution is far more difficult than

---

[22] In a letter to Senator Wilson C. Nicholas on September 7, 1803, Jefferson stated:

When an instrument admits two constructions, the one safe, the other dangerous, the one precise, the other indefinite, I prefer that which is safe & precise. I had rather ask an enlargement of power from the nation, when it is found necessary, than to assume by a construction which would make our powers boundless. Our peculiar security is in the possession of a written Constitution. Let us not make it a blank paper by construction. . . . I confess, then, I think it important, in the present case, to set an example against broad construction by appealing for new power to the people.

Jefferson eventually agreed not to push for an amendment to the Constitution, saying that "the good sense of our country will correct the evil of construction when it shall produce ill effects." Quoted in Everett S. Brown, *The Constitutional History of the Louisiana Purchase, 1803–1812* (Berkeley: University of California Press, 1920), p. 28. For a contemporary example of rule-of-law constitutionalism, see Raoul Berger, *Government by Judiciary* (Cambridge: Harvard University Press, 1977).

passing ordinary legislation, there is a recurring argument over when an amendment is necessary. Those who oppose any important policy change argue that it requires an amendment. Even if they are only a small minority, their demand must be satisfied. If it is not, the minority claims that the Constitution is being improperly amended through a controversial interpretation that has no legitimacy. This destroys rule-of-law constitutionalism because the point of the doctrine is to guarantee that everyone has the same understanding of what the Constitution means. If many such minorities are satisfied, however, then the Constitution would quickly become loaded down with specific regulative rules. The Constitution would increasingly resemble ordinary legislation and would simply reproduce the conflicts of day-to-day politics rather than structure them. Since this would undermine the distinction between constitutional law and ordinary politics, it appears that rule-of-law constitutionalism is self-defeating.

James Madison posed another strong objection to rule-of-law constitutionalism in *The Federalist*, No. 49 by arguing that frequent recourse to the amending process would undermine the stability of the government because it would imply that the Constitution was seriously defective.[23] Madison noted that the Constitution would benefit from "that veneration which time bestows on everything,"[24] and that this veneration would enhance the stability of government generally. Frequent amendment would have the effect of constantly putting the fundamental structure of the government up for grabs as ordinary political struggles were transformed into constitutional crises.

The objections to rule-of-law constitutionalism suggest that the unique status of the Constitution as a policy-structuring document cannot be maintained through the procedures appropriate to statutory change. Either important constitutional changes will have to occur through non-Article V means, or the nature of the document as primarily constitutive will be altered. Both alternatives would be explored in the two centuries that followed ratification of the Constitution.

II. The Constitution in Practice—the Nineteenth Century

Formulating standards to judge how well the Constitution has worked is not an easy task, and it is especially difficult for American lawyers. Lawyers tend to regard the Constitution as *the* set of ultimate normative standards appropriate for judging any political practice. The Constitu-

---

[23] *The Federalist*, No. 49 (James Madison), ed. Clinton Rossiter (New York: New American Library, 1961), pp. 313–15. See Levinson, " 'Veneration' and Constitutional Change," 21 *Texas Tech Law Review* 2443 (1990).

[24] Ibid., p. 314.

tion occupies so much normative space that it is hard to see anything else. The Constitution is "a machine that [goes] of itself,"[25] and policy disasters and even constitutional crises are not evidence of a failure of the document, but only that Americans have failed its high expectations.

What generally prevents a realistic assessment of the Constitution is the habit of treating it simply as a document under glass rather than as a text-based system of institutions. Political institutions can succeed or fail, work well or badly, change incrementally or through radical reform. We must judge the collectivity of institutions known as the Constitution by the same standards we apply to political institutions generally. Thus the Constitution can be criticized when it can be causally linked with events that have harmful effects. Here a problem can arise if we disagree over what political theory should be used to specify what constitutes a harmful effect. Different political theories can obviously lead to different assessments of the Constitution's performance. This difficulty will be avoided here by employing standards for criticism that seemingly enjoy wide agreement. At a minimum, it can be agreed that the Constitution should fulfill its purposes as stated in the Preamble, should ensure a stable and well-ordered polity, and should not lead to political outcomes that are in no one's interest (such as frequent coups d'état or other breakdowns in public order). From this perspective, amendments, radical shifts in interpretation, and constitutional crises are prima facie evidence that the Constitution is not working well.

A national government was successfully established under the Constitution in 1789 and quickly proved superior to the government under the Articles of Confederation. But the nature of the federal union proved ambiguous. Was the United States a perpetual union of states subordinate to national authority, or was it a league of states, any one of which could secede at will?[26] Partly because of this ambiguity, well into the nineteenth century, "the most common perception of the Union was as an experiment whose future was uncertain at best."[27] Citizens owed their primary allegiance to the separate state governments, and state and local governments did most of the actual business of governing throughout the nineteenth century.[28]

This last fact is crucial to an assessment of the constitutional order of the nineteenth century. Political institutions cannot be judged as working well or badly when they are not given any substantial tasks to per-

[25] Kammen, *A Machine That Would Go of Itself*, p. 18 (quoting James Russell Lowell).

[26] See Kenneth M. Stampp, "The Concept of a Perpetual Union," *Journal of American History* 65 (1978): 5, 11, 19–20.

[27] Ibid., p. 20.

[28] See Phillip S. Paludan, "The American Civil War Considered as a Crisis in Law and Order," *American Historical Review* 77 (1972) 1013, 1021.

form. Yet apart from the Civil War and Reconstruction, this accurately describes the moribund condition of the national government through-out the nineteenth century.[29] The main administrative task of the national government seems to have been simply to deliver the mail.[30] Before the Civil War, it was far from clear whether the national govern-ment even had the ability to enforce national laws and federal court judgments.[31] Although the Civil War briefly expanded the power and potential authority of the national state, it did not fundamentally alter the duties and structure of the government, which remained essentially unchanged until after the turn of the century.[32] By contrast, "states built and subsidized a transportation infrastructure, set money and banking policies, established a legal structure for business growth, defined and punished crime, alleviated poverty, and determined the extent of peo-ple's moral and religious freedom."[33]

In this context, any assessment of the Constitution as working well or badly is relatively meaningless. The complex system of government cre-ated by the Framers was not given a true test for most of the first 140 years of the nation's history because the federal government was not re-quired to do very much. On the other hand, since state governments did most of the actual governing, their statutes and constitutions took the full impact of the various social and economic changes in the new na-tion. The discussion of constitutionalism in Part I argues that constitu-tions generally adjust to historical change either through non-Article V means or by losing their primarily constitutive character. American state constitutions are well known for displaying the latter effect. Starting in the 1820s, many new constitutions were written in response to social and economic change that resembled statutory codes and contained far more regulative rules than their eighteenth-century counterparts.[34] Adapting to historical change forced state constitutions to become more like ordinary legislation and thus undermined, at least on the state level, the reasons for having a constitution in the first place.[35]

---

[29] See ibid.; see also Loren P. Beth, *The Development of the American Constitution, 1877–1917* (New York: Harper and Row, 1971), pp. 249–50.

[30] See Paludan, "The American Civil War."

[31] See William E. Nelson, *The Fourteenth Amendment: From Political Principle to Judi-cial Doctrine* (Cambridge: Harvard University Press, 1988), pp. 27–30.

[32] See Harold M. Hyman, *A More Perfect Union: The Impact of the Civil War and Re-construction on the Constitution* (New York: Alfred A. Knopf, 1975), pp. 546–47; Morton Keller, *Affairs of State: Public Life in Late Nineteenth Century America* (Cambridge: Har-vard University Press, 1977), pp. 35, 289, 312, 318.

[33] Nelson, *The Fourteenth Amendment*, p. 27.

[34] See Kermit L. Hall, *The Magic Mirror: Law in American History* (New York: Oxford University Press, 1989), pp. 102–4.

[35] As well demonstrated by Donald Lutz's article in this volume, state constitutions have

The national Constitution faced its first real test when the acquisition of territory during the Mexican War and the Wilmot Proviso of 1846 forced the issue of slavery onto the national agenda in a way that could not be ignored. The continuing controversy over slavery showed the American constitutional order to be unstable in a fundamental way. The Constitution itself can be viewed as a compromise on this issue and the slavery question caused a recurrent series of crises and compromises—the Missouri Compromise of 1820, the nullification crisis of 1833, the admission of Texas into the Union, the Compromise of 1850—that eventually resulted in a civil war between the states.[36] From the introduction of the Wilmot Proviso to the end of Reconstruction three decades later, the nation was almost continuously in a political uproar as one constitutional crisis succeeded the next.[37]

The crises and the increasingly desperate attempts at compromise of the 1850s revealed that the "United States" was essentially a league of states without a central authority powerful enough to resolve a question that could not be settled by compromise. All the branches of the national government were eventually brought into play, as Congress repeatedly tried to get the federal courts to settle the matter, with the resulting disaster of the *Dred Scott* case.[38] This attempt to resolve the crisis "was an implicit admission that political processes had broken down, and that the dominant political question of the period had proved beyond the capacity of the political system to resolve."[39] The confluence of constitutional ambiguity and political tensions meant that doctrines such as interposition, nullification, and secession, which were inimical to the national constitutional order, could not be effectively discredited.[40] By the session of Congress that began in December 1859, the House of

---

with some frequency been subjected not only to "amendment," but also to outright substitution by successor documents drafted by state constitutional conventions.

[36] See William M. Wiecek, "The Witch at the Christening: Slavery and the Constitution's Origins," in *The Framing and Ratification of the Constitution*, ed. Leonard W. Levy and Dennis J. Mahoney (New York: Oxford Press, 1987), pp. 167, 183–84. See also Richard E. Ellis, *The Union at Risk: Jacksonian Democracy, States' Rights, and the Nullification Crisis* (New York: Oxford Press, 1987); William Freehling, *The Road to Disunion: Secessionists at Bay* (New York: Oxford Press, 1990).

[37] See Arthur Bestor, "The American Civil War as a Constitutional Crisis," reprinted in *American Law and the Constitutional Order: Historical Perspectives*, ed. Lawrence M. Friedman and Harry N. Scheiber (Cambridge: Harvard Press, 1978), p. 219.

[38] See William M. Wiecek, *The Sources of Antislavery Constitutionalism in America, 1760–1848* (Ithaca: Cornell University Press, 1977), p. 285.

[39] Ibid.

[40] See Alfred H. Kelly, Winfred A. Harbison, and Herman Belz, *The American Constitution: Its Origins and Development*, 6th ed. (New York: Norton, 1983), pp. 290–91; Ellis, *The Union at Risk*, pp. 183, 185.

Representatives barely functioned as a deliberative body, as many members and spectators came armed, with the expectation that the war would start in the Capitol itself.[41] When southern states seceded a year later, it seemed clear to many that the constitutional experiment had failed.[42] "The 'new light' the War was shedding onto the 'principles and meaning' of the Constitution revealed that before 1861 American government had been untested. Now, 'when it is for the first time subjected to the test of a severe ordeal, its defects are becoming manifest.' "[43]

The "constitutional catastrophe" of the Civil War,[44] which cost over 620,000 lives, decimated the South's economy,[45] and affected national development well into the twentieth century, was one of the greatest political failures in world history that can be linked to a constitution, possibly only exceeded by the failure of the Weimar Constitution of 1919 in 1933.[46] The war became a revolutionary struggle to end slavery and destroy the Old South, establish a national guarantee of civil rights, and terminate the agrarian republic of the Framers.[47] As James McPherson has written, secessionists "were correct" in protesting that "they were acting to preserve traditional rights and values" and "to protect their constitutional liberties against the perceived northern threat to overthrow them." It was the North's, rather than the South's, conception of republicanism that had changed since the period of the Founding. "With complete sincerity the South fought to preserve its version of the republic of the founding fathers—a government of limited powers that protected the rights of property and whose constituency comprised an independent gentry and yeomanry of the white race undisturbed by large cities, heartless factories, restless free workers, and class conflict." For white southerners, the coming to power of a new Republican party, ideologically committed to "competitive, egalitarian, free-labor capitalism, was a signal to the South that the northern majority had turned irrevocably towards this frightening, revolutionary future." Thus, says McPherson, "secession was a preemptive counterrevolution

---

[41] See David M. Potter, *The Impending Crisis, 1848–1861* (New York: Harper and Row, 1976), p. 389.

[42] Ibid., p. 471; Kammen, *A Machine That Would Go of Itself*, p. 63.

[43] Hyman, *A More Perfect Union*, p. 111 (quoting constitutionalist Sidney George Fisher, writing in 1862).

[44] Bestor, "The American Civil War," p. 220.

[45] See James M. McPherson, *Battle Cry of Freedom: The Civil War Era* (New York: Oxford Press, 1988), pp. 818–19, 854.

[46] On the problems of the Weimar Constitution that helped Hitler seize power, see Gordon A. Craig, *Germany, 1866–1945* (Oxford: Clarendon Press, 1978), pp. 415–24.

[47] See McPherson, *Battle Cry of Freedom*, pp. 233, 358, 558; Eric Foner, *Reconstruction: America's Unfinished Revolution, 1863–1877* (New York: Harper and Row, 1988), pp. 244–45.

to prevent the Black Republican revolution from engulfing the South."
James B. D. DeBow and Jefferson Davis were thus correct in insisting,
"We are not revolutionists. We are resisting revolution. . . . We are
conservative."[48]

The crises of secession and civil war were only the beginning of the
constitutional disasters of the mid-nineteenth century. Because the Constitution did not provide for emergency government or clearly identify
the duties of Congress and the president in the event of sudden invasion
or rebellion, President Lincoln was forced to institute a "quasi dictatorship" in order to prosecute the war effectively.[49] The three amendments
to the Constitution that were the fruits of war would not have been
ratified under normal conditions and were forced on the southern states
as a condition of readmission.[50] Under the Military Reconstruction Act
of 1867, the South was occupied by thousands of federal troops commanded by officers who had the power to dismiss local officials and state
governors.[51] President Andrew Johnson attempted to subvert congressional Reconstruction by refusing to enforce the law, and became the
only president to be impeached and nearly convicted for his failure to
carry out his constitutional duties.[52] In the South, a reign of terror was
instituted by whites as the war continued after 1865 in guerrilla fashion.
Federal laws were openly violated and "whole sections of Southern
states experienced breakdowns in law and order."[53] "More so than at
any other time in the history of the United States, terrorism and murder
became a frequent adjunct of the political process."[54] Federal authorities
were unable to stem this wave of counterrevolutionary terror and, by
1875, the forces of resistance were strong enough so that Democratic
whites could openly crush the Mississippi Republican party without fear
of retribution.[55] Reconstruction culminated in the presidential election
crisis of 1876, which the Constitution exacerbated by failing to provide

---

[48] McPherson, *Battle Cry of Freedom*, pp. 860–61 (footnote omitted).

[49] Kelly, Harbison, and Belz, *The American Constitution*, pp. 300, 306.

[50] See Richard B. Bernstein with Jerome Agel, *Amending America* (New York: Times
Books, 1993), pp. 102–3, 109, 115. This reality is, of course, a basic foundation of Bruce
Ackerman's argument about constitutional change in the United States, as summarized in
this volume and set out more fully in *We the People* (Cambridge: Harvard University Press,
1991).

[51] See Keller, *Affairs of State*, p. 207.

[52] See Harold M. Hyman and William M. Wiecek, *Equal Justice Under Law: Constitutional Development, 1835–1875* (New York: Harper and Row, 1982), pp. 455–56.

[53] Robert J. Kaczorowski, *The Politics of Judicial Interpretation: The Federal Courts, Department of Justice and Civil Rights, 1866–1876* (New York: New York University Press,
1985), p. 54.

[54] Keller, *Affairs of State*, p. 224.

[55] See Foner, *Reconstruction*, p. 245, 425–26, 442–44, 558–63.

any mechanism for judging disputed returns and allowing for no delay in inauguration.[56] This is not an enviable constitutional record.

At a minimum, the crisis of the Union constituted a serious indict-ment of the constitutional order created by the Framers. The nation was not unified by fundamental law, but by military force. The national state created by the Constitution of 1787 was simply too weak to resolve im-portant issues that divided the nation or even to maintain order when the need arose. Although the Civil War Amendments increased the potential authority of the national government somewhat, the question of how an active national state could be reconciled with an eighteenth-century constitutional order was avoided as most of the agencies created by the war disappeared after 1865.[57]

To an astonishing degree, however, the reputation of the Constitu-tion did not suffer. Patriotic feeling fused the Constitution and the na-tion, so that when Lincoln responded effectively to the outbreak of war, the Constitution was once again judged to be adequate.[58] This response and the reverence for the Constitution that grew after the war were not based on any realistic assessment of political institutions, but rather re-flected the general glorification of the nation characteristic of the late nineteenth century.[59] The Constitution did not undergo any important tests after the end of Reconstruction in the nineteenth century, as the national government was again not required to do very much.[60] Funda-mental change in the Constitution began to occur only after the elec-toral realignment of the 1890s and the events that followed—the slow demise of the early American state and the construction of a new na-tional bureaucratic order.[61]

III. The Constitution in Practice—the Twentieth Century

One reason the Constitution is typically accounted a success is that the text has changed very little since the Bill of Rights was ratified in 1791.[62] Although more than ten thousand amendments have been proposed,

---

[56] See Hyman and Wiecek, *Equal Justice Under law*, p. 493; Keith Ian Polakoff, *The Politics of Inertia: The Election of 1876 and the End of Reconstruction* (Baton Rouge: Louisiana State University Press, 1973), pp. 223–24.

[57] See Hyman, *A More Perfect Union*, pp. 380–82.

[58] Ibid., pp. 136–37.

[59] See Keller, *Affairs of States*, p. 42.

[60] Ibid., pp. 312, 318.

[61] See Stephen Skowronek, *Building A New American State: The Expansion of National Administrative Capacities, 1877–1920* (New York: Cambridge University Press, 1982), pp. 165–69.

[62] See Van Alstyne, "Notes on a Bicentennial Constitution," pp. 941–42.

only seventeen were adopted, and a good argument can be made that most of these amendments did not alter the fundamental structure of the three branches of government created by the framers. Only the Seventeenth Amendment, providing for the direct election of senators, changed a key element of the framers' design.[63] We must assess this claim, however, in the light of the need of change and the methods of constitutional change available.

As we have seen, the most important reason the Constitution did not experience significant change in the nineteenth century was that little was expected of the national government. The Civil War Amendments were approved under special circumstances and their potential for expansion of national authority was quickly nullified by the profound localism and antigovernment attitudes typical of nineteenth-century politics.[64] The weight of the enormous social and economic changes of the late nineteenth century was borne by state governments, and state constitutions continued to change at a rapid pace. As the people attempted to restrict the powers of state legislatures, state constitutions became even more codelike.[65] If constitutionalism rests on the idea that there must be a clear difference between ordinary legislation and the provisions of the constitution, then the experience with state constitutions in the nineteenth century indicated that constitutionalism could not survive historical change.

In light of the dramatic changes in state constitutions as state governments assumed new powers and roles in response to events in the nineteenth century, the key question of the twentieth century would be how the constitutional-political system would change as the national government assumed many duties that the states had previously shouldered alone and as it assumed completely new responsibilities, such as fighting world wars and maintaining a global military and intelligence establishment. The experience of state governments in the nineteenth century indicates that a change in the kind and level of government activity inevitably leads to constitutional change. The increase in government activity at the state level meant that state constitutions lost their constitutive character—how would the federal Constitution change in response to similar pressures?

The short answer to this question is that the federal Constitution underwent massive changes in the twentieth century, but that this happened, in the main, through non–Article V means. The twentieth

[63] See Alan P. Grimes, *Democracy and the Amendments to the Constitution* (Lexington, Mass.: Lexington Books, 1978), p. 2.

[64] See Keller, *Affairs of State*, pp. 35, 106, 289.

[65] Ibid., pp. 111–13, 319–20.

century opened with a series of constitutional amendments largely spon-
sored by the Progressive movement (Amendments Sixteen to Nineteen),[66] but only two (the income tax and the direct election of senators)
arguably had significant policy-structuring effects. More important,
there were no amendments to the Constitution with significant constitutive effects after Franklin Roosevelt took office in 1933. That is, during the period when the national constitutional order experienced the
greatest changes in its history, the text of the Constitution changed
hardly at all. The crucial constitutional fact of the twentieth century is
that all significant change in the structure of the national government
after the New Deal occurred through non–Article V means.[67]

Why should this be the case? This is best answered by examining the
conflict between the New Deal and the Supreme Court. One need not
believe in rule-of-law constitutionalism to think that the changes in the
role of the national government in the regulation of the economy proposed by President Roosevelt were so fundamental that they should
have been authorized through appropriate amendments. The New Deal
reforms were likely the most significant changes in the constitutional
system made in the twentieth century, yet one cannot tell from the text
of the Constitution that any change occurred at all. Roosevelt's reasons
for not asking for amendments are instructive, because they apply with
equal force to all of the significant constitutional changes that came after
the New Deal and show why these changes could not have occurred
through amendment.

Roosevelt carefully considered the amendment option from the summer of 1935 to the end of 1936.[68] He eventually rejected this option for
three reasons. First, after two years of study there was still no agreement
in the executive branch on the language of any amendment.[69] We can
infer why this was the case. No one could anticipate what law the Court
would strike down next, or what general rationales it would use. Also,
no one could anticipate what kind of expansion in governmental power
might be required by future events. Any amendment would therefore

[66] See Grimes, *Democracy*, p. 96.

[67] Thus Ackerman describes the New Deal as America's third great "constitutional
moment," following only the 1787–88 convention and ratification of the original
Constitution and the addition of the Reconstruction Amendments between 1865 and
1870.

[68] See William E. Leuchtenburg, "The Origins of Franklin D. Roosevelt's 'Court-Packing' Plan," *Supreme Court Review* (1966): 347, 362–65, 384. See also the excellent article
by David E. Kyvig, "The Road Not Taken: FDR, the Supreme Court, and Constitutional
Amendment," *Political Science Quarterly* 104 (1989): 463–81.

[69] Leuchtenburg, "The Origins of Franklin D. Roosevelt's 'Court-Packing' Plan,"
p. 384.

have to be drafted in broad terms, but a broad amendment increased the risk of unforeseen effects.[70] The New Dealers could not afford to be as confident as the framers in drafting new constitutional provisions because they were trying to influence a complex governmental system that was already operating.

Second, any new amendment would still be subject to judicial interpretation.[71] An amendment drafted in broad terms might be undermined by the Court through a narrow construction of its vague provisions. If, on the other hand, the amendment was drafted narrowly to send an unmistakable message to the Court, then it might not apply to all the circumstances in which the government needed new powers.

Third, the amending process specified in the Constitution was too cumbersome. It would take much too long and would not have a clear chance of success, since a minority of state legislative houses could defeat any amendment.[72] "It would require an adverse vote by only one house in thirteen legislatures to defeat an amendment, and the state legislatures were known to overrepresent conservative interests."[73] Any amendment therefore required an extraordinary degree of national consensus. While Roosevelt may have had that degree of consensus behind him as a national leader, he could not be certain that the consensus would persist on any particular reform issue, especially when it involved an important change to the Constitution.

A fourth reason can be inferred from Roosevelt's strategy in the 1936 presidential election. The election was Roosevelt's best chance to win popular support for needed amendments, but he kept the Democratic platform ambiguous on this critical issue.[74] Proposing amendments would constitute not only a criticism of the Court, but would suggest that the Constitution was not adequate to meet the crisis. Because the public generally respected the Court as an institution and revered the Constitution, this would give the Republicans a strong campaign issue.[75] Republicans would be able to cast themselves as defenders of the constitutional faith and denounce the Democrats as destroyers of the Constitution.[76] Partly because Roosevelt himself believed the Constitution already authorized his reforms, he concluded that it was the mem-

[70] Kyvig, "The Road Not Taken," pp. 473–76.

[71] Leuchtenburg, "The Origins of Franklin D. Roosevelt's 'Court-Packing' Plan," p. 386.

[72] Ibid., pp. 384–85.

[73] Ibid., p. 384.

[74] Ibid., p. 378.

[75] See ibid., p. 368; William Lasser, *The Limits of Judicial Power: The Supreme Court in American Politics* (Chapel Hill: University of North Carolina Press, 1988), p. 144.

[76] Ibid., pp. 151–52.

bership of the Court that was the problem and moved to the "Court-packing" option.[77]

This last reason is especially interesting for our purposes, because it provides concrete evidence that rule-of-law constitutionalism is self-defeating. The rule of law needs respect for law in order to work properly, but respect too easily becomes reverence when the law in question is the fundamental law of the nation. Such a law is seen as an ideal normative standard and becomes identified with the nation itself. It thus is the focus of strong patriotic sentiments. Such sentiments prevent even reasonable constitutional changes when they become necessary, because proposed changes imply that the national political order and its values are seriously defective. Since Americans do not believe that the values endorsed by the framers and solemnly reaffirmed by subsequent generations are defective, this creates an enormous roadblock to rational constitutional reform. Rule-of-law constitutionalism requires that the Constitution be changed through amendment in response to significant change in the duties and responsibilities of government, but this kind of change is rendered impossible by the reverence that the rule of law inspires.[78]

An even more important consequence flows from this reverence feedback effect and the other arguments against amending the Constitution considered by Roosevelt. The option available to state governments of responding to change by inserting specific regulative rules into the constitutional text is closed for the national government. All of the significant constitutional changes initiated by the national government in the twentieth century had to occur through non-Article V means. This bias against change through amendment was further reinforced by the growing institutionalization of American politics over time, especially after the New Deal.[79] "As the Republic has matured, its government has become further established and resistant to change. Citizens and groups have become increasingly attached to established practices," not to mention the commitment of officeholders themselves to the political status quo.[80] Any amendment with significant policy-structuring effects

[77] Ibid., p. 152.

[78] I leave aside the issue, which I consider elsewhere, of whether this reverence exists primarily among the mass public or political elites. See Stephen M. Griffin, "What Is Constitutional Theory? The Newer Theory and the Decline of the Learned Tradition," *Southern California Law Review* 62 (1989): 493, 525–29.

[79] See generally John E. Chubb and Paul E. Peterson, "Realignment and Institutionalization," in John E. Chubb and Paul E. Peterson, eds., *The New Direction in American Politics* (Washington, D.C.: Brookings Institution, 1985), p. 1. See also Stephen Skowronek, *The Politics Presidents Make* (Cambridge: Harvard University Press, 1993).

[80] Chubb and Peterson, "Realignment and Institutionalization," p. 6.

is thus bound to attract substantial opposition. Since a large degree of consensus is required to pass any constitutional amendment, passing any important constitutive change is practically impossible.[81]

Taken together, the various changes in the structure of the national government made through non-Article V means during the New Deal, World War II, and the Cold War amounted to a major program of constitutional reform. The political branches were given plenary authority to maintain a welfare state and generally provide for the nation's economic well-being.[82] The presidency experienced the greatest change. Under Roosevelt, the president became chief legislator as Congress looked to him to take the initiative in proposing measures to cope with the Depression.[83] The president was also in charge of the permanently large military and intelligence bureaucracy and became accustomed to taking unilateral military action during the Cold War.[84] Once the public demanded action on a perceived policy problem, there appeared to be no important limits to the new power of the political branches.

"Non-Article V means" thus does not stand primarily for judicial interpretation. Since amendments were not passed clarifying the Civil War Amendments with respect to the equal rights of black citizens or providing for regular reapportionment of state legislatures, the Supreme Court was forced to take on these tasks.[85] But the sheer scale of the changes required in the duties of the national government after the New Deal precluded the Court from having a dominant role with respect to delineating the new powers of the political branches in domestic and foreign affairs. After the New Deal, the Court generally let Congress define the boundaries of its own authority by refusing to read constitutional grants of power as limits on legislative power.[86] Indeed, the major reforms of the New Deal could not properly take root until the Court recused itself from any significant role in reviewing legislation affecting the economy under the Constitution. "In the years after 1937, the Supreme Court essentially offered the Congress *carte blanche* to regulate

---

[81] See James L. Sundquist, *Constitutional Reform and Effective Government* (Washington, D.C.: Brookings Institution, 1986), pp. 13–14.

[82] See Kelly, Harbison, and Belz, *The American Constitution*, pp. 485–86, 509, 518, 665.

[83] See William E. Leuchtenburg, *Franklin D. Roosevelt And The New Deal, 1932–1940* (New York: Harper and Row, 1963), pp. 327, 331. James L. Sundquist, "The Question *Is* Clear, and Party Government *Is* the Answer," *William and Mary Law Review* 30 (1989): 425, 427.

[84] See Kelly, Harbison, and Belz, *The American Constitution*, p. 574.

[85] See, e.g., Brown v. Board of Education, 347 U.S. 483 (1954); Reynolds v. Sims, 377 U.S. 533 (1964).

[86] See Laurence H. Tribe, *American Constitutional Law*, 2d ed. (Mineola, N.Y.: Foundation Press, 1988), pp. 304, n.13.

the economic and social life of the nation, its actions subject only to the requirements of the Bill of Rights."[87] Much the same thing happened in the countries that adopted new constitutions after World War II. In order to facilitate acceptance of the welfare state, these countries avoided placing language into their constitutions that could be read by the judiciary as an invitation to hold economic-regulatory legislation unconstitutional.[88] The Court also consistently refused to put significant restraints on presidential discretion in the area of military conflicts and foreign affairs.[89]

The pattern here seems clear enough. Once the political branches made the determination to assume new powers, the Supreme Court was in no position to resist this development for long. The Court did not even have the alternative of maintaining a minimal standard of review— it simply had to stay out of the way. The experience of other nations suggests that, once a welfare state is created, judicial interference with economic matters cannot be tolerated. Because it could not regularly review whether the political branches were legitimately exercising their new powers under the Constitution, the Court became a policy specialist, largely concerning itself with whether state legislation met the national moral standards found to be implicit in the Bill of Rights and Civil War Amendments.[90] The political branches were thus primarily responsible for determining the scope of their own powers through a process of argument, negotiation, and compromise.[91]

This is what is meant by the move from "theory" to "politics." American constitutionalism has moved from the theory that the entire Constitution could remain separate from politics to a situation, caused by the transformation of the national government in the twentieth century, where the meaning and point of most of the key constitutive provisions of the Constitution are determined through the normal interaction of the political branches, usually without recourse to judicial review. While it is possible for the political branches to change their interpretations of the Constitution through legalistic procedures involving carefully reasoned written arguments (as change is supposed to occur in the judicial

[87] Ibid., p. 386 (footnote omitted).

[88] See Edward McWhinney, *Supreme Courts and Judicial Law-Making: Constitutional Tribunals and Constitutional Review* (Boston: M. Nijhoff, 1986), p. 222.

[89] See Richard A. Watson and Norman C. Thomas, *The Politics of the Presidency*, 2d ed. (Washington, D.C.: CQ Press, 1988), p. 355.

[90] See Lawrence Baum, *The Supreme Court*, 2d ed. (Washington, D.C.: CQ Press, 1985), pp. 160, 172. For a more detailed presentation of this theme, see Stephen M. Griffin, "Politics and the Supreme Court: The Case of the Bork Nomination," *Journal of Law and Politics* 5 (1989): 551.

[91] See generally Louis Fisher, *Constitutional Dialogues: Interpretation as Political Process* (Princeton: Princeton University Press, 1988).

branch), change does certainly not have to happen in this manner, and one suspects usually it does not. Instead, the political branches alter the Constitution in the course of ordinary political struggles, often without much attention to what the legal profession would surely claim are independent constitutional values.

Since the judiciary is the only branch of government capable of providing an interpretation of the Constitution that does not simply reflect the balance of power between Congress and the president, the original hope of the framers that there would be a strict separation between constitutional law and politics is now preserved, albeit potentially, only with respect to those provisions of the Constitution that the Supreme Court regularly interprets. It has already been noted that these provisions are largely contained in the Bill of Rights and Civil War Amendments and that they are usually applied only to state legislation. It is worth briefly noting why this has to be the case. If the Supreme Court were to attempt to develop standards (as it did before the New Deal) that could routinely alter outcomes agreed to by the political branches, Roosevelt's "Court-packing" plan would revive and the members of the Court responsible for these new standards would soon find themselves outvoted as Congress increased the size of the Court by appointing justices more attuned to the needs of the political branches.[92] The political branches cannot tolerate continuous interference with their ongoing process of partisan mutual adjustment. Historical change has confined the promise of constitutionalism to a narrow area of policy.

Another consequence of the fact that most constitutional change occurs through non–Article V means is that, as time goes on, the text of the Constitution is less and less informative about the way the government actually operates, as most change occurs "off-text." There has been a convergence in this respect between the constitutional traditions of the United States and Great Britain—as the British constitution became more written and formalized over time, the American Constitution became encrusted with political compromise and judicial interpretation.[93] More constitutional truth can be obtained by examining the way government operates than by reading the document. To develop a new model of the way the U.S. constitutional-political system operates, we must take the political branches into account, since judicial review affects only a comparatively small portion of the Constitution.

To understand the structure of post–New Deal constitutionalism, it is necessary to make two crucial distinctions: (1) a distinction between the

[92] See the discussion in Daniel A. Farber and Philip P. Frickey, *Law and Public Choice* (Chicago: University of Chicago Press, 1991), p. 71.

[93] See Carl J. Friedrich, *The Impact of American Constitutionalism Abroad* (Boston: Boston University Press, 1967), p. 12.

constitutional change that occurs in the course of the interaction of the political branches (which includes most significant twentieth-century constitutional change) and the change that is initiated by the judiciary in the "sphere of adjudication," and (2) a distinction within the sphere of adjudication between decisions of the Supreme Court that affect the national government and those that affect the states. Without the first distinction, it is difficult to understand constitutional developments that only tangentially affect the judiciary—such as Watergate, the resurgence of Congress, and the general crisis of confidence in government experienced during the 1970s. Without the second distinction, it is difficult to appreciate the special role of the Supreme Court in the American constitutional system. Most of the controversial Court decisions after the New Deal concerned state legislation, and the Court has what power it has largely because it has not directly opposed the political branches and has taken issues off the national legislative agenda that politicians would prefer not to deal with.[94] The second distinction suggests that in cases involving civil rights and civil liberties there are, in effect, two sets of constitutional standards: a relatively stringent set of standards for state governments and a much looser, deferential set of standards for the national government. One is more likely, for example, to encounter stronger civil libertarian language and unanimity in the Court's opinion when state legislation is in play than when acts of the executive branch are in question.[95]

The American constitutional-political system has this two-tier structure because of the dominance of the political branches in the post–New Deal landscape. The New Deal reforms may have been justifiable under the Constitution, but the political branches were not interested in allowing the judiciary even a minimal role in reviewing important policies and thus taking the chance that the Supreme Court would again begin striking down needed legislation. So most constitutional change occurred through non-Article V, nonjudicial means, and when the judiciary did review the actions of the political branches, it usually adopted a deferential posture. The Court gradually discovered, however, that deference was not necessary when it reviewed state legislation. Once it became apparent that there were severe deficiencies in state and local government after World War II, the Court was able to inaugurate a new era of judicial activism.[96] The Court applied constitutional standards to

---

[94] For this analysis, see Griffin, "Politics and the Supreme Court." See also Mark Graber, "The Non-Majoritarian Difficulty: Legislative Deference to the Judiciary," *Studies in American Political Development* 7 (1993): 35.

[95] Compare, for example, Brandenburg v. Ohio, 395 U.S. 444 (1969), with New York Times v. United States [The Pentagon Papers Case], 403 U.S. 713 (1971).

[96] The Court's main areas of activism are summarized in Griffin, "Politics and the Su-

the states that it never would have been able to apply to the national government.

In its initial commitment to a written constitution and some version of rule-of-law constitutionalism at the national level and its later turn to complete reliance on non-Article V means to cope with significant constitutional change, the United States is unique. Great Britain rejected the idea of a written fundamental law from the eighteenth century onward, and other liberal-democratic nations adopted new constitutions in the twentieth century that differed from the American model in that they were longer, contained more regulative rules, were easier to amend, and took more explicit account of the need for a powerful national state.[97] The United States adapted to historical change not by creating a new constitutional text but by ensuring that the new powers of the national government would not be subject to independent constitutional review by the judiciary. Nevertheless, the difficulty of amendment may be one of the most serious political problems facing the United States as the Constitution enters it third century.

IV. The Constitution in Its Third Century

We are now in a better position to assess claims of the U.S. Constitution's success. It is apparent that the standards that are often used to support claims of success are inappropriate. Claiming that the Constitution has been a success because of its longevity means little because not much was required of the constitutional system for most of the first 140 years of its existence. And as Joyce Appleby once remarked, even if we stipulate that the Constitution "still works after 200 years," we must never forget "that it was in the shop for at least four of those years between 1861–65," and if we count the heyday of Reconstruction, for almost a dozen years.[98] Claims of success based on the relative infrequency of important amendments are unfounded because all significant

---

preme Court," pp. 583–84. They included: (1) civil rights for black citizens, including decisions respecting desegregation and school bussing; (2) reapportionment of congressional districts and state legislatures; (3) prohibition of mandatory prayer in public schools; (4) increased constitutional protection for those accused of criminal offenses; (5) protection through the right of privacy for reproductive activities and family relationships.

[97] See, e.g., Mary Ann Glendon, *Rights Talk* (New York: Free Press, 1991), pp. 145–70. See also Donald Lutz's essay in this volume, especially Table 12 on the relative difficulty of amending various national constitutions.

[98] Appleby made this remark while participating in a Smithsonian Institution symposium on the Constitution's bicentennial in 1987, in reference to a button—"Still Working After 200 Years"—worn by Michael Kammen (eyewitness testimony supplied by Sanford Levinson).

constitutional change that took place after the national government assumed important responsibilities occurred through non-Article V means. The analysis presented in Part I seems valid: Since rule-of-law constitutionalism cannot work, the Constitution cannot be adapted to change by altering its important constitutive provisions. Change can only occur by loading the Constitution with regulative rules that reflect the political compromises of the day, or through non-Article V means. State governments were free to employ the former course because they were not burdened by undue reverence for their constitutions. Partly because of the reverence for the federal Constitution, however, the political branches found that they had to employ the latter course during the New Deal.

The whole idea that the Constitution has worked fairly well, to say nothing of being an outright success, begins to look quite fraudulent. The constitutional disasters of the mid-nineteenth century make any realistic on-balance assessment a draw at best. Most claims of the Constitution's success or adequacy, however, are not realistic. They are better understood as expressions of national ideology and patriotic sentiment, rather than as a cold evaluation of American political institutions. Such claims do not refer to a fallible constitutional system, but express an identification of the Constitution with the nation. As such, they are really claims that the American nation has been a success, that the American people have been a success, or that American history has been a success.

More important, since most of the change in the American constitutional system occurs through the interaction of the political branches, an evaluation of how that system is working cannot be independent of an evaluation of present U.S. politics and political outcomes. Since evaluations of the way the American political system is working are usually far more critical than evaluations of the Constitution, this implies that there may be far more to be said for making changes in present constitutional arrangements than is usually thought. Although important constitutive changes have occurred without formal amendment, there are certain constitutive changes (such as altering the terms of members of Congress, changing the ballot format to abolish ticket splitting, or moving to a parliamentary system) that can be made only formally.[99] If it is the case that present policy difficulties can be resolved only through constitutive amendments of this kind, then the United States may be in serious trouble.

The recent revival of proposals for constitutional reform are largely motivated by the persistence of gridlock in government (including a long period of a government divided between a Democratic Congress

[99] For a review of these proposals, see Sundquist, *Constitutional Reform.*

and a Republican president) and various policy disasters of the past two decades.[100] Such proposals are not presently being given serious discussion in national politics, but this could easily change. The United States may be entering a period similar to the Progressive Era (roughly 1900–1920), in which far-reaching changes in the structure of the economy will lead to significant changes in the constitutional-political system. In the Progressive Era the concern was that the national government was unprepared to deal with the challenges posed by new forms of business organization (the trusts). The Sixteenth and Seventeenth Amendments were one form of response to these challenges.[101] The motivation for constitutional change in the present may be the sense that the U.S. standard of living is declining relative to other nations (such as Japan and Germany) whose state and corporate structures are better integrated than our own.

Even if political elites and a majority of the public perceive a problem with the structure of American government, however, it is not at all clear that the necessary amendments could be approved. All of the difficulties that stymied proposals for amendments during the New Deal are still present (with the possible exception of judicial hostility).[102] Fortunately for the New Deal, the constitutive changes required could occur without recourse to Article V. The United States may not be so fortunate in the future. The United States may come to a point where the need for a constitutive change that can be made only through formal amendment is clearly recognized, yet because of the opposition of a minority of citizens in a minority of state legislative houses, change is still impossible. This would be a kind of ultimate constitutional failure. The tradition of American constitutionalism would have failed because it makes fundamental change too difficult.

If it is the case that important constitutive amendments cannot be made, then it may be that the United States has come to the end of constitutionalism as a distinctive and meaningful political idea—not the end in the sense that the Constitution is irrelevant to present political outcomes, for clearly it is quite relevant, but, rather, in the sense that Americans have lost the confidence, present in the late eighteenth century, that they have the ability rationally to diagnose fundamental prob-

---

[100] See Robinson, *Reforming American Government*. See also the articles in John E. Chubb and Paul E. Peterson, eds. *Can the Government Govern?* (Washington, D.C.: Brookings Institution, 1989).

[101] See Grimes, *Democracy*. The Sixteenth Amendment, adopted in 1913, gave Congress the power to impose an income tax. The Seventeenth Amendment, also adopted in 1913, provided for the direct election of senators by the people, instead of by state legislatures.

[102] See James L. Sundquist, *The Decline and Resurgence of Congress* (Washington, D.C.: Brookings Institution, 1981), pp. 466–67.

lems of their political order, discuss those problems openly, and resolve them through a special political process that results in changes to the text of the Constitution. Ironically, the framers of the Constitution began this process by identifying the Constitution with the nation and initiating the slow institutionalization of American politics. Whether this victimization by history will actually help cause a national decline in wealth and power is another question, but present circumstances do not look favorable.[103]

If constitutionalism is understood in terms of the principle that the government must be restrained through written provisions that have the force of law, the American experience with the activist state raises serious questions about the viability of this principle. To restrain government, such provisions must have a meaning independent of the shifting balance of power between the political branches, but such an independent meaning can only be guaranteed by the judiciary. Since the new powers assumed by the political branches were insulated from judicial review, the provisions of the Constitution cannot function as restraints on government in any strong sense. It appears that the eighteenth-century concept of constitutionalism is compatible only with the kind of limited government the framers were familiar with. The Constitution that the framers created may well prevent Americans from making the kind of structural reforms that may be necessary to cope with the policy challenges of the next century.

[103] See generally Paul Kennedy, *The Rise and Fall of the Great Powers: Economic Change and Military Conflict from 1500 to 2000* (New York: Random House, 1987).

Four

Higher Lawmaking

BRUCE ACKERMAN

The Prophetic Voice

My fellow Americans, we are in a bad way. We are drifting. Our leaders are compromising, compromised. They have lost sight of government's basic purposes.

It is past time for us to take the future into our hands. Each of us has gained so much from life in America. Can we remain idle while this great nation drifts downward?

No: We must join together in a movement for national renewal, even if this means self-sacrifice. We will not stop until the government has heard our voice.

The People must retake control of their government. Our representatives must act decisively to bring the law in line with the deeper meanings of American life.

Since the first Englishmen colonized North America, this voice has never been silent. We have never lived for long without hearing its diagnoses of decline, its calls for renewal. For good and for ill, there can be no thought of silence—no way to proclaim that our generation has reached the promised land. Americans have become too diverse, too free, to suppose their struggle over national identity will end before the death of the Republic. The voice will remain—calling upon Americans to rethink and revitalize their fundamental commitments, to recapture government in the name of the People. It is this voice that will concern us here, as well as the distinctive attitude Americans have cultivated in its exercise. While we have long since learned to live with prophets in our midst, we have not learned to love them.

Talk is cheap. The normal American's reaction to some politico's claim of a popular "mandate" is incredulity, not commitment. It is easy for a self-proclaimed savior to persuade himself to lead a movement for national renewal. It is quite another thing for him to convince others—millions and millions of others—to work together to renew and redefine the collective sense of national purpose in the name of the People of the United States.

Authority to speak for the People cannot be lightly presumed. It must be earned through years of work in the political wilderness—arguing, mobilizing, recruiting a broadening commitment to a revitalized understanding of the public good. Even relatively successful movements have seen their efforts meet with vastly different fates. Sometimes Americans have responded to the call for renewal by giving a ringing endorsement to the Constitution-as-it-was; sometimes, by adopting important, but interstitial, constitutional amendments; sometimes, by endorsing sweeping constitutional transformations.

The twists and turns of centuries have done more than reshape the substance of our political identity. They have defined and redefined constitutional processes through which Americans have engaged the prophetic voice, granting lawmaking authority to a few movements while withholding it from countless others that would speak the People's name. The earliest calls for spiritual renewal expressed themselves in the accents of Protestant Christianity.[1] But since the Revolution and Founding, national debate has been conducted primarily in secular terms. The constitutional system has not allowed transformative movements to excommunicate nay-sayers in the name of a jealous God. It has required would-be spokespersons for the People to take seriously the skeptical doubts of their opponents; to give them a fair chance to mobilize their own supporters in the country. Only after the innovators carried their initiative repeatedly in deliberative assemblies and popular elections has our Constitution finally awarded them the solemn authority to revise the foundations of the polity in the name of We the People.

I shall be asking two questions about this extraordinary process of democratic definition, debate, and decision. How has it worked in the past? How should it work in the future?

Foundations

These questions are important in the study of any democratic constitution. But they are especially significant in America. This country's Constitution focuses with a special intensity on rare moments when movements for constitutional transformation earn broad and deep support for their initiatives. Once a movement survives its period of institutional trial, the Constitution tries to assure that its new constitutional solutions will have a central and enduring place in the future life of the polity. Elected politicians will not normally be allowed to undermine the Peo-

---

[1] See Sacvan Bercovitch, *The American Jeremaiad* (Madison: University of Wisconsin Press, 1978); Perry Miller, *Errand into the Wilderness* (Cambridge, Mass.: Harvard University Press, 1956).

ple's solemn commitments through everyday legislative compromise. If they wish to revise preexisting constitutional principles, they must return to the People and gain the deep, broad, and decisive popular support that earlier movements won during their own periods of arduous instititutional testing.

This focus upon successful moments of mobilized popular renewal distinguishes the American Constitution from most others in the modern world. It motivates a distinctive system of government involving the construction of two lawmaking tracks. The normal lawmaking track is designed for the countless decisions made in the absence of mobilized and politically self-conscious majority sentiment. The higher lawmaking system imposes specially rigorous tests upon political movements that hope to earn the heightened sense of democratic legitimacy awarded to spokespersons for the People. When this two-track system is operating well, it is continually encouraging Americans to distinguish between ordinary decisions made by government and considered judgments made by the People. I have this distinctive constitutional aspiration in mind in describing America as a dualist democracy.

The historical origin of dualism is the Founding generation's revolutionary experience. Washington, Madison, and the rest had initially been given the opportunity to play the normal political game according to the rules laid by Imperial Britain. They refused, but were not rewarded by the life of frustration, exile, and death that usually accompanies such a revolutionary rejection. After long years of war and political effort, they lived to see most of their fellow countrymen support their vision of a federal union—but only after a period of heated debate climaxed by a complex and arduous process of constitutional ratification. Little wonder, then, that they thought their own exercise in revolutionary mobilization had achieved something special, something that set its constitutional solutions apart from the normal give-and-take of political life. Nor were they content to look on passively as their great achievements were eroded by politicians who had failed to gain the mobilized and deliberate assent of the People that marked (in their eyes at least) their revolutionary triumph. As children of the Enlightenment, they used the best political science of their time to write a two-track Constitution— and thereby set the terms for the future development of dualistic democracy by subsequent generations.

Combining history with philosophy, I argued in my book *We the People: Foundations* that this two-track idea still makes sense, perhaps even more sense than it did two centuries ago. Dualism responds to a characteristic complexity in the modern American's approach to politics. On the one hand, most of us recognize a responsibility to do our part as citizens—talking about the issues of the day at home and at work, pay-ing our taxes, coming out to vote. On the other hand, we do not normally place an exceptionally high value on these obligations when they compete with other responsibilities—to our family and friends, church and labor unions. Normal politics is a sideline that competes with other sidelines: national sports, the latest movies, and so forth.

And yet, unlike these other sidelines, politics can take center stage with compelling force. The events catalyzing a dramatic rise in political consciousness have been as various as the country's history—war, economic catastrophe, or urgent appeals to the national conscience. The crucial point is that they have endowed political talk and action with an urgency and breadth lacking most of the time. Normally passive citizens become more active—arguing, mobilizing, and sacrificing their other interests to a degree that seems to them extraordinary.

While this ebb and flow has been noted by social scientists,[2] *We the People: Foundations* made it the basis of a normative argument. Dualistic government seems especially appropriate for a citizenry whose engagement with politics varies substantially from decade to decade, generation to generation. During periods of constitutional politics, the higher lawmaking system encourages the engaged citizenry to focus on the fundamental issues and determine whether any of the proposed solutions can gain the considered support, and therefore the accompanying political legitimacy, of a mobilized majority. During periods of normal politics, the system prevents the political elite from undermining the hard-won achievements of the People "behind the citizenry's back"—requiring leaders to return to the People and mobilize their considered support before foundational principles might be revised in a democratic way.

The aim is to learn what history can teach about the ways in which Americans have translated the heady rhetoric of constitutional politics into enduring judgments of higher law. Only after canvassing our past two centuries of practice can we look intelligently to the future: Is our existing system of higher lawmaking in good repair? If not, how should it be reformed?

The Professional Narrative

Our search requires a critical reexamination of the conceptual tools we use to interpret the constitutional past. Modern Americans are entirely familiar with the fact that their Constitution has changed fundamentally over the course of two centuries. But they have been taught to conceptualize these changes in ways that trivialize their character.

---

[2] See Albert Hirschman, *Shifting Involvements* (Princeton: Princeton University Press, 1982).

The principal source of trivialization has been the legal profession. Day after day, the courts try to control our most powerful elected officials by searching out the meaning of decisions made in the name of the People a century or two ago. The things they allow themselves to see in the past determine, sometimes dramatically, what all of us can do in the here and now. It is their professional narrative, as I shall call it, that blocks insight into the character of our historical experience in constitutional transformation.

The problem does not involve the outright denial of fundamental change. No serious judge, lawyer, or scholar has trouble recognizing that the Constitution of the late twentieth century is very different from the eighteenth-century version. Nor do they experience difficulty in identifying crucial periods of constitutional reorganization. While particular doctrines owe their origins to the work of many different generations, two historical periods stand out. The first is the Reconstruction Republicans' transformation of the Union in the aftermath of the Civil War. The second is the New Deal Democrats' legitimation of activist national government in the aftermath of the Great Depression of the 1930s.

As with the original Founding, neither of these sweeping transformations came about overnight. Each was preceded by a generation and more of political agitation that eroded the perceived legitimacy of preexisting constitutional arrangements. This lengthy period of critique prepared the way for a decade of intensive constitutional reorganization. In 1860, constitutional lawyers could endlessly argue about secession of the states and slavery in the territories; by 1870, such questions were no longer open to fair dispute. The agonies of civil war had been translated into new constitutional meanings that would shape legal discourse for generations.

The same pattern—lengthy critique capped by a transformational decade—also marks the process by which the activist welfare state gained constitutional legitimacy. As late as 1931, the power of the United States government to regulate the economy was subject to a complex set of fundamental limitations—whose precise character served as the centerpiece of ceaseless doctrinal debate. By 1941, this intricate web had disintegrated and the Constitution now allowed ongoing governmental intervention in social and economic life. The agonies of the Great Depression had provoked a fundamental reworking of our preexisting constitutional identity.

After these two transformations, American government was very different from anything the Founders had experienced. No longer had We the People established a decentralized federal system that allowed white men to pursue their self-interest within a market economy. Americans had constituted a powerful national government with unquestioned

constitutional authority to secure the legal equality and economic welfare of all its citizens regardless of the state in which they happen to
reside.

So much, I take it, is common ground for all students of the American
constitution—citizens no less than scholars, politicians no less than
judges. Whenever some new current of opinion gains political promi-
nence, the popular mind—as if by reflex—recurs to these great historical
achievements in an effort to measure the new movement's significance.
If asked to state the fundamental question raised by the Reagan presidency, I can do no better than: To what extent did it succeed in leading
the American People to repudiate the welfare state legitimated during
the New Deal? The modern civil rights movement cannot be understood without recognizing the power of the question: Is it not past time
for the American People to redeem the promise of equality made after
the Civil War?

My problem arises when we turn from constitutional substance to
higher lawmaking process: How did Americans of the nineteenth and
twentieth centuries define, debate, and finally decide to support the
transformative proposals championed by their respective parties of constitutional renewal?

The Existing Story Line

Today's Americans come to this question at a great disadvantage. As far
as Reconstruction is concerned, they are entirely at the mercy of specialists. The great struggles of the nineteenth century are now beyond the
recall of our grandparents. As I write these words, darkness is settling
over the New Deal. The constitutional meaning of the 1930s will soon
be determined exclusively by Americans whose first acquaintance with
the facts was gained in half-remembered conversations with elders, in
tenth-grade civics, in books of history, political science—and in the professional narrative retold daily in the nation's courtrooms.

Here is where the lawyers have let their fellow citizens down. To measure their collective act of trivialization, I shall use as a benchmark the
orthodox story that lawyers tell themselves about the Founding. If anything, modern constitutionalists are increasingly prepared to recognize,
and reflect upon, the revolutionary redefinition of the higher lawmaking
process attempted by the Philadelphia convention. After all, the convention did not come together in a Lockean state of nature, but in a dense
legal environment established by the existing constitutions in each of
the thirteen states, joined in "perpetual Union" through the Articles of
Confederation. If the Federalists had played the game defined by these
rules, their Constitution never would have been ratified.

In response to their predicament, the Federalists asserted the right to redefine the rules in the name of the People. Even more remarkably, most of their opponents went along with this effort to redefine the rules of the game. The Articles of Confederation, solemnly ratified by all thirteen states only a few years before, seemingly required an extraordinarily formidable higher lawmaking process if they hoped to gain legitimacy for their exercise in revision. Its thirteenth Article required the Founding Federalists to gain the unanimous consent of all thirteen state legislatures to their sweeping constitutional proposals. Only then would the Articles recognize them as valid amendments to the decisions made previously.

The Federalists responded to this textual demand by rejecting it. They revolutionized the process, no less than the substance, of constitutional order. The Federalists owed their success to a distinctive process of institutional adaptation. While they played fast and loose with the existing rules, they did not break entirely with the preexisting institutional matrix. Instead they bootstrapped their way to legitimacy by using old institutions in new ways to enhance their claim to speak for the People.[3] This fascinating process of *unconventional adaptation* will be the central object of our study. Americans owe their remarkable constitutional continuity only to their repeated success in unconventional adaptations of preexisting institutions at moments of grave crisis.

For the moment, however, it is enough to contrast existing treatments of the Founding with the received interpretation of subsequent transformations. Quite simply, the professional narrative obliterates all trace of a similar bootstrapping process when dealing with Reconstruction and New Deal. When lawyers turn to the great Civil War Amendments, they treat Reconstruction Republicans as if they had obediently

---

[3] Akhil Reed Amar's essay in this volume usefully explores the way in which the Federalists used the principles of popular sovereignty to help justify their end run around existing institutions. Unfortunately, he does not try to explore the legal objections aggressively advanced by anti-Federalists. Nor does he move beyond doctrinal arguments to explore the fascinating, if irregular, institutional processes through which the fundamental debate was resolved in a way that ultimately allowed the losers to concede, very grudgingly, the legitimacy of the new Constitution.

Instead, Amar treats the dispute as if he were arguing before a hypothetical Supreme Court; he provides a document that resembles a legal brief seeking to assure the nonexistent justices that the Federalist end run was perfectly legal. I remain convinced, however, that a more balanced presentation of the anti-Federalist argument would reveal that the constitutional convention was engaged in a deeply problematic effort to play fast and loose with the preexisting rules of the game. Rather than denying the seriousness of the problems, it is more enlightening to determine how eighteenth-century Americans managed to resolve their bitter legal argument without the existence of a Court. I shall explore this aspect of the matter at greater length in my forthcoming book, *We the People: Transformations* (Cambridge, Mass.: Harvard University Press, 1996), for which this essay will serve, in modified form, as the first chapter.

followed down the formal tracks for constitutional amendment established by Article V of the 1787 Constitution.

The New Deal is treated even more dismissively. At least lawyers are
willing to admit that the Civil War Amendments changed the substantive law in fundamental ways; in contrast, they tell themselves a story
about the New Deal that denies that anything creative was going on.
They treat the constitutional struggles of the 1930s as if they were the
product of an intellectual mistake made by a handful of holdover Republicans on the Supreme Court. These laggards lacked the wit to recognize that John Marshall, even James Madison, were crypto–New Dealers
who authorized the creation of the modern welfare state. On the reg-
nant view, the epic battles between the Old Court and the New Deal
should never have happened. The Court should have immediately
dressed the Roosevelt regime up in the clothes of the Founding Fathers.
The anti-Roosevelt majority on the Supreme Court were fools or knaves
to imagine the contrary.

Combining these stories about the Founding, Reconstruction, and
New Deal, the overarching message is a continuing decline in constitutional creativity. Apparently, the most sweeping transformation of the
twentieth century is best understood through a myth of rediscovery—
it was not Franklin Roosevelt, but James Madison, who laid the constitutional foundations for the New Deal. Even the Civil War and Reconstruction are not to be understood as a second American Revolution—at
least from a legal angle, the proposal and ratification of the Fourteenth
Amendment are no different from the most trivial amendment in our
sacred text. The last time the American People engaged in unconventional forms of popular sovereignty was at the Founding.

Revision

American lawyers are a contentious bunch. Curiously, however, they
have reached a rare unaninimity in endorsing this grim diagnosis of the
American condition. Every time a lawyer rises in court to tell familar
stories about the Founding, Reconstruction, and New Deal, he is casting modern Americans as tired epigones, without an ongoing experience
of successful constitutional politics. Such an insult would be acceptable,
I suppose, if it were based on the hard truth. But if it isn't true, how
can serious lawyers continue to aid and abet in this collective act of civic
trivialization?

I will be pointing to some large professional advantages resulting
from a revision of the reigning narrative. A new approach to the past
will greatly clarify the interpretive dilemmas judges face in the modern

practice of judicial review; it will allow new insights into the dilemmas confronted by judges in past eras; it will open up new dimensions of interdisciplinary collaboration with historians, political scientists, and philosophers. But all these specialist advantages pale when compared to the simple question of integrity: Can lawyers allow themselves to abuse their special knowledge and power by systematically demeaning the political creativity of their fellow citizens?

But it would be naive to rely on the force of this question to carry the day. The received constitutional narrative has one priceless advantage in its struggle for survival. It exists as a pervasive cultural reality in the life of the law, and you can't beat something with nothing. If we hope to do better, constitutionalists must return to their sources, and discover that they tell a very different story. They reveal both Reconstruction Republicans and New Deal Democrats refusing to follow the path for constitutional revision set out by their predecessors; like the Federalists before them, they transformed existing systems of higher lawmaking—what is more, they were perfectly aware of the unconventional bootstrapping operation in which they were engaged. It is we, not they, who have suppressed the telltale evidence. Even at the end of this study, many questions and gaps will remain. It will be more than enough to establish that there *is* a deeper story yearning to be told—if only we worked together to make its meanings clear.

Indeed, it would be a mistake to plunge immediately into the details. Since each of the crucial episodes is fascinating in its own right, there is a danger of losing sight of the whole. Let me begin, then, with an orienting sketch.

The Meaning of Article V

Wherever we may end our story, it is clear where we should begin: the fifth article of the original Constitution provides future generations with a special set of higher lawmaking procedures for constitutional amendment. These Founding rules are dimly familiar to all Americans who have survived the terrors of high school civics: Future movements in constitutional politics are invited either to gain the support of two-thirds of both houses of Congress for their initiative, or invoke an onerous procedure that will lead to the convocation of a new constitutional convention. Even if they persuade Congress or a convention to endorse their initiatives, they confront a second obstacle. They must gain the assent of three-fourths of the states, acting through legislatures or conventions. Only then does the article explicitly authorize them to enact their proposals into higher law in the name of the People.

As one might expect, these rules are not so clear as high school civics might suggest. But the crucial question is more fundamental: Should modern Americans read Article V as if it described the only mechanisms they may appropriately use for constitutional revision at the dawn of the twenty-first century?

The text does not answer this question explicitly. None of its 143 words says anything like "this Constitution may only be amended through the following procedures, and in no other way." The Article makes its procedures sufficient, but not necessary, for the enactment of a valid constitutional amendment. It is up to us, not the text, to decide whether to convert a sufficient condition into a necessary one and give the Founding rules a monopoly over the methods of amendment.

Given the importance of this decision, we should not make it arbitrarily. Much of the lawyer's craft involves the thoughtful resolution of such textual indeterminacies. We will be ranging over the full range of interpretive disciplines—from the intention of the Framers to the decisions of the modern Supreme Court. For this introductory sketch, it will be enough to confront the monopolistic reading with the challenge posed by Reconstruction. This, I shall suggest, should suffice to render the monopolistic reading unacceptable and move the argument to a second, and more constructive, phase.[4]

[4] I should note, however, the support that Akhil Amar's essay in this volume gives to my project. Placing Article V against its eighteenth-century context, Amar persuasively argues that the American Founders should not be read as insisting upon a monopoly for their rules of revision. Instead, it is the fundamental principle of popular sovereignty, not the rules of Article V, that should serve to guide us in articulating the "rules of recognition" organizing American law. (For more on *grundnormen* and rules of recognition, see Frederick Schauer's essay in this volume.)

Amar and I differ, at least in our emphasis, when taking the next step: Given the non-exclusive character of Article V, how should lawyers go about elaborating the additional ways the American Constitution may be legitimately amended? At least in his work thus far, Amar answers with his eyes firmly focused upon the eighteenth century and seeks to establish that the Founding generation had a clean and crisp answer: the Founders thought that the People were always entitled to convene special constitutional conventions; they also believed that the political majority at such conventions were automatically authorized to speak for the People.

While Amar is right to emphasize the importance of the constitutional conventions, my reading of eighteenth-century practice is more complex. I do not believe that it can be reduced to a few simple rules of the kind that Amar proposes. I will pursue this point at greater length in *We the People: Transformations*, but it is more important here to note a second, and more important, methodological point. As the text suggests, I deny that the lawyerly search for the appropriate supplements to Article V should focus exclusively upon the eighteenth century. It is more important to consider the ways that Americans moved beyond Article V to revise the Constitution during Reconstruction and the New Deal. These great historical precedents must be analyzed thoroughly by any serious legal efffort to elaborate the modern American law of higher lawmaking. Thus far at least, Amar has not

Some simple mathematics introduces the problem confronted by the Republicans during Reconstruction. During the 1860s, there were never more than thirty-seven states in the Union. Under the terms of Article V, this gave an absolute veto over constitutional initiatives to any ten states—one-fourth plus one. Despite the Union's victory in the Civil War, it was all too easy for the Republicans to see how such a veto bloc might be assembled. There were no less than eleven states returning to the Union from the former Confederacy—as well as a number of northern states whose assent to Republican constitutional initiatives could not be guaranteed. The Republicans' opponents—and there were millions in the North as well as the South—were confident of victory as long as constitutional amendments were processed in the way envisioned by Article V. They insisted that the Republicans play the game in strict accordance with the traditional rules, confident that the Founders had dealt them a losing hand.

The Republican leadership responded as one might expect—with anxiety, and yet with grim determination. As the constitutional crisis reached its climax in the struggle over the Fourteenth Amendment, they refused to allow their opponents' legalistic interpretation of Article V to block Reconstruction. In the face of dramatic challenges by conservatives, they gained popular support to press the rules of Article V beyond their breaking point. Only in this way did they finally win the constitutional authority to validate the Fourteenth Amendment in the name of the People.

A large chunk of my forthcoming book, *We the People: Transformations,* will be required to establish this single conclusion. If, however, I persuade you that the Republicans did not follow the Founding principles, I think I have earned the right to dismiss the monopolistic interpretation of Article V. After all, the original Constitution does *not* explicitly try to monopolize the procedures used by future generations; indeed, as Akhil Amar argues in the next chapter, such a suggestion is inconsistent with fundamental principles of popular sovereignty. Why, then, read such a demand into the text at the cost of delegitimizing the Fourteenth Amendment?

It is far more plausible to adopt a pluralistic reading of the Founding text, one that permits its harmonious coexistence with the Reconstruc-

---

attempted such an analysis, but he seems to suppose that he may adopt eighteenth-century precedents to the twenty-first century without fundamental consideration of any intervening efforts by the American People to exercise their popular sovereignty. To this extent, Amar is far more originalist than historicist in his constitutional sensibility. See Morton J. Horwitz, "The Supreme Court, 1992 Term—Foreword: The Constitution of Change: Legal Fundamentality without Fundamentalism," *Harvard Law Review* 107 (1993): 32.

tion experience. Pluralists understand the rules for amendment laid down in 1787 as facilitative devices, which remain available when the American People choose to use them. But they deny that these rules exhaust the repertoire of legitimate techniques for constitutional revision. If we aim for a *comprehensive* statement of the modern law, we must move beyond the Founding and consider Reconstruction as a fundamental precedent in the evolving law of higher lawmaking.

This means, first, that we should try to state the relevant facts as dispassionately as we can: What problems did Republicans confront in using Article V and what were their available alternatives? Second, we must consider how each of the authoritative decision makers dealt with the problems they confronted. Third, we must organize individual responses to particular problems into larger patterns of constitutional decision. By the end, we shall be in a position to reflect upon the basic constitutional principles implicated by the larger patterns of practical decision making we have uncovered.

While this fourfold task requires some work, it should seem familiar to any competent lawyer. In principle, it is no different from the job she might do in examining the basic precedents defining the law of free speech (or the common law of automobile accidents, for that matter). If there is anything distinctive, it has less to do with legal method and more with the identity of the actors whose words and deeds are at the center of the constitutional stage. While decisions of the Supreme Court play a part in our story, a larger part will be played by presidents and Congresses—and their efforts to gain the support of the American People at general elections. We will be studying congressional committee reports, presidential proclamations, and party campaign platforms with the same care that lawyers usually reserve for Supreme Court opinions.

This shift in focus is only natural, given the nature of our question. Our subject is the law of constitutional lawmaking, not the way courts and others should interpret the law once it has been enacted. How, then, did nineteenth-century Americans define, debate, and finally decide which proposals for Reconstruction deserved to gain the authority of We the People of the United States? What is the relationship between these constitutional processes and those marked out by the Federalists in the original Constitution?

The Facts

First and foremost, the Republicans' process was more nation-centered than its Federalist predecessor. The rules of 1787 envision an equal partnership between the national government and the states in the process of higher lawmaking: while national actors dominate at the proposal stage, constitutional dialogue moves to the state level during ratification. During the 1860s, the Republicans used national institutions to call into question, ever more profoundly, the equal status of the states in our higher lawmaking system.

During the constitutional debate over slavery, the presidency served as the principal vehicle for the Republicans' assault on the Federalist premise. Not only did Abraham Lincoln's Emancipation Proclamation shift the constitutional status quo in 1863 before the Thirteenth Amendment was formally proposed; Andrew Johnson's role was, in many ways, even more remarkable. Johnson did not allow the southern states to suppose that the original Federalist idea of an equal nation-state partnership applied to their consideration of the Emancipation amendment. The president placed extraordinary pressures on the South. While these actions violated original Federalist principles, they fell short of pure military coercion. They did not, for example, deter Mississippi from formally rejecting the Thirteenth Amendment—though they significantly contributed to ratification by other states of the former Confederacy. The process is best described as a presidentially led ratification effort that diminished, but did not eliminate, the role of the states in the higher lawmaking process—an artful weave of old Federalist and new presidential patterns that culminated in Secretary Seward's proclamation of December 1865, declaring the Thirteenth Amendment part of our higher law.

This precedent will prove especially important when we encounter the New Deal—which represents yet another quantum leap in the development of the *model of presidential leadership*. As we turn to the Fourteenth Amendment, however, our analysis must take a different turn. Johnson refused to give this amendment the unconventional kinds of support that he had deployed on behalf of the Thirteenth in the preceding year. Instead, he opposed all further unconventional actions on the higher lawmaking front. This principled act of presidential opposition led to a dramatic struggle with the Reconstruction Congress for the mantle of national leadership left in the wake of Lincoln's assassination. The result was the elaboration of a second higher lawmaking pattern. The struggle over the Fourteenth Amendment generated a *model of congressional leadership* in which the Republicans on Capitol Hill finally gained the acceptance of the president (and the Supreme Court) of Congress's claim to speak for the American People.

The interbranch struggle evolved in four distinct stages. During most of 1866, Congress and the president struggled to an impasse from their citadels on either end of Pennsylvania Avenue: each issuing an escalating series of official messages that not only questioned their antagonists' substantive vision of the Union, but also challenged the very right of their opponent to speak on fundamental matters in the name of We the People of the United States.

This first period of constitutional counterpoint induced the contending parties to transform the next regular election into one of the great higher lawmaking events of American history. The congressional leadership proposed the Fourteenth Amendment as the platform on which they called upon the American People to renew their mandate. Andrew Johnson used all the resources of the presidency to mobilize constitutional conservatives against the Republicans, calling upon the People to repudiate the proposed Fourteenth Amendment by electing solid conservatives to Congress.

The result of these competing mobilizations was a decisive electoral victory for the party of constitutional reform. This inaugurated the second stage of the process. The returning Republicans claimed a mandate from the People for the Fourteenth Amendment; the conservatives, led by President Johnson, denied that the People had spoken decisively. The president successfully led ten southern state governments to exercise the veto seemingly offered them by the Federalists' Article V.

This put Congress in an awkward position, since these very same governments had been instrumental in giving the Thirteenth Amendment its three-fourths majority. Nonetheless, the Republicans in Congress refused to accept the legitimacy of Federalist constitutional norms. They sought to override the veto by destroying the southern governments that had rejected the amendment. They required all reconstructed governments in the South to ratify the amendment before gaining constitutional legitimacy.

This effort inaugurated the third phase of the process, which I will call the challenge to dissenting institutions. It begins with the enactment of the Reconstruction Act of March 2, 1867, and continues through the impeachment of Andrew Johnson one year later. During this period, Congress claimed a mandate from the People to destroy the autonomy of any institution—including the southern governments, the presidency, and the Supreme Court—that opposed the legitimation of the Fourteenth Amendment. In response, these dissenters remained free to resist congressional demands until the next round of elections in 1868—in the hope that constitutional conservatives might gain the decisive victory at the polls that had thus far eluded them.

And resist is precisely what the dissenters did until they confronted their moment of truth in March 1868: when the voters in the South, the constitutional conservatives on the Supreme Court, and, most crucially, President Andrew Johnson were forced to engage in some of the most pivotal decisions in our constitutional history. The central event was the president's impeachment trial, precipitated by Johnson's effort to slow down the ratification of the Fourteenth Amendment sufficiently so that it could remain a campaign issue in the upcoming 1868 elections. Would the president continue to resist the Republicans' vision of the Union—and thereby suffer impeachment at the hands of the Senate? Or would he try to save the presidency by making a belated "switch in time" in which he would accept Congress's effort to achieve ratification of the Fourteenth Amendment by un-Federalist means?

The president chose the latter course, inaugurating the final stage—the "switch in time." No longer did he attempt to frustrate congressional demands for a speedy reconstruction. He allowed southern ratification of the Fourteenth Amendment to proceed according to congressional directive. Only after he announced this "switch" did he gain sufficient Republican support in the Senate to avoid conviction at his impeachment trial. Virtually simultaneous "switches" by the other dissenting institutions also allowed them to preserve their institutional autonomy. As a consequence of all these switches, a new institutional situation emerged in the months after the impeachment trial. The fourth stage concludes with the president and the Court recognizing that the Republican Congress, after winning its decisive electoral victory of 1866, had indeed gained the constitutional authority to speak for the People in demanding ratification of the Fourteenth Amendment.

The Reconstructed Pattern

So much for the constitutional struggles that loom behind every legal citation to the Thirteenth and Fourteenth Amendments. For now, step back from this outline to define the decisive aspects of the Republicans' challenge to the preexisting Federalist system of higher lawmaking.

A major sticking point is clear enough. The Republicans challenged the Federalists' view that the states should be an equal partner in the amendment process, with the right to veto any innovation that did not meet with their overwhelming approval. This partnership made sense in an era when the relationship between national and state citizenship was itself deeply controversial—to the point where many believed that the citizens of a state could repudiate their membership in the Union through a collective act of secession. Given these pervasive uncertainties, it made sense for Article V to play it safe and provide for independent approval by states as well as the nation to fundamental change.

After the Civil War, however, the Republicans were prepared to end this uncertainty. The first sentence of their Fourteenth Amendment proclaimed the primacy of federal over state citizenship. When this assertion of primacy was threatened by a state veto under Article V, they gained the popular support necessary to challenge the article's premise that states were equal partners in the process of constitutional decision. In short, both the substance of the Fourteenth Amendment and the process through which it was enacted are grounded on the very same point: that We the People of the *United* States were now a nation that could express itself politically on fundamental matters independently of the will of the individual states.

Once we grasp the fundamental character of this shift toward nation-centered patterns of higher lawmaking, the next challenge is to define the Republican innovations with greater clarity. Three basic points are crucial. First, the nineteenth-century patterns involved the rise of the *separation of powers* to a new role in the higher lawmaking system. Under the original Federalist constitution, the basic building block for higher lawmaking was the division of powers between the national government and the states. While the separation of powers between Congress, president, and Court was crucial in normal lawmaking on the national level, it had no comparable role in the Federalist understanding of higher lawmaking. In the aftermath of Civil War, the contending constitutional movements transformed the national separation of powers into a process through which the protagonists might test each others' claims to a decisive "mandate" from the People on behalf of their rival visions of the reconstructed Union.

Second, the rise of the separation of powers led the contending movements to give a new meaning to *national elections* that are a regularly scheduled part of the constitutional calendar. While the ideological meaning of these elections is normally diffused by a host of local and regional issues, a prolonged period of constitutional conflict in Washington may induce the protagonists to break the impasse by mobilizing their forces in the country in an effort to oust their opponents from their positions of strength in the separation of powers. When this leads to a clear and decisive victory for one side or another, as in 1866, the terms of the struggle for higher lawmaking authority will shift: the winners will claim a mandate for their constitutional initiative from the People and may demand that the dissenting branches reconsider their previous patterns of resistance. When faced with threats by the victorious branch to their normal operation in the separation of powers, the dissenting branches may find it more appropriate to recognize that the victors *do* speak for the People than to continue resisting in the hope that the voters will come to their assistance at the next election.

My first two points focused on the new institutional principles implicated in the Republicans' act of constitutional creation. The third focuses on the way separation of powers and national elections interact with one another over time to make up a four-stage schema of constitutional debate and decision. During the first stage—constitutional impasse—the constitutional protagonists contend with one another on relatively equal terms from different citadels of strength in the separation of powers. The effort to break the impasse generates the second stage—an electoral struggle to win a popular mandate—in which the contenders mobilize their forces in the country for a decisive political victory. While such victories prove notoriously illusive, occasions do arise when one or another contender can plausibly claim a "mandate" from the People on behalf of their constitutional initiative. If, as may well happen, the electoral losers in the other branches remain skeptical of the breadth and depth of their opponents' popular support, the electoral victors may provoke a third stage in the transformative process by challenging the normal institutional independence of dissenting branches.

During this third stage—the challenge to institutional legitimacy—the incumbents of the challenged branches are faced with a hard choice. As in the impeachment trial of Andrew Johnson, they must decide whether they should stick to their guns and appeal once more to the People for vindication at the next regularly scheduled national election or whether they should protect the autonomy of their office by accepting the new constitutional order.

The final stage of the process—the "switch in time"—is reached if all the relevant branches decide that further resistance will lead only to institutional destruction rather than electoral vindication by the People. Here, President Johnson and the leaders of other dissenting institutions call off their resistance. As a consequence, the constitutional reformers allow them their institutional autonomy within the new regime that they have established.

To summarize this four-stage process in terms of a simple schema: Constitutional Impasse → Electoral "Mandate" → Challenge to Dissenting Institutions → the "Switch in Time."

From Reconstruction to New Deal

To recapitulate my argument: First, modern lawyers must confront Reconstruction as a fundamental precedent in the American law of higher lawmaking and refuse to allow the 143 words of Article V of the original Constitution to monopolize their understanding. Second, I outlined salient features of the process through which Americans debated and decided the constitutional meaning of the Civil War. The third step of my argument involves the use of the Reconstruction precedent as a tool for analyzing subsequent transformations in American history—most notably, the New Deal. Once we have rediscovered the process through which the Republicans won their authority to speak for the People, we can grasp a series of remarkable parallels between the 1860s and the 1930s. The New Deal Democrats were obliged to expose themselves to a four-stage process of debate and decision that was broadly similar to the one encountered by the Reconstruction Republicans.

The New Deal Pattern

Roosevelt's first term culminated in a constitutional impasse between the branches similar to the one that set constitutional reformers and constitutional conservatives at loggerheads in 1866. Once again, the separation of powers provided a key mechanism for channeling constitutional debate—allowing the conservatives institutional space to raise basic questions of legitimacy and challenge the reformers to go to the People if they hoped for ultimate success. As in 1866, this invited the constitutional reformers to use the next regularly scheduled election as a device to break the constitutional impasse. When the New Dealers gained a crushing victory in the presidential and congressional elections of 1936, they claimed a mandate from the People in support of their new activist vision of American government.

As with the Reconstruction Republicans, they made this claim by demanding the rapid transformation of personnel at the helm of the leading conservative branch. Since the leading conservative branch during Reconstruction was the Presidency, the Republicans threatened Johnson with impeachment unless he accepted their constitutional reforms. Since the leading conservative branch in the 1930s was the Court, the Democrats threatened the justices with court packing if they continued to defend the principles of laissez-faire constitutionalism: freedom of contract and limited national government. While impeachment and court packing differ in legal form, their constitutional function was identical: to confront the leading conservative institution with a distinctive, and fundamental, question. Should it continue supporting the older constitutional tradition at the risk of permanent damage to its institutional autonomy?

In both cases, the decision of the conservative branch was the same. President Johnson and the Supreme Court made a "switch in time" in the late 1860s and 1930s. On both occasions, this allowed the triumphant spokesmen for the People to validate their fundamental constitutional revisions. As in 1868, the New Deal transformation ended with all three branches accepting the new vision of constitutional government that had been so bitterly controverted during the preceding period of debate, mobilization, and decision.

As the constitutional conservatives gave ground, the reformers allowed the dissenting branch—the presidency during Reconstruction, the Supreme Court during the New Deal—to escape grave, long-term damage. If Johnson had been impeached, or the Supreme Court packed, the presidency or the Court would have been permanently impaired. Instead, once the switch was made, the reformers narrowly failed to convince the Senate to impeach the president or pack the Court. This not only enabled the separation of powers to survive. It encouraged the endangered branch to rehabilitate itself over time by playing a constructive role in the elaboration of the new constitutional order.

What Was New about the New Deal?

The New Deal pattern is best viewed, then, as a variation on historic precedents established during Reconstruction. It was the Reconstruction Republicans, not the New Deal Democrats, who first combined the separation of powers with decisive electoral victories to gain the constitutional authority to speak in the voice of We the People of the *United* States—a voice distinct from, but no less authentic than, the voice of We the People of the United *States* expressed through the Federalist rules of Article V. But, of course, it is crucially important to clarify the variations introduced in the 1930s—since they mark the parameters of modern constitutional development. I shall be emphasizing three themes.

The first, and most important, involves the role of the presidency. While Presidents Lincoln and Johnson played unprecedented roles in the constitutional emancipation of the slaves, presidential leadership came to an end with Andrew Johnson's defection during the struggle over the Fourteenth Amendment. In contrast, Roosevelt survived all assassination attempts. This meant that the New Deal Democrats could rely on the presidency to provide ongoing constitutional leadership.

The Democrats' good fortune gave them more lawmaking options. They did not need to follow the example of the Reconstruction Congress as it destroyed state governments when they vetoed the Fourteenth Amendment. Nor did they need to threaten a hostile president with impeachment. Instead, Roosevelt could target the Supreme Court and codify the New Deal vision by flooding it with new justices prepared to endorse a radical transformation of traditional constitutional doctrine.

This led to a second fundamental change—the self-conscious use of *transformative judicial appointments* as a central tool for constitutional change. Roosevelt introduced this device in his famous court-packing proposal of 1937—which would have given the president the right to make six new nominations immediately, allowing the Court to expand from nine to fifteen. When the Old Court switch took the political wind out of this radical proposal, president and Congress elaborated a more gradual, but similar, approach. As traditionalist justices resigned or died, they were systematically replaced by appointments prepared to support and elaborate a transformative vision of constitutional law. This new mechanism for presidential leadership gave a new importance to the Senate hearings. Previously, it was considered improper for the Senate to call nominees personally to testify about their views. After 1937, it became an accepted part of constitutional practice—with Felix Frankfurter the first nominee required to run this gauntlet.

By the early 1940s the stage had been set for the third change. Given the Senate's support of a transformative appointments strategy, the Supreme Court had been reconstituted. No longer was the fate of New Deal legislation resolved by close votes that turned on the manipulation of traditional legal categories. Instead, the Court now unanimously swept away entire doctrinal structures. *Lochner v. New York* was not only rejected, but was demonized as a symbol of an entire constitutional order that had been dominant only a decade before. This order was now displaced by *transformative opinions* that gave ringing validation to activist governmental management of economic and social institutions.

These opinions operate today as the functional equivalent of formal constitutional amendments. Indeed, *Lochner* is a far more powerful constitutional symbol than many of those inscribed into the text by the Founding Federalists or Reconstruction Republicans. Judges are far more respectful of the New Deal precedents, for example, than they are when it comes to interpreting the Republicans' guarantee to all citizens of their "privileges [and] immunities" or the Federalists' demand that the "obligations of contract" be protected.

I do not claim that this New Deal jurisprudence is an unchangeable element of our Constitution—but then again, neither is most of the formal text.[5] My central claim is this: If and when these New Deal principles are radically transformed, debate and decision will occur through a higher lawmaking process comparable to the one led by President Roosevelt in the 1930s.

From Roosevelt to Reagan—and Beyond

The central significance of this New Deal model has been paradoxically confirmed during the last decade. As in the 1930s, so in the 1980s: Ronald Reagan, like Franklin Roosevelt, refused to put the presidency's principal energies behind formal amendments—in this case, amend-

[5] For further discussion of the problem of amendability, see Ackerman, *We the People: Foundations* (Cambridge: Harvard University Press, 1991), pp. 13–16, 320–21; and Ackerman, "Rooted Cosmopolitanism," forthcoming in *Ethics* (Spring 1994).

ments to balance the budget and overrule *Roe v. Wade*. Like Roosevelt, he claimed a mandate from the People for a new breed of Supreme Court justice—and sought to fulfill this mandate through a series of transformative judicial appointments that would jolt constitutional doctrine out of its rut. The aim, as in the Roosevelt years, was to gain a commanding judicial majority for transformative opinions that would demonize the leading cases of the prior era: If Justice Scalia had his way, *Roe* would be treated with the same contempt that the New Deal Court reserved for the leading cases of the *Lochner* era.

The parallel ends at this point. The Reagan effort at presidential leadership does not culminate in transformative opinions proclaiming a decisive break with the past. Rather than demonizing *Roe*, as the New Deal Court demonized *Lochner*, the reconstituted Court of the 1990s pledged its continued fidelity to the past. The crucial decision here is *Planned Parenthood v. Casey*—in which Reagan-Bush justices cast the decisive votes to preserve *Roe* against the angry dissent of Justice Scalia.

While the outcome of the 1980s was different from the 1930s, the process by which the American people debated their constitutional future was uncannily similar. In both cases, the presidency served as the institutional focus of an effort to lead the American People to a revised understanding of their constitutional identity; in both cases, the critical question was the extent to which the president could convince Congress and the Court to accept his demand for fundamental change in the name of We the People of the United States; in both cases, the fate of the president's higher lawmaking pretensions was climaxed by a struggle in the Senate over his effort to make transformative appointments to the Supreme Court.

The substantive views of Robert Bork were different from Felix Frankfurter's. But the two nominations played uncannily similar functions in the evolving practice of presidential leadership. Both men were nominated by transformative presidents in the seventh year of their tenures; both were archetypal transformative appointments—immensely capable scholars who had provided intellectual leadership to the political movements ascendant in the White House, they were transparently eager to write transformative opinions that repudiated key elements of existing doctrine. Just as Frankfurter provided intellectual leadership in the New Deal Court's repudiation of *Lochner*'s jurisprudence, so too would Bork play a similar role in the repudiation of *Roe*, and the entire jurisprudence that made *Roe* plausible.

The failure of the Bork nomination had profound consequences upon the next stage of constitutional development. Instead of following up with another transformative appointment, the Reagan-Bush administration retreated and began to nominate solid professionals who were uninterested in a radical constitutional break with the past. Thus, by the end of the Bush administration, the juridical scene looked very different from the end of Roosevelt's third term. Instead of unanimous transformative opinions demonizing leading cases of the past era, the Reagan-Bush Court was proclaiming the importance of *stare decisis* and insisting on the need for continuity with the past. The fact that Roosevelt succeeded, and Reagan-Bush failed, in their efforts at transformative practice should not blind us to the striking similarity in the processes through which they both sought to revolutionize our higher law in the name of We the People.

Having isolated a recurring model of presidential leadership, and placed it in deeper historical context, I conclude by considering its reform. Should the precedents inherited from the Roosevelt and Reagan years be radically repudiated, interstitially modified, wholeheartedly accepted?

Beyond Formalism

My arguments require reference to lots of history, some political science, and a little philosophy—so much that it threatens to obscure the fundamentally legal character of my quest. For I am asking myself a single legal question: If Americans of the 1990s wish to revise their Constitution, what are the *legal* alternatives they may legitimately pursue?

Now, it would be nice if a thoughtful lawyer could answer this very important question in a page or two or ten. Such a clear and crisp statement would not only satisfy lawyers, whose desires for conceptual neatness sometimes verge on the pathological. It would also yield very real advantages for all Americans. The first of these is fair notice. From the very beginning, each side knows precisely what it must do in order to emerge victorious from the constitutional struggle that lies ahead. As a consequence, partisans are given a fair opportunity to marshal their political forces at the critical moments. This makes it harder for them to explain away defeat by saying that they didn't know that a critical decision was about to be made and so held some of their political forces in reserve. A formalist process has the further merit of signaling the point at which a particular exercise in constitutional lawmaking comes to an end—at a predetermined point the new amendment will turn out either a clear winner or a clear loser. While committed activists retain the right to begin again from the beginning, the rest of the citizenry can choose to relax their political attention and turn to other things.

In a dualist democracy, this is no mean achievement. One of dualism's guiding principles is the economy of virtue:[6] the Constitution cannot, and should not, try to force citizens to remain in a constant state of constitutional agitation. Normal Americans have a right to assert their constitutional will in politics without making this project their life's work; by bringing constitutional exertions to an unambiguous end, the formalist does as much service as when he permits a new movement to signal a new set of constitutional intentions to the public at large.

And yet, for all this, formalism cannot escape the vices of its virtues. Formalism achieves clarity and structure only at the cost of *presuming* the existence of a mobilized and considered popular judgment by pointing to some readily observable institutional criteria—say, the affirmative vote of two-thirds of Congress and three-fourths of the state legislatures. Underlying this presumption is something I shall call the theory of institutional resistance. The idea is that an elaborate institutional obstacle course will exhaust all political groups that fail to mobilize and sustain the massive public-regarding support required for constitutional legitimacy. Institutional resistance, in short, will frustrate the cynical manipulation of the idea of a higher law by coalitions of narrow pressure groups. While there is something to this idea, the design of the perfect obstacle course is transparently a tricky business. For the obstacle course cannot be so exhausting that it resists even a massive public-regarding majority on those rare occasions when the People-with-a-capital-P *do* have something new to say.

To put the point scientistically, any formalist rule system suffers two dangers. The first danger is the *false positive*: Here the formal system signals that the People have spoken, although the supporters of the initiative have not in fact mobilized the sustained and considered support that dualist principles require of a new constitutional solution. This is a very bad thing, and thus any formal rule system should be designed to make it unlikely.

As this risk is diminished, however, it inevitably increases the risk of a *false negative*: By making it hard for a momentary special-interest coalition to impersonate the People, the formalist's obstacle course may stifle the expression of constitutional movements that, after years of mobilized debate that has penetrated deeply into the consciousness of ordinary citizens, won the sustained support of a decisive and sustained majority.[7] This is also a very bad thing—indeed, if lawyerly elites were allowed to use the rules to stifle the considered judgments of constitutional politics, it could lead most Americans to despair at the very idea

---

[6] See Ackerman, *We the People: Foundations*, esp. chaps. 7–10.

[7] For an extended discussion of the characteristics required of a majority before it has the authority to legislate a new constitutional solution, see ibid., chap. 9.

that We the People can meaningfully give our governors their marching orders.

Formalists might dismiss this second danger if, after two centuries of history, it has proved merely hypothetical. But the truth is different. At two of the greatest crises in their constitutional history, Americans were face to face with a very grave risk of a false negative. If they chose to play punctiliously by the rules of Article V, Reconstruction Republicans and New Deal Democrats confronted the clear and present danger that their long and successful struggle to mobilize the People for fundamental change would be stifled by legalistic nitpicking. In response, they sought to win the support of the People for a change in the rules of revision.

Thus the need for extended argument. I want to establish that these fascinating efforts to modify the rules in midstream, to bootstrap the movement to constitutional legitimacy, were not themselves lawless. This claim, of course, supposes that there is more to law than rules. But this is a very uncontroversial notion in jurisprudence.[8] Every thoughtful legal analyst, I would hope, recognizes that law includes the study of principles and precedents no less than rules—and that he or she must try to state the law in a way that takes all three into account.

Sometimes it may prove possible to set the principles, precedents, and rules into a neatly ordered sequence—with the leading precedents falling under crisp rules, which are in turn illuminated by fundamental principles. While such neoclassical reasoning structures aren't fashionable right now, they sometimes can be cogently developed. But sometimes they can't be. After two centuries of unruly but creative constitutional politics, neoclassical order is simply unattainable. The great historical precedents simply do not fall under crisp rules.

But they do display important family resemblances. As long as we do not expect to reduce these precedents to simple-seeming rules, it is possible to elaborate fundamental criteria that political movements must satisfy before gaining higher lawmaking authority.

This is the purpose of the model of presidential leadership—to provide historically rooted criteria for appraising future efforts by political movements to use the White House as a springboard for a new beginning in constitutional law. The next time that a president comes forward aggressively to claim some sweeping mandate from the People, constitutionalists should be far better prepared to use the experience of the past to test the inevitable claims of a sweeping mandate that will emerge from the White House. Despite the rise of presidential leadership in the modern republic, the chief executive has not (yet) won the authority to jolt

---

[8] See Ronald Dworkin, *Taking Rights Seriously* (Cambridge: Harvard University Press, 1978), chaps. 2, 3; Karl Llewellyn, *The Common Law Tradition: Deciding Appeals* (Boston: Little Brown, 1960).

the Constitution into a new direction on the basis of a victory or two at the polls. The precedents continue to constrain profoundly the occasions upon which the separation of powers may be used to legitimate a new constitutional beginning in the name of We the People. The challenge for the legal community (and for the American people) is to begin a serious conversation now that will allow us to play a disciplined role in the next crisis of presidential leadership.

Five

Popular Sovereignty and Constitutional Amendment

AKHIL REED AMAR

> We hold these truths to be self-evident, that all
> men are created equal, that they are endowed by
> their Creator with certain unalienable Rights. . . .
> That . . . Governments . . . deriv[e] their just
> powers from the consent of the governed. That
> whenever any Form of Government becomes
> destructive of [its] ends, it is the right of the
> People to alter or abolish it, and to institute
> new Government, laying its foundations on
> such principles and organizing its Powers in such
> form, as to them shall seem most likely to effect
> their Safety and Happiness.

IF UNDERSTOOD—and taken seriously—these words from the Declaration of Independence require a fundamental rethinking of conventional understandings of the U.S. Constitution. Concretely: The U.S. Constitution is a far more majoritarian and populist document than we have generally thought; and We the People of the United States have a legal right to alter our government—to amend our Constitution—via a majoritarian and populist mechanism akin to a national referendum, even though that mechanism is not explicitly specified in Article V.[1]

This essay is a highly abridged version of the Southmayd Inaugural Lecture, delivered at Yale Law School on November 30, 1993, and published as "The Consent of the Governed" in *Columbia Law Review* 94 (1994): 457. The interested reader is urged to consult that article for more extensive quotation, documentation, and analysis.

[1] Specifically, I believe that Congress would be obliged to call a convention to propose amendments if a majority of American voters so petition; and that an amendment could be lawfully ratified by a simple majority of the American electorate.

What Article V Does Not Say and Cannot Do

Let us first consider the text of Article V[2] and, more particularly, what it does *not* say: that it is the *only* way to amend the Constitution. Of course, we often read the enumeration of one mode (or in this case four modes, if we multiply the two Article V mechanisms for proposing amendments by the two Article V mechanisms for ratifying them) as impliedly precluding any other modes. Congress, for example, cannot pass laws other than via bicameralism and presentment. But there is an alternative way of understanding the implied exclusivity of Article V: It enumerates the only mode(s) by which ordinary *government*—Congress and state legislatures—can change the Constitution, and thereby free themselves from various limits on their power imposed by the Constitution itself. (Without Article V, government would have no such power.)[3] But under this alternative view, Article V nowhere prevents the *People* themselves, acting apart from ordinary government, from exercising their legal right to alter or abolish government, via the proper legal procedures. Article V presupposes this background right of the People, and does nothing to interfere with it. It merely specifies how ordinary government can amend the Constitution *without* recurring to the People themselves, the true and sovereign source of all lawful power.

The conventional view of Article V sees it as *implementing* Jefferson's formulation of consent by the governed, rather than *supplementing* it; but this makes hash of Jefferson's language and logic. Article V is *government*-driven: If exclusive, it gives ordinary government officials— Congress and state legislatures—a monopoly on initiating the process of constitutional amendment. By contrast, Jefferson's self-evident truth is *People*-driven. It cannot be satisfied by a government monopoly on amendment, for the government might simply block any constitutional change that limits government's power, even if strongly desired by the People. (Elections for government officials do not solve this problem; in the 1780s, not all members of the polity were even eligible to vote for, say, state senators, who in turn helped elect U.S. senators; but all members of the polity—"freemen," in 1787—were by definition part of "the People" eligible to participate in People-driven constitutional change.)[4]

[2] For the text of Article V, see this volume, p. 5.

[3] Gordon Wood, *The Creation of the American Republic* (Chapel Hill: University of North Carolina Press, 1969), pp. 273, 276, 277, 290, 306, 337.

[4] Ibid., p. 289. The problem remains, even today. If a legislator in any given district refuses to support a constitutional change voters favor, voters in that district can throw the rascal out only by depriving the district of legislative seniority and clout, in a kind of prisoner's dilemma.

Second, and related, Article V is *minoritarian*. Precisely because ordinary government is distrusted, it may not amend the Constitution without amassing an extraordinary bloc of government officials. A mere minority of officials may often stymie constitutional change. But as we shall see below, Jefferson's self-evident truth was universally understood in 1787 as *majoritarian*. A simple majority of the People themselves—members of the polity—had a legal right to alter government and amend constitutions. If exclusive, Article V betrays this right.

There are, then, two plausible interpretations of Article V: (1) the conventional reading that it enumerates the only mode(s) by which the Constitution may be amended, and (2) an alternative reading that it enumerates the only mode(s) by which *ordinary government* may amend the Constitution. How shall we decide which is the better reading? By widening our focus beyond the narrow text of Article V, to consider other parts of the original Constitution, various glossing provisions of the federal Bill of Rights, and various Article V analogues in state constitutions.

Widening our frame will also help cure an underlying anxiety that, I think, may wrongly tilt lawyers toward the conventional reading of Article V exclusivity. The Constitution is supreme law, and the legal rules it establishes for its own amendment are of unsurpassed importance, for these rules define the conditions under which all other constitutional norms may be legally displaced. It is comforting to believe that Article V lays down these all-important legal rules with precision. If we stick close to Article V, we are safe; if we go beyond it, we are at sea.

But this is an optical illusion. Article V is far less precise than we might expect. What voting rule must an Article V proposing convention follow? What apportionment ratio? Can an amendment modify the rules of amendment themselves? If so, couldn't the "equal suffrage" rules be easily evaded by two successive "ordinary" amendments, the first of which repealed the equal suffrage rules of Article V, and the second of which reapportioned the Senate? Could a legitimate amendment generally purport to make itself (or any other random provision of the Constitution) immune from further amendment? If so, wouldn't that clearly violate the legal right of future generations to alter their government? Wouldn't the same be true of an amendment that effectively entrenched itself from further revision by, say, outlawing criticism of existing law? But if *that* would be unconstitutional, haven't we in effect made the narrow and hard core of our First Amendment *itself* unamendable?

If determinate answers to these and other questions exist, they lie outside Article V, narrowly construed—in other provisions of the Constitution, in the overall structure and popular sovereignty spirit of the document, in the history of its creation and amendment, and in the history of the creation and amendment of analogous legal documents, such as state constitutions. And once we consult these sources, we will find that we are in fact *not* at sea. The very sources that render Article V rules determinate also clarify the equally determinate rules for People-driven, majoritarian amendment outside Article V. By 1787, at least, the legal rules underlying Jefferson's right of the People to alter or abolish were no murkier or more mysterious than those encoded in Article V.

What the Rest of the Constitution Does Say and Do

In considering the "Constitution" as a whole, we must remember that it is not simply a text, but an act: the found-ing and constitut-ing—in the Preamble's phrase, the "ordain[ing]" and "establish[ing]"—of a new nation and a new regime of governance. And more: This act of founding, of constitution, was—and was universally understood to be in 1787—itself an act of "the People" exercising and implementing their "self-evident" right to "alter or abolish" existing government "and to institute new government, laying its foundations on such principles and organizing its Powers in such form, as to them shall seem most likely to effect their Safety and Happiness." What does the act of constituting say and do—for it does by saying and says by doing—about the legal right of We the People to alter or abolish what We have legally ordained and established?

The Legality of the Constitution

One camp of modern scholars might quickly answer, "Nothing at all." For some claim that the Constitution of 1787 was itself the product of an illegal process; if true, then its genealogy tells us nothing about the People's *legal* right to alter or abolish.[5] Under this "illegal" argument, the Constitution was a second American revolution, different only from the first, and its 1776 Declaration, in that the second was bloodless.

In contrast to the Declaration, however, the Constitution submitted itself to a popular vote in each state, under principles of majority rule. Unlike American Loyalists in 1776 who took up arms against the Declaration, the loyal opposition to the Constitution in 1787 fought the

[5] See, e.g., Bruce Ackerman, "The Storrs Lectures: Discovering the Constitution," *Yale Law Journal* 93 (1984): 1013, 1058 (ratification of the Constitution was, under preexisting law, "plainly illegal"); Richard S. Kay, "The Illegality of the Constitution," *Constitutional Commentary* 4 (1987): 57.

good fight in conventions and not on battlefields. And when outvoted—often by simple majorities—anti-Federalists in every single state in the end accepted the outcome because, deep down, they too understood the Federalists' claim that the Constitution had been *legally* ratified.[6]

But not before trying to brand the proposed Constitution "illegal" early in the game. The "illegal" gambit took two forms, but both gambits properly failed.

LEGALITY AND THE CONFEDERATION

The first gambit focused on the inconsistency between Article VII of the proposed Constitution and Article XIII of the Articles of Confederation. Begin with Article VII, the last section of the Constitution, which explains its first section, the Preamble. The Preamble says that "We the People *do* ordain and establish this Constitution," and Article VII says *how* we do this:

> The Ratification of the Convention of nine States shall be sufficient for the *Establishment of this Constitution* between the States so ratifying the Same.[7]

Now contrast Article XIII of the Articles of Confederation:

> And the Articles of this confederation shall be inviolably observed by every state, and the Union shall be perpetual; nor shall any alteration at any time hereafter be made in any of them; unless such alteration be agreed to in a congress of the United States, and be afterwards confirmed by the legislatures of every state.

These provisions are undeniably inconsistent. The Constitution speaks of nine states; the Articles, of all thirteen. The Constitution relies on state conventions, yet the Articles require approval by state legislatures. But inconsistency is not illegality. The Articles of Confederation were nothing more than a tight treaty among thirteen otherwise independent states—a self-described "firm *league* of friendship" in which each state expressly "retains its sovereignty." Like the later Congress of Vienna, its "Congress" was merely an international assembly of ambassadors, sent, recallable, and paid by state governments with each state casting a single vote as a state. It nowhere described itself as a "government" or "legislature," or its pronouncements as "law." By 1787, the Articles had been routinely and flagrantly violated on all sides.[8] And under well-estab-

---

[6] The "illegal" argument cannot account for any of this.

[7] U.S. Constitution, Art. VII (emphasis added). I add this emphasis to highlight the connection between the Preamble and Article VII.

[8] See, e.g., James Madison, "Vices of the Political System," in Marvin Meyers, ed., *The Mind of the Founder* (Indianapolis, Ind.: Bobbs-Merrill, 1981), pp. 57–59.

lished legal principles in 1787, these material breaches freed each com-pacting party—each state—to disregard the pact, if it so chose. Thus, Blackstone wrote in his best-selling *Commentaries* that in a "foederate alliance"—that is, a confederation, or league of otherwise sovereign states—an infringement of fundamental conditions "would certainly re-scind the compact."[9]

Nor does Article XIII's declaration that "the Union shall be perpet-ual" change the analysis, for in fact this clause was itself yoked to a mandate that the Articles "shall be inviolably observed by every state." Following standard principles of international law, each of these yoked mandates was a condition of the other. When inviolable observation lapsed, so did perpetual union under the Articles. (Indeed, international law principles help explain why perpetuity and inviolability were point-edly paired.) To put the point another way, the key point about the Arti-cles was that it was a league, a treaty. The word *perpetual* said what kind of league it would be: the strongest, the firmest of leagues—as leagues go—but a league nonetheless. And the rule Blackstone invoked applied to all leagues, weak or strong, firm or mushy. In the words of the Swiss jurist Emmerich de Vattel, whose *Law of Nations* was widely read and cited in America, "several sovereign and independent states may unite themselves together by a perpetual confederacy without each in particu-lar ceasing to be a perfect state."[10]

Here, then, is a powerful rejoinder to the first "illegal" gambit: The Constitution did not "illegally" depart from Article XIII, because that Article and the other Articles of Confederation were by 1787 no longer legally binding for any state that chose to exercise its legal right to rescind the compact. This powerful rejoinder is no mere twentieth-century fabrication. On the contrary, when pressed, leading law-trained friends of the Constitution repeatedly resorted to this rejoinder in 1787–88.

Space limitations prevent laying out all of the evidence in this venue. Consider, though, the following four statements by James Madison to the Philadelphia convention,[11] the first delivered on June 5: "As far as the Articles of Union were to be considered as a Treaty only of a partic-ular sort, among the Governments of Independent States, the doctrine might be set up that a breach of any one article, by any of the parties,

---

[9] William Blackstone, *Commentaries*, 1:97 note (added in 1766 ed.).

[10] Emmerich de Vattel, *The Law of Nations* (London, 1760), bk. 1, chap. 1, sec. 10. The leading modern historian of the era, Gordon Wood, agrees with my assessment of the Arti-cles here. See Wood, *The Creation of the American Republic*, p. 355.

[11] These ideas were first developed by Madison in his now-famous critique, "Vices of the Political System." They would be developed further for public consumption in *The Feder-alist*, No. 43.

absolved the other parties from the whole obligation."[12] And two weeks later: "Clearly, according to the Expositors of the law of Nations, . . . a breach of any one article, by any one party, leaves all the other parties at liberty, to consider the whole [compact] as dissolved. . . . [T]he violations of the federal articles had been numerous & notorious. . . . He did not wish to draw any rigid inferences from these observations."[13] On June 30, and more tartly: "In reply to the appeal of Mr. E. to the faith plighted in the existing federal compact, he remarked that the party claiming from others an adherence to a common engagement ought at least to be guiltless itself of a violation."[14] And later still, on July 23, when Madison may well have his copy of Blackstone in hand as he sharply distinguished, as had Blackstone, "between a *league or treaty*, and *a Constitution*": "The doctrine laid down by the law of Nations, in the case of treaties is that a breach of any one article by any of the parties, frees the other parties from their engagements. In the case of a union of people under one Constitution, the nature of the pact has always been understood to exclude such an interpretation."[15]

To be sure, substantial political delicacy was involved in making this argument. To mention only one problem, conclusive establishment of the relevant breaches in effect dissolving the confederation would have required lots of awkward and nasty fingerpointing—hardly the kind of thing conducive to the launching of a new nation in the spirit of harmony and goodwill. Madison's arguments, especially when presented publicly later in *The Federalist*, were thus restrained and cautious. But politics aside, the argument was, legally, an apparent winner. Indeed, not a single anti-Federalist, to my knowledge, contradicted Madison and other Federalists on this key point.[16] When the issue was joined, the anti-Federalists caved; when pressed to put up or shut up, they shut up.[17]

LEGALITY AND STATE CONSTITUTIONS

But the very failure of the first "illegal" gambit leads to the second, far more interesting one. If indeed the Articles of Confederation were a

[12] Max Farrand, ed., *The Records of the Federal Convention of 1787* (New Haven: Yale University Press, 1937), 1:122–23.

[13] Ibid., 1:315.

[14] Ibid., 1:485. "Mr. E" is Oliver Ellsworth.

[15] Ibid., 2:93.

[16] Alexander Hamilton had expressed some early reservations about the breached treaty argument at Philadelphia. Farrand, *Records*, 1:324. But these had apparently lapsed by the time of his Publian collaboration with Madison.

[17] As states' rightists, most anti-Federalists were hardly in a position to rebut the states' rights gloss placed on the Articles by the breached treaty rejoinder, and by the Constitution's own Article VII. See note 18, below.

mere treaty among otherwise independent nations,[18] we must carefully consider the laws of these nations—the thirteen states—and their relation to the Constitution. Undeniably, the U.S. Constitution, when adopted, would effect important changes in the internal governance of each state. The key question thus became: By what legal right would Article VII ratification of the Constitution in the, say, Maryland convention alter the existing Maryland Constitution? The Maryland Constitution of 1776 had its own explicit amendment clause, and it, too, looked rather different from the federal Constitution's Article VII:

> That this Form of government, and the Declaration of Rights, and no part thereof, shall be altered, changed, or abolished, unless a bill so to alter, change or abolish the same shall pass the General Assembly, and be published at least three months before a new election, and shall be confirmed by the General Assembly, after a new election of Delegates, in the first session after such new election.[19]

Note the obvious differences between this Maryland Constitution clause, and the U.S. Constitution's Article VII. The Maryland clause requires two votes; Article VII, one. The Maryland clause looks to the ordinary government; Article VII, a special convention of the people of Maryland.

Here, then, was the anti-Federalists' second "illegal" gambit: (1) The Maryland Constitution clause specified the exclusive mode by which the Maryland Constitution could be lawfully altered or abolished. (2) Ratification of the federal Constitution in Maryland would indeed alter important aspects of the state constitution. But (3) the Article VII ratification mechanism did not satisfy the Maryland exclusive clause. Thus,

---

[18] The legally independent status of the states prior to adoption of the Constitution is supported by all the major legal documents of the era, and by broad historical evidence. For 150 years prior to independence, the individual colonies had of course been separate, having been founded at different times and with different, unique charters and forms of government. The Declaration of Independence proclaimed itself in the name of "free and independent states"—independent even of each other, save as they chose to concert their action. Given the predominance of Montesquieu's vision that a single republic could not extend over a vast geographic, cultural, and climatic range, it is somewhat fanciful to think that, legally, a continental nation was formed in 1776 with virtually no discussion, and with the patriots' continental assembly pointedly calling itself a "congress." The language of individual state constitutions, and the centrality accorded them by revolutionary Americans, further attests to the independence and sovereignty of states prior to 1788. So, too, the Treaty of Peace with Britain recognized the legal independence of individual states. Finally—and revealingly—so did Article VII of the Constitution itself, which made clear that prior to joining the Constitution's "more perfect union" each state spoke for itself and only itself, and was legally free to go its own way. Further supporting documentation and analysis appears in Akhil R. Amar, "Of Sovereignty and Federalism," *Yale Law Journal* 96 (1987): 1425, 1444–62, and in Wood, *The Creation of the American Republic*, 354–59.

[19] Maryland Constitution of 1776, Art. 59.

ratification via Article VII would be illegal under preexisting and binding Maryland law.

But once again, the Federalists had a compelling rejoinder.

Popular Sovereignty

In the Philadelphia convention, Maryland's Daniel Carroll "mentioned the mode of altering the Constitution of Maryland pointed out therein, and that no other mode could be pursued in that state."[20] But listen carefully to Madison's bold yet lawyerly reply: "The difficulty in Maryland was no greater than in other States, where no mode of change was pointed out by the Constitution. . . . The people were in fact, the fountain of all power, and by resorting to them, all difficulties were got over. They could alter constitutions as they pleased. It was a principle in the Bills of rights that first principles might be resorted to."[21]

Whereas Carroll read the Maryland amendment clause as the exclusive mode of lawful constitutional change—"no other mode could be pursued"—Madison read it more narrowly; it specified only the way *ordinary government* could amend the constitution (by two ordinary votes of two ordinary legislatures) but did not exclude the People themselves—"the fountain of all power"—from altering or abolishing their government "as they pleased." Especially revealing is Madison's analogy to those sister states of Maryland—such as Madison's own Virginia—"where no mode of change was pointed out by the [state] Constitution." Surely, Madison suggested, that did not mean that the Constitution could never be changed. It meant only that the People themselves—and not ordinary government—could amend. And so the addition of the Maryland clause gave ordinary government an amending power it would not otherwise have had, but it was not best understood as depriving the People of their preexisting legal right to alter or abolish at will. For that preexisting right, proclaimed Madison, was one of the "first principles" of the legal order.[22]

During the ratification period, the Carroll-Madison exchange was in effect reenacted in several states—this time in the public spotlight. Pointing to state constitutions, various leading anti-Federalists played the "state illegality" card, to be met in turn by Madisonian responses, including those in *The Federalist*, Nos. 22, 39, 40, and 78.[23]

[20] Farrand, *Records*, 2:475.

[21] Ibid., 2:476.

[22] Versions of Madison's argument were replicated at Philadelphia by Alexander Hamilton, no friend of popular government, and by George Mason. See Amar, "Consent of the Governed," p. 471.

[23] *The Federalist*, No. 78 was, of course, written by Hamilton, as was No. 22. Hamilton's willingness to endorse "the fundamental principle of republican government which admits the right of the people to alter or abolish the established constitution whenever they

The most important such response was that of James Wilson during the Pennsylvania ratifying convention. Though less famous today than some of his companions, Wilson deserves our most careful attention. He was one of only six men to sign both the Declaration of Independence and the Constitution. At Philadelphia, he played a role second—if that— only to Madison. As Gordon Wood has written, Wilson was the Federalists' preeminent popular sovereignty theorist;[24] and it was his hand that first penned the bold first three words of the Constitution, "We the People."[25] In the 1780s, Wilson was universally regarded as perhaps the most brilliant, scholarly, and visionary lawyer in America; he delivered the most important and celebrated lectures on law ever given in eighteenth-century America and was a natural choice by President Washington when picking the initial membership of the U.S. Supreme Court.

Wilson dominated the Pennsylvania ratifying convention in a one-man tour de force. Early on, he laid down first principles:

> There necessarily exists, in every government, a power from which there is no appeal, and which, for that reason, may be termed supreme, absolute, and uncontrollable.
>
> . . . Perhaps some politician, who has not considered with sufficient accuracy our political systems, would answer that, in our governments, the supreme power was vested in the constitutions. . . . This opinion approaches a step nearer to the truth, but does not reach it. The truth is, that in our governments, the supreme, absolute, and uncontrollable power *remains* in the people. As our constitutions are superior to our legislatures, so the people are superior to our constitutions. Indeed the superiority, in this last instance, is much greater; for the people possess over our constitution, control in *act*, as well as right.
>
> *The consequence is, the people may change the constitutions whenever and however they please. This is a right of which no positive institution can ever deprive them.*[26]

Wilson's elaboration of the popular sovereignty rejoinder was not some newly minted, half-baked, ad hoc apology for Article VII. Rather, as his immediate audience well understood, Wilson's speech built on arguments he and his allies had been crafting in Pennsylvania for almost a

---

find it inconsistent with their happiness" only underscores the extent of the consensus on this crucial point.

[24] Wood, *The Creation of the American Republic*, p. 530 ("more boldly and fully than anyone else, Wilson developed the [popular sovereignty] argument that would eventually become the basis of all Federalist thinking").

[25] Farrand, *Records*, 2:150.

[26] J. Elliot, *The Debates in the Several State Conventions on the Adoption of the Federal Constitution* (1901), 2:432 (emphasis added).

decade. As early as 1777, they had articulated—and acted upon—the theory that the Pennsylvania amendment clause was not exclusive, and that popular sovereignty first principles required that the People themselves, acting in special conventions, retain the right to amend their Constitution at any time and for any reason.[27]

Declarations of Rights

Here, then, was the Federalists' emphatic popular sovereignty rejoinder to the anti-Federalists' second "illegal" gambit. Now that we understand its *substance*, we must investigate its *source*: From whence did the Federalists derive these "first principles"?

Recall once again Madison's precise, lawyerly response to Carroll: "It was a principle in the Bills of rights, that first principles might be resorted to." Madison was of course not referring to what we today call "the Bill of Rights"—the first set of amendments to the federal Constitution—for *that* bill was not even proposed until 1789. What, then, did Madison have in mind? The bill of rights of each state. And when we closely examine the various bills of rights and declarations of rights issuing from the states between 1776 and 1790, we will see a dramatic pattern: Each state had explicitly endorsed at least one statement—and in many cases several—that established popular sovereignty as that state's legal cornerstone. These formulations both overlapped and varied. Again, space considerations prevent offering more than a tip of the iceberg.[28]

Consider, though, the opening chords of Virginia's Declaration of Rights—the first and most influential of all the state declarations, adopted in June 1776, one month before Jefferson's Declaration. Among the "rights . . . of the good people of Virginia" constituting "the basis and foundation of government" were these:

Sec. 2. That all power is vested in, and consequently derived from, the people. . . .
Sec. 3 . . . of all the various modes and forms of government, that is best which is capable of producing the greatest degree of happiness and safety. . . . *[W]hen any government shall be found inadequate or contrary to these purposes, a majority of the community hath an indubitable, inalienable, and indefeasable right to reform, alter, or abolish it, in such manner as shall be judged most conducive to the public weal.*[29]

[27] See Geoffrey Seed, *James Wilson* (1978), pp. 123–24; and the eye-opening forthcoming essay by Matthew Herrington, *Temple Law Review* (1994).

[28] For further elaboration and documentation, see Amar, "The Consent of the Governed," pp. 475–81.

[29] Virginia Constitution of 1776 (Declaration of Rights), preamble, secs. 2–3 (emphasis added).

As the Federalist statesman and historian David Ramsay gushed in his 1791 *History of the American Revolution*: "It is true, from the infancy of political knowledge in the United States; there were many defects in their [state] forms of government; but in one thing they were all perfect. They left the people in the power of altering and amending them, whenever they pleased."[30]

To be sure, the language of state constitutions differed, and at least some omitted specific language of a right of the People to alter or abolish in favor of more general pronouncements of popular sovereignty. If the various state declarations were legislative codes, then we might well read them narrowly, under principles of *expressio unius*. But these state declarations were emphatically *not* legislative codes. They did not claim to create new rights but to declare ones the People already had, in reason or in custom.[31] By their very nature, not all the rights of the People could be specified, and so it would be silly to make too much of a silence or omission—especially if omitted language merely clarified a logical corollary of explicit language, as the right of the People to alter or abolish logically flowed from popular sovereignty. (The later federal Ninth Amendment would explicitly confirm the silliness of reading Bills of Rights in narrow *expressio unius* fashion.) These declarations were quasi-judicial utterances, declaring the true common law—common to all American states.

At the very least, a contrary inference—i.e., that the People were *without* the right to alter their government—should require an emphatically clear, explicit rejection of Virginia's (and every state's) premise of popular sovereignty. None of the states came close to this, unless the reader falls into the *expressio unius* trap.

Majority Rule

One clever counterploy to this Federalist rejoinder would try to read the various state amendment clauses not as excluding, but as *implementing*—exclusively!—the People's right to alter or abolish. But this clever counterploy fails. The Maryland amendment clause empowered ordinary government—the legislature—and not the People themselves.[32] In both Massachusetts and Pennsylvania, the amendment clause speci-

---

[30] Russell and Russell (1793; reprint, Athenian House, 1968), 1:355; first edition quoted in Wood, *The Creation of the American Republic*, pp. 613–14.

[31] In the words of the anti-Federalist pamphleteer the Federal Farmer, "We do not by declarations change the nature of things, or create new truths." Letters from the Federal Farmer (16), in Herbert Storing, ed., *The Complete Anti-Federalist* (Chicago: University of Chicago Press, 1981), 2:324. For more elaboration of this declaratory theory, see Akhil R. Amar, "The Bill of Rights and the Fourteenth Amendment," *Yale Law Journal* 101 (1992): 1193, 1205–12.

[32] So too with Delaware and South Carolina.

fied certain dates for amendment—in Massachusetts, 1795; in Pennsylvania, every seven years—whereas first principles required that the People be able to alter or abolish at any time. Sensing this, an anti-Federalist pamphleteer who played the illegality gambit in Massachusetts explicitly conceded that 1795 was not exclusive, and need not be read as such.[33] But by similar grammatical logic, the entire amendment clause was nonexclusive; its date was syntactically intertwined with its other rules, and so the concession gave away the game.

But far more fundamentally, the Massachusetts clause could not be considered as implementing first principles since the clause expressly required a supermajority of popular support—and so too, with the Pennsylvania clause[34]—whereas first principles required that a *simple majority* of the People be empowered to alter or abolish. This simple majority could occur in a "convention" of the People; popular sovereignty theory, for good reasons,[35] sharply distinguished special conventions—chosen in a special election of the entire polity, for the sole purpose of effecting constitutional change—from ordinary, everyday legislatures, and assimilated these special convention assemblies to "the People" themselves. But first principles clearly demanded that a simple, deliberate majority of the polity—50 percent plus one—would suffice. The Massachusetts and Pennsylvania clauses clearly failed this requirement, and thus had to be viewed as nonexclusive as a matter of first principles.

The majority rule corollary of popular sovereignty and the right to alter or abolish appeared most obviously in George Mason's celebrated Virginia Declaration, with its explicit emphasis on the "indubitable, unalienable, and indefeasible" right of "a *majority* of the community." No other state declaration addressed the issue explicitly, and clearly none explicitly took issue with Virginia's Declaration.

This last point is not some lawyer's trick to prevail only by shifting the burden of proof. In the 1780s, the special status of majority rule was extraordinarily well understood. Both as a general default rule in the absence of specific language to the contrary, and as a specific corollary of popular sovereignty, it literally went without saying in a variety of declarations precisely because it was so obvious. Thus, Jefferson's 1776 Declaration spoke only of "the right of the People to alter or abolish" without specifying a precise voting rule; but clearly Jefferson believed that popular sovereignty, best understood, meant majority rule—it went

---

[33] A Republican Federalist (3), in Storing, 4:172.

[34] New Hampshire's Article V analogue, based on the Massachusetts model, also had this defect; and likewise specified a certain date for amendment.

[35] I have explored these reasons in detail elsewhere. Simply put, there are far fewer agency costs between convention and people—much like today's presidential electors. See Amar, "Philadelphia Revisited," *University of Chicago Law Review* 55 (1988): 1043, 1094–95.

without saying. Indeed, for Jefferson "the first principle of Republican-ism is, that the lex majoris partis is the fundamental law of every society of equal rights." This entailed "consider[ing] the will of the society enounced by the majority . . . as sacred as if unanimous."[36]

These views were near universal in the 1780s, for anyone who had read Locke knew that majority rule stood as a basic default principle of all assemblies.[37] But more concretely: Americans understood the unique status of majority rule for implementing popular sovereignty and the right to alter or abolish.[38]

Even anti-Federalists shared this belief in majority rule as a clear cor-ollary of popular sovereignty. Thus we find the very same Pennsylvania anti-Federalists who tried to play the "illegal" card appearing to concede in the very next paragraph that perhaps the Pennsylvania Constitution could be altered if "a majority of the people should evidence a wish for such a change."[39] (The anti-Federalists denied that such a majority had evidenced such a desire, pointing to the low voter turnout in electing convention delegates; the obvious Federalist counterargument would be that in a properly called election, a majority of those voting—not of those eligible—should prevail.) So too, Federal Farmer, perhaps the leading anti-Federalist pamphleteer, wrote that "it will not be denied, that the people have a right to change the government when the major-ity chuse it, if not restrained by some existing compact"[40]—i.e., a valid treaty. In Virginia the firebrand Patrick Henry seemed to concede that the proposed Constitution's Article V was in theory not exclusive—a point to which we shall return—but worried that in practice it would be.[41] And if exclusive as a practical matter, it would, Henry argued, clearly violate first principles, for a popular majority might not prevail

---

[36] Paul Leicester Ford, ed., *The Writings of Thomas Jefferson* (1899), 10:89 (Letter of June 13, 1817, to Baron F. H. Alexander Von Humbolt). Further elaboration of Jeffer-son's commitment to majoritarianism can be found in Amar, "The Consent of the Gov-erned," 482–83.

[37] See John Locke, *Second Treatise*, sec. 96; Jefferson, *Notes on the State of Virginia* ("*Lex majoris partis* is founded in common law as well as common right. It is the natural law of every assembly of men") (citing Brooke, Hakewell, and Pufendorf); Wood, The Creation of the American Republic, pp. 62–64 (citing Bernard Wishy, "John Locke and the Spirit of '76," *Political Science Quarterly* 73 (1958): 413–25; Walter Berns, "The Con-stitution as a Bill of Rights," in *How Does the Constitution Secure Rights?*, ed. Robert Gold-win and William Schambra (1985), 58–59; Wilmore Kendall, *John Locke and the Doctrine of Majority Rule* (1959). See also Russell Caplan, *Constitutional Brinksmanship* (New York: Oxford University Press, 1988), pp. 120–21.

[38] For many examples, see Amar, "The Consent of the Governed," pp. 483–85.

[39] The Address and Reasons of Dissent of the Minority of the Convention of Pennsylva-nia to their Constituents, in Storing, 3:145, 149.

[40] Letters from the Federal Farmer (17), in Storing, 2:330, 336.

[41] Elliot, *The Debates*, 3:51.

under it. Henry quoted Virginia's Third Declaration verbatim, stressing its commitment to simple majority rule, and labeling it "the genius of democracy."[42]

Perhaps most clear and most dramatic of all were the words of the great James Wilson in his 1790 lectures on law in a passage that was as clear then as it is unknown now:

> As to the people, however, in whom sovereign power resides, . . . [f]rom their authority the constitution originates: for their safety and felicity it is established; in their hands it is clay in the hands of the potter: they have the right to mould, to preserve, to improve, to refine, and to finish as they please. If so; can it be doubted, that they have the right likewise to change it? A majority of the society is sufficient for this purpose.[43]

So much for the Founders' words. If we turn instead to their deeds, we see an even more vivid picture. Article VII as a text nowhere specified that within each state convention a simple majority would rule. But this was the universal understanding in every state. I know of not a single leading anti-Federalist who tried to claim that, somehow, the convention should follow supermajoritarian—that is, minority veto—principles. On the contrary, men such as Patrick Henry explicitly conceded that they "must submit" to the opinion of the convention "majority."[44] And in state after state, anti-Federalists in the final analysis acted on this understanding, accepting the legitimacy of the ultimate outcome. The point here, though often overlooked today, is absolutely vital, for in many states the convention vote was a squeaker: 30–27 in New York; 187–168 in Massachusetts; 57–47 in New Hampshire; and 89–79 in Henry's own Virginia, for example. With so many clever and ardent folk opposed to ratification, why did no one try to make hay of the omission in the text of Article VII? *Because majority rule really did go without saying.*[45]

The Meaning of the Constitution

Though setting out merely to establish the basic legality of the act of constitution, before closely parsing the text of constitution, we have in fact done much more. We have seen how that act itself reflected and

[42] Ibid., 3:49–51. See also ibid., 3:55 (stressing simple majority rule for constitutional amendment).

[43] *The Works of James Wilson*, Robert G. McCloskey, ed. (1967), 1:304. For further discussion of majority rule, see 1:242, 2:507–9.

[44] Elliot, *The Debates*, 3:50.

[45] Actually Edmund Randolph in the Virginia convention did say something, when he

embodied—self-consciously—first principles of the legal order, popular sovereignty and majority rule. Further, we have confronted various state constitutional clauses that look remarkably like our federal Article V and seem, at first blush, to set out the exclusive mode of state constitutional amendment. But after more careful inspection, we learned that these Article V analogues were and are *not* best read as exclusive. As a matter of first principles the polity had retained the legal right to alter or abolish outside these analogues, by simple majority vote.

And so the obvious question is: Why is the same not true for Article V itself? Why does not a simple majority of the national People—for the Constitution forms one national People from the formerly distinct thirteen state peoples—retain an analogous legal right to alter or abolish its Constitution outside Article V?[46] (Once again, Article V cannot be read as *implementing* that right, because it is both *government*-driven and *minoritarian*; its rules may well thwart sensible constitutional changes strongly desired by a deliberate majority of the American polity.)

There are indeed clear texts in the U.S. Constitution—texts outside Article V but very much inside (indeed, fundamental to) the Constitution, understood as a unified document—that confirm the right we have rediscovered. When properly read, these texts say the very same thing and serve the very same function at the national level as the state declarations in the context of state Article V analogues.

THE PREAMBLE

Begin at the beginning. Do not the words "We the People of the United States . . . do ordain and establish this Constitution" say it all? What We, acting by simple majority in convention assembled (see Article VII), have ordained and established, cannot We, acting similarly, alter or abolish? Of course, because the Constitution formed previously separate state peoples into one continental People—Americans!—by substituting a true (and self-described) Constitution for a true (and self-described) league, the relevant majority after ordainment and establishment should be national, not state by state, as it was before ordainment and establishment, under Article VII. An easy modern day analogy comes from corporate law: Company A and company B agree to merge, with the merger approved by lawful majorities of each company's shareholders; but after merger, we look to the lawful majority of shareholders of the

---

thought that the anti-Federalist minority might try to break a quorum: "An idea of refusing to admit to the decision of the majority is destructive of every republican principle." *Elliot's Debates*, 3:597.

[46] I intentionally gloss over some important federalism issues here, which I have addressed in considerable detail elsewhere, and to which I shall return at the end of this essay.

newly formed company, United A&B. (And we should not forget that Massachusetts, New Jersey, and Connecticut had themselves each been formed by mergers of previously separate colonies, prior to the American Revolution.) To be sure, the Constitution redefined the relevant polity, but that redefinition cannot change the basic nature of popular sovereignty. If it did, no state prior to 1787 could have been grounded on popular sovereignty, for every new day brought a slight redefinition of the polity, with some voters dying and others coming of age, with western borders being relentlessly pushed back and new settlers brought in.

But, of course, every text finds itself embedded in a historical context. Did the Founders themselves recognize the Preamble as a textual declaration of popular sovereignty and the People's right to alter or abolish? Indubitably. Once more I can present only a fraction of the relevant evidence,[47] beginning with the man who wrote the first draft of the Preamble, James Wilson: "What is the necessary consequence [of the Preamble]? Those who ordain and establish have the power, if they think proper, to repeal and annul."[48]

And listen to Edmund Pendleton, the great lawyer who headed the Virginia ratifying convention, as he evoked the Preamble to prove that the People would retain a legal right to alter or abolish. Article V, said Pendleton, simply set out *one* "easy and quiet" mechanism of amendment; but because it was government-driven, it could not be exclusive:

> We, the people, possessing all power, form a government, such as we think will secure happiness and suppose, in adopting this plan, we should be mistaken in the end; where is the cause of alarm on that quarter? In the same plan we point out an easy and quiet method of reforming what may be found amiss. No, but, say gentlemen, we have put the introduction of that method in the hands of our servants, who will interrupt it from motives of self-interest. What then? . . . Who shall dare to resist the people? No, we will assemble in Convention; wholly recall our delegated powers, or reform them so as to prevent such abuse; and punish those servants who have perverted powers, designed for our happiness, to their own emolument.[49]

The leader of the Virginia anti-Federalists, Patrick Henry, appeared to concede Pendleton's legal analysis, but predicted that a federal standing army would prevent the People from ever exercising their legal right to "assemble" in convention.[50] In light of the Pendleton-Henry exchange, the declaration issued by the entire Virginia convention to accompany

---

[47] For elaboration, see Amar, "The Consent of the Governed," pp. 489–92.

[48] Ibid., 2:434–35 (emphasis in original).

[49] Ibid., 3:37. Logic suggests that Pendleton is referring here to a convention *outside* Article V, *see* Amar, "Philadelphia Revisited," pp. 1056–57.

[50] *Elliot, The Debates*, 3:51.

its ratification takes on added significance: "The powers granted under the Constitution, being derived from the people of the United States, may be resumed by them, whenever the same shall be perverted to their injury or oppression."[51]

And if we need still further proof, we shall find it in the first Congress, where James Madison proposed various "declaratory and restrictive" amendments to the Constitution.[52] Although our federal Bill of Rights was eventually tacked on to the end of the original document, Madison initially proposed to interweave new clauses directly into the original fabric. One of these proposals was to append a prefix to the Preamble, which included the following: "That the people have an indubitable, unalienable and indefeasible right to reform or change their government."[53] Not one representative quarreled with Madison on the substance of this claim, but the prefix was eventually dropped precisely because its detractors deemed it redundant, given the broad meaning of the Preamble itself.[54]

THE NINTH AND TENTH AMENDMENTS

Closely related to the Preamble were words that eventually became the Ninth and Tenth Amendments:

> The enumeration in the Constitution, of certain rights, shall not be construed to deny or disparage others retained by the people.
>
> The powers not delegated to the United States by the Constitution, nor prohibited by it to the states, are reserved to the states respectively, or to the people.

Conventional wisdom misses this close triangular interrelation. The Ninth is said to be about unenumerated individual rights, like personal privacy; the Tenth, about federalism; and the Preamble, about something else again. But look again at these texts. All are at their core about popular sovereignty. All, indeed, explicitly invoke "the people." In the Preamble, "We the people . . . *do*" exercise our right and power of popular sovereignty, and in the Ninth and Tenth amendments, expressly "retain" and "reserve" our "right" and "power" to do it again. If the Ninth is mainly about individual rights, why does it not speak of individual "persons" rather than the collective "people"? If the Tenth is only about states' rights, why does it stand back to back with the Ninth, and

[51] Ibid., 1:327.

[52] *Documentary History of the Constitution of the United States of America* (Washington: Department of State, 1894), 2:321.

[53] Bernard Schwartz, ed., *The Bill of Rights* (New York: McGraw Hill, 1971), 2:1026.

[54] See Amar, "The Consent of the Governed," pp. 491–92, for elaboration.

what are its last three words doing there, mirroring the Preamble's first three? In fact, both amendments trace their lineage to declarations in the ratifying conventions, including New York's, with strong popular sovereignty overtones:

> That the powers of government may be reassumed by the People, whensoever it shall become necessary to their Happiness; that every Power, Jurisdiction and right, which is not by the said Constitution clearly delegated to the Congress of the United States, or the departments of the government thereof, remains to the People of the several States, or to their respective state governments to whom they may have granted the same.[55]

Similarly, James Wilson had emphasized that the people, who "never part with the whole" of their "original power, . . . may always say, WE *reserve* the right to do what we please."[56]

THE RIGHT OF THE PEOPLE TO ASSEMBLE

The popular sovereignty motif sounded by the words "the People" in the Preamble and Amendments Nine and Ten should alert us to the words and music elsewhere in the Constitution. And once alerted, we hear yet another clear affirmation of the first principles of majority-rule popular sovereignty: the First Amendment "right of the people to assemble."

As Gordon Wood has observed, "conventions . . . of the people . . . were closely allied in English thought with the people's right to assemble"—thus, for example, we find Blackstone describing how in 1688 the British people, through Parliament, "assemble[d]" in "Convention."[57] And in revolutionary America, we almost invariably find the ideas and words "people," "assemble," and "convention" tightly clustered in discussions of popular sovereignty.[58] Recall Edmund Pendleton's pointed phrase that if dissatisfied with Article V, "the people" will "assemble in convention"—clustered words repeated by Patrick Henry in his apparent concession of the point. Members of the First Congress clearly understood all this in 1789, as evidenced by a casual reference in Congress itself to "assembling in convention."[59] Thus, a core meaning of "the right of the people to assemble" in 1789 was their right to as-

---

[55] Elliot, *The Debates*, 1:327.

[56] Ibid., 3:437 (emphasis added).

[57] Blackstone, *Commentaries*, 1:147–48.

[58] Further documentation appears in Amar, "Philadelphia Revisited," 1058–60; and Akhil Reed Amar, "The Bill of Rights as a Constitution," *Yale Law Journal* 100 (1991): 1131, 1152–55.

[59] Schwartz, 2:1022 (remarks of John Page).

semble *in convention*.[60] To be sure, this was not the only meaning, for the text radiated beyond this core, just as the text of the Ninth Amendment radiated beyond the core right of the People to popular sovereignty. But there is no doubt that in both places the words "the people" do indeed mean—at least—just that.

Objections and Conclusions

I thus state the following theorem: Just as first principles and various state declarations required us to rethink and ultimately reject the seeming exclusivity of state analogues to Article V, so too do first principles and various other parts of the federal Constitution require us to abandon the seeming exclusivity of Article V itself.

If this is correct, we need to seriously rethink much of constitutional law. But as I have learned over the years, many doubt its validity. I take up some of the possible objections.[61]

The Novelty Objection

This can be summarized as follows: Given the magnitude of the claim, which goes to the very essence of our constitutional order, why has it not been offered before or, even more to the point, acted upon by my beloved "People"? It has not, and they have not. Thus it is just too novel to be true.

Not surprisingly, I disagree. Even if one stipulates that my theorem is novel to most contemporary readers, it would surely have not been so to "We the People" of 1787 who did ordain and establish our Constitution. As I hope I have shown, they understood and self-consciously acted upon the theorem and its underlying principle of majority-rule popular sovereignty. Perhaps the impression of "novelty" is, alas, a result of ignorance of the thought of our constitutional ancestors.

Our entire perspective on the place of majority rule in our Constitution may be askew, in part because of our post-*Lochner* preoccupation with the "countermajoritarian difficulty" posed by judicial review and, concomitantly, the emphasis on the "majoritarian" nature of Congress and state legislatures. Instead of dwelling on the relationship between

[60] See also Barron v. Baltimore, 32 U.S. (7 Pet.) 843, 250–51 (1833) ("a convention would have been assembled" to amend state constitutions); McCulloch v. Maryland, 17 U.S. (4 Wheat.) 326, 403 (1819) ("the people . . . assembled" in "convention" in the "several states" to ratify constitution).

[61] For further discussion of these and other objections, see Amar, "The Consent of the Governed," pp. 494–508.

legislatures and courts, we need to see how the People ordained the supreme law by majority-rule popular sovereignty. And we must ask if the People can do this again.

Indeed, we have spent far too little attention generally pondering the processes of constitutional change. Analytically, much of our constitutional order exists in the shadow of constitutional amendment rules, yet these rules have received far less serious theoretical attention than their special status demands. And to understand how the Constitution can be legally amended, we must better understand how it was legally brought into existence. The majoritarian Preamble and Article VII—literally the original Constitution's textual and performative alpha and omega—stand on an analytically higher plane than "countermajoritarian" provisions such as those in Article III.

When sophisticated theorists do touch on the Preamble, or Article VII, it is too often with a cynical smirk on their lips: who but a rube could take seriously the winkingly democratic phrase "We the People"? But—Charles Beard notwithstanding—the act of the constitution was not some antidemocratic, Thermidorian counterrevolution, akin to a coup d'état, but was instead the most participatory and majoritarian event the planet had ever seen (and lawful to boot). Looking backward from today, we see all the painful exclusions—of women, of slaves—but often miss the breadth of inclusion, looking backward from 1787. Americans did not receive their supreme law from On High, from some Great Man claiming a pipeline to God—Moses, Solon, Lycurgus—or from some conclave of fifty-five demigods in Philadelphia (which merely proposed a piece of paper). Nor did Americans simply inherit their supreme law from immemorial custom. Rather, Americans did ordain and establish their supreme law—peacefully, deliberately, and lawfully—by majority-rule popular sovereignty. The act electrified Europe and doomed the ancien regime. The novelty objection, in short, suffers from remarkable amnesia concerning the Constitution's words and deeds.

The obvious overlaps between state declaration of rights and the federal bill should remind us of the general importance of the state constitutional experience in shaping American constitutional discourse. Yet here, too, the mainstream suffers from amnesia. To my knowledge, no modern legal scholar has carefully examined the state Article V analogues from 1787 and pondered their significance for Article V itself. And perhaps because of the pervasive nationalism of today's law schools, few constitutional scholars are even aware of the dramatic pattern of majority-rule popular sovereignty in amending state constitutions after 1787.

As Massachusetts Assistant Attorney General Roger Sherman Hoar documented in a 1917 book, innumerable amendments to state constitutions occurred in a wide variety of states in the nineteenth century by modes of state popular action not explicitly authorized by preexisting state constitutions, and often in the teeth of what at first seemed exclusive Article V analogues.[62] In short, in both word and deed, majority-rule popular sovereignty was alive and well throughout the nineteenth century, if we only know where to look.

The Deliberation Objection

Another objection: Does the theorem mean that the majority can do anything it wants? Instantaneously? Surely majority rule must at least be deliberate rather than whimsical. And so multiple vote and minority veto rules should be permitted, as long as they truly do induce deliberation.

It does not necessarily follow from the theorem that the majority can simply do whatever it likes. Majority rule does not necessarily imply majority will or majority whim. James Wilson, for example, clearly stated that the People stood *under* God and natural law; and that a majority was not entitled to do simply whatever it pleased.[63] There is no paradox or contradiction here. Wilson is simply reminding us that, just as Parliament as sovereign was both supreme legislature and supreme judiciary in England, so in America were the People. As judges they were indeed bound by the higher law of God; but legally, they were the earthly *judges* of that law, the True and Ultimate Supreme Court. Sitting in their judicial capacity, they had duties as well as rights, and could not simply do whatever they pleased if doing so would indeed trench on inviolable rights. And in exercising their judicial judgment, as in exercising their legislative will, the People act by simple majorities—as do inferior legislators and courts, as a general rule. (The Supreme Court, under Article III, acts by majority rule among the justices; but that does not mean that, in theory, the justices may simply do whatever they please.)

In order to properly deliberate—legislatively as well as judicially—the People must indeed be exposed to and must engage opposing ideas; the majority should attempt to reason with and persuade dissenters, and vice versa. Majority-rule popular sovereignty presupposes a deliberate majority of the collective "People," not a mere mathmatical concatenation of atomized "persons." In the words of Publius's opening sentence: "You are called upon to *deliberate* on a new Constitution for the United States."[64]

---

[62] Roger Sherman Hoar, *Constitutional Conventions* (Boston: Little, Brown, 1917), pp. 39–40. This book is a must read for those who continue to have doubts about the nonexclusivity of state Article V analogues.

[63] *The Works of James Wilson*, 7:153.

[64] *The Federalist*, No. 1 (Alexander Hamilton) ed. Clinton Rossiter (New York: Mentor 1961), p. 33 (emphasis added).

Because the requisite convocations and deliberations could not occur en masse in 1787 among all voters, the Founders relied on smaller conventions to speak as and for the People. Direct special election for a single purpose would minimize the "agency gap" between convention and electors; but the convention could carry on extended deliberations and discussions that would be difficult in the polity at large. In 1787, a referendum would have been a *less* true index of the will and judgment of a deliberate majority, given that many voters in the referendum would not have had the benefit of focused discussion from the most articulate proponents of varying views.

Today, because of vast improvements in communication and transportation technology—radio, television, cable, fiber-optics, electronic town meetings, etc.—there may be ways to retain the deliberation of the convention while providing for even more direct popular participation, akin to referenda. There thus remains considerable room for flexibility in implementing the deliberation requirement, including, perhaps, a requirement for two separate votes, spaced far enough apart to allow true conversation and conversion to occur, and for second thoughts to cool fleeting fancy. But there can be no similar compromise on the principle of simple majority rule. As the framing generation well understood, and modern political science has reaffirmed, simple majority rule has unique mathematical properties. It is the only workable voting rule that treats all voters and all policy proposals equally.[65] And once it is abandoned, there is no logical stopping point between, say, a 50 percent plus *two* rule, and a 99.9 percent rule. And the latter, of course, surely is not rule by the People.

Thus, in the pregnant phrase "deliberate majority," there is no unique mechanism for ensuring deliberation, but majority rule does have a unique instantiation. The people must talk, listen, and vote, and that takes time. (The people's right to alter or abolish "at any time" cannot, by its very nature, be *instantaneous*.) But when they do vote, a majority, however small, must in the end prevail over a minority.

The Individual Rights Objection

But what about individual rights?

In the end, individual rights in our system are, and should be, the products of ultimately majoritarian processes. Once again, there is noth-

---

[65] *See* Kenneth O. May, "A Set of Independent Necessary and Sufficient Conditions for Simple Majority Decision," *Econometrica* 20 (1952): 680, 683: simple majority rule is the only mechanism that does not (1) favor one individual over another, (2) favor one alternative or another, (3) fail to generate a definite result in some situation, or (4) fail to respond positively to individual preferences.

ing paradoxical about this. Sloppy philosophical rhetoric notwithstanding, there is nothing in the ontological character of a "right" that requires that it be vested in an "individual" or "minority" *against* the "majority." It is perfectly intelligible to speak of majority rights. And historically, many of the most important rights in the federal Bill of Rights and its state counterparts have been majoritarian rights of the people. Through majoritarian processes, We the People have also recognized rights of individuals and minorities, and extended the right to be part of We the Polity to formerly excluded elements of society such as black men and women of all races.

Conventional wisdom emphasizing "countermajoritarian" judicial review to protect unpopular rights is also shortsighted. Presidents select judges, and presidents are elected by majorities. In the long run, rights will only be safe if they are understood and accepted by the polity, and not just the judges.

The individual rights objection may also prove too much, for at least some variants are opposed to *any* amendment of certain rights. But the question before the house is not *whether* amendment can occur, but *how*. Why do individual rightists trust government with the power to amend but not the People? To be sure, government must act with super-majorities—but that is precisely because government officials often have interests separate from their constituents, in ways that often threaten liberty.

The Geographic Objection

But doesn't Article V exist to protect geographic minorities?

No. Analytically, the rules of Article V may be satisfied even if an amendment is fiercely opposed in one geographic section of the country. And the analytic point has powerful empirical support. The leading political science study of the federal amendments since the Founding, authored by Alan Grimes, concludes that a dominant "characteristic of amendment politics has been the sectional or regional aspect of the political struggle."[66] The very titles of Grimes's chapters are devastating to the geographic objection. Amendments One through Twelve are labeled the "Southern Amendments"; Thirteen through Fifteen, the "Northern Amendments"; Sixteen through Nineteen, the "Western Amendments"; and Twenty-three through Twenty-six, the "Urban Amendments."

[66] Alan P. Grimes, *Democracy and the Amendments to the Constitution* (New York: University Press of America, 1987), p. 26.

Indeed, the Framers explicitly rejected the premise underlying the geographic objection. In response to concerns at Philadelphia that one day, the population of western states would overwhelm the East, James Wilson proclaimed:

> Conceiving that all men wherever placed have equal rights and are equally entitled to confidence, [I view] without apprehension the period when a few States should contain the superior number of people. The majority of people wherein found ought in all questions to govern the minority. If the interior country should acquire the majority they will not only have the right, but will avail themselves of it whether we will or no.[67]

That a majority within a polity should rule, regardless of geographic distribution, is confirmed not just by the leading Founder's words but—here too—by the act of constitution itself. Georgia's Article V analogue required a majority within each Georgia county and yet the analogue, like those of its sister states, was supplanted by Article VII's simple majority vote of the state convention as a whole regardless of geography.[68]

The Federalism Objection

But are states within the union truly akin in counties within states? Perhaps the theorem is indeed true as a matter of state constitutional law; but doesn't the *federal*—or, at least, mixed—nature of our continental union render state Article V analogues ultimately *not* analogous?

Here, at last, we come to the hardest objection to my theorem. We have reached a fork in the road, and must choose one of three paths. And that choice will make all the difference.

Path no. 1 was Jefferson Davis's: The people of each state remained sovereign even after union, and as such, retained the inalienable right—notwithstanding Article V—to alter or abolish their government, and even withdraw from the Union, by simple majority-rule popular sovereignty state by state.

Path no. 2 was James Wilson's: After ratification under Article VII, We the People became—if we were not already before—a truly continental people. As far as the continental Constitution was concerned, majority-rule popular sovereignty outside Article V meant a national majority. State peoples continued to exist, and in effect enjoy sovereign powers over their own state legislatures and state constitutions. And

---

[67] Farrand, *Records*, 1:605.
[68] Georgia Constitution of 1777, Art. 63.

thus, for state constitutional purposes, state peoples continue to retain the right to alter or abolish outside their state Article V analogue. But the state peoples are clearly subordinate to the national People, just as state constitutions are subordinate to the national Constitution. The people of a single state may not nullify the federal government's action; but the national People may. Unilateral secession by the part is void, but the whole People can peacefully agree to divide, just as they can agree to merge with other peoples—for example, by admitting Texas.

Path no. 3 was James Madison's: Ordinary government under the Constitution was neither wholly "national" nor purely "federal"— "federal" here meaning leaguelike, as in the Articles of *Confederation*. As with ordinary government, so too with constitutional amendment. Neither the people of each state nor the People of the nation were wholly sovereign. Sovereignty had somehow been divided, with Article V embodying the precise—exclusive—terms of the divison.

Which path is most plausible? Not, I think, Jefferson Davis's. For the text of the Constitution made clear in Article VI that any state constitutional provision—even if adopted by majority-rule popular sovereignty in a state—was clearly inferior to the federal Constitution. And Article V makes clear that a state people can be bound by a federal amendment even if that state people in state convention explicitly reject the amendment. (Here, Article V differs dramatically from Article VII.) Both of these provisions are logically inconsistent with the sovereignty of the people of each state. And if we examine the Constitution of 1787 as an act, and not a mere text, we will find no one—on either side of ratification—asserting that after ratification a state people could unilaterally secede at will.[69]

That leaves us with a choice between the Constitution's two greatest architects, James Madison and James Wilson. And on this vital question, Wilson—though less celebrated and studied today—was the truer prophet, seeing further and more clearly. Wilson built his argument axiomatically on the idea that sovereignty was absolute and indivisible. This view was almost universally held in the 1780s. Divided sovereignty was seen as logical contradiction, a "solecism."[70] Indeed, as far as I can tell, Madison was the only major figure who believed in it.

Why did virtually no one follow Madison's lead in this point? Perhaps because they understood that "divided" or "mixed" popular sovereignty

[69] For more documentation, see Amar, "Of Sovereignty and Federalism," pp. 1425, 1457–66. For analysis of the geostrategic logic undergirding all this, see Akhil R. Amar, "Some New World Lessons for the Old World," *University of Chicago Law Review* 58 (1991): 483, 485–91.

[70] See Amar, "Philadelphia Revisited," p. 1063, n. 71; Wood, *The Creation of the American Republic*, p. 345.

was no popular sovereignty. A fundamental principle for republican government was that the majority should rule, and divided sovereignty betrayed that fundamental principle. The formal principle of popular sovereignty, in other words, cannot tell us whether we should be a state people, or a national People, but it does insist that we be one or the other. (And since Davis was wrong, Wilson must be right.) For if sovereignty can indeed be divided—as only Madison believed—then We the People today cannot control our fate. This is not popular self-rule; it is rule from the cold graves of dead men of constitutions past. Self-evidently, that is not what Jefferson meant in 1776, what Wilson meant in 1787, or what we should accept today.

Six

The Plain Meaning of Article V

DAVID R. DOW

LAW is composed of a variety of ambiguous texts.[1] Some of our texts, including provisions of the Constitution such as the equal protection clause of the Fourteenth Amendment, invite virtually unending debates about meaning. Other constitutional provisions, however, seem rather straightforward. Consider, for example, Article I, section 1, which forecloses the possibilities of Congress's consisting of fewer or more than two houses; the terms for senators being other than six years; or a twenty-year-old serving even as a representative, let alone president. These texts seem clear. Of course, one can cavil. Must a presidential aspirant be thirty-five at the time of election or inauguration? Nevertheless, though questions can perhaps be tortuously raised, the text itself is fundamentally clear,[2] and if we can debate meaning at all, it is only at the periphery.

The meaning of Article V—arguably the single most important procedural provision in the Constitution, governing, as it does, how we may alter the Constitution—is an example of yet another text the meaning of which is essentially clear.[3] To be sure, it is not altogether without ambi-

My work on this project was supported by a grant from the University of Houston Law Foundation. This chapter is a substantially abridged (and slightly revised) version of my argument originally published as "When Words Mean What We Believe They Say: The Case of Article V," *Iowa Law Review* 76 (1990): 1.

[1] By "ambiguous," I do not mean that the text is without meaning, but that it is subject to several plausible meanings. See, e.g., Stanley Fish, *Is There a Text in this Class?* (Cambridge: Harvard University Press, 1980), pp. 97–111, 303–21; Willard Van Orman Quine, *Word and Object* (Cambridge: Technology Press of the Massachusetts Institute of Technology, 1960), pp. 125–56. This does not mean, of course, that *any* interpretation is possible, but simply that more than one is acceptable. Others have argued that although more than one interpretation may be acceptable, one will almost always be the best. See, e.g., Ronald Dworkin, "Law as Interpretation," *Texas Law Review* 60 (1982): 527, 546.

[2] The meaning is clear at the core, at any rate. Debates may arise concerning meaning at the margins, or at what I prefer to call the periphery. The very idea of "easy cases" suggests that any number of texts mean precisely what they say. See generally Frederick Schauer, "Easy Cases," *Southern California Law Review* 58 (1985): 399, 414–31 (clear "language is significantly important in producing easy cases").

[3] The text of Article V is set out above at p. 5.

guity. "Two thirds of both Houses" could mean two-thirds of each house, that is, two-thirds of each the House and the Senate, or it could mean two-thirds of the two houses sitting together. Further, the use of the phrase "Intents and Purposes" seems nearly to invite readers of constitutional amendments to dig beneath the words on the parchment. Nevertheless, the *procedure* delineated in Article V as to modes of originating proposed amendments and of subsequent ratification seems quite clear. Questions remain,[4] yet questions are also answered—or so it appears from the text. Indeed, I argue that the mechanism outlined in Article V clearly and unequivocally sets out an exclusive mode of constitutional amendment.

The Countermajoritarian Difficulty and the Nature of Our Foundational Beliefs

Federal courts—by definition nonmajoritarian institutions—periodically strike down acts of the legislature on the grounds that the legislative enactments contravene certain provisions of the Constitution. This so-called "countermajoritarian difficulty" has caused constitutional scholars a great deal of consternation. It is, I think, what drives efforts—represented in this volume especially in the essays of Ackerman, Amar, Griffin, and Levinson—to justify extra-Article V theories of amendment. Advocates of judicial review have struggled to reject Alexander Bickel's characterization of the Supreme Court as a "deviant" institution—deviant because in our basically democratic polity, the Court at times thwarts the ostensible will of the majority.[5] Both judges and academicians have struggled mightily, but fruitlessly, to resolve the difficulty.[6]

The so-called "difficulty," however, is not resolvable.[7] Bickel, as well

---

[4] For example, questions as to how long an amendment may languish without being ratified before it dies, questions as to the power of a convention called for the purpose of proposing specific amendments, and even questions as to the justiciability of these very issues. As Sanford Levinson explains in his Introduction, these extremely interesting and important questions are beyond the scope of this volume.

[5] Alexander Bickel, *The Least Dangerous Branch* (Indianopolis: Bobbs-Merrill, 1962).

[6] See, e.g., Bowers v. Hardwick, 478 U.S. 186, 191 (1985) (noting that the Court is "striving to assure itself and the public that announcing rights not readily identifiable in the Constitution's text involves much more than the imposition of the Justices' own choice of values on the States and the Federal Government"). The scholarly efforts that have addressed this issue are vast. See generally John Hart Ely, *Democracy and Distrust* (Cambridge: Harvard University Press, 1980); Paul Brest, "The Fundamental Rights Controversy: The Essential Contradictions of Normative Constitutional Scholarship," *Yale Law Journal* 90 (1981): 1063.

[7] Brest, "The Fundamental Rights Controversy." In contrast to Brest, I have argued that although the paradox is not resolvable, countermajoritarianism ought not to be

as his answerers, have failed to appreciate that the countermajoritarian difficulty simply illustrates that we hold competing beliefs. In the United States, we believe in,[8] and our political institutions reflect, majority rule. At the same time, we also believe that not everything ought to be subject to it. Following the majority *because it is the majority* is sometimes obligatory; resisting the majority *even though it is the majority* is sometimes required. Two competing principles constitute the essence of our political being, and this raises a terribly difficult question: How do we know which to follow when?

In recent years scholars, most certainly including Ackerman and Amar, have seized upon the notion of popular sovereignty as the tool of reconciliation.[9] The notion of popular sovereignty and the principle of majority rule are conceptually distinct. When we talk of popular sovereignty in the United States, we usually mean to refer to some power held by the people.[10] By sovereignty, specifically, we mean "unfettered power of legislation."[11] The very idea of popular sovereignty acquires meaning by virtue of its juxtaposition to theories holding that the source of legislative authority is other than the people—that it lies, for example, in the king or in God.[12] By *popular* sovereignty, therefore, we mean that the people, in contradistinction to God or the king, hold this power.[13]

Once sovereignty is understood to be popular—once the power of legislation is understood to be in the hands of the people—it follows

---

regarded as a problem. Dow, "Hillel's Dilemma and Wisdom: The Paradigmatic Instance of the Counter-Majoritarian Difficulty and the Judaic Resolution," *National Jewish Law Review* 4 (1989): 59, 66; Dow, "Constitutional Midrash: The Rabbis' Solution to Professor Bickel's Problem," *Houston Law Review* 29 (1992): 543.

[8] When I say "we believe in," as I do throughout this essay, I am making an empirical assumption concerning the ideas that are prevalent in our culture: concerning, more specifically, the ideas that define our culture, that are its essence rather than merely its attributes. Insofar as these empirical assumptions are flawed or erroneous, my argument suffers accordingly.

[9] See, e.g., Akhil Reed Amar, "Philadelphia Revisited: Amending the Constitution Outside Article V," *University of Chicago Law Review* (1988): 1043–44; Bruce Ackerman, "The Storrs Lectures: Discovering the Constitution," *Yale Law Journal* 93 (1984): 1013, 1014–16; Ackerman, "Constitutional Politics/Constitutional Law," *Yale Law Journal* 99 (1990): 453, 456; Ackerman, *We the People: Foundations* (Cambridge, Mass.: Harvard University Press, 1991).

[10] *The Federalist*, No. 40 (J. Madison), ed. C. Rossiter (New York: New American Library, 1961), p. 253.

[11] Dennis Lloyd, *Introduction to Jurisprudence*, 3d ed. (London: Stevens, 1972), p. 152, n.1.

[12] See, e.g., Ernest Kantorowicz, *The King's Two Bodies: A Study in Medieval Political Theology* (Princeton: Princeton University Press, 1957), pp. 43–45; Edmund Morgan, *Inventing the People: The Rise of Popular Sovereignty in England and America* (New York: Norton, 1988), p. 15.

[13] Morgan, *Inventing the People*, p. 15.

ineluctably that the law comes *from the people*.[14] The definition of "people" poses an initial obstacle, but because the theory pertains solely to the *source* of legislative authority, it need not preclude an evolving or expanding conception of "people." We can say, in other words, that the framers held an impoverished notion of "people" without saying, necessarily, that their parochial notion of people belied their commitment to the idea of popular sovereignty.

Recent work indeed suggests that the Framers were committed to this idea.[15] However, it is quite difficult to ascertain whether the theory was viewed by the Framers—or, for that matter, whether contemporaries view it—as a prescriptive or descriptive proposition. Do we (or did the Framers) believe that law *ought* to come from the people, or only that it *does?* The question is not entirely academic, because any legal theory that rests upon the Framers' intent presumes that the Framers believed that they were shaping the polis and not merely describing it.

In any event, the idea of popular sovereignty does *not* entail rule by majority will. Although popular sovereignty *can* be understood as 50 percent plus one, it can also be understood as a plurality, a supermajority, or even the will of an appointed oligarchy of lawmakers. In addition, even at the level of pure political theory, the rule of the majority is not coextensive with popular sovereignty since the majority acts out its desires through legislatures, and legislatures may represent the popular will only imperfectly.[16] Majority rule is a practical (and normative) rule of who wins. Popular sovereignty is a theoretical view of who does, or who ought to, have power. Neither notion entails the other.

Students of political thought tend to locate the ascendancy of theories of popular sovereignty in the sixteenth-century reformist movements.[17] However, since popular sovereignty and majoritarianism are

[14] This proposition can present a problem insofar as the people who constitute the sovereign might continue to believe in some type of natural law.

[15] See Morgan, *Inventing the People*; see also Thomas Pangle, *The Spirit of Modern Republicanism* (Chicago: University of Chicago Press, 1988), pp. 131–279 (emphasizing the Lockean orientation of framers and the applicability of this orientation to current political issues).

[16] See, e.g., James Buchanan and Gordon Tullock, *The Calculus of Consent* (Ann Arbor: University of Michigan Press, 1962); Armatya Sen, *Collective Choice and Social Welfare* (San Francisco: Holden-Day, 1970). The potential for agency abuse is Amar's justification for the supermajority requirements on Congress and state legislatures (or conventions).

[17] See Quentin Skinner, *The Foundations of Modern Political Thought* (New York: Cambridge University Press, 1978), 1:113–14. More specifically, Skinner argues strongly for the influence of Calvinist thought on the development of notions of popular sovereignty (1:225–37). Skinner sees the roots of Calvinist ideology in Catholic scholasticism (pp. 321–22). Calvin understood that the doctrine he espoused had roots going back at least to Cicero (2:230–31). As I argue in the text, the roots could well be located in the Torah, and in the Talmudic development of its majority rule principle.

conceptually distinct, these historical inquiries do not help us to determine when majoritarianism emerged or how a majoritarian democracy ought to operate from an ethical point of view, or, more important, how the Framers intended it to operate.[18] Theories of sovereignty are political theories (or perhaps religious theories). Majority rule is practical politics (though it may be defensible from the standpoint of secular morality as well).[19] As a practical matter, then, what is primarily significant in the United States is not so much our putative belief in popular sovereignty as our commitment to majoritarianism. This is significant because, as is obvious (albeit philosophically problematic), our commitment to majoritarianism is severely circumscribed.

Consider one of the earliest discussions of majority rule, which occurs in the Torah and ensuing commentary by the rabbis. Exodus 23:2 warns that we "not follow a multitude to do evil." From this negative injunction, the talmudic rabbis inferred that, except when the majority is doing evil, it is commanded to follow the majority.[20] At the same time, and in contrast, the most general, overarching principle of Jewish law is not to follow the majority, but to do what is just and good.[21] In many instances and numerous contexts, the legal code defines what it is that is just and good, but not always. As a result, the just-and-good desideratum can act as an exception to a particular rule; it even can act as an exception to a rule enunciated by a majority. The principle of majority rule does not override the overarching commandment to do what is "just and good."[22]

Implicit in this legal structure is protection of minority interests. That is, it may be "just and good" to protect the minority even when the majority would not be so inclined.[23] Similarly, as Walter Murphy insists

---

[18] See generally Donald Lutz, *The Origins of American Constitutionalism* (Baton Rouge: Louisiana State University Press, 1988), pp. 28, 60, 81, 102. Lutz defines popular sovereignty as "the idea that the community and its government originate in the consent of the people" (p. 81). Even as this belief was emerging, however, it was accompanied by the idea, which was well in place by the 1780s, that even the majority could be bound by fundamental law (p. 60).

[19] Indeed, Jefferson argued that majority will is an aspect of natural law. Thomas Jefferson, *Notes on the State of Virginia*, ed. W. Peden (Chapel Hill: University of North Carolina Press, 1954), pp. 124–25. Even so, the practical features of this principle are paramount, for any other focus proceeds at so high a level of abstraction as to be utterly unhelpful in resolving contemporary problems.

[20] B. Talmud, Baba Mezia 59b. For a detailed examination of the role of majority rule in Jewish society, see A. Schreiber, *Jewish Law and Decision Making: A Study Through Time* (Philadelphia: Temple University Press, 1979), pp. 316–27.

[21] Deuteronomy 6:17–18.

[22] Ibid. It would be possible, of course, to define "just" as coterminous with majority will: to say that something is just *because* it is supported by a majority. This is not the talmudic view.

[23] As Maimonides recognized, although talmudic law ordinarily follows the majority (of

in his essay in this volume, our American political commitment to majoritarianism is likewise qualified and not absolute. We are, after all, a *constitutional* democracy. Despite our general commitment to majority rule, mere majorities may not *legitimately* do whatever they want simply because they are majorities.[24]

The idea of popular sovereignty is not helpful as a tool for constitutional explication because it has no value in reconciling our two elemental beliefs. Do we not believe that we can agree today to bind ourselves tomorrow, and, further, that we can agree today that we shall not have the right tomorrow to change our minds?[25] Do we not agree that a majority can (i.e., it has the authority to) agree today that it will take more than a mere majority tomorrow to interfere with the freedom of the press? Do we not believe that a majority can agree today that accused wrongdoers will have certain rights tomorrow even if tomorrow a bare majority of us no longer believes that a particular accused should? Indeed, we believe in each of these propositions, for these make up what our Constitution is.

Ackerman and Amar

Congress, according to Article V, shall propose amendments to the Constitution when "deemed necessary" by two-thirds of both houses. Alternatively, Congress shall call a convention for the purpose of proposing amendments when called upon to do so by two-thirds of the states. These are the two exclusive mechanisms for proposing amendments; irrespective of which is employed, a proposed amendment becomes part of the Constitution when ratified by three-fourths of the states. Amending the Constitution is thus made purposefully difficult; advocates of amendment are required to muster broad, substantial, and widespread geographic support for their proposals. Nevertheless, amending the Constitution might not be especially arduous if there is an alternative to Article V, if there is some way to circumvent the rigor ostensibly demanded by the language of the text.

---

sages), there must be exceptions, as when the minority view is "better reasoned." M. Maimonides, Commentary on the *Mishnah: Tractate Sanhedrin*, mishnah 6, trans. F. Rosner (1981), p. 11.

[24] The operative word, of course, is *legitimate*. A majority *can* often work its way, but this is simply a statement about raw power.

[25] Cf. H.L.A. Hart, *The Concept of Law* (Oxford: Clarendon Press, 1961), pp. 64, 70–76 (arguing that some restrictions placed on the legislature narrow the scope of the power to amend). See generally Jon Elster, *Ulysses and the Sirens: Studies in Rationality and Irrationality* (New York: Cambridge University Press, 1979).

Amar's Popular Vote Theory

Amar's theory bypasses, for ratification purposes, the states. He allows a national majority of individuals to ratify a proposed amendment. This could mean that if the citizens of, say, Texas, California, New York, Florida, and Illinois voted overwhelmingly to ratify, it would not matter that mere majorities of voters in the other forty-five states voted against ratification. Moreover, if the ratification *is* valid for some reason of political theory, then presumably the process might extend to the prior step: A majority of citizens could compel Congress to call the convention.[26] Amar's proposal starkly departs from the text of Article V.

For Amar, the notion of popular sovereignty provides the predicate for the legitimacy of the existing Constitution. It provides as well a mechanism for amending the Constitution outside of Article V. "The People," Amar argues, are "sovereign, and . . . a majority of them enjoy[] the inalienable legal right . . . to alter or abolish their form of government whenever they please."[27] Article V, he concludes, "makes constitutional amendment by ordinary governmental entities possible and thus eliminates the *necessity* of future appeals to the People themselves. However, future appeals to the People remain *sufficient*, as a general matter, to effect constitutional change."[28] Article V "should not be understood as binding" the people.[29]

The first thing we need to do is to be clear about what we are talking about. Amar equivocates between the assertion that the people retain the "right" to amend outside Article V and the claim that they possess the power to do so. Rights and powers are, of course, quite different.[30] Statements about power are statements about physics, and I am not concerned with addressing them here. The people may well have the power to alter the Constitution, but this does not establish that in exercising that power they have acted lawfully. They have acted lawfully only insofar as they have the right to act; hence, Amar's more pertinent argument is that the people retain the right to amend the Constitution and that this right is inalienable.

The normative basis for this argument, however, is quite unclear.[31]

---

[26] Amar acknowledges this point. Amar, "Philadelphia Revisited," p. 1065. This concession seems to me to underscore the implausibility of his thesis.

[27] Ibid., p. 1050. Here it is clear that Amar is, inappropriately, using sovereignty and the principle of majority rule interchangeably.

[28] Ibid., p. 1054 (footnote omitted).

[29] Ibid., p. 1055.

[30] See Dow, "Individuals, Governments, and Rights," *South Texas Law Review* 30 (1989): 369, 372–73, n.21.

[31] Amar might be defining sovereignty as inalienable; that is, he might be making a

On one hand, Amar's claim about the inalienability of the right to amend outside Article V might be justified by an argument that: (1) this is so under the framers' theory of popular sovereignty; (2) the framers embodied their political theory (i.e., popular sovereignty) in the Constitution as a normative proposition; (3) we therefore have available to us, *for reasons rooted in the Constitution*, a certain political theory.[32] On the other hand, Amar's claim might rest on a noninterpretivist basis and posit either that the theory of popular sovereignty is simply true, or that we (either as Americans or as human beings) enjoy a natural or fundamental right that we are without the power to alienate. Under this view, extra-Article V methods of amendment are legitimated not because they are enshrined in the Constitution, but because of our extraconstitutional beliefs.

Amar is apparently not an intentionalist, although it is not clear that he rejects the interpretivist argument. Nevertheless, the interpretivist argument seems readily dispatched by an examination of the primary source of the framers' intent, which speaks not a whisper about any other mode of amendment.[33] Moreover, Amar also deploys his argument as a justification for the original ratification of the Constitution (despite the fact that the procedure utilized departed from that demanded by the Articles of Confederation). Amar's theory cannot be rooted in the Constitution; it must have its origin elsewhere.

The remaining argument, and the more difficult one to dispatch, is that which is rooted in the transcendent truth of popular sovereignty. But popular sovereignty is an esoteric notion, irrelevant to constitu-

---

statement of positive law. On the other hand, he might be making a philosophical point about natural law. His position is unclear. As a proposition of political philosophy, the claim traces its modern roots to Jean-Jacques Rousseau, *The Social Contract*, trans. D. Cress (Indianapolis: Hackett Pub. Co., 1983), bk. 2, chaps. 1–2. This view, however, is inextricably tied to Rousseau's notion, which is not prevalent in American constitutionalism, that sovereignty is the exercise of the general will. Further, Rousseau additionally holds to the view—which is also quite alien to us—that the entire self can somehow be alienated to the general will (bk. 1, chaps. 6–7). For the influence (or, more properly, relative lack of influence) of Rousseau on the framers, see Lutz, *The Origins of American Constitutionalism*, pp. 139–49.

[32] Of course, this argument would suffer from all the problems attendant to intent-based theories generally. See, e.g., Paul Finkelman, "The Constitution and the Intentions of the Framers: The Limits of Historical Analysis," *University of Pittsburgh Law Review* 50 (1989): 349; Daniel Farber, "The Originalism Debate: A Guide for the Perplexed," *Ohio State Law Review Journal* 49 (1988): 1085.

[33] The primary source of the contemporaneous views of the framers is Max Farrand, ed., *The Records of the Federal Convention of 1787* (New Haven: Yale University Press, 1937). Also useful is J. Elliot, ed., *The Debates in the Several State Conventions on the Adoption of the Federal Constitution* (Philadelphia, J. B. Lippincott, 1901). I review these materials in detail below, under "The Plain Meaning of Article V."

tional interpretation. What matters is the meaning of our normative commitment to majoritarianism, and our commitment to this principle is only partial. We quite clearly believe that the power to amend is alienable; it may be restricted to the mode authorized by Article V.

Ackerman's Theory of Structural Amendment

Ackerman argues that the Constitution can be amended through what he calls a "structural amendment."[34] Although Ackerman does not define this term with rigor, structural amendments are additions to or deletions from the Constitution that come about through the behavior of the voters rather than through the formal amendment mechanism. The relevant behavior of voters is that displayed during elections, particularly presidential elections.

These structural amendments are not written down anywhere or even expressly articulated; they simply "emerge" from the political process, which is to say that they are redacted and ratified as a by-product of elections.[35] The basic point is that voters' attitudes, as those attitudes are expressed in (presidential) elections, can operate to amend the Constitution in a manner consistent with their attitudes.[36]

Ackerman's theory posits a distinction between normal politics and constitutional politics. Typically, but not always, constitutional politics consists of episodes such as the constitutional convention and the formal amendment (Article V) mechanism. The characteristics of constitutional politics include predominance of the public over the private and concern for broad interests rather than more narrow concerns. Hence, constitutional politics may, but they need not, operate through the formal Ar-

[34] Ackerman, "Storr's Lectures," pp. 1051–57.

[35] Not all elections, and not all presidential elections, are connected to proposed constitutional amendments. Typically, elections do *not* have constitutional significance. Such ordinary, routine politics Ackerman refers to as "normal" politics. Ibid., pp. 1022–23. Although Ackerman's delineation of the structural amendment focuses on presidential elections, his theory does not dictate that structural amendments emerge exclusively from presidential politics. Presumably, congressional elections might also be a source of constitutional amendments. This would raise even more serious difficulties than those I enumerate in the text.

[36] Ackerman is also interested in the behavior and attitudes of elected representatives, namely congresspersons and senators, especially in Ackerman, "Constitutional Politics," pp. 503–10. I do not think that the shift in focus from voters to elected officials affects the thrust of my critique. Moreover, it seems odd that newly elected or returned members of Congress could enact an "unconstitutional" statute after an election in which the voters, by participating in the very congressional elections that sent the representatives and senators to Washington, were engaging in "constitutional" politics. This paradox strikes me as terribly serious, but it is not the focus of this essay.

ticle V mechanism. What is important finally is that the benchmarks of constitutional politics be present.

By studying electoral politics closely, one can ascertain when normal politics has ended and when constitutional politics has begun. Once one has the vision to do this, one can also divine the content of the structural amendment that the voters have enacted through their participation in the process of constitutional politics. Indeed, this apparently is the only way to discern that constitutional politics is operating outside of the Article V mode. Moments of constitutional politics, for Ackerman, amount to "glorious reenactment[s] of the American Revolution."[37]

Ackerman utilizes the conceptual dualism between normal and constitutional politics to "dissolve the 'countermajoritarian difficulty.'"[38] Judges are no longer seen as frustrating majorities when they declare acts of Congress unconstitutional; they instead reflect that the people have acted: that the people, by engaging in constitutional politics, have altered the constitutional text and signaled a shift that itself invalidates the legislative enactment under scrutiny. Ackerman locates historical moments tantamount to formal amendment of the Constitution and argues that these moments have effected constitutional change. The first of these moments comprises the framing of the original Constitution together with *Marbury v. Madison* and *McCulloch v. Maryland*; the second moment consists of events surrounding the Civil War, including the judicial failure manifested by *Dred Scott* followed by the Civil War Amendments; the third episode is the emergence during the New Deal of the modern welfare state.[39] "Time and again," Ackerman maintains, "we return to these moments; the lessons we learn from them control the meaning we give to our present constitutional predicaments."[40]

Interpretation of historical episodes or eras is thus a key element of the theories of both Ackerman and Amar. For Amar, studying eighteenth- (or perhaps sixteenth-) century history is primarily important as a means to ascertain the dictates of the theory of popular sovereignty, which purportedly underlies the Constitution. Ackerman's use of history is more sweeping; he suggests that both the Civil War Amendments and the economic legislation of the New Deal era have acquired the status of constitutional law by virtue of the historical circumstances surrounding these moments. Amar's use of history is ultimately connected to matters of political theory, whereas Ackerman's use of history is connected more directly to politics. Amar's history is intellectual history; Ackerman's

[37] Ackerman, "Storrs Lectures," p. 1020.
[38] Ibid., pp. 1044, 1049–57.
[39] Ibid., pp. 1051–52.
[40] Ibid., p. 1052.

is social or political history. Criticizing their respective uses of history therefore involves somewhat different approaches. My discussion of Ackerman's theory will hew to the political moments upon which he seizes. I shall suggest that, at a minimum, his inferences from those moments are dubious. When I turn to Amar's theory, I shall focus more on the theory of our Constitution and suggest that his proposal fundamentally misapprehends our constitutional structure. Both theories ignore the nature and the content of our beliefs.

The Plain Meaning of Article V

Interpretation cannot proceed without accepted hermeneutical techniques. In American law, both statutory as well as constitutional, one such basic rule is the principle *expressio unius est exclusio alterius*: The expression of one thing is the exclusion of another.[41] It is true, of course, that the applicability of this maxim of interpretation depends upon the intentions of the parties who drafted the document, but I shall argue below that the Framers must be understood to have intended Article V to be exclusive. Even were their intent unfathomable, however, the invocation of this maxim would be appropriate, for Article V must be understood as exclusive not precisely because the framers expected it to be, but because the structure of the government they established *depends* upon its exclusivity. Consequently, insofar as the primary obstacle to applying the maxim is that it is not always an accurate reflection of the drafters' intentions,[42] this caveat is altogether inapposite in the present context. Article V must be exclusive because if it is not, then the notion of rights collapses of logical necessity.

The stark implication of the Amar or Ackerman proposals is that supermajorities are one mechanism, but simple majorities will also suffice. That implication renders Article V supererogatory. Hence, if the Constitution is to continue to be the ultimate source that protects individual rights against encroachment by government power and political majorities, then the affirmative words in Article V must be understood to negative other conceivable modes of amendment.[43]

[41] See generally Herbert Broom, *A Selection of Legal Maxims*, ed. R. H. Kersey (London: Sweet and Maxwell Ltd., 1939), pp. 443–54.

[42] See Potomac Passengers Ass'n v. Chesapeake & Ohio Ry., 415 U.S. 453 (1974). See generally Note, "Intent, Clear Statements, and the Common Law: Statutory Interpretation in the Supreme Court," *Harvard Law Review* 95 (1982): 892, 895, n.28, 899–900, nn. 58–62.

[43] William Van Alstyne, "A Critical Guide to *Marbury v. Madison*," *Duke Law Journal* (1969): 1 (Article V must be understood to negate other conceivable modes of amendment); cf. *Marbury*, 5 U.S. (1 Cranch) 137, 174 (1803).

In *The Federalist* No. 43, Madison described the amendment mechanism as one that would mediate between a Constitution too fixed and one too transient.[44] While amending the Constitution must be possible, the process must not be facile. Amendments must be attended by deliberation. Similarly, Hamilton implied in *The Federalist* No. 85, that the proposed ratification procedure aspired to ensure widespread geographic support.[45] Though amending the Constitution would be easier than establishing the Constitution in the first instance, the requirement that ten of the thirteen states approve the proposed amendment would achieve widespread geographic support.[46] A desideratum of the amendment process, then, was that it proceed slowly and deliberately, and that it insist upon widespread geographic support. These same values also appear in the discussion of the process at the constitutional convention, though, as was the case with the Federalist Papers, the issue of the Article V amendment process received comparatively little attention at the convention.[47] Significantly, apparently at no time did any of the convention delegates express any interest in popular participation in the amendment process,[48] i.e., submission of proposed amendments directly to the people. This is not surprising since we would rarely expect to find in ordinary popular elections the degree of deliberation that is attendant to legislative voting.[49] By insisting, then, that the amendment procedure

[44] As Madison put it: "The mode [of amendment] preferred by the convention seems to be stamped with every mark of propriety. It guards equally against that extreme facility, which would render the Constitution too mutable; and that extreme difficulty, which might perpetuate its discovered faults." *The Federalist*, No. 43 (Madison), p. 278. All of the citations are taken from the 1961 edition edited by Clinton Rossiter.

[45] Hamilton asserted that subsequent amendments would be easier to achieve than initial acceptance of the Constitution (though his argument in this regard appears fallacious since the Constitution itself provided that it would become effective upon consent by nine states), but he reiterated that states would be protected by virtue of the supermajority requirement. *The Federalist*, No. 85 (Hamilton), pp. 524–25.

[46] *The Federalist*, No. 43 (Madison), pp. 278–79.

[47] The following list reflects the entirety of references in the records of the constitutional convention to the amendment process. Some of the references are to the formulation of Article V itself, while others appertain to discussion of amendment procedure in general. Farrand, *Records*, 1:22, 28, 117, 121–22, 126, 194, 202–3, 206, 227, 231, 237, 476, 478; 2:84, 87, 133, 136, 148, 152, 159, 174, 188, 461, 467, 555–59, 578, 602, 629–31, 634, 662; 3:120–21, 126, 357, 367, 400, 575; 4:49, 61, 93–103; Farrand, *Records*, supplement, ed. James Hutson (New Haven: Yale University Press, 1987), pp. 191–92, 270.

[48] I say "apparently" because it is notoriously difficult to ascertain the framers' intentions from the extant records of the convention, particularly since these records depend almost entirely on Madison's notes. In the context of Article V, the problem is especially acute. See Note, "Good Intentions, New Inventions, and Article V Constitutional Conventions," *Texas Law Review* 58 (1979): 131, 149–56.

[49] Which is not to say that all legislative voting is thoughtful or deliberate.

be conducted entirely through the legislatures,[50] the delegates at Philadelphia emphatically underscored the value of deliberation.

In addition, the delegates declined to give Congress power to frustrate the states. The language of Article V is mandatory, meaning that if the requisite number of states (thirty-four) so demand, Congress *must* call a convention.[51] The delegates purposefully utilized the word *shall* to express that Congress is required to call the convention if the conditions are satisfied.[52] Other references to the importance of widespread geographic and sectional assent are fairly common.[53]

The framers wanted the Constitution to be amendable but not *too* amendable. They wanted their work to be subject to revision, but they did not want it to be jettisoned in moments of passion. The requirement of supermajorities, the distinctive core feature of Article V, achieves the framers' goal of making the amendment process a slow, deliberative one. At the same time, it reflects the belief, prevalent among the framers and prevalent now, that certain rights are not subject to interference by mere majorities.

The majority in our democracy is not entirely free to do as it desires, and it is permitted at time $t-1$ to agree that only a supermajority will have the lawful power to legislate on certain subjects at time $t-2$. Jefferson, of course, *was* troubled by the fact that the Constitution would persist into generations that had not ratified it,[54] though this concern seems to have provoked little scholarly attention. Instead scholars since Bickel have fastened on the Madisonian dilemma: the removal by the Constitution of certain issues from the majoritarian process. This dilemma is, as we now know, unresolvable because we believe in both the premises that together make it up.

This suggests that attempts to dissolve the countermajoritarian diffi-

---

[50] On the subject of whether the word *legislature* in Article V can plausibly be construed to mean "the people," see Note, "The Unconstitutionality of Voter Initiative Applications for Federal Constitutional Conventions," *Columbia Law Review* 85 (1985): 1525 (arguing that it cannot).

[51] See ibid., p. 1525, n. 3.

[52] See Farrand, *Records*, supplement, p. 190.

[53] See, e.g., Max Farrand, *The Framing of the Constitution of the United States* (New Haven: Yale University Press, 1913), p. 190; Farrand, *Records*, 1:476, 478 (noting the framers' concerns that factions based on the sizes and geographic locations of states would arise); Farrand, *Records*, 2:631 (noting the concerns of one member of the convention that the Constitution gave too much power to Congress).

[54] "Every constitution, then, and every law, naturally expires at the end of 19 years." Letter from Jefferson to Madison, September 6, 1789, in *Papers of Thomas Jefferson*, ed. J. Boyd (Princeton: Princeton University Press, 1958), 5:395–96. This letter was not sent until January 9, 1790. See D. Malone, *Jefferson and the Rights of Man* (Boston: Little, Brown, 1951), p. 179.

culty (like Amar's and Ackerman's) commit the same fallacy that underlies the ostensible difficulty itself. The fallacy of the difficulty is that it
rests on a misunderstanding of the ontology of a higher law system:[55] It
undervalues the extent to which a higher law system, even one fundamentally democratic, intends, on occasion, to frustrate majority will.
Displaying the same myopia, Amar and Ackerman endeavor to dissolve
the difficulty by transforming even the amendment process into a majoritarian exercise.[56]

Both Amar and Ackerman dissolve the presumed countermajoritarian
difficulty by bowing to majorities; they ease the Madisonian dilemma by
dissolving the Constitution. Ackerman ignores the text entirely. Amar,
on the contrary, does seek to root himself in the political theory that
underlies the text, yet he misapprehends that very theory. In supposing
that sovereignty provides an adequate rationale for going outside the
text of Article V, and in supposing that this sovereignty is somehow inalienable, Amar, as I discuss below, slights additional structural assumptions also implicit in the Constitution.

Extra–Article V Theories

Ackerman and Amar ultimately ground their arguments on a historical
analogy. The analogy is as follows. The ratification of the Constitution
was not in accordance with the plain meaning of the positive law that
existed in the colonies in the late eighteenth century. Nevertheless, the
Constitution is legitimate, and was even viewed by contemporaries as
legitimate, because positive law does not provide the sole means for altering governments. Popular sovereignty (or, for Ackerman, constitutional politics, which amounts to the same thing) also provides a means,
and it can be exercised today, even outside the confines of Article V.

The problem here is manifest: Amar, and to a lesser degree Ackerman
as well,[57] argue that the ratification was defensible despite apparent con-

---

[55] See Dow, "Constitutional Midrash"; Dow, "Hillel's Dilemma." See generally Hart,
The Concept of Law, pp. 92–107 (discussing primary and secondary rules as the foundation
of a higher legal system); Hans Kelsen, *General Theory of Law and State*, trans. Anders
Wedberg (1945), pp. 110–34 (discussing the role of norms in higher legal systems; in particular, Kelsen describes the relationship between basic norms and the Constitution); Hans
Kelsen, *Pure Theory of Law*, trans. Max Knight (Berkeley: University of California Press,
1967), p. 198–201. Both Hart and Kelsen make clear that a (the) master rule can only be
ontological, not deontological.

[56] Amar is by no means oblivious to this criticism, and I do not mean to imply that he
has overlooked it. See Amar, "Philadelphia Revisited," pp. 1096–1100.

[57] Ackerman might resist my assertion that one of his premises assumes the illegality of
the Constitution. While he does argue that it must be seen as "illegal," he adds that his

flict with existing state law. However, we simply do not know what the outcome of a legal challenge to the legitimacy of the Constitution would have been in 1791. All we can say in retrospect is that Article VII of the Constitution *seems* illegal in light of the Articles of Confederation, that it *appears* to be at odds with the then-governing law, and that the ratification of the proposed Constitution by several states apparently violated their own constitutions. Perhaps the theoretical justification that Amar proposes could have been proffered in the 1790s, but it was not. We cannot say, therefore, that a challenge to the Constitution in light of the Articles or a particular state constitution would have failed. Yet that is precisely what we *must* say if the argument Amar and Ackerman make is to work. The underlying assumption that the Constitution itself is somehow "illegal," critical as it is to Ackerman's theory, is simply wrong.[58]

STRUCTURAL AMENDMENTS AND THE (AB)USE OF HISTORY

It is clear, I think, that the meaning of constitutional language, indeed the meaning of constitutional lacuna, often resides in constitutional structure, a point that Ackerman and Amar would not dispute. This structure is bound to a particular historical context, which suggests, derivatively, that constitutional language and lacuna also derive their meaning, at least in part, from constitutional history. That is surely so; the question raised by Ackerman's proposal, however, is not whether history is significant to constitutional interpretation, but whether we can tell—with anything close to certainty—nearly as much from political history as he supposes. Ackerman's own treatment of the historical record suggests that the answer is no.

Ackerman focuses on three historical periods, the late eighteenth to early nineteenth century; the Civil War period; and the Roosevelt era.[59] He argues that during each period constitutional politics displaced and predominated over normal politics and consequently altered the consti-

---

"larger project" does not depend on this assumption that the convention's arguments "would be rejected as *clearly* erroneous by any self-respecting court." Ackerman, "Storrs Lectures," p. 1017 n. 6 (emphasis in original). I confess that this argument loses me. The error strikes me as crucial. Without it, Ackerman is left with a naked normative argument, ungrounded in either text or constitutional history.

[58] To restate the point somewhat, the word *illegal* is a term of art. It does not mean illegitimate, or contrary to a philosophical tenet or principle. It means that there has been a particular judicial finding.

Amar's most recent work, including his essay written for this volume, rejects Ackerman's argument that the ratification process was "illegal." Consideration of Amar's new arguments is beyond the scope of this essay.

[59] See Ackerman, "Storrs Lectures," pp. 1051–57.

tutional text. In scrutinizing the politics of the Roosevelt era, for example, Ackerman concludes that the voters were engaging in constitutional deliberation about the legitimacy of the welfare state. The Constitution, under Ackerman's theory, may be amended even when there is no text to guide those who must interpret and enforce it.

The basic problem with postulating a theory whereby the political climate yields constitutional text is that reading electoral politics is only slightly less fatuous than reading tea leaves. Consider, for example, the folly of attempting to infer voter intent from the political climate of the Civil War era. In the election of 1860, four candidates had four different views on the two central questions of the day: slavery and union. The Constitutional Union party, a new name for the old Whigs, nominated John Bell on a platform that eulogized "the Constitution of the country, the union of the states, and the enforcement of the laws."[60] The Democratic party split. The northern Democrats nominated Stephen Douglas; the southern wing chose John Breckenridge. Douglas refused to run on a platform that explicitly protected slavery.[61] Yet he did insist on the right of popular sovereignty (which he linked, not surprisingly, to the states), thereby undercutting the need for secession by providing a basis for the southern states to protect their own interests. That was not concession enough to mollify the southern Democrats, however, so Breckenridge ran on a platform that expressly demanded nothing less than federal protection of slavery.

Rounding out the field was the Republican candidate, Abraham Lincoln. Even Lincoln's personal views are the subject of continuing controversy,[62] but the ideology of the Republicans as a party is far more elusive, due primarily to the extraordinarily eclectic nature of the group. One extreme consisted of the Radical Republicans. They abhorred slavery, castigated the slave states in virulent language, and refused utterly to compromise or placate the southern interests merely for the sake of preserving the Union. Although it is true that during Reconstruction the Radicals became fervent Nationalists, it is also true that in 1860,

[60] John Morton Blum et al., *The National Experience*, 4th ed. (New York: Harcourt Brace and World, 1977), 1:314. Unless otherwise indicated, the discussion immediately below is based on this reference (pp. 314–15).

[61] See David Potter, *Division and the Stresses of Reunion* (Glen View, Ill.: Scott, Foresman, 1973), p. 90.

[62] It has been said that more has been written about Lincoln than about any other human being, so it is almost pointless to pick out one or two works for citation. Nonetheless, for a good recent discussion, see James M. McPherson, *Abraham Lincoln and the Second American Revolution* (New York: Oxford University Press, 1991), pp. 3–63. Of course, delineation of Lincoln's own views does not enable us to know with any precision how they were perceived and interpreted by his contemporaries—which is, ultimately, central to Ackerman's theory.

rather ironically, the Radicals continued to exalt the power of the state governments over the federal. In uneasy alliance with the Radicals were the conservative Republicans. Led by Henry Clay and Daniel Webster, the conservatives, while not approving of slavery, were anxious to find a compromise rather than see the Union torn asunder. Maintaining the Union was paramount—more important to the conservatives than ending slavery.[63]

The party's third strand, the Democratic-Republicans, represented defectors from the Democrats. This faction remained tethered to its Jacksonian roots and resisted the encroachment of federal power upon the states. The Democratic-Republican opposition to the *Dred Scott* decision, for instance, was based less on the merits of that decision than on what was perceived as the Court's effort to foist its own (nationalistic) constitutional views on the states. To the Whigs among the Republicans, the Democratic-Republicans came too close to endorsing the Virginia and Kentucky Resolutions and the Doctrine of Nullification.[64]

Lincoln himself maintained both that slavery had to go *and* that the Union had to be preserved. Yet Lincoln's nomination followed the rejection of William Seward, who had made the "irrepressible conflict" speech and whose outspoken opposition to slavery ensured a violent confrontation between North and South were he to be elected.[65] How Lincoln would respond to secession was difficult to predict in advance of his election. Indeed, not until his inauguration speech, *after* he had been elected, did his rhetoric contain the ominous "clank of metal," which boded disaster. Even then, however, Lincoln would not take the first step; it would be the South that would decide "the momentous issue of Civil War."[66]

A vote in 1860 for Abe Lincoln was thus hardly a ringing endorsement for anything. In addition, the vote totals make it still more treacherous to attempt to infer what the voters were saying. Bell, the Unionist candidate, received fewer than 600,000 votes—less than one-third Lincoln's total. Douglas, on the other hand, the vocal proponent of popular sovereignty (linked to the states), ran second, with 1.3 million votes, to Lincoln's 1.8 million.[67] Lincoln's victory was made possible by his carrying the conservative border states (Indiana, Illinois, and Pennsylvania), which the 1856 Republican candidate, John Fremont, had lost to Buchanan. Popular sentiment in these pivotal swing states did strongly

[63] Blum, *National Experience*, 1:273–74.

[64] Ibid., 1:217. My discussion in this paragraph also draws on Allen Nevins, *Ordeal of the Union*, 2 vols. (New York: Scribner, 1947).

[65] Blum, *National Experience*, 1:314.

[66] Ibid., 1:318.

[67] Ibid., 1:315.

favor the Union, but inferring a national attitude from the views of voters in three states is dubious. Further, Lincoln won only 39 percent of the popular vote—a far cry from the supermajority demanded by Article V.[68] At a minimum, then, it is safe to say that Lincoln did not command the broad, widespread popular assent at which Article V's three-fourths requirement patently aims. It is equally safe to say that Lincoln stood for many things; precisely which particular things commanded endorsement from his discrete supporters is not knowable. Only Ackerman's highly dubious notion that what the Republican party stood for (as a matter of constitutional theory) was clear to the voters[69] allows him to make the wholly untenable suggestion that the Thirty-ninth Congress may properly "be viewed as a constitutional convention."[70]

Attempting to infer the content of voters' constitutional beliefs from the elections in the 1930s, which Ackerman's theory also proposes, is equally hazardous. From Roosevelt's election over Hoover in 1932, coupled with his resounding defeat of Alf Landon in 1936, Ackerman concludes that the voters first sanctioned the New Deal experiment, and then ratified the policies in 1936.[71] It is, of course, relatively safe to say that the voters knew what they were voting for in 1932: Roosevelt favored national economic planning, federal control over public utilities, federal development of public power, and he was willing to endure budget deficits if needed to ameliorate human suffering.[72] Hoover, in contrast, sanctioned austere restraint.[73] Yet if we want citizens to ponder constitutional amendments dispassionately, as Ackerman does, if we want citizens to be motivated by national interests rather than self-interest (assuming there is a difference) when engaging in constitutional politics, as Ackerman does, then using 1932 is deeply problematic.

At least 11 million Americans were out of work at the time of the 1932 election, and manufacturing wages had declined nearly 60 percent between 1929 and 1933.[74] A vote for Roosevelt in 1932 is therefore rather easy to regard as a vote for self-interest. Further, given the prevailing economic emergency in 1932, the most we can say, even if we can say with confidence that "the people" voted for "national" interests rather than "selfish" concerns, is that drastic measures were needed to

[68] Potter, *Division and the Stresses of Reunion*, pp. 82, 93.

[69] See ibid., pp. 1065–68.

[70] Ackerman, "Storrs Lectures," p. 1065.

[71] Ibid., pp. 1051–57.

[72] Blum, *National Experience*, 2:314. My discussion of this era is also informed by Frank Freidel, *Franklin Roosevelt: The Triumph* (Boston: Little, Brown, 1956); Charles Kindeberger, *The World in Depression* (Berkeley: University of California Press, 1973); Arthur Schlesinger, *The Politics of Upheaval* (Boston: Houghton Mifflin, 1960); Howard Zinn, ed., *New Deal Thought* (Indianapolis: Bobbs-Merrill, 1966).

[73] Blum, *National Experience*, 2:630–31.

[74] Ibid., 2:618.

combat an unprecedented catastrophe. That is quite different from saying that the voters wanted to institutionalize—to constitutionalize—those measures.

So what of the 1936 election: Does it not illustrate, as Ackerman intimates, ratification of the New Deal? Ackerman answers the question affirmatively, but his answer rests upon tenuous footing. For in addition to the fact that the economy was still ailing after four years of the Roosevelt experiment[75]—meaning that we must still ferret out self-interest from national interest motivations—the more serious difficulty is that Roosevelt's opponent did not initially challenge the constitutionality of the New Deal legislation (which the Court persisted in striking down until 1937).[76] Roosevelt countered attacks by critics who termed the New Deal legislation radical by describing it as moderate. Further, as Carl Degler has noted, "Virtually all of the truly experimental activities of the New Deal . . . were ultimately abandoned because of hostility from Congress—that is, from the immediate representatives of the people."[77] Voters may have felt comfortable with Roosevelt even if his programs were radical because of their confidence that Congress would reject anything *too* radical.

For Ackerman, the electorate signaled its assent to radical measures; in fact, it constitutionalized them. For Degler, the electorate would have rejected anything radical. In truth, the New Dealers lacked a coherent theory; they were purposefully ambiguous, intentionally understating their innovativeness. In light of this obfuscation—some intentional, some not—drawing conclusions about what the people said, about what they intended their vote to signify, is simply not possible.[78]

Ackerman's theory is an example of bad history being used for questionable reasons.[79] His description of the 1860s and 1930s is not disinterested, which is what one would hope for from a historian; it is instead patently instrumental, designed to buttress a particular political argument. Ironically, the method Ackerman utilizes is a two-edged sword: For just as history can give, so too can it take away. Arguably, having gone through twelve years of the Reagan-Bush era, Ackerman's own generation of Americans has acted to make unconstitutional many

---

[75] Ibid., 2:643.   [76] Ibid., 2:647.

[77] Carl Degler, "Introduction: What Was the New Deal?" in *The New Deal*, ed. C. Degler (Chicago: Quadrangle Books, 1970), p. 23.

[78] Of course, we can conclude that they intended to signify a preference for that candidate for whom they voted. I mean to suggest only that we can safely conclude no more.

[79] What I mean by questionable reasons is that one does not expect the historian's account to be instrumental. See Thomas Haskell, "Objectivity Is Not Neutrality: Rhetoric vs. Practice in Novick's *That Noble Dream*," *History and Theory* 2 (1990): 129, 151. Moreover, even if Ackerman's history were "good" history, in the sense of being a fair and accurate telling of the story, his theory would still suffer from many of the criticisms made of intent-based theories of constitutional interpretation.

restrictions on free-market capitalism. And as the problem of drugs becomes increasingly intractable, perhaps the people will do away with the
Fourth Amendment, if this has not occurred already. The historical argument is not difficult to make.

SOVEREIGNTY AND THE ALIENABILITY OF POWER

The core requirement of Article V, which is the fundamental cause of
the countermajoritarian difficulty, is the insistence upon supermajorities
for purposes of amendment. Unless we reject this core, then it follows
that sovereignty is indeed alienable. This conclusion may well be inconsistent with the descriptive theoretical content of sovereignty prior to
the creation of the Constitution of the United States, but it is what we
believe. And it is what our Constitution is. Indeed, the Federalists'
"greatest achievement" was in resolving the erstwhile "apparent paradox of sovereign states in a sovereign union."[80] This is a crucial point:
The structure of the Constitution reflects the notion that sovereignty is
alienable. This is what it means to say that certain rights are fundamental. Even from a purely originalist point of view, the framers themselves,
by establishing the supermajority requirement, demonstrated their belief that sovereignty is alienable.[81] The people may agree today that a
mere majority tomorrow will lack the lawful power to alter the Constitution. When the people do this, they have alienated a portion of their
sovereignty.

As noted earlier, that the Constitution *can* be altered in other ways,
that it can be changed or disregarded even without acquiring a supermajority, says nothing constitutionally significant. Whereas statements
about power are statements about physics, statements about rights are
statements about philosophy—and hence about law. The Constitution
does not speak to questions of physics. It does speak to issues of right,
and it speaks clearly and emphatically when it says that a mere majority
is not sufficient to amend the constitutional text, and when it establishes, through its complex structure, that a majority may (has the right
to) bind itself in such a way that its will may not be exercised unless it
becomes a supermajority.

[80] Peter Onuf, *The Origins of the Federal Republic* (Philadelphia: University of Pennsylvania Press, 1983), p. 198. See generally pp. 198–209.

[81] The assertion in the text is true even if Article V were not understood as the exclusive
mode of amendment, for sovereignty would continue to be alienated on those occasions
when Article V was utilized. It merits emphasizing at this point that my argument distinguishes conceptually between the theory of popular sovereignty and majoritarianism, for
the core idea of Article V is that even when a group constituting a political majority has the
power to effect change, it agrees not to—it binds itself to the status quo—unless and until
it can become a supermajority.

The normative proposition that "the 'power' to amend the Constitution is not alienable" can be true for two, and only two, reasons. First, the Constitution itself might, implicitly or explicitly, recognize the truth of the proposition. Second, irrespective of the positive law, the proposition might be true as a principle of fundamental or natural law.[82] Clearly the text of the Constitution does not explicitly recognize the truth of this proposition. This implies that insofar as Madison and the people of Virginia, Pennsylvania, and Maryland believed (prior to the ratification of the Constitution) in some amorphous "right" of the people to alter or abolish their governments, to the extent they believed in some right unconnected to those legal rights recognized by existing state constitutions or the Articles of Confederation—and to the extent Amar believes this as well—what was being expressed was a belief in natural law.[83] Similarly, Amar does not argue that the truth of the proposition (that sovereignty is not alienable) is acknowledged explicitly or implicitly in the Constitution, either through penumbras or emanations or some other less manifest constitutional source. He simply asserts that it is true. Thus, only if one believes in natural law, or some other nonwritten law, is it accurate to say, as Amar does say, that the right to amend the Constitution is inalienable.[84]

This is not at all self-evident. In fact, it is seemingly belied by the final words of Article V, which render two issues—American participation in the international slave trade and the equality of states in the Senate—nonamendable.[85] More generally, unless one believes in natural law, or believes that the Constitution embodies or recognizes it, the very idea of inalienability is problematic. Even for Locke, who did believe in natural

[82] This proposition would be the same if one believes that the Constitution, either through the Ninth Amendment or generally, incorporates natural or fundamental law.

[83] See generally John Finnis, *Natural Law and Natural Rights* (New York: Oxford Press, 1980).

[84] Presumably it was Locke from whom emerged the idea of "right" to alter one's government. See Oscar Handlin, "Who Read John Locke?" *The American Scholar* 58 (Fall 1989): 546. Handlin concludes, interestingly, that the framers, though they cited Locke when convenient, probably had not read his *Second Treatise*. They were apparently more familiar with Locke's epistemology, as put forth in the *Essay Concerning Human Understanding*.

It might be the case that Amar's argument concerning the inalienability of sovereignty is an asserted postulate of his overarching theory. Yet it does seem to me that Amar is making an independent normative claim. For discussions of sovereignty generally, see John Austin, *The Province of Jurisprudence Determined*, ed. H.L.A. Hart (New York Noonday Press, 1954), lecture 5 (1861–1863); Hart, *The Concept of Law*, pp. 49–76.

[85] Amar argues that even these issues would be amendable. Amar, "Philadelphia Revisited," pp. 1067–71. Congress can, under Article V, prohibit participation in the international slave trade after 1808, but, until then, it was presumably forbidden to Congress to do so. See Douglas Linder, "What in the Constitution Cannot Be Amended?" *Arizona Law Review* 23 (1981): 717.

law and who is still presumed to have had *some* influence on the framers, the agreement to enter into civil society involves an agreement to be bound by the majority.[86] "Every man, by consenting with others to make one body politic under one government, puts himself under an obligation to every one of that society, to submit to the determination of the majority, and to be concluded by it."[87] It is true that Locke holds that no man can "subject himself to the *arbitrary* power of another,"[88] but this does not preclude him from entering into civil society in the first place, which entails obeisance to the majority. This surrender of sovereignty must be understood as non-arbitrary, and Locke would permit it.[89] In Locke's theory, the people do retain the power to change a government even when their surrender of power has not been arbitrary,[90] but this does not change the fact that they have the right—even the natural right—to submit to be governed by a majority. There is no reason, either in the text of Locke or in theory generally, to believe that it is necessarily arbitrary to agree to be governed by a supermajority rather than a mere majority. Hence, when Amar, like Madison, speaks of the right to alter one's government irrespective of laws requiring supermajorities, it is more accurate to say that the people have the *power* to alter or abolish their governments. This is *not* equivalent to a legal *right* to do so.

Perhaps the people do have the power to alter their government; perhaps they do not. The answer lies in history and on the battlefield, not in constitutional explication. If, on the other hand, Amar supposes that the people retain the lawful power to alter their government outside of Article V, his point is quite specifically a point about rights[91] and, thus, a point about constitutional explication. It bears, however, the heavy burden of overcoming specific textual language as well as our basic constitutional structure.

---

[86] J. Locke, *Second Treatise*, chap. 8.

[87] Ibid., par. 97.

[88] Ibid., chap. 11, par. 135 (emphasis added).

[89] Ibid., chap. 15, par. 172.

[90] Ibid., chap. 13, par. 149; see also chap. 19.

[91] Assuming that Amar's point is a point about rights, the first question to ask is: Whence the source of this right? If the source, for Amar or for the early republicans, is natural law, then continued adherence to this notion is deeply problematic; if the source is the explicit text of the Constitution, then words (namely those of Article V) must be redefined. Only one source remains: The Constitution, by virtue of embodying republican principles, thereby embodies a certain right—the right of the people to alter their government whenever a majority so demands. This, ultimately, is the essence of Amar's claim. The inescapable difficulty is that it disregards the language of the text, the apparent intent of the framers, the core of what we believe today, the benign policies underlying the text, and, most fundamentally, the structure of sovereignty.

At the constitutional convention, the framers agreed that "provision ought to be made for the amendment of the [Constitution] whensoever it shall seem necessary."[92] The drafting committee initially proposed that Congress call a convention for the purpose of proposing amendments when requested to do so by two-thirds of the states. The concerns expressed about the committee's proposal addressed the ease of the process. While some delegates expressed the view that the process seemed too easy, others, like Hamilton, seemed concerned that the Constitution would be too difficult to amend. Madison assuaged the concerns of both groups by proposing that no amendment become part of the Constitution until ratified by three-fourths of the states, and by further proposing that Congress itself be permitted to originate amendments upon a vote of two-thirds of both houses.[93] Rutledge, from South Carolina, a slave state, proposed that the amendment provision preclude interference with the slave trade before 1808,[94] which Article V reflects was agreed upon. Sherman's concern that the big states would somehow find a way to abolish the smaller ones resulted in the provision in Article V that each state shall continue to have equal representation in the Senate.[95]

What is unmistakably clear is that the delegates to the convention consciously and intentionally approved an amendment process that would bar mere majorities from altering the Constitution. The participants in the process understood that they were drafting and agreeing to be bound by a document that could be changed only upon the garnering of a supermajority. Not a single delegate raised a philosophical objection to this proposal; not a single delegate asserted that this scheme was for any reason unenforceable or "illegal" in view of higher law. The understanding manifested by the framers, moreover, accords with our understanding today. We continue to believe in the truth of the principle embodied in the language of Article V.[96] The durability of the Constitution derives in no small measure from the fact that Article V means what it says.

[92] Elliot, *The Debates*, 1:170 (quoting a resolution unanimously adopted on July 23, 1787).

[93] Ibid., 5:531 (Mr. Gerry stated that by allowing two-thirds of the states to propose amendments the national government would be subverted to the will of the states).

[94] Ibid., 5:532.

[95] Ibid., 1:315–17, 5: 551.

[96] Ironically, Amar's claim that sovereignty continues to reside in the people despite their efforts (despite their *legal* efforts) to alienate it is reminiscent of (even identical to) the argument used by Calhoun to construct his doctrine of nullification. See John C. Calhoun, *A Discourse on the Constitution of the United States, a Disquisition on Government*, ed. C. G. Post (New York: Liberal Arts Press, 1953), pp. xi–xii.

States and Sovereignty

In their discussion of the amendment process, the delegates reflected a concern for another structural feature of the Constitution that Amar and Ackerman also slight: the states. Our government is not national; it is federal. States play critical theoretical and practical roles. Most fundamentally, despite Amar's rejection of the idea of divided sovereignty,[97] states are central components of the constitutional concept of sovereignty. The Supreme Court has recognized this structural point in a variety of contexts. In *Oregon v. Mitchell*,[98] for example, the Court rejected the conclusion that Congress's power was broad enough to "blot out all state power." Neither the original Constitution nor the Civil War Amendments transformed the nature of our government into "a central government of unrestrained authority."[99]

The Court could have easily quoted Madison on this point. Writing George Washington, Madison stated "that a consolidation of the whole into one simple republic would be as inexpedient as it is unattainable." He described himself as having "sought for a middle ground, which may at once support a due supremacy of the national authority" while "not exclud[ing] the local authorities whenever they can be subordinately useful."[100] More publicly, in *The Federalist*, No. 39 he expressly rejected the structural conception of government that underlies Amar's theory. The Constitution, Madison explained, is

> neither wholly *national* nor wholly *federal*. Were it wholly national, the supreme and ultimate authority would reside in the *majority* of people of the Union; and this authority would be competent at all times, like that of a majority of every national society, to alter or abolish its established government. Were it wholly federal, on the other hand, the concurrence of each State in the Union would be essential to every alteration that would be binding on all. The mode provided by the [Constitution] is not founded on either of these principles. In requiring more than a majority, and particularly in computing the proportion by *States*, not by *citizens*, it departs from the *national* and advances toward the *federal* character; in rendering the concurrence of less

[97] See Amar, "Philadelphia Revisited," p. 1063.

[98] 400 U.S. 112 (1970).

[99] Ibid., p. 128. Of course, the Civil War Amendments did significantly affect our governmental structure. This is among Ackerman's most compelling points.

[100] Letter from James Madison to George Washington, April 16, 1787, reprinted in *Papers of James Madison*, ed. Robert Rutland (Chicago: University of Chicago Press, 1975), 9:383. Madison wrote a similar letter to Edmund Randolph on April 8, 1787, reprinted in ibid., 9:368, 369.

than the whole number of States sufficient, it loses again the *federal* and partakes of the *national* character.[101]

This is extraordinary language, and in using it, Madison expressly dismissed the theories later adopted by both Amar and Ackerman. Similarly, in *The Federalist* No. 43, Madison reiterated the role of state governments in originating proposed amendments, and he observed that the guarantee of equal representation in the Senate was "probably" a concession to residual state sovereignty.[102] Even Hamilton, especially in *The Federalist* No. 85, likewise recognized the residual sovereignty retained by the states, and he argued that it would make the national government figures especially responsive.[103] He also observed the profound difference between drafting and ratifying the Constitution in the first instance and subsequently amending it (a difference that neither Ackerman nor Amar appreciates).

Finally, the anti-Federalists shared the Federalists' conception of the structure of sovereignty. Said Patrick Henry: "The assent of the people in their collective capacity is not necessary to the formation of a Federal Government. The people have no right to enter into leagues, alliances, or confederations: They are not the proper agents for this purpose: States and sovereign powers are the only proper agents for this kind of Government."[104]

In light of the constitutional structure of sovereignty, relying on a national majority to ratify proposed amendments rather than on majorities in discrete states is unconstitutional in the truest sense: It departs from the unmistakable language of the text as well as the concerns underlying the choice of such language. It is also inconsistent, not merely with the words of the Constitution, but with the constitutional structure of sovereignty and with those of our beliefs from which that structure emanates. Transforming the ratification process, as Amar does, from a state-based procedure to one based on a national majority is therefore more than merely at odds with the unambiguous language of the Constitution; it is radically at odds with the structure of our polity. Smaller governmental units *do* contain residual sovereignty distinct from that which animates the larger body. The Constitution also recognizes, structurally if not explicitly, this relationship. Article IV guarantees to

[101] *The Federalist*, No. 39 (Madison), p. 246.

[102] *The Federalist*, No. 43 (Madison), p. 279.

[103] *The Federalist* No. 85 (Hamilton), pp. 525–26.

[104] Ralph Ketcham, ed., *The Anti-Federalist Papers and the Constitutional Convention Debates* (New York: New American Press, 1986), p. 207 (speech of Patrick Henry, June 5, 1788).

the states a republican form of government, and the Tenth Amendment speaks of power retained by the states. This power is precisely a residue of sovereignty—a residue that, when it comes to amending the Constitution, is vested by Article V with immense significance. The suggestion that Article V is not the exclusive mode of amendment contradicts that bedrock principle of federalism and leads inexorably to the disappearance of states.[105]

Conclusion: Living with Conflicting Beliefs

Thought is false happiness: the idea
That merely by thinking one can,
Or may, penetrate, not may,
But can, that one is sure to be able—

That there lies at the end of thought
A foyer of the spirit in a landscape
Of the mind, in which we sit
And wear humanity's bleak crown;

In which we read the critique of paradise
And say it is the work
Of a comedian, this critique;
In which we sit and breathe

An innocence of an absolute,
False happiness, since we know that we use
Only the eye as faculty, that the mind
Is the eye, and that this landscape of the mind

Is a landscape only of the eye; and that
We are ignorant men incapable
Of the least, minor, vital metaphor, content,
At last, there, when it turns out to be here.[106]

The voice of the people, it is sometimes said, is the voice of God. How better, then, to conclude this essay than by looking at one treatment of the classic paradox that man has free will and that all is foreseen by an omniscient God. Rabbi Akiba said, "Everything is foreseen [by

[105] Whether the Amar and Ackerman proposals thus contradict the language of the Tenth Amendment itself is an issue I do not address.

[106] W. Stevens, "Crude Foyer," in *The Collected Poems of Wallace Stevens* (New York: Vintage, 1982), p. 305.

God], and freedom of choice is given."[107] Akiba's language is remarkable. So unperturbed, so unaffected, so untroubled was the great rabbi by the ostensible contradiction that Akiba did not even use the word *but* as his grammatical conjunction; he used *and*. For a man dedicated to law, as Akiba was, this repose is extraordinary, for the tension that did not disturb him pervades Torah and can deeply arouse our modern sensibilities.

"Scripture," David Winston points out, "makes no attempt to harmonize the moral freedom of the individual with God's effective action in all things, but remains content to affirm both."[108] Scripture is not troubled by the tension, nor are the faithful: those who believe. If one believes in an omnipotent, omniscient God, as the ancients did and some moderns do, then talk of human responsibility, of *individual* responsibility, is inapt. Yet if one cares about human morality, about individual ethics, as the talmudic rabbis did and some moderns do, then, it would seem, one must confront this paradox. As Akiba testifies, however, and as his life affirms, one need not resolve it; all one need do is reconcile oneself to living with it. This repose is difficult for the modern, frustrated by the coexistence of paradoxical beliefs; instead, one seeks reconciliation.

Paradoxes emerge from beliefs and meanings, not merely from words. Article V and the entire Constitution acquire meaning from our beliefs, which we translate only imperfectly into language. Through interpretation, we attempt to say what the words mean. The bounds of acceptable interpretation are circumscribed by context and by the fact that the Constitution is a legal document.[109] Still, in interpreting we are driven to resolve. From the need to interpret there can be no escape. The current aim of interpretation, on the contrary, which is largely to resolve, can be altered. It should be.

Legal interpretation will benefit when the interpreters heed Wittgenstein's exhortation that we look instead of think.[110] When we look at the structure of the Constitution, and in particular at Article V, what we see is that our political essence reflects an individualist commitment to majoritarianism coupled, concomitantly, with a radical individualist commitment to the sanctity of certain principles. We believe in majority will,

---

[107] B. Talmud, Avot III:15 (in the prayer book, this text appears at III:19). The Hebrew is *ha-kol tsa-fu v'hareshut netunah* (author's transliteration).

[108] David Winston, "Free Will," in *Contemporary Jewish Religious Thought*, ed. Arthur Cohen and Paul Mendes-Flohr (New York: Scribner, 1987), pp. 269–70.

[109] See generally Richard Posner, *Law and Literature: A Misunderstood Relation* (Cambridge: Harvard University Press, 1988), pp. 209–68.

[110] Wittgenstein, *Philosophical Investigations*, trans. G. Anscombe, 3d ed. (Oxford: Basil Blackwell, 1968), secs. 134–37.

and we believe in the idea that certain ideals transcend the vicissitudes of majority will. We believe in the alienability of sovereignty, at some level, and we believe that no person can bind him or herself to slavery. We can see paradox, but no amount of thinking can resolve it. Constitutional theory will be better off when constitutional theorists learn, like Akiba, to live with the conflict.

Seven

Amending the Presuppositions of a Constitution

FREDERICK SCHAUER

WHAT makes a constitution constitutional? Nothing, we most plausibly answer, nor does or can anything make a constitution unconstitutional. Constitutions establish the grounds for constitutionality and unconstitutionality, and in so doing they simply cannot themselves be either constitutional or unconstitutional.

Yet although it thus appears illogical to inquire into the constitutionality of a constitution, there may be a point in framing a question in this manner, especially in the context of thinking about the process of constitutional amendment. For although constitutionalists often assume that something *in* a constitution provides the grounds for distinguishing between a valid and an invalid amendment, scholars who focus on large-scale political and constitutional transformation just as often maintain that the process of amending an entire constitution, of discarding it and replacing it with another one, takes place outside of both the new and the old constitutions. But if displacing a constitution takes place outside of that constitution, then is it possible that displacing part of it may take place outside the constitution as well, and, if so, that amending it may also occur outside the constitution?

These questions are not just logicians' puzzles, but logical questions that have considerable import for how we view just what it is that constitutes a constitution.[1] I mean to explore these questions here, guided

This essay was completed while I was a visiting fellow of the Research School of Social Sciences, Australian National University. I am grateful for both financial and intangible support to the Australian National University, and also to the Joan Shorenstein Barone Center on the Press, Politics and Public Policy. An earlier version was presented at the Academica Sinica, Taipei, Taiwan, and I am grateful for the audience comments on that occasion.

[1] The relationship between the problems of amendment and the logical paradoxes of self-reference are well known. See, for example, Peter Suber, *The Paradox of Self-Amendment: A Study of Logic, Law, Omnipotence and Change* (London: Peter Lang, 1990); Patrick Fitzgerald, "The 'Paradox' of Parliamentary Sovereignty," *Irish Jurist*, n.s., 7 (1972): 28–48; J. C. Hicks, "The Liar Paradox in Legal Reasoning," *Cambridge Law Journal* 29 (1971): 275–91; N. Hoerster, "On Alf Ross's Alleged Puzzle in Constitutional Law," *Mind* 81 (1972): 422–27; Alf Ross, "On Self-Reference and a Puzzle in Constitutional

substantially by my readings of the implications of Hans Kelsen's concept of the *grundnorm* and H.L.A. Hart's of the ultimate rule of recognition. I will not, however, engage in exegesis of Kelsen or Hart, and thus it is no part of this project to try to remain faithful to Kelsen's or Hart's intentions, especially since those intentions remain obscure and the results of those intentions appear at times confused. Nor, therefore, will I take Kelsen's or Hart's views as authoritative, in the sense of using a citation as a substitute for an argument. Still, their views on the extra-legal foundations of a legal system are suggestive of an approach to the problem of amendment, an approach I propose to develop in the pages to come.

The Limits of Internalist Analysis

It is a characteristic of most existing treatments of the process of constitutional amendment, American and non-American, that those treatments are *internal* to the constitution itself. They take a constitution's own provisions, however defined,[2] as the sole source of legitimate amendment.[3] Commonly the starting point for such an analysis is a specific amending clause. As with almost all other constitutions, the Constitution of the United States specifies the conditions for its own amendment, and the Constitution is most easily read as implying that its own specified conditions for valid amendment are to be treated as exclusive. Although Article V does not specify in so many words that the procedures specified therein shall be the sole method of amending the Constitution, nor does it contain the words "inter alia," any fair literal reading of the text of Article V produces the conclusion that nothing *in* the

---

Law," *Mind* 78 (1969): 1–14; Ilmar Tammelo, "The Antinomy of Parliamentary Sovereignty," *Archiv für Rechts-und-Sozialphilosophie* (1958): 495–513.

[2] I mean to encompass a great deal by "however defined." That is, I do not mean to limit my notion of "internal" to a text-based approach to constitutional interpretation. Rather, my notion of "internal" encompasses any interpretive methodology that its proponder would claim to be an interpretation *of this* constitution, rather than an interpretation of some other constitution, and rather than a political or moral proposal its proponent admitted could not be connected to the constitution.

[3] Good examples would include Walter Dellinger, "The Legitimacy of Constitutional Change: Rethinking the Amendment Process," *Harvard Law Review* 97 (1983): 386–432; Walter Dellinger, "Constitutional Politics: A Rejoinder," *Harvard Law Review* 97 (1983): 446–50; Gerald Gunther, "The Convention Method of Amending the Constitution," *Georgia Law Review* 14 (1979): 1–25; Laurence H. Tribe, "A Constitution We Are Amending: In Defense of a Restrained Judicial Role," *Harvard Law Review* 97 (1983): 433–45; Katherine Swinton, "Amending the Canadian Constitution: Lessons from Meech Lake," *University of Toronto Law Journal* 42 (1992): 139–69; George Winterton, "An Australian Republic," *University of Melbourne Law Review* 16 (1988): 475–78.

Constitution textually authorizes methods of amendment other than the two alternative procedures established in Article V itself.[4]

Because Article V appears on its face to exhaust the possibilities for amending the Constitution consistent with the Constitution itself, existing American attempts to explain how the 1993 Constitution might legitimately be different from the 1787 Constitution, as amended, other than *by* amendment in conformity with the procedures specified in Article V, have involved heroic efforts to explain either how other provisions of the Constitution might also allow amendment in different ways, or how different readings of Article V itself might suggest a broader conception of what it takes to amend the Constitution. Bruce Ackerman, for example, castigates an attempt to read Article V according to the historical meaning of "Convention" as "formalistic," arguing that an updated notion of "Convention" allows the Constitution to be structurally amended by a range of engaged public deliberative actions—constitutional "moments"—that are to be treated as "Conventions" in a less formal sense of that word.[5] And Akhil Amar reaches similar conclusions about the nonexclusivity of Article V by relying both on the history of the Constitution's creation and on his reading of the Preamble, Article VII, and the First, Ninth, and Tenth Amendments.[6]

My concern here is not with the soundness of efforts such as Ackerman's and Amar's, but rather with their impetus. More specifically I am concerned with why it is that "exclusivists" such as Dow, Dellinger, Gunther, Tribe, and Vile, and "nonexclusivists" such as Ackerman, Amar, and Levinson,[7] all suppose that the internal resources of the Constitution, however those internal resources are defined, provide the only or most appropriate way of thinking about the process of constitutional change. By contrast, I argue that constitutions rest on logically antece-

[4] See David R. Dow, "When Words Mean What We Believe They Say: The Case of Article V," *Iowa Law Review* 76 (1990): 4, 39–44; John R. Vile, "Legally Amending the United States Constitution: The Exclusivity of Article V's Mechanics," *Cumberland Law Review* 21 (1991): 271–307; John R. Vile, "Judicial Review of the Amending Process: The Dellinger-Tribe Debate," *Journal of Law and Politics* 3 (1986): 21–50; John R. Vile, "The Amending Process: Alternative to Revolution," *Southeastern Political Review* 11 (1983): 49–96; John R. Vile, "American Views of the Constitutional Amending Process: An Intellectual History of Article V," *American Journal of Legal History* 35 (1991): 44–69.

[5] Bruce Ackerman, "The Storrs Lectures: Discovering the Constitution," *Yale Law Journal* 93 (1984): 1013–72; see also Ackerman's "Constitutional Politics/Constitutional Law," *Yale Law Journal* 99 (1989): 453–96, and *We the People: Foundations* (Cambridge, Mass.: Harvard University Press, 1991).

[6] Akhil Reed Amar, "Philadelphia Revisited: Amending the Constitution Outside Article V," *University of Chicago Law Review* 55 (1988): 1043–1104.

[7] Sanford Levinson, "Accounting for Constitutional Change (Or, How Many Times Has the United States Constitution Been Amended? (A) <26; (B) 26; (C) >26; (D) All of the Above)," *Constitutional Commentary* 8 (1991): 409–31, reprinted, in expanded form, as Chapter 2, above.

dent presuppositions that give them their constitutional status. As a result, constitutions can and do change not only when they are amended according to their own provisions or their own history, however broadly those provisions or that history may be understood, but whenever there is a change in these underlying presuppositions—political and social, but decidedly not constitutional or legal.[8] Constitutions are thus necessarily always subject to amendment as their supporting presuppositions are amended, even though it cannot be the case that the amendment of those supporting presuppositions can be thought of in anything other than factual or other prelegal terms.

Grounding the Constitution

Although the issues I address pertain equally to all constitutions, and thus to all national constitutions, to all subnational constitutions such as those of the states in the United States, and to the constitutions of private associations, I will use the Constitution of the national government of the United States as my primary continuing example. Consider, then, the question of the validity of a particular action by or decision of an administrative agency. Because agencies typically have their own rules purporting to govern all of their own actions, the normal test for the validity of an administrative action is whether that action is authorized by and consistent with the agency's own regulations. The first question about the validity of an administrative action, therefore, is whether it is authorized by some higher (but not very much higher) law, here the set of regulations of the agency itself.

Even if some administrative action were valid according to an agency's own regulations, however, the question would then arise about the validity of those administrative regulations themselves. Administrative agencies are not of course sovereign bodies, and we know, to oversimplify, that the validity of an administrative regulation is a function of its falling (or not) within the scope of some authorizing act of Congress. An administrative regulation is thus itself valid only insofar as it is authorized by some higher law, here an act of Congress.

[8] By drawing this distinction I plead guilty to legal positivist predispositions. See Frederick Schauer, "Constitutional Positivism," *Connecticut Law Review* 25 (1993): 797–828. Nevertheless, nothing in this article assumes any stronger a positivist perspective than even, say, Ackerman and Amar presuppose. As long as they and others seek to situate their conclusions in *a* reading of the constitutional text, or in a reading of history that focuses more on events related to that text than to other historically contemporaneous events, then they have accepted the broad extensional disequivalence between the realms of the constitutional/legal on the one hand and the social/political on the other that is presupposed in my argument.

Although administrative regulations are valid only insofar as they are authorized by acts of Congress, what is it, however, that makes an act of Congress valid? Here we move one step up the chain, and we know that just as administrative regulations are valid only insofar as they are authorized by acts of Congress, then so too are acts of Congress valid only insofar as they are authorized by and consistent with the Constitution.

But if we are searching for the foundations of law, we might then go one step further, and ask what it is that makes the Constitution valid? It is at this point that some of the most enduring questions of jurisprudence are engaged, and it is here that those questions are directly relevant to the question of constitutional amendment. For when we ask what it is that makes the Constitution valid, the work of Hans Kelsen would indicate that the validity of the Constitution is established by the *Grundnorm*, whose validity is in turn *presupposed* or *hypothesized* as valid. Thus to Kelsen the *Grundnorm* is the presupposition without which the whole notion of legal validity makes no sense, and which is necessary for statements such as "this is the law" to have any meaning. For Kelsen the *Grundnorm* functions as sort of a Kantian transcendental understanding, not a fact capable of empirical investigation, but just a way of thinking that is necessary for a range of statements and conclusions about the law to make any sense at all.[9]

Just what it is that Kelsen meant by the *Grundnorm* is notoriously obscure.[10] Still, the main points are that constitutions need grounding as much as they supply it, and that it is therefore a mistake to think of a constitution as itself being the last or ultimate word. But since Kelsen's ideas here get a bit mysterious, and since my aim in this essay is not to engage in Kelsenian exegesis, it may be more useful to look instead at H.L.A. Hart's derivative but clearer idea of the ultimate rule of recognition.[11] Among the secondary rules that combine with primary rules to

[9] On the questions I discuss here, the primary Kelsenian text is Hans Kelsen, *General Theory of Law and State*, trans. Anders Wedberg (New York: Russell & Russell, 1961), especially pp. 115–36. See also Hans Kelsen, *Pure Theory of Law*, trans. Max Knight (Berkeley: University of California Press, 1967), pp. 46–50, 202–11; Hans Kelsen, "On the Pure Theory of Law," *Israel Law Review* 1 (1966): 1–7; Hans Kelsen, "Professor Stone and the Pure Theory of Law," *Stanford Law Review* 17 (1964): 1128–48.

[10] For a sampling of the commentary, see J. W. Harris, *Law and Legal Science: An Inquiry into the Concepts Legal Rule and Legal System* (Oxford: Clarendon Press, 1979); Joseph Raz, *The Concept of a Legal System: An Introduction to the Theory of Legal System*, 2d ed. (Oxford: Clarendon Press, 1980); Julius Stone, *Legal System and Lawyers' Reasonings* (Sydney: Sweet and Maxwell, 1964), pp. 132–34, 202–5; George C. Christie, "The Notion of Validity in Modern Jurisprudence," *Minnesota Law Review* 48 (1964): 1049–79; J. W. Harris, "When and Why Does the Grundnorm Change?" *Cambridge Law Journal* 29 (1971): 103–33.

[11] H.L.A. Hart, *The Concept of Law* (Oxford: Clarendon Press, 1961), especially pp. 97–114, 245–47. Hart's ideas about the ultimate rule of recognition are usefully explained

make a legal system, Hart says, are rules of recognition by virtue of which citizens and officials can know what is a law and what is not. Acts of Congress such as the Administrative Procedure Act, therefore, function in part as rules of recognition determing which administrative regulations are to be *recognized* as valid and which are not. So too with the Constitution, which similarly functions as a rule of recognition determining the validity of state and federal laws. And when we ask what makes the Constitution valid, Hart says, we look to something different, the *ultimate rule of recognition*, which might specify, for example, that the document commonly known as "the Constitution of the United States of America," the original version of which was ratified in 1787 and is now to be found in the National Archives in the District of Columbia, is the measure of the validity of all other laws in the United States.

But what if we want to know what makes the ultimate rule of recognition valid? Although Kelsen thinks that this is an answerable question, Hart maintains simply that we have asked the wrong question, because the very notion of validity presupposes some higher legal norm against which a subordinate legal norm might be measured. When we run out of legal norms we have exhausted the concept of legal validity (although we might still use the word *valid* to refer to some other norm system, such as a moral one),[12] and thus the question about the status of the ultimate rule of recognition is a question of fact. The ultimate rule of recognition is a matter of social fact, and so determining it is for empirical investigation rather than legal analysis.[13]

In referring to the ultimate rule of recognition as a *rule*, Hart has probably misled us. There is no reason to suppose that the ultimate source of law need be anything that looks at all like a rule, whether simple or complex, or even a collection of rules, and it may be less distracting to think of the ultimate source of recognition, following Brian Simpson, as a *practice*.[14] The ultimate source of law, therefore, is better

---

and at times criticized in Neil MacCormick, *H.L.A. Hart* (Stanford, Calif.: Stanford University Press, 1981), and in P.M.S. Hacker, "Hart's Philosophy of Law," in P.M.S. Hacker and J. Raz, eds., *Law, Morality and Society: Essays in Honour of H.L.A. Hart* (Oxford: Clarendon Press, 1977), pp. 1–25.

[12] Thus Stone, *Legal System and Lawyers' Reasonings*, pp. 202–5, maintained that what Stone called the "apex norm" could still be measured by "socioethical" standards.

[13] The precursor to both Kelsen and Hart was Salmond, who noted that the ultimate rule of law was "historical only, not legal." J. Salmond, *Jurisprudence*, 12th ed. (London: Sweet and Maxwell), p. 111.

[14] A.W.B. Simpson, "The Common Law and Legal Theory," in A.W.B. Simpson, ed., *Oxford Essays in Jurisprudence*, 2d ser. (Oxford: Clarendon Press, 1973), pp. 77–99. And at one point Hart himself says that the ultimate rule of recognition "exists only as a com-

described as the practice by which it is determined that some things are to count as law and some things are not.

Hart's analysis is also thin on the question of just *whose* determination and whose practice makes for the existence of the ultimate rule of recognition. Hart says that the ultimate rule of recognition exists in what officials, particularly judges, recognize as the sources of law,[15] but here Hart's own argument against the Realists may be used against him.[16] Just as saying that law is what the judges say it is tells us nothing about why the judges say what they say, or what judges look at in determining what the law is, or what arguments might be usable in legal argument, so too does identifying as the ultimate rule (or practice) of recognition what the judges actually take to be the sources of law tell us little about where judges will look to determine what the legitimate sources of law are. This, it turns out, is a question of considerable importance in cases of revolution or commensurate transformation, for it may then be the task of judges to try to determine just what the ultimate rule of recognition is. Perhaps they just choose sides on political grounds of their own, but perhaps in some cases they also try to determine whether the people in general, or other officials in general, or just law-enforcing officials, have shifted in what *they* believe the ultimate source of law to be, such that the judges are looking externally as well as internally in determining the content of the ultimate rule of recognition.[17] And this is why at the

---

plex, but normally concordant, practice of the courts, officials and private persons in identifying the law by reference to certain criteria." Hart, *The Concept of Law*, p. 107.

[15] The act of recognition on the part of judges and other officials may not be explicit, but may just consist in what officials use and apply in making their decisions. See Roger Shiner, *Norm and Nature: The Movements of Legal Thought* (Oxford: Clarendon Press, 1992), pp. 170–74.

[16] Hart, *The Concept of Law*, pp. 121–50.

[17] There is a remarkable series of cases in which postrevolutionary judges, required just after a period of major political upheaval to decide what body of law, what legal system, they were supposed to enforce, relied quite explicitly on Kelsenian ideas in framing their inquiries. The most famous of these cases arose out of the Unilateral Declaration of Independence (UDI) of what was then Southern Rhodesia, Madzimbamuto v. Lardner-Burke N.O., JD/CIV/23/66, 9 Sept. 1966 (1968) 2 S.A. 284 (App. Div.) [1969] A.C. 645 (P.C.), and earlier and similar issues arose in Pakistan, State v. Dosso (1958) 2 Pakistan S.C.R. 180, and in Uganda, Uganda v. Commissioner of Prisons, ex parte Matovu (1966) E.A. 514. There has been an extensive and jurisprudentially sophisticated commentary on these cases, and much of it is germane to the issue of amendment. Good examples are J. M. Eekelaar, "Splitting the Grundnorm," *Modern Law Review* 30 (1967): 156–75; J. M. Eekelaar, "Rhodesia: The Abdication of Constitutionalism," *Modern Law Review* 32 (1969): 115–18; Harris, "When and Why Does the Grundnorm Change?" A. M. Honore, "Reflections on Revolution," *Irish Jurist*, n.s., 2 (1967): 268–78; S. A. de Smith, "Constitutional Lawyers in Revolutionary Situations," *Western Ontario Law Review* 7 (1968): 93–110.

level of determining what the ultimate rule of recognition is, questions of *efficacy* are central, because only with some degree of efficacy in fact (Kelsen said that the existence of a legal system required that the laws of that system were obeyed and applied "by and large")[18] is it possible to say that some norm or practice exists as all or part of the ultimate rule of recognition. As Ilmar Tammelo put it, "The foundation rules of a legal system can never be derived from within the system itself; they are a political fact."[19]

For purposes of thinking about the process of amendment, not all of these complications need be pursued to the same extent that we might pursue them were we concerned with the total displacement of legal systems. Still, the central import of this line of thought is recognition of the necessarily *factual* basis of the ultimate rule of recognition, and recognition of the associated point that something preconstitutional as well as factual is the logical predicate for the truth of the proposition that the document in the National Archives is the Constitution of the United States.

A New Constitution?

I want to illustrate this point with a bizarre, but I hope still useful, example. Let me, right here on these pages, offer a constitution for the United States:

The Constitution of the United States of America

We the People of the United States, in order to place our welfare and our future in the soundest possible hands, grant to Frederick Schauer, of the City of Cambridge, County of Middlesex, Commonwealth of Massachusetts, the plenary and sovereign powers of governance, without limitation, over the territory known in 1994 as the United States of America.

Article I. Frederick Schauer or those he may designate shall possess all of the legislative powers of the United States.

Article II. Frederick Schauer or those he may at any time designate shall hold all powers of enforcement and application of the laws.

Article III. All judicial powers shall be exercised by judges appointed by whoever at the time holds power under Article II of this Constitution.

Article IV. The powers under Articles I, II, and III shall descend according to the laws of descent and distribution in force in the Commonwealth of Massachusetts on December 31, 1992.

---

[18] Kelsen, *General Theory of Law and State*, pp. 118, 437.
[19] Tammelo, "The Antinomy of Parliamentary Sovereignty," p. 504.

Article V. This Constitution may be amended only with the joint consent of those then exercising power under Articles I and II.

Article VI. This Constitution shall be established and in force upon signing by the individual named in Article I.

/s/

Frederick Schauer

There you have it. Not only have I just presented a document entitled "The Constitution of the United States of America" purporting to be the constitution *for* the United States of America, but I have also ensured that it is valid and in force according to its own terms, just as the document to be found in the National Archives is also valid and in force according to *its* own terms. And as a result of my having drafted this constitution and satisfied its own internal conditions for validity, I can state with confidence that there now exist within the territory known as the United States (at least) two internally valid documents, each purporting to be the Constitution of and for the United States of America.

We know, of course, that the document in the National Archives is, more or less (which I will get to presently), the Constitution of the United States, and we know just as well that the silly collection of words just above is not. But how do we know this? We know this not because of anything internal to one document or the other, because internally they are equally valid. Rather, we know that one is the Constitution and the other is not because of what we know empirically and factually about the world, because we know that one is efficacious and the other not, because we know that one document has been accepted by the American people, by American officials, and by American judges, while the other has been accepted by no one, not even its author. Yet had the facts, and only the facts, been reversed, the conclusion would be just the opposite. Had the American people and the American officials accepted my constitution as governing law rather than the thing in the National Archives, then the document above would *be* the Constitution of the United States. Thus a change in the raw fact of efficacy or acceptance could make my document the Constitution while the thing in the National Archives would be but a legally irrelevant historical relic.

Recognizing a Constitution

Although my example is both simple and silly, it nevertheless resembles more closely than might at first appear a number of genuine issues that arise whenever there is a case of dramatic constitutional transformation. Whenever there is a revolution, or whenever there is some other form of dramatic change in government, there is usually an attempt by the successor government to substitute a new ultimate rule of recognition for the one that had been in force prior to the transformation. As with the choice between my constitution and the existing U.S. Constitution, however, the question of whether the ultimate rule of recognition has indeed been changed by revolution is a question that the internal resources of neither the old nor the new constitutions can answer.[20] The fact of constitutional displacement is just that—a fact—and the social choice between the new and the old is just like the social choice between the existing U.S. Constitution and some other, such as mine.[21]

Most of the existing literature about the transformation of legal systems has focused on full-scale displacements of just this type. As with the cases in Pakistan, Uganda, and Southern Rhodesia, courts and various international bodies have been required to determine whether the ultimate rule of recognition had changed, in order to make the logically subsequent determination of which particular constitution was then in force. And in making this determination, it is clear that courts could not rely on anything *in* either of the contesting legal systems, for the status of the very documents was exactly what was at issue.

[20] There is a curious literature addressing the question of whether the existing U.S. Constitution is illegal according to the Articles of Confederation. Those arguing that the 1787 Constitution was illegal according to the Articles of Confederation include Bruce Ackerman, "Discovering the Constitution," pp. 1017, n.6, 1058; Richard S. Kay, "The Illegality of the Constitution," *Constitutional Commentary* 4 (1987): 57–80; John Leubsdorf, "Deconstructing the Constitution," *Stanford Law Review* 40 (1987): 181, 186–88; and those maintaining that the 1787 Constitution can be taken to have been ratified consistent with the authorization of the Articles include Amar, "Philadelphia Revisited," and Julius Goebel, *History of the Supreme Court* (New York: Columbia University Press, 1971), pp. 198–204. The debate is curious, however, because both the debate and the reason for having it are again external to the resources used by the combatants. No amount of illegality according to the Articles would render the 1787 Constitution any less the law now, and conversely no amount of legality according to the Articles would make the 1787 Constitution the law absent the necessary factual preconditions of acceptance and efficacy. It is likely, therefore, that the debate is premised on the mistaken supposition that the only options are violent and armed revolution, on the one hand, and legal continuity, on the other. Yet if we accept the fact that there can be peaceful, orderly, and deliberative revolutions (consider the current legal orders in some number of countries that were formerly members of the Soviet Union), then one can recognize the illegality of the 1787 Constitution under the Articles while still not concluding that the Framers of the 1787 Constitution were "lawless" in the sense of that word that implies violence or tyrannical usurpation of power rightfully held by others.

[21] This is decidedly not to say, however, that the task of a judge in such circumstances is limited to determining the social or political fact of the efficacy of a new legal system. The judge is herself part of the very efficacy that determines whether the ultimate rule of recognition has been transformed, and thus there is an unavoidable normative component in a judge's determination that a new ultimate rule of recognition should replace and has replaced the old one.

Yet although the history and the literature typically focus on cases of total constitutional displacement, the essential point about the externality (to a constitution) of the determination of constitutional change applies equally to partial displacement. We understand now that the determination that Constitution *B* has replaced Constitution *A* cannot be made on the basis of anything *in* Constitutions *A* or *B*, but the same lesson holds in the case of partial rather than total replacement. Suppose that Constitution *A* contained two parts, Part A.1 outlining the structure of government and Part A.2 being a bill of rights limiting the powers of government. And suppose as well that Constitution *B* also contained two parts, again one establishing the structure of government and the other constraining that government with a bill of rights, these two parts being designated B.1 and B.2. Now suppose that at some time a population has decided that its existing constitution, *A*, is unsatisfactory, because it contains a defective bill of rights. Revolutionary forces have proposed *B* as a substitute, there is some fighting, and then there is a cease-fire. The result is that the competing forces agree, with widespread public support, that the country should henceforth be governed according to a combination of the structure of government provisions of the earlier constitution and the bill of rights of the proposed replacement, that is, A.1 and B.2.

Were all of this to happen, and were this resolution of the conflict thus accepted by the people and by officials, the content of the ultimate rule of recognition would be such that it then recognized as the supreme law this combination of A.1. and B.2. If, therefore, the ultimate rule of recognition were to recognize as supreme law this A.1/B.2 constitution, then the correct answer to the question "What *is* the constitution?" would be "the combination of A.1 and B.2."

Once we accept that "the constitution" according to the ultimate rule of recognition need not be something written at one time,[22] we see Kelsen's mistake in assuming that the only two possible *Grundnormen* are a changeable one in countries such as Great Britain, New Zealand, and Israel, which have no single document titled "the Constitution," or what he referred to as the "historically first constitution."[23] Where there is a written constitution, Kelsen asserted, "coercive acts ought to be carried out only under the conditions and in the way determined by the 'fathers' of the constitution or the organs delegated by them."[24] As the

---

[22] On the way in which the constitution of a country is more than just the document it labels as "the Constitution," see W. R. Lederman, "The Supreme Court of Canada and Basic Constitutional Amendment: An Assessment of *Reference Re Amendment of the Constitution of Canada* (Nos. 1, 2 and 3)," *McGill Law Review* 27 (1982): 527–40.

[23] Kelsen, *Pure Theory of Law*, p. 50.

[24] Kelsen, *General Theory of Law and State*, pp. 115–16.

father of the Austrian Constitution of 1930, it is understandable why Kelsen would promote this view, but it is nevertheless a poor interpretation of Kelsen's own idea of the *Grundnorm*, and independently mistaken in its own right. Although Kelsen's quoted view *could* be the *Grundnorm* or ultimate rule of recognition in a country with a written constitution, and although we well understand why the drafter of a constitution would wish for this to be the *Grundnorm*, there is no reason why the *Grundnorm* *must* be one that treats the law-recognizing functions of a particular written constitution as exclusive. If the *Grundnorm* were "coercive acts ought to be carried out only under the conditions and in the way determined by the 'fathers' of the constitution or the organs delegated by them, or whenever such acts are authorized by a referendum of 90 percent of the population," this would still qualify as a *Grundnorm* or ultimate rule of recognition, and were this the *Grundnorm* actually in force in some society, then coercive acts authorized by 90 percent of the population in a referendum would qualify as "valid law" even though those acts would not comport with the requirements of the written constitution taken in isolation.[25]

What all of this shows, of course, is that once we recognize that constitutional displacement takes place outside of the constitution, then so can partial displacement take place outside of the constitution. And the next step is no step at all, or at least a very small one. If partial displacement can take place outside of the "primary" written constitution, then so too can partial "supplementation" take place outside of the written constitution. Thus it is quite likely, as Kent Greenawalt has developed at length, that the ultimate rule of recognition in the United States may refuse to recognize parts of the written Constitution of 1787 as valid law, and most certainly recognizes as valid law sources of law not traceable to or through the Constitution of 1787.[26] And thus if law can exist outside of the Constitution, then so too can it be amended outside of that Constitution. Moreover, since the Constitution thus rests on the extraconstitutional foundations that make up the ultimate rule of recognition, then the Constitution necessarily can be amended by the extraconstitutional process of amending, socially and politically, those extraconstitutional foundations.[27] To take an example, if the American

[25] For a similar critique of Kelsen, see Raz, *The Concept of a Legal System*, p. 138.

[26] Kent Greenawalt, "The Rule of Recognition and the Constitution," *Michigan Law Review* 85 (1987): 621–71.

[27] Thus it may be important to distinguish what appears to be Ackerman's and Amar's question—"Can the Constitution be amended outside of a literal reading of Article V consistent with a certain internal and accepting attitude toward the Constitution as a whole?"—from the quite different question of whether the Constitution can be amended outside of a literal reading of Article V. Putting the question in the former way, and thus

people came to the realization that the Second Amendment's seeming protection of the right to keep and bear arms was simply obsolete and unwise in light of the realities of 1994, and if that view were shared by legislative, executive, and judicial officials, and if all proceeded to treat the Second Amendment as a nullity despite the fact that it had not been repealed according to the provisions of Article V, then it would be accurate to say that the Constitution of the United States did not contain the provision designated as "Amendment II" in most versions of the document titled "the Constitution of the United States." The small *c* constitution would thus have been amended by virtue of this amendment to the ultimate rule of recognition, even though it could also be accurately said that the large *C* Constitution had not been validly amended according to its own terms.

Presuppositions and Rules

Nothing I have said in the foregoing analysis is intended to take a position on whether it would be a good idea, in a country having a canonical written constitution, to adopt this type of somewhat more open-ended ultimate rule of recognition instead of the more bounded one that Kelsen preferred. Although Kelsen was mistaken in supposing that the existence of a historically first written constitution mandated a *Grundnorm* treating that historically first constitution (and therefore its amending clauses) as exclusive, it might still be a wise course of action, as a matter of social/constitutional policy, for a nation having a written constitution with internally comprehensive pretensions to treat that constitution as the exclusive "supreme criterion"[28] for the recognition of all other laws. This is almost certainly not the American approach, but that is not to say that it could not be a quite plausible one.

My primary goal here is to explain why the choice between a written constitution as an exclusive or a nonexclusive supreme criterion of law is antecedent and external to the constitutional text (and therefore also to the history of that text) rather than to explore the reasons why a polity should choose one or the other. Still, it is worth noting that at this antecedent level the issue is merely an instantiation of the familiar questions about the desirability of rule-based constraint, albeit at one remove and

---

trying to get out of a literal reading of Article V only by use of the Constitution's own internal resources, may signal a certain kind of "pro" attitude toward the existing Constitution not necessarily shared by the explanatory theorist, and not necessarily shared by a population inclined toward large-scale change in their constitution.

[28] Hart, *The Concept of Law*, p. 103.

in a slightly different setting. For just as the amendment power itself grows out of a rule-based view of legal or constitutional constraint (were rules merely rules of thumb then there would be no need to amend those rules to take care of the instances in which the rules produced a suboptimal result),[29] a *Grundnorm* treating the amendment power as exclusive would be a rule-based view that it is better to have some ideally desirable amendments not take place because of the constraints of the amendment procedure than to have too many unwise amendments take place because of an excessively permissive environment that treated the amendment power as merely establishing a rule of thumb.

Alternatively, some society might recognize that rules, including the rules of amendment, are necessarily either actually or potentially both under- and overinclusive vis-à-vis their background justifications, or vis-à-vis the best all-things-considered decision for the case at hand, such that there might be circumstances in which the rules of amendment, if followed faithfully, would turn out either to be insufficiently or excessively stringent. Recognizing this, and not wishing to be bound in the way that rules bind, this society might choose instead an ultimate rule of recognition that treated the amendment provision as merely hortatory, or simply as a rule of thumb, or presumptive but not conclusive, or perhaps even to be dispensed with entirely.[30]

Insofar as a society feared its own excess willingness to amend its constitution outside of the ways designated by that constitution, it might prefer the former approach to the latter, seeking to bind itself, at least presumptively but perhaps even conclusively, to an amendment process premised on textual exclusivity. As should now be clear, however, this state of affairs cannot be accomplished simply by writing that exclusivity into a constitutional text, for that writing would itself be subject to the very kind of antecedent amendment of presuppositions that I have been exploring here.[31] Nevertheless, entrenchment can be accomplished psy-

---

[29] I have developed elsewhere the picture of rules that undergirds the brief statement in the text. Frederick Schauer, *Playing By the Rules: A Philosophical Examination of Rule-Based Decision-Making in Law and in Life* (Oxford: Clarendon Press, 1991).

[30] Descriptively, my own view is that the American legal and constitutional culture treats the procedures of Article V as presumptively but not conclusively constraining, just as that same culture treats most written legal norms in just this presumptive way. See Frederick Schauer, "Rules and the Rule of Law," *Harvard Journal of Law and Public Policy* 14 (1991): 645–94.

[31] Thus, the supposed paradox of self-amendment is either no paradox at all, or is only a paradox within a closed domain whose presuppositions are stipulated not to be subject to alteration. But the fact that a change at one level might be inconsistent with something said at another level is simply not paradoxical. See Hoerster, "On Alf Ross's Alleged Puzzle in Constitutional Law," Tammelo, "The Antimony of Parliamentary Sovereignty" Thus there is nothing paradoxical about a change in constitutional presuppositions having the

chologically even if not logically, and so a society with this rule-based approach to the amendment process might choose to adopt and publicly articulate as its *Grundnorm* that the textually designated amendment process was to be taken as exclusive.[32] Were that to happen, it is likely that the very act of public articulation and public written canonization would serve to make it substantially more psychologically difficult to amend that presupposition than would have been the case without that public commitment. Just as making even an internal New Year's resolution may produce a resolve to keep that resolution stronger than would have existed for the same conduct without the crystallized internal articulation of the resolution, and just as publicly announcing that resolution may create an informal but still effective interpersonal enforcement mechanism that is even more constraining than an internal resolution,[33] so too may publicly announcing and discussing the importance of retaining textual exclusivity in the amendment process serve to entrench psychologically an ultimate rule of recognition that, as we have seen, cannot be entrenched by legal or constitutional means.

The case of constitutional amendment, therefore, turns out to exemplify the familiar (although often abused) point that rules cannot determine their own application. Rules exist against a background of presuppositions—such as the presupposition that when confronting an arrow on a highway one should drive in the direction of the point rather than the tail,[34] or the presupposition that the language in which a rule is written should, or should not, be interpreted as ordinary nontechnical English—that are themselves subject to change. Amendment provisions are of course written in a language, and it is a mistake to assume that the

---

effect of repealing some provision in a text, or giving it a meaning different from its ordinary language meaning.

[32] As should be clear by now, an ultimate rule of recognition could treat the entire constitution as exclusive, and thus necessarily treat its amendment clause as exclusive. But a different ultimate rule of recognition, indeed the one advocated by Walter Dellinger, "The Legitimacy of Constitutional Change," pp. 389, 418–19, and seemingly presupposed by many other commentators, could treat all of a constitution as nonexclusive except for its amendment provision, which it would treat as exclusive. Such an approach, however, puts the greatest strain on any distinction between interpretation and amendment, because at some point the interpretive freedom allowed by such an approach through all of the rest of the constitution will turn into the very kind of nonexclusive approach to the amendment process that this combination of views seeks to avoid. See Chapter 2 in this volume, by Sanford Levinson.

[33] See Thomas C. Schelling, "The Intimate Contest for Self-Command" and "Ethics, Law, and the Exercise of Self-Command," in *Choice and Consequence* (Cambridge, Mass.: Harvard University Press, 1984), pp. 57–112.

[34] Ludwig Wittgenstein, *Philosophical Investigations*, trans. G.E.M. Anscombe (Oxford: Basil Blackwell, 1958).

contingency of linguistic meaning entails a world in which there is a possibility of frictionless linguistic change. Moreover, it is also a mistake to assume that the difficulties in explaining the grounding *of* language entail either the indeterminacy of language, or the indeterminacy of rules that may be written in it.

As an empirical matter, the amendment provisions of most constitutions do have identifiable semantic content sufficient to indicate an outcome in a large number of potential instances. Where an amendment provision is this concrete, as Article V of the Constitution of the United States has proved to be, where the public commitment to recognition of the constitution containing those provisions is strong, and where the public commitment to recognition of that amendment provision in particular is equally strong, then an amendment provision could reflect public recognition of the desirability of an exclusive approach to that amendment provision, especially if its words are also taken to be understood literally. In other words, a polity could make a New Year's resolution about the exclusivity of its amending clause, and that resolution could make a difference in the degree of entrenchment of that exclusivity. But all of this is contingent, and all of this is therefore subject to change. A society could, for example, shift from a literal to a nonliteral understanding of its amendment provisions, and given the prevalence of nonformal and nonliteral modes of legal and constitutional interpretation in the United States,[35] this may in fact be what has happened. Or it could shift from an exclusive to a nonexclusive approach when confronted with a situation in which its amending clause was widely understood to have proved unsatisfactory. But whether and when these eventualities have occurred are not issues that can be determined by looking *at* the Constitution, however the Constitution is defined. And if these presuppositions are to change, the resources for that change are again not something that any amount of massaging of the Constitution itself can produce.

The process of constitutional amendment, therefore, can take place on one of two levels. On the constitutional level, it can take place within the contours of the constitution itself, either according to a literal reading of an amending clause, or according to an interpretive understanding consistent with the understanding of just what the constitution encompasses. But because constitutions owe their "constitutionality" to logically and politically antecedent conditions, the process of constitutional amendment may also take place at another level, when these

---

[35] The point in the text is exemplified by works such as Guido Calabresi, *A Common Law for the Age of Statutes* (Cambridge, Mass.: Harvard University Press, 1984), and contrasted with other approaches in Robert Summers and Patrick Atiyah, *Form and Substance in Anglo-American Adjudication* (Oxford: Clarendon Press, 1986).

logically and politically antecedent conditions are themselves amended. Because these antecedent conditions are not themselves legal or constitutional in any important sense of those terms, however, it remains necessarily the case that constitutions are always subject to amendment by changes—amendments—in the practices of a citizenry, in the practices of its officials, and in the practices of its judges. Whether these changes have occurred will be a question of social and political fact and not a question of law, constitutional or otherwise. And whether these changes should occur will be the necessarily political and moral question of what status a constitution should have, and what status its particular provisions should have. There may not be any harm in thinking of these questions as constitutional ones, but neither is there any harm—and there may indeed be some good—in recognizing the way in which thinking about the presuppositions of a constitution is quite different from thinking about constitutionalism against the background of assumed presuppositions.

Eight

Merlin's Memory: The Past and Future Imperfect of the Once and Future Polity

WALTER F. MURPHY

> The very attempt to make *perpetual*
> constitutions, is the assumption of a right to
> controul the opinions of future generations; and
> to legislate for those over whom we have as little
> authority as we have over a nation in Asia.[1]

SOME scholarly essays attempt to describe events or introduce concepts, some test hypotheses against data or analyze doctrines, others define or defend norms. This chapter frets. It worries about stability and change, though more about change, in a constitutional democracy:[2] what it was, what it is, and what it will become. I edge around the margins and below the surface of problems of constitutional change.[3]

I am indebted to James Sigmund of the Princeton class of 1995 and Adriana Alberti of the University of Bologna for research assistance; as usual, Rosemary Allen Little of the Firestone Library for help in navigating that labyrinth; Helen Wright of Princeton, the sharpest eyes in the East, for proofreading; and my colleague Andrew Koppelman for critically analyzing the manuscript. The William Nelson Cromwell Fund of Princeton and Boesky Family Fund of the Center of International Studies provided financial support. This chapter is part of a larger study of constitutionalism underwritten by the American Council of Learned Societies and the Ford Foundation.

[1] "Bills of Rights," in Noah Webster, *Collection of Essays and Fugitive Writings on Moral, Historical, Political and Literary Subjects* (Boston: Thomas & Andrews, 1790), p. 47 (emphasis in original).

[2] I have insisted, ad nauseam, that the United States and most nations popularly called "democracies" are really constitutional democracies. Each is based on a pair of normative principles, constitutionalist and democratic theory, which advocate similar goals but also sometimes conflicting means. For a fuller discussion, see my "Constitutions, Constitutionalism, and Democracy," in Douglas Greenberg, Stanley Katz, et al., eds., *Constitutionalism and Democracy* (New York: Oxford University Press, 1993).

[3] Because several times before, I have made arguments similar to some of those this chapter addresses, I repeat only enough of those arguments here for them to make sense. See "An Ordering of Constitutional Values," *Southern California Law Review* 53 (1980):

The Problem of Time

"It's a long, long while from May to September," Jo Stafford used to wail back in the 1940s. For Americans it's a longer time from 1787 to 1993 and much longer for the English from the Barons at Runnymede to the romantic romps of the current and not so merry wives of Windsor. Even many younger constitutional democracies, such as Austria, the Federal Republic of Germany, India, Ireland, Italy, and Japan, have aged to the point where few, if any, members of the founding generation are still politically active.

Furthermore, we cannot simply move, as some "originalists" would like to believe, from the moment of creation to the present—a fact that soon ensnares all efforts to retrieve the founding of a constitutional democracy, even those of Spain after the demise of fascism in the 1970s; Argentina, Brazil, Chile, and Uruguay after the collapse of military rule in the 1980s; and the nations of Eastern Europe after the self-destruction of Marxist hegemony in 1989. We cannot make that simple move because constitutions undergo more or less constant, if uneven, development, a lesson Pierre Trudeau and his Liberal party painfully relearned in the years after 1982. They wrote their vision of the good Canadian society into the parchment of the Constitution Act but failed to implant that vision into the political culture of Quebec.[4]

Now

Most human beings, in and out of public office, display a solemn concern for that slice of time called the present. But, as is the concept of time itself, that of "now" is problematic. More than six decades ago, the

---

703; "*Slaughter-House, Civil Rights,* and Limits on Constitutional Change," *American Journal of Jurisprudence* 21 (1986): 1; "The Right to Privacy and Legitimate Constitutional Change," in Shlomo Slonim, ed., *The Constitutional Bases of Political and Social Change in the United States* (New York: Praeger, 1990); "Consent and Constitutional Change," in James O'Reilly, ed., *Human Rights and Constitutional Law* (Dublin: Round Hall Press, 1992); "Staggering toward the New Jerusalem of Constitutional Theory," *American Journal of Jurisprudence* 37 (1992): 337; "Constitutions, Constitutionalism, and Democracy"; "Excluding Political Parties," in Paul Kirchhof and Donald P. Kommers, eds., *Germany and Its Basic Law* (Baden-Baden: Nomos, 1993).

   [4] For careful analyses of Canada's constitutional agony during the decade following adoption of that act, see Peter H. Russell, *Constitutional Odyssey* (Toronto: University of Toronto Press, 1992); and R. Kent Weaver, ed., *The Collapse of Canada?* (Washington, D.C.: Brookings Institution, 1992). Kenneth McRoberts argues that Canada's constitu-

historian Carl L. Becker warned readers about the speciousness of "the present."[5] Somewhat like Gertrude Stein's Oakland, California, there's no there there. At the very instant we speak the word *now*, it changes to the most recent of a vast multitude of "thens."[6] For Heraclitus's assertion that we never bathe in the same river twice, a brash legal realist might substitute the contention that we live only fleetingly under the same constitution once. Such a claim may be exaggerated, but it contains more truth than would please citizens who prefer stasis.

Then

"Continuity with the past," Oliver Wendell Holmes once said, "is not a duty, it is only a necessity."[7] The "course of human events" is likely to bring hardships as well as benefits. A political system has to be able to survive bad times as well as good, though individual officials might not be so fortunate. It is one thing to vote a party or a president out of office because of severe economic distress; it is quite another to vote a constitution or even a constitutional text out of existence.

In order to survive, a system needs not only the support from its people that comes from gratification of immediate wants, but also a deeper attachment, what some political scientists call "diffuse support,"[8] loyalty

---

tional difficulties have worsened because Trudeau's efforts to create an attachment to one nation largely succeeded among English-speaking citizens and failed among French-speaking citizens. McRoberts, *English Canada and Quebec* (North York, Ont.: Robarts Center for Canadian Studies, 1991).

[5] See especially Carl L. Becker, *The Heavenly City of the Eighteenth Century Philosophers* (New Haven: Yale University Press, 1932), chap. 4.

[6] On the other hand, some postmodernists have dubbed the present "our one and only eternity." Agnes Heller and Ferenc Feher, *The Post-Modern Condition* (Cambridge, Eng.: Polity Press, 1988), pp. 3–4. Other postmodernists believe, Pauline Marie Rosenau says, that "we live in the present-as-text, in a fragmented 'series of perpetual presents,' where the future is only an 'anticipated presence and the past a former presence.'" Rosenau, *Post-Modernism and the Social Sciences* (Princeton: Princeton University Press, 1992), p. 64 (citations omitted).

[7] Oliver W. Holmes, "Learning and Science," in *Collected Legal Papers* (New York: Harcourt, Brace, 1920), p. 139.

[8] The seminal work on this problem was that of David Easton, especially *A Systems Analysis of Political Life* (New York: Wiley, 1965) and "A Re-Assessment of the Concept of Political Support," *British Journal of Political Science* 5 (1975): 435. See also Dean Jaros and Robert Roper, "The United States Supreme Court: Myth, Diffuse Support, and Legitimation," *American Political Quarterly* 8 (1980): 85. The late Joseph Tanenhaus and I tried to operationalize the distinction between "specific" and "diffuse" support: "Public Opinion and the United States Supreme Court," *Law and Society Review* 2 (1968): 357;

and perhaps affection that will be strong enough to sustain devotion during crises. To build up that sort of commitment, it is *probable* that a nation requires a sense of continuity, of communion with a hallowed past—"the American way of life," "the glory of France," or "the culture of Italy"—which provides a model of moral strength and patriotic vigor.

In at least two respects, the American constitutional text of 1787 was less radical than many Anti-Federalists charged. First, it was part of a tradition of social and political contracts, reaching back a century and a half to the Mayflower Compact of 1620.[9] Second, the new Constitution rested on a younger but marked trend among colonists toward nation building. The Articles of Confederation had formalized a loose league born of common heritage and grievances, signified first by committees of correspondence, then by a Continental Congress, sanctified by the Declaration of Independence, and sealed by a victorious war of liberation. The new agreement of 1787–88 tried to restructure this embryonic political system by strengthening its center, but it was not something created out of nothing.

And the product of the Philadelphia convention itself soon became a revered institution. As early as 1791, Senator William Maclay was complaining that one might have thought that "neither Wood grew nor Water run in America, before the late happy Adoption of the New Constitution."[10] The reverence persists, not only for the document but also for its drafters. In fact, for some judges as well as many lesser folk, "the intent of the framers" or "original understanding" solves most problems of constitutional interpretation. But even for those of us who do not dance to these notes, the message that the Framers—especially James Madison—disapproved of a particular interpretation inflicts a serious if not mortal wound on that proposal.

Concerns for continuity may echo even from the mouths of revolutionaries. In 1861, for instance, when the Confederate States of America seceded from the United States, they adopted as their basic law the text of 1787 as amended, though with certain alterations to repair some of

---

"Explaining Diffuse Support for the United States Supreme Court," *Notre Dame Law Review* 49 (1974): 1037; "Patterns of Public Support for the Supreme Court," *Journal of Politics* 43 (1981): 24; "Publicity, Public Opinion, and the Court," *Northwestern University Law Review* 84 (1990): 985; and (with Daniel Kastner) *Public Evaluations of Constitutional Courts: Alternative Explanations* (Beverly Hills, Calif.: Sage, 1973).

[9] See Donald S. Lutz, *The Origins of American Constitutionalism* (Baton Rouge: Louisiana State University Press, 1988); and Lutz, "The Preamble to the Constitution of the United States," 1 *this Constitution* 23 (Sept. 1983).

[10] Kenneth R. Bowling and Helen E. Veit, eds., *The Diary of William Maclay and Other Notes on Senate Debates, March 4, 1789–March 3, 1791* (Baltimore: Johns Hopkins University Press, 1988), p. 399.

the "mistakes" the Committee on Style had made in 1787 and John Marshall had exacerbated.[11] Thus Southerners could claim it was they who were conserving the *real* Constitution. "We are upholding the true doctrines of the Federal Constitution," Jefferson Davis insisted. "We are conservative."[12] No less a historian than James B. McPherson believes that Davis and his confederates were correct.[13] I think they were wrong; at most, they were upholding a peculiar blend of Anti-Federalist fear of centralized government and Federalist fear of democratic rule. The point, however, is not whether Southerners were right or wrong; rather it is that they tried to weave a conservative pattern into their revolution's cloak and to do so appealed to the nation's venerable covenant.

We can see similar phenomena in Europe. Since 1989 Poles have often spoken of the constitution of May 3, 1791, as if it had been morally, albeit not legally, operative during much of the intervening two centuries; and Hungarians have earnestly tried to link their new texts to the Golden Bull of 1222. Shortly after World War II, the Germans in the nascent Federal Republic had drawn their version of federalism from the Holy Roman Empire and their political philosophy from Immanuel Kant. These myths of continuity with a resplendent past lose little for being fictions. Indeed, it may be that one essential element of statesmanship is inventing a glorious tradition to continue.[14]

[11] See, for example, Marshall L. DeRosa, *The Confederate Constitution of 1861* (Columbia: University of Missouri Press, 1991); Drew Gilpin Faust, *The Creation of Confederate Nationalism* (Baton Rouge: Louisiana State University Press, 1988); Emory M. Thomas, *The Confederate Nation, 1861–65* (New York: Harper, 1979). See also Don E. Fehrenbacher, *Constitutions and Constitutionalism in the Slaveholding South* (Athens: University of Georgia Press, 1989).

[12] Quoted in James B. McPherson, "AnteBellum Southern Exceptionalism," *Civil War History* 29 (1983): 230, 244.

[13] Ibid., p. 243:

> When secessionists protested that they were acting to preserve traditional rights and values, they were correct. They fought to protect their constitutional liberties against the perceived Northern threat to overthrow them. The South's concept of republicanism had not changed in three-quarters of a century; the North's had. With complete sincerity the South fought to preserve its version of the republic of the founding father—a government of limited powers that protected the rights of property and whose constituency comprised an independent gentry and yeomanry of the white race undisturbed by large cities, heartless factories, restless free workers, and class conflict. . . . Therefore secession was a preemptive counterrevolution to prevent the Black Republican revolution from engulfing the South.

[14] There is a growing literature on political invention. See, for example, William Chapman, *Inventing Japan* (New York: Prentice Hall, 1992); Faust, *The Creation of Confederate Nationalism*; Eric F. Hobsbawn and Terence Ranger, eds., *The Invention of Tradition* (New York: Cambridge University Press, 1992); Edmund S. Morgan, *Inventing the People* (New York: Norton, 1988); Vladimir Tismaneau, *Reinventing Politics: Eastern Eu-*

The Future

My rather mundane claim so far has been that some elements of continuity are useful for, probably crucial to, political stability and therefore
likely to be present in all systems that long survive. But *some* continuity
does not imply a rigid state. Probably such a constitution would quickly
be terminated with extreme prejudice. It was, after all, Edmund Burke,
the prophet of conservatism, who asserted that "a state without the
means of some change is without the means of its own conservation."[15]
The chief justice of India put the point more mystically: "A Constitution
is only permanent and not eternal."[16]

In all modern political systems, much does and must remain constant,
but much does and must change. Like law in Roscoe Pound's jurisprudence, a constitution must be stable, yet it cannot stand still. Since the
adoption of Canada's Constitution Act, 1982, the basic text of every
constitutional democracy establishes procedures for formal constitutional change. In 1943, Wendell Willkie went so far as to argue before
the U.S. Supreme Court that "a person can be attached to the Constitution no matter how extensive the changes are that he desires, so long as
he seeks to achieve his ends within the framework of Article V."[17]

As will become evident, I think Willkie was wrong. I begin with the
simplistic point that *some* change is not the same as *any* change. Acceptance of the necessity, even inevitability, of change tells us nothing
about the political desirability, the procedural propriety, or the substantive legitimacy of any specific proposal for change. Difficult and thus interesting problems arise only when we discuss how a political system
adopts amendments and the substance of particular alterations.

Procedurally, a constitutional democrat might postulate a hierarchy
of change. For shifts likely to effect major, structural modifications, he
or she might demand a formal constitutional amendment, meticulously
following whatever institutional procedures text or tradition prescribes.
William F. Harris II would go further and require meaningful popular

---

rope from Stalin to Havel (New York: Free Press, 1992). In 1978 Edward W. Said angrily
accused Western scholars of inventing and reinventing the Near East in terms that fed current national interests: *Orientalism* (New York: Pantheon, 1978).

[15] Edmund Burke, *Reflections on the Revolution in France* (1790; reprint, New York:
Dutton, 1910), pp. 19–20.

[16] Golak Nath's Case, [1967] A.I.R. 1643, 1670.

[17] Schneiderman v. United States, 320 U.S. 118 (1943). Displaying the prudence for
which they are famous, the justices found no need "to consider the validity of this extreme
position" (p. 140). As in so many things, I am indebted to Sanford Levinson for this example: *Constitutional Faith* (Princeton: Princeton University Press, 1988), p. 138.

participation in adopting such far-reaching innovations.[18] For changes that partake more of clarification, interpretation by some authoritative body, such as a constitutional court, might suffice. For "changes" that fill in lacunae or carry out textual orders that permit some discretion, the practices that public officials adopt might be adequate.

The real world is not so neat, alas. Formal amendments may address important practical problems but without affecting the foundations of the political system. The Twentieth Amendment to the U.S. Constitution, for example, met a serious need when it reduced the time of presidential transitions from four months to two; but certainly that modification did not affect the structure, processes, or principles of the political system. Constitutional interpretation, on the other hand, may alter the polity quite radically. Cases such as *Marbury v. Madison* (1803), *McCulloch v. Maryland* (1819), *Gibbons v. Ogden* (1824), *Brown v. Board of Education* (1954), and even *Dred Scott v. Sandford* (1857) were far more important than many amendments in (re)shaping the American nation.

And such interpretations need not solely or even principally be judicial products. One might reasonably argue that Abraham Lincoln precipitated[19] the most important restructuring in American constitutional history when he declared in 1861: "I hold that in contemplation of universal law, and of the Constitution, the Union of these States is perpetual."[20] He did not say "the Supreme Court has held" or "I infer from the Constitution and/or the Court's interpretations"; rather Lincoln, a careful lawyer, said "I hold."[21] And he went on to argue that there were

[18] William F. Harris II, *The Interpretable Constitution* (Baltimore: Johns Hopkins University Press, 1993), chap. 4.

[19] I deliberately choose the term *precipitated*. In politics not only are most slopes slippery, but the law of unanticipated consequences works with vengeance. Seldom, if ever, does any single act create systemic change. What is far more probable is that an act will (help) trigger a chain reaction.

[20] "First Inaugural Address," March 4, 1861, in *Abraham Lincoln: Speeches and Writings, 1859–1865* (New York: Library of America, 1989), p. 217.

[21] It is likely that today most Americans who have thought about the matter, probably even most scholars, accept Lincoln's dictum as positing another of those self-evident truths on which their polity rests. Like most human creations, however, nations and the constitutions that constitute them may decay. Even for constitutional democracies, fission is no less a political fact than is fusion, as the recent history of the Federal Republic of Czechs and Slovaks demonstrates (and possibly that of Canada will also). The Soviet Union and Yugoslavia show that nations trying to make a transition away from authoritarian rule may experience even more traumatic deconstruction. In the specific American case, the issue is certainly contestable, at least as a question of constitutional interpretation. A people who had solemnly constituted themselves into "a perpetual union" under the Articles of Confederation and then unconstituted themselves and proposed to reconstitute those members of the former "perpetual union" who wished to join "a more perfect union" would be hard

real limits to how far the Supreme Court's constitutional interpretation bound the other branches of the national government.

For Germany, the Federal Republic's government and the voters of East Germany, not the *Bundesverfassungsgericht*, decided to incorporate the East under Article 23 of the Basic Law, which provides for the admission of new *länder*. A more dramatic alternative, but one no less and perhaps more consonant with the text, was to invoke the procedures Article 146 had anticipated for reunification: a call for a convention from the two Germanys to draft a new constitutional text.[22]

More basically, constitutional interpretation is inherently creative, for at very least it attempts to make clear what was unclear, to provide one meaning where several were plausible, or to correct previous misunderstandings. The persistence of that creative element is cause enough for fretting, but it is a simply one of what Holmes called "can't helps." The world and people's perceptions of their world change. As Noah Webster explained: "Unless the advocates for unalterable constitutions of government can prevent all changes in the wants, inclinations, the habits and the circumstances of the people, they will find it difficult, even with all their declarations of unalterable rights, to prevent changes in government. A paper declaration is a feeble barrier against the force of national habits and inclinations."[23]

Framers of the West German and Japanese constitutional texts could

---

put to explain why, later, members could not avail themselves of the same "right" to reconstitute an even more perfect union. See Mark E. Brandon's chapter in this volume and his "Free in the World: American Slavery and Constitutional Failure" (Ph.D. diss., Princeton University, 1991).

[22] The State Treaty on Monetary, Economic, and Social Union (1990) agreed to several modifications of the Basic Law, including a change in Article 146. With the amendment within brackets, that article now reads: "This Basic Law [, which is valid for the entire German people following the achievement of the unity and freedom of Germany,] shall cease to be in force on the day on which a constitution adopted by a free decision of the [united] German people comes into force." The State Treaty also committed Germany to consider constitutional changes within five years, when the question of reunification itself would no longer be on the agenda. Other changes in the constitutional text entailed a realignment of votes in the Bundesrat and revised Article 143 to allow the Eastern *länder* a delay of two to five years in adhering to some provisions, such as those relating to abortion, property, and *Bund-land* relations. For a comprehensive analysis of the process, see Peter E. Quindt, "The Constitutional Law of German Unification," *Maryland Law Review* 50 (1991): 475; Donald P. Kommers, "The Basic Law and Reunification," in Peter Merkl, ed., *Germany at Forty-Five* (New York: New York University Press: 1993); and Kommers, "The Basic Law Under Strain," in Christopher Anderson et al., eds., *Domestic Politics of German Unification* (Boulder, Colo.: Lynne Reiner, 1993).

[23] "On Government" (1788), in Webster, *Collection*, p. 64. For a discussion of Webster's constitutional theories, see Gordon S. Wood, *The Creation of the American Republic, 1776–1787* (New York: Norton, 1969), especially pp. 372–83.

not have predicted the economic miracles that would quickly restore their devastated nations any more than the people who drafted and ratified the American text of 1787 could have divined the economic and political evolution of their nation and the rest of the world. To achieve and maintain prosperity together with political stability, it has been necessary for leaders to reinvent their nations and to adapt and amend provisions of their constitutional texts.

Virtual Reality

These changes have not been linear, but they have seemed to move in one temporal direction, that is, from then to now and beyond. Some postmodernists, however, might brand such an account as "chronophonistic," what Pauline Marie Rosenau defines as accepting "the modern assumption that time is chronological or linear."[24] These people might see the problem here as more complicated than my description indicates. Time, they might "reason," if they would allow that term, can run in either direction.[25] We all recall from our childhood that Merlin claimed to live backward and to remember the future. Stephen W. Hawking admits the possibility that "what we call real time is a figment of our imaginations."[26] Nevertheless, he argues, although "the laws of science do not distinguish between the forward and backward directions of time," in fact: "at least three arrows of time . . . do distinguish the past from the future. They are the thermodynamic arrow, the direction of time in which disorder increases; the psychological arrow, the direction of time in which we remember the past and not the future; and the cosmological arrow, the direction of time in which the universe expands rather than contracts."[27]

This reassurance that common sense had it right all the time allows most of us to sleep easier, though not without a tinge of regret that Merlin was putting Arthur (and us) on. Although we would acknowledge that the present and the future may change views we hold about the past, we nonetheless would reject the notion that the future can affect the past.

Still, one might wonder whether constitutional interpreters always and fully accept that proposition and might not, instead, be toying with

[24] Rosenau, *Post-Modernism*, p. xi. Rosenau, I should note, is a critic of postmodernism.

[25] See, for example, Martin Amis's fascinating novel *Time's Arrow or The Nature of the Offence* (New York: Harmony Books, 1991).

[26] Stephen W. Hawking, *A Brief History of Time* (New York: Bantam Books: 1988), p. 139.

[27] Ibid., p. 152.

conceptions of virtual reality. The American case of *Bolling v. Sharpe* (1954) provides a curious example.[28] There the Supreme Court held that the Fifth Amendment, ratified in 1791, incorporated at least some of the equal protection clause of the Fourteenth Amendment, ratified in 1868.[29] There are, of course, other possible interpretations of *Bolling*, but none quite so intriguing[30] or, to those of us who wish we could go back and correct our errors, quite so appealing.

Are There Limits to Valid Constitutional Change?

So far we have been discussing change *within* an existing constitutional democracy, shifts that may be quite important in and of themselves. Because of their effects on economic and social interests, these sorts of amendments inevitably breed sharp, even bitter, differences of opinion. At another level, prudential judgments about particular proposals for change *within* the existing paradigm will also divide proponents and opponents: What is the probability that a proposed amendment will accomplish its goal? Even if successful, will its costs outweigh its benefits for the nation as a whole?

These concerns are vexing. Political improvement is a constant need. "Surely," Oliver Wendell Holmes once remarked, "it cannot show a lack of attachment to the principles of the Constitution that [a person] thinks it can be improved. I suppose that most intelligent people think that it might be."[31] But degeneration poses an equally constant peril. "Change," as John Randolph of Roanoke liked to say, "is not reform."[32]

---

[28] 347 U.S. 497.

[29] Similarly, Hammer v. Dagenhart, 247 U.S. 251, 275 (1918), rewrote part of the history of the Bill of Rights. The First Congress had three times declined to include the words "expressly delegated" in what became the Tenth Amendment, but the Court in *Hammer* said that amendment reserved to the states and the people "the powers not expressly delegated to the National Government." See also Hans v. Louisiana, 134 U.S. 1 (1890), correcting the oversight of the framers of the Eleventh Amendment in not excluding from federal jurisdiction suits commenced against a state by a citizen of that state.

[30] Especially since the Court had earlier several times held that the Fifth Amendment did not include "an equal protection component." See, for example, Hirabayashi v. United States, 320 U.S. 81, 100 (1943): "The Fifth Amendment contains no equal protection clause and it restrains only such discriminatory legislation by Congress as amounts to a denial of due process." Detroit Bank v. United States, 317 U.S. 329, 337 (1943): "Unlike the Fourteenth Amendment, the Fifth contains no equal protection clause and it provides no guaranty against discriminatory legislation by Congress."

[31] United States v. Schwimmer, 279 U.S. 644, 654 (1929) (dissenting opinion).

[32] Quoted by Russell Kirk, *John Randolph of Roanoke* (Chicago: University of Chicago Press, 1951), p. 148. Randolph made this remark at Virginia's constitutional convention of 1829, but the thought reverberates through his entire public life.

Even assuming wise judgment on such issues, a much more basic question of change may arise: whether to abolish constitutional democracy. That sort of transformation would raise problems of an entirely different order—not only questions of gored oxen and sage policy but of principle and legitimacy as well. The very question of what sort of changes would fall within and outside the parameters of constitutional democracy is itself sometimes difficult, aggravated by the fact that no polity, however well intentioned, does more than approach that sort of political system. Polyarchy, Robert A. Dahl concedes,[33] is about as close to representative democracy as nations actually get. One could say much the same about constitutional democracy: We may aspire to it but will never fully achieve it.

For the sake of coherence, I shall first try to illustrate, though I shall not be able to define in a complete way, what I mean by changes *within* and *outside* the paradigm of constitutional democracy. After that discussion, I shall move to an argument about limits on legitimate constitutional transformation. Legitimacy, as I use that term here, refers not to popular support but to grounding in the existing system's fundamental normative principles.[34]

As already indicated, radical transformations need not be products of constitutional amendments; but, for the sake of space, I limit discussion to replacements by such formal means. I also leave aside questions of physical force. As unlikely as a truly popular revolution may be, it is a possibility. Some sort of coup in which the bulk of the people passively accepted the overthrow of the polity is more probable. Both would produce problems for constitutional theory as well as practical affairs, but not as stark as those my scenario would generate.

The Scope of Changes within Constitutional Democracy

Amendments may trigger immense changes within a polity, shifting allocations of resources to favor some groups of private citizens and/or public officials while disadvantaging others. But amendments can have such effects without transforming a constitutional democracy into a different kind of political system. One immediately thinks of adopting a protective bill of rights that would include recognition of voting rights for people previously denied suffrage, spell out substantive restrictions on governmental authority, define some rights more broadly and per-

---

[33] Robert A. Dahl, *Polyarchy* (New Haven: Yale University Press, 1971), especially p. 8; see also his *Democracy and Its Critics* (New Haven: Yale University Press, 1989), part 5.

[34] When we speak of consent as an, if not *the*, indicium of legitimacy, we are, of course, speaking from within a set of contested normative principles.

haps others more narrowly than would current practice.[35] In attempting to demarcate public authority, amendments might create or remove self-denying limitations on the use of armed forces, limit the consecutive number of terms of office elected officials could hold, set retirement ages for judges, require the government to balance its budget, or (re)allocate power among governmental agencies.

Other amendments could make more sweeping structural changes in the political system without abandoning constitutional democracy. A polity might, for example, switch from a presidential to a parliamentary form of government or adopt something in between, along the lines of the French model. So, too, a polity might embrace or abandon federalism. Because constitutional democracy has functioned quite well under each of these arrangements, the issues would be largely ones of prudence, of adapting particular arrangements to a people's capacities and needs.[36]

Far different is a situation in which a nation faces proposals for systemic transformation. It is hardly inconceivable, for instance, that in time of dire economic distress a charismatic leader might appear who would promise prosperity if only citizens were willing to abolish constitutional democracy. "Grant me and my party full power to rule and we shall restore this nation to greatness" could be a persuasive appeal. "People who are hungry and out of a job," as Franklin D. Roosevelt said, "are the stuff of which dictatorships are made."[37]

Let us assume that the charismatic leader would persuade the people and/or their duly elected representatives to effect, with fastidious observance of every prescribed procedure for amendment, a constitutional transformation to a near-totalitarian dictatorship of some sort. Political participation might continue, but only of the kind and with the results the leader would deign to permit. All "rights" of individuals would tarnish into privileges. In sum, citizens would become denizens.

Such a change might well be effective in the sense of controlling the

[35] Although many or even most thoughtful American constitutional democrats might oppose a constitutional change that would ease restrictions on the capacity of "public figures" to sue for libel or eliminate the exclusionary rule for illegally seized evidence, it would be difficult to make a persuasive argument that both changes would transform the United States from a constitutional democracy into some other kind of system.

[36] I do not mean to gloss over the risks such changes present. Every action (and perhaps inaction as well) is likely to spawn unforeseen effects. Dangers are likely to be acute both with amendments that seek systemic restructuring and with those that try to reallocate authority within existing structures. On such occasions, prudence would require painstaking analysis and sensitive judgment about the implications of the new order for constitutional democracy.

[37] Franklin D. Roosevelt, "Message to Congress on the State of the Union," January 11, 1944; in Samuel I. Rosenman, ed., *The Public Papers and Addresses of Franklin D. Roosevelt* (New York: Harper & Bros., 1950), 13:41.

nation, and the system it produced might cope with economic distress so as to increase dramatically the level of prosperity while minimizing inequalities across all strata of society. Can the people agree to this transformation? The answer is obvious: Of course they can. Might may not make right, but it can establish national borders, create national institutions, and coerce much outward conformity. There are, however, other relevant questions: *May* a people who accepted constitutional democracy democratically or constitutionally authorize such a political transmutation? *May* the new system validly claim to draw its authority from the consent of the governed? My answer is no to these questions.

The Bases of Arguments for Limitations

Because I have often if not well argued for limitations on valid constitutional change,[38] I shall only summarize the principal contentions here. It should be obvious that these justifications sometimes overlap one another.[39]

PROHIBITIONS EXPLICIT IN THE TEXT

A constitutional document may itself forbid some kinds of change. Insofar as that document is authoritative—itself a potentially serious problem, because no operative constitutional text is completely so—those terms, I would contend, bind both the constituted people and their public officials. For example, the American text's outlawing amendments that would eliminate, without a state's consent, "its equal Suffrage in the Senate" appears straightforward,[40] and that document is generally authoritative.

[38] See the essays cited in note 3, above.

[39] One interesting problem could not arise under the scenario I have sketched: an amendment being "adopted" by other procedures. Some committed constitutional democrats might argue that, as the history of the adoption of the constitutional text of 1787 and later of the "ratification" of the Fourteenth Amendment illustrate, this omission is serious, but not necessarily fatal. See, for example, Akhil Reed Amar, "Philadelphia Revisited: Amending the Constitution Outside Article V," *University of Chicago Law Review* 55 (1988): 1043; Bruce Ackerman, "Discovering the Constitution," *Yale Law Journal* 93 (1984): 1013, 1063–69; and Ackerman, "Constitutional Politics/Constitutional Law," *Yale Law Journal* 99 (1989): 499–507. For the checkered history of the adoption of the Fourteenth Amendment, see, among others, Ferdinand F. Fernandez, "The Constitutionality of the Fourteenth Amendment," *Southern California Law Review* 30 (1966): 378; Joseph James, "Is the Fourteenth Amendment Constitutional?" *Social Science* 50 (1975): 3; and Walter B. Suthon, "The Dubious Origin of the Fourteenth Amendment," *Tulane Law Review* 28 (1958): 22. I shall try to address this problem in another place.

[40] The prohibition against amending the clause forbidding regulation of the importation of slaves self-destructed in 1808. One might also argue that the First Amendment

Some constitutional texts impose broader restrictions. Article 79(3) of Basic Law of the Federal Republic of Germany forbids changes that would challenge the "dignity of man" or destroy the democratic and federal nature of the *Bund*. Article 139 of the Italian text reads: "The republican form of the State cannot be the subject of constitutional amendment." Norway's constitutional document imposes limitations that are perhaps more sweeping. After laying out procedures for amendment, Article 112 adds: "Such amendment must, however, never contradict the principles embodied in this Constitution, but merely relate to modifications of particular provisions which do not alter the spirit of this Constitution."

Each of these provisions, including the relatively clear American ban, poses fascinating interpretive problems, even for people who abjure deconstructionism.[41] In all constitutional democracies,[42] however, constitutional exegesis is a flourishing industry. The existence of such problems complicates, but does not negate, the argument that, to the extent a text is authoritative, its terms shackle public and official discretion.

TEXTUAL DISTINCTIONS AMONG AMENDING, REVISING,
AND TRANSFORMING

A generation ago, Herman Finer claimed that it was reasonable to "define a constitution as its process of amendment. For to amend is to de-

---

prohibits its own repeal, at least via an amendment proposed by Congress. A constitutional amendment is by definition law and that amendment says, "Congress shall make no law . . ." For general agreement, see Amar, "Philadelphia Revisited." The response that Congress does not alone enact constitutional amendments might be countered by pointing out that the president is part of the normal legislative process, so Congress does not, except when overriding a veto, "make law" by itself when passing a statute. The Indian Supreme Court used similar reasoning in *Golak Nath's Case*, though the justices later reversed that interpretation in *Kesavananda Bharati's Case*, [1973] S.C.R. 1 (supp.) (Ind.). My colleague Andrew Koppelman raises the question whether the "no-law" reasoning would hold in the United States for a constitutional amendment proposed by a national convention rather than by Congress.

[41] In the American case, the meaning of "equal suffrage" in the Senate may be both subtle and complex. Furthermore, a narrow positivist might propose eliminating equal suffrage in the Senate, of whatever kind, by amending the text to eliminate the prohibition in Article V. At that point, Congress might propose a new amendment to reapportion "suffrage" in the Senate.

[42] I want to avoid the question of whether such nations as New Zealand and the United Kingdom, which lack constitutional texts, are nevertheless constitutional democracies. If they are not, it is not simply because of this institutional omission. But, whatever they are, their officials often and publicly engage in constitutional interpretation. Works on the British constitution abound; for an insightful comparative study, see Gary J. Jacobsohn, *Apple of Gold: Constitutionalism in Israel and the United States* (Princeton: Princeton University Press, 1993).

constitute and reconstitute."[43] Finer was mistaken, I believe. He conflated two (or perhaps three) very different concepts. The word *amend*, which comes from the Latin *emendere*, means to correct or improve; amend does not mean "to deconstitute and reconstitute," to replace one system with another or abandon its primary principles. Thus changes that would make a polity into another kind of political system would not be amendments at all, but revisions or transformations. In sum, valid amendments can operate only within the existing political system; they cannot deconstitute, reconstitute, or replace the polity. Most constitutional texts authorize only amendments, though a few others, like those of Spain and some American states, also provide for revision and the German Basic Law allows for its own replacement by a new text.[44]

In 1990, the Supreme Court of California drew these sorts of distinctions to strike down an amendment, adopted by referendum, that would have required state judges, when interpreting the *state* constitution, to follow the U.S. Supreme Court's interpretations of similarly worded clauses in the national constitutional text. That change, the justices held, would so fundamentally transform California's status as a member of a federal union as to effect a constitutional revision; and the text provided that "revisions" could be accomplished only by special conventions.[45]

PROHIBITIONS EMBEDDED IN THE STRUCTURE OF THE TEXT[46]

The *Bundesverfassungsgericht* has offered two solutions to problems of incoherence that drafters' carelessness, compromise, or deliberate inconsistency might leave in a constitutional text. First, the court has proposed reconciliation through structural interpretation: "Taken as a unit, a constitution reflects certain overarching principles and fundamental decisions to which individual provisions are subordinate."[47] Second,

[43] Herman Finer, *The Theory and Practice of Modern Government*, rev. ed. (New York: Holt, 1949), p. 127.

[44] Article 146. Note 22, above, quotes this article.

[45] Raven v. Deukemejian, 801 P.2d 1077 (1990). See Sanford Levinson's essay in this volume, "How Many Times Has the U.S. Constitution Been Amended?" for further discussion of this case.

[46] To save space, I leave aside considerations of the structure of the political system, but I do, in the next section, "Prohibitions Imposed by the Normative Theory in the Constitution," take up considerations imposed by a constitution's normative theory. See William F. Harris II, "Bonding Word and Polity," *American Political Science Review* 76 (1982): 34, and Harris, *The Interpretable Constitution*.

[47] The Southwest Case, 1 BVerfGE 14 (1951), trans. and ed. in Walter F. Murphy and Joseph Tanenhaus, *Comparative Constitutional Law* (New York: St. Martin's Press, 1977), pp. 208ff.

that a constitutional provision itself may be null and void is not conceptually impossible just because it is part of the constitution. There are constitutional principles that are so fundamental and to such an extent an expression of a law that precedes even the constitution that they also bind the framer of the constitution, and other constitutional provisions that do not rank so high may be null and void, because they contravene those principles.[48]

Madison had made a pair of parallel points in *The Federalist*, No. 40, where he referred to "two rules of construction, dictated by plain reason, as well as founded on legal axioms." The first is that "every part of the expression ought, if possible, to be allowed some meaning, and be made to conspire to some common end." The second holds that "where the several parts cannot be made to coincide, . . . the less important should give way to the more important part; the means should be sacrificed to the end, rather than the end to the means."

PROHIBITIONS IMPOSED BY THE NORMATIVE THEORY
IN THE CONSTITUTION

The *Bundesverfassungsgericht*'s assertions, if not Madison's, bleed into questions about the limiting force of the normative theories on which a constitutional democracy is based. Amendments that would destroy or cripple the values of constitutional democracy, judges as well as academics have argued, are invalid.[49] When such a polity consciously, seriously, and systematically violates its fundamental principles, it destroys its justification for existence, and public officials lose their authority to speak as agents of the people.

Again we face difficult prudential as well as normative problems. Because there is no single "democratic theory," a nation would not necessarily be bound to any particular form of democracy; a polity could shift from one type to another, providing continued conformity to basic democratic principles.[50] Nevertheless, the argument runs, a people could not

---

[48] Ibid. The court was quoting with approval the Bavarian constitutional court.

[49] For Germany: In addition to the *Southwest Case*, see the dissenting opinion in the *Privacy of Communications Case* (1970), in Murphy and Tanenhaus, *Comparative Constitutional law*, p. 659. (The court divided 4–4, but its rules require a majority to invalidate a law, so the amendment remains part of the Basic Law.) For India: *Golak Nath's Case*; *Kesavananda Bharati's Case*, reversing the basis of *Golak Nath*'s holding that a constitutional amendment was invalid but reasserting that authority on different grounds; and *Minerva Mills v. v. Union of India*, [1980] S.C.R. 1789. For discussions of the instances in which the Indiana Supreme Court invalidated constitutional amendments, see Upendra Baxi, *Courage, Craft, and Contention* (Bombay: Tripathi, 1985); H. M. Seervai, *Constitutional Law of India*, 3d ed. (Bombay: Tripathi, 1984), especially 2:2635–2705; and Lloyd I. and Suzanne Hoeber Rudolph, *In Pursuit of Lakshmi* (Chicago: University of Chicago Press, 1987), chap. 3.

[50] For discussion of the basic institutional conditions necessary for democracy to oper-

legitimately use democratic processes to destroy the essence of democracy—the right of others, either of a current majority or minority or of
a minority or majority of future generations,[51] to meaningful participation in self-government.[52]

So, too, there is no single theory of constitutionalism. Moreover, the
nature and extent of rights needed to protect fundamental values such as
human dignity are problematic, for those rights often compete with one
another. Therefore a people who accept constitutionalism might make
and at other times remake agreements that fashion different tradeoffs
among duties and among rights as well as between duties and rights.
But, the argument goes, those tradeoffs must always be reasonably designed to protect the basic goals of constitutionalism. Any change that
would transform the polity into a political system that was totalitarian,
or even so authoritarian as not to allow a wide space for human freedom,
would be illegitimate, no matter how pure the procedures and widespread the public support.

---

ate, see Walter F. Murphy, James E. Fleming, Sotirios A. Barber, and William F. Harris II,
American Constitutional Interpretation, 2d ed. (Westbury, N.Y.: Foundation, 1995),
chap. 3; see also Dahl, *Democracy and Its Critics*, pp. 1–9, and *Polyarchy*, chap. 1.

[51] For discussions of the temporal dimension of democratic theory, see James G. March
and Johan P. Olsen, *Rediscovering Institutions* (New York: Free Press, 1989), pp. 118,
146–47, and sources cited; and Dahl, *Democracy and Its Critics*, p. 71 and chaps. 12–13.
As March and Olsen say,

> Unless a democratic system can solve the problem of representing the future, changing
> interests of the unborn, it violates a rather fundamental underlying premise of democ-
> racy—that those who bear the costs of decision should have their interests adequately
> reflected in the choice.
>
> If aggregative democracy cannot be extended to the unborn, or to the future
> (changed) preferences of current citizens, the criterion of political equality is compro-
> mised as a foundation of democracy. Aggregative democracy based on subjective politi-
> cal equality among current citizens appears to be only a crude approximation to political
> equality. It is conceivable that it is the best practical solution to a complicated problem.
> But the assertion of practicality is a claim that the flaws of such a system as an instrument
> of the ideals of democracy are less than the flaws of procedures that seek to provide some
> kind of basis for interpersonal and intertemporal comparisons; and such a claim is not
> self-evidently justified. (Pp. 146–47)

[52] The intergenerational argument is appealing, and, like others, I have sometimes
adopted and adapted a version of it. See especially my "Excluding Political Parties." But
the argument also has weaknesses. If this generation should not limit the capacity of future
generations to make basic political choices, by what authority can future generations restrict our choices about such matters? If our bodies must respect their ghosts, why do not
their ghosts have the same obligation to respect our bodies? One response would reason
that in "denying" us the right to destroy our right to make additional political choices—
indeed, our right to have rights—future generations would be enlarging rather than restricting our range of choices. It is obvious, except perhaps to an extreme postmodernist,
that even the specious present *can* inflict much more grievous harm on the future than the
future can inflict on the past.

The reasoning behind this conclusion is simple, though not obvious. Because I have spelled it out elsewhere,[53] I offer only a summary. Like democracy, constitutionalism rests on the notion of human worth. Thus a people's freely given consent is a critical element of legitimacy for constitutional democracy.[54] Consent does not, however, function as a magic wand that can cast a benevolent spell over all political arrangements. A system that denies human worth cannot claim consent as the foundation of its legitimacy, for what is worthless can confer nothing. The argument here parallels that of John Rawls regarding toleration of the intolerant:[55] As a person cannot reasonably ask others to respect what he or she does not respect, so, too, a system that would treat men and women as mere "things" cannot logically (or justly) insist that others respect its hegemony over those "things" because those "things" have given the consent that only human beings, morally responsible and worthy of deep respect, could give.

PROHIBITIONS IMPOSED BY NATURAL LAW, JUSTICE, AND RIGHTS

These sorts of limitations usually exist outside the constitutional system. Occasionally, however, a text, as does Ireland's, may make them part of the positive law of the land.[56] The basic constitutional document of the Fifth Republic of France explicitly incorporates the Declaration of the Rights of Man of 1789; and so judges of the Conseil Constitutionnel, as well as scholars, are increasingly arguing for the constitutionalization of a broad version of natural rights.[57] The constitutional text of the United States explicitly sets the establishment of justice as one of the polity's goals. One might also logically infer that, insofar as American tradition implants the nation's founding document, the Declaration of Independence, into the larger Constitution, natural rights impose binding standards on public officials.

Accordingly, Irish, French, and even American constitutional inter-

---

[53] Murphy, "Consent and Constitutional Change."

[54] How a people might give their consent and how both academics and public officials might recognize that consent present enormous problems, which I gleefully pass over.

[55] John Rawls, *A Theory of Justice* (Cambridge: Harvard University Press, 1971), pp. 216–21.

[56] Especially the Preamble and Articles 41–43; see McGee v. Attorney General, [1974] I.R. 284, in Murphy and Tanenhaus, *Comparative Constitutional Law*, p. 398; and In Re Art. 26 and the School Attendance Bill, 1942, [1943] I.R. 334, in ibid., p. 477.

[57] For analyses, see especially Alec Stone, *The Birth of Judicial Politics in France* (New York: Oxford University Press, 1992); Michel Troper, "The Interpretation of the Declaration of Human Rights by a Constitutional Judge," *Scandinavian Law Review* (forthcoming); and George Vedel, "Interpretation of Old Constitutional Texts in Contemporary Societies," *Scandinavian Law Review* (forthcoming).

preters could rely heavily, perhaps completely, on positivistic reasoning for protection of "natural" rights and even for applying principles of natural law to judge the validity of constitutional changes. The argument would be spare: Whatever one's opinion of the intellectual worth of natural law and natural rights, the text of the supreme law of the land recognizes and protects them. Thus officials who take seriously their oath to support that constitutional document are bound to try to give those norms practical effect.[58]

Interpreters who would rely on natural law or natural rights in the absence of firm textual grounding might deploy the classic natural-law theory that an unjust enactment, of whatever sort, is not law at all but a mere act of arbitrary will, incapable of imposing obligation. Additionally or alternatively, such interpreters might utilize Jefferson's argument in the Declaration regarding the right to revolt against a government that fails its basic purpose of protecting its citizens' natural rights.[59]

Some Objections and Implications

Rather than expand on these overlapping lines of reasoning, let me explore a few objections to them and several of the implications these arguments suggest.

States of Emergency

Many constitutional democracies authorize declarations of "states of emergency" or "states of siege," which suspend all or some constitu-

---

[58] For a different view, see Anthony J. Sebok, "Legal Positivism and the Growth of Twentieth Century American Jurisprudence" (Ph.D. diss., Princeton University, 1993), especially pp. 262ff.

[59] In the American case, a Jeffersonian argument need not be nontextual. Walter F. Berns has claimed that a right to return to "first principles"—certainly close to a right to revolution—is one of the unlisted rights the Ninth Amendment protects. "The Framers' Judiciary and the Ninth Amendment," the Fourth Thomas P. O'Neill, Jr. Symposium in American Politics, Boston College, 1988, pp. 40–47. This argument becomes stronger when one adds the final words of the Tenth Amendment about undelegated powers being reserved not merely to the states but, alternatively, "to the people." See also Wayne D. Moore, "Constitutional Rights and Powers of the People" (Ph.D. diss., Princeton University, 1992). Cf. John Marshall's oblique reference in *McCulloch v. Maryland* to the Declaration, the right of rebellion, and the adoption of the Constitution of 1787: "It has been said that the people had already surrendered all their powers to the state sovereignties, and had nothing more to give. But, surely, the question whether they may resume and modify the powers granted to government does not remain to be settled in this country" (4 Wheaton 316, 404 [1819]).

tional processes and rights in order to cope with crises such as foreign invasion, rebellion, or terrorism.[60] When such declarations are in effect, the political system operates, at best, as a substantially modified constitutional democracy and perhaps even as a dictatorship. Could such changes, even if specifically provided for by the constitutional text, be valid under the theory I have outlined?

The short answer is "only with great difficulty." The practical problems are enormous. Emergencies sometimes do disrupt normal processes of governing and exercise of rights, but the cure may be as deadly as the crisis itself. Authority to assume emergency powers poses one set of problems, what range of powers that assumption invokes creates another. Allowing, for instance, the executive to rule by decree risks erosion, even destruction, of constitutional democracy, and a wide ambit or long life for such decrees heightens those dangers. There is a large and useful literature on these problems, which we need not review here.[61] Let us, instead, focus on the issue of legitimate change when: (a) a crisis, in fact, threatens mortal harm to the polity; and (b) the institution invoking emergency power has moved with punctilious observance of the procedures the constitutional text prescribes.

If the normal rules and rights were modified or suspended only for the duration of a real emergency, the change would, by definition, not be permanent. The emergency might very well last a long time, but it may be the price of constitutional democracy over a much longer haul. John Maynard Keynes may have spoken eternal truth when he said that in the long run we are all dead; but, as long as we do live, it is likely to be in a world of restricted choice. And the list of options may be limited to (i) temporarily modified constitutional democracy or (ii) no constitutional democracy at all.[62]

---

[60] For instance, the constitutional texts of the United States, Art. I, sec. 8, clause 15, sec. 9, clauses 1–2, and Art. IV, sec. 4; the Federal Republic of Germany, Arts. 12a, 53a, 80a, 81, 87a, 91, and 115a–5l; Ireland, Arts. 15.8, 24.1, and 28.1–3; and Italy, Art. 77. The Canadian Constitution Act of 1982 contains no explicit grant of emergency powers, but Article 33 allows Parliament to declare expressly that a particular statute shall stand despite its conflict with many of the enumerated rights of citizens (those recognized in Articles 2 and 7–15). Under the British North America Act of 1867, much of which remains in force as one of Canada's constitutional documents, there would be little serious question about the government's authority to suspend rights and utilize court-martials when it perceived an emergency.

[61] For bibliographies, see, for example, John E. Finn, *Constitutions in Crisis* (New York: Oxford University Press, 1991), and Murphy, Fleming, Barber, and Harris, *American Constitutional Interpretation*, chap. 19.

[62] The Canadian War Measures Act provides one model for control. In the event of "war, invasion, or insurrection," the act authorizes the government to issue a proclamation suspending a wide range of civil liberties and to promulgate "orders and regulations" that have "the force of law." The statute also stipulates that the prime minister shall "forthwith"

The one important qualification I would add is that, although an emergency may allow government to operate outside many of the restrictions imposed by constitutional text, tradition, interpretation, and practice, government still must respect what John E. Finn calls "constitutive, or preconstitutional, principles, of which any constitutional text is but a specific and historically contingent articulation."[63] At the very least, emergent governmental action would have to respect the basic value of constitutional democracy, the dignity of human beings. How specific decisions would carry out that general precept presents, of course, an array of complex practical problems.

Closely related is the question of what happens when the state of emergency ends. Victory by the defenders of the constitutional order that preexisted the crisis does not necessarily imply a need to return to the status quo. The defenders may have the power to change the political system, as Union forces did after the American Civil War. For the immediate transition back to normalcy, the North restricted political participation by ex-Confederate officials and imposed rigorous conditions for readmission to the Union by those states that had supposedly never left in the first place. Much more significantly, the Radical Republicans pushed through the Thirteenth, Fourteenth, and Fifteenth Amendments, fundamentally changing the structure of the Union and creating what Justice Noah Swayne prematurely termed "a new Magna Charta."[64]

Making such changes may be exceedingly prudent. As was the case in the United States, the text itself, authoritative interpretations of it, or the practices that surrounded it may have individually or collectively fed the roots of the crisis. On the other hand, circumstances might exist under which governing groups, either because of internal divisions or the slimness of their margin of victory, would be unable to effect any real changes. But the main questions over which this chapter frets involve but do not directly focus on either power or prudence. The central problem for this section is a much simpler one: Would most species of either constitutionalist or democratic theory require that the system return to the same constitutional form and text that were operative before the emergency? The answer must clearly be no. All that most combinations of constitutionalist and democratic theory would require is that

---

lay such a proclamation before Parliament for debate. If that body does not give its approval, the proclamation and regulations issued under it cease to have legal force. Pierre Trudeau's invocation of the act in 1970 to cope with terrorism by the Front de Libération du Quebec illustrate the operations of this statute. See the materials collected in Murphy and Tanenhaus, *Comparative Constitutional Law*, pp. 686–93.

[63] Finn, *Constitutions in Crisis*, p. 7.

[64] Slaughter-House Cases, 16 Wall. 36, 125 (1873)(dissenting opinion).

the new or modified system continue to approach constitutional democracy, a qualification that imposes real restraints but still allows a wide range of institutional and procedural changes.[65]

Stifling Advocacy

If some kinds of constitutional transformations are invalid in a constitutional democracy, may such a polity legitimately forbid and punish advocacy of such proposals? This question grates against political liberalism; and although I am not a liberal by some definitions of that term, this issue troubles me as well. In responding, it helps to return to the distinction implicit in the last section, that between legitimate governmental action and wise governmental action.

THE LEGITIMACY OF RESTRAINING ADVOCACY

The logic of this chapter's argument marches toward the conclusion that neither mainstream democratic nor constitutionalist theories would forbid government's trying to stifle proposals for constitutional change that would crush constitutional democracy. If both sets of theories disallow systemic transformations that would destroy the capacity of citizens either to participate in self-government or to be entitled to those substantive rights necessary to human dignity, neither theory could, with much consistency, forbid government to try to prevent such changes. "Justice," John Rawls argued, "does not require that men must stand idly by while others destroy the basis of their existence."[66] Neither does constitutionalist or democratic theory require a polity's quiet submission to its own extinction or its citizens' meek acceptance of slavery.

I have spelled out the steps of such an argument elsewhere, with details about the concept of "militant democracy" and the ban by the Basic Law of the Federal Republic of Germany on parties that advocate destruction of constitutional democracy.[67] The reasoning of the Canadian Supreme Court in *The Queen v. Keegstra* (1990), sustaining the federal

[65] I think my reasoning on this point is quite consonant with that of Finn, especially in chap. 1 of *Constitutions in Crisis*.

[66] Rawls, *A Theory of Justice*, p. 218.

[67] Murphy, "Excluding Political Parties." Like the other contributors to Kirchhof and Kommers, *Germany and Its Basic Law*, I prepared my paper for an October 1989 conference that celebrated the fortieth anniversary of the Basic Law, shortly before the Wall came down. Were I to redo that essay now, almost four years later, I would, I hope, make a more nuanced argument, but would reiterate its essential reasoning.

law against hate speech,[68] fits this argument much more closely than does that of Justice Antonin Scalia's opinion for the U.S. Supreme Court in *R.A.V. v. St. Paul* (1992),[69] striking down a somewhat similar ordinance.

THE WISDOM OF RESTRAINING ADVOCACY

That each of the theories would condemn destruction of constitutional democracy (or at least the segment of that political hybrid that its norms support) and *allow* government to try to prevent that destruction does not tell us much about how either would *require* the polity to cope with threats of systemic eradication. In many circumstances, tolerating such proposals might be the most effective defensive strategy. Justice Felix Frankfurter liked to remind his readers of the folly of equating constitutionality with wisdom.[70] Many unwise, mischievous, or hurtful policies can pass muster under the terms of a constitutional text—and even be congruent with democratic and constitutionalist principles. Worse, one cannot make, in the abstract, many sure prudential judgments about the desirability, utility, or even feasibility of particular limitations on communication and association in a constitutional democracy.

My prejudices would run strongly against a restrictive governmental policy. Still, prudence and prejudice are only accidental companions. Jefferson could eloquently preach that those who would destroy the Union or "change its republican form" should "stand undisturbed as monuments of the safety with which error of opinion may be tolerated where reason is left free to combat it."[71] But to generalize from the America of 1801 across time to the rest of the world would require a whistling walk among the tombstones of failed constitutional democracies. Their "truth" has not always triumphed in the free competition of a marketplace of ideas, perhaps because that forum has so seldom been open. After the end of the Cold War, we might all agree with Justice William O. Douglas's claim in 1951 that American Communists were merely "miserable merchants of unwanted ideas."[72] On the other hand, we cannot so easily dismiss the threat the Nazis posed for Weimar Germany, Neo-Nazi and Stalinist parties posed for West German constitu-

---

[68] [1990] 3 S.C. 697.

[69] 112 S.C. 2538. The concurring opinions of Justices Byron R. White and John Paul Stevens come closer both to my reasoning and that of the Canadian Supreme Court.

[70] See, for example, his concurring opinion in Dennis v. United States, 341 U.S. 494, 553–56 (1951).

[71] "First Inaugural Address," reprinted in Henry Steele Commager, ed., *Documents of American History* (New York: Crofts, 1938), p. 187.

[72] Dennis, v. United States, 341 U.S. 494, 589 (1951) (dissenting opinion).

tional democracy in the 1950s, or the revised edition of the Communist party of the Soviet Union posed for the Russian Federal Republic in 1991, after the attempted coup, when President Boris Yeltsin banned it by decree, or in December 1992, when the new Russian constitutional court partly sustained that order.[73]

One can concede the reality and enormity of such dangers and still be uncomfortable about limiting freedom of political communication. First, a terrible temptation tugs at public officials to brand honest differences on policy *within* the four corners of constitutional democracy as threats to that political order, as the cases of the elder Adams, the older Richard Nixon, and their minions so vividly illustrate. Second, public officials are also apt, for good as well as evil motives, to exaggerate the magnitude of threats posed by those who would, even by peaceful means, attempt to overthrow constitutional democracy.

Third, curbing political expression or participation is likely to steepen the slope down which a polity may slide from the ideals of constitutional democracy. One need look no further than to the American experience from 1945 to 1955, when Joe McCarthy, Karl Mundt, James O. Eastland, and Francis Walter joined the younger Richard Nixon in scouring the country in search of Communists in government and private life. Those worthies discovered few if any threats to national security, but they generated a brood of their own: They curbed freedom of expression, twisted substantive policies in domestic and foreign affairs, and denigrated constitutionalist as well as democratic values.[74]

CONSTITUTIONALIZING WISDOM?

Suppose a polity were to decide that the potential costs of allowing government to outlaw advocacy of radically transformative systemic change so grossly outweighed the potential benefits as to justify inserting a clause in the constitutional text forbidding such action. Would both constitutionalist and democratic theory permit such a clause? I think the answer would be yes. I would, however, add two observations, neither

[73] "Court Issues Compromise Ruling in CPSU Case," *Current Digest of the Soviet Press*, no. 48 (1992): 11–13; "Constitution Watch: Russia," *East European Constitutional Review* 1 (Summer 1992): 6–7; "Constitution Watch: Russia," *East European Constitutional Review* 1 (Fall 1992): 9–10.

[74] The Federal Republic of Germany suffered from a similar pathology during the 1950s, though the imminence of a Soviet military threat and the ubiquity of East German agents within the West German government make fears for national security, though not necessarily the government's specific policies, appear less foolish. For details, see Donald B. Kommers, *The Constitutional Jurisprudence of the Federal Republic of Germany* (Durham, N.C.: Duke University Press, 1989), pp. 229–44, and the sources cited in my "Excluding Political Parties."

of them original. First, it is difficult to institutionalize prudence. Second, the existence of a crystalline clause in the American constitutional text—"Congress shall make no law"—did not prevent the Sedition Act of 1798, the banning of abolitionist literature from the mails before the Civil War, Lincoln's heavy-handed treatment of those who disagreed with his vision of the nature of the Union, the Sedition Act of 1917, the Great Red Scare that followed the First World War, or the longer and fiercer Red Scare that followed the Second World War.

To What Extent Can the People Bind Themselves?

A critic might respond to this chapter by saying that it relies on the contention, undefended above, that the people can bind themselves. But, the critic might continue, popular sovereignty denies that the people can bind themselves, for to be sovereign means to be subject to no higher authority. Sovereigns are legally, if not always physically, free to do what pleases them. Thus, as sovereigns, the people cannot make irrevocable commitments. We can only speak in a figurative sense of their "binding" themselves.[75]

This argument, I would respond, rests on a fiction and a confusion; furthermore, it proves too much. The fiction is the concept of "sovereignty," popular or otherwise. In international relations, nation-states make grand claims to being free from the will of other nation-states; but often, perhaps typically, these assertions ring hollow. In domestic politics, governments fare somewhat better. Yet even at the height of the divine right of kings, the monarch was supposedly subject "to God and the law." Government under law, if not under God, lives on as an ideal of constitutional democracy. A basic function of constitutionalism—and a source of tension with democratic theory and therefore within constitutional democracy—is to restrain government, even when it accurately reflects the popular will. Generations ago most students of American politics gave up trying to locate sovereignty within that system.

The critic's confusion is to equate democracy with anarchy and so to prove too much: If the people cannot bind themselves, there can be neither a large-scale, peaceful, ordered society nor any constitution that is authoritative beyond declaring that the will of the people is the supreme law of the land. That "people" would always remain free to act as they wished at any particular moment. Mob rule would not merely be a possibility, it would be a *legitimate* option to which the mass of the people

[75] I may do Akhil Reed Amar an injustice, but I believe his argument in "Philadelphia Revisited," which I admire in many respects (and which is also spelled out in his contribution to this volume), leads in this direction.

might resort whenever it pleased or profited them. To modify the extreme claims of popular sovereignty by admitting a people could bind themselves either to operate under a particular framework to allow determination of their will or to follow certain procedures in defining that will does not help the argument. Either the people can or they cannot bind themselves. If they cannot, they cannot bind themselves procedurally, and the legitimacy of mob rule persists. If they can bind themselves procedurally, there is no reason they cannot do so substantively as well and thus can set limits on their own authority both to alter the stakes of politics and to change the rules of the political game. The alternatives are either that the people can restrict their "sovereignty" or that anarchy is an authentic outcome for democracy.

Some people have lived and still live in anarchy, and all societies are vulnerable to slipping into it. The real question is whether humanity is doomed to that condition. If we could not bind ourselves, we would be so condemned. Thus it is not unreasonable to contend that men and women can fully bind themselves, at least conditionally; that is to say, they can fully bind themselves to act in certain specified ways, providing that their fellow citizens or public officials behave in other specified ways.

If the people can bind so themselves, then the rule of certain kinds of law becomes possible, law that relies on reason rather than force and respects particular substantive values along with decision-making procedures. Given human nature, mob rule always remains a danger possible; but if the people can and do bind themselves, it becomes an illegitimate option.

Conclusion: Reason and Systemic Transformation

Do the democratic and constitutionalist strands of this chapter combine to beget a perverse paradox? Do they, in the name of keeping the possibility of political change open, eliminate the validity of systemic transformation? Does the logic of this essay require the conclusion that, once a people have adopted constitutional democracy, they as well as future generations are forever trapped in that sort of political system?

To some extent the answer must be yes, and that response provides additional cause for fretting.[76] Let me back up a bit: We are intelligent

[76] I mention in passing two other such causes. First is the problem of gradual systemic transformation from constitutional democracy. The reasoning I have used here would apply to that situation, but the practical difficulties, including but not limited to those of recognition of the change, would be far more serious. Second is the problem, however open or rapid the attempt at transformation, of whose duty it is to stand up and shout foul.

men and women who think we can choose our form of government by
"reflection and choice." We arrive at constitutional democracy, we like
to believe, because reason and experience convince us that it is the best
form of government for achieving those values that Benjamin N. Cardozo summed up under the rubric of "ordered liberty."[77] Not only does
reason lead us to try to create a constitutional democracy, but that sort
of system depends heavily for its maintenance on reasoned argument
rather than threats of violence. Thus it has a double appeal to people
who value reason. Indeed, Noah Webster claimed that constitutional
government created "the empire of reason."

But does not the primacy of reason raises additional problems for my
argument? Sotirios A. Barber, for example, maintains that a full commitment to reason allows only a provisional commitment to constitutional
democracy because we must be open to rational persuasion about the
moral necessity, or at least desirability, of systemic transformation of the
polity.[78] A plenary commitment to reason does not, however, permit
every sort of systemic transformation, only to that which will, at least
equally as well as constitutional democracy, protect the capacity of humans to reason about basic values and political change and an opportunity to carry out changes that reason indicates.

Thus, constitutional democracy would allow a transformation to another system that would enlarge reason's empire or strengthen its reign.
But a move from constitutional democracy to dictatorship, again except
in true emergencies and then for only limited periods, would restrict
reason's ambit for all citizens except the ruler and his coterie; worse,
such a system would not even push that elite to rule by reason.[79]

Dictatorial and would-be totalitarian systems aside, the question
would remain about what other kinds of transformations might be validly open to a constitutional democracy. And here I would offer a simple, "I haven't yet seen any such metamorphosis." I do not, however,

---

The short answer is "all citizens, in and out of public office." A long answer would have to
take into account the institutional structure and responsibilities of specific constitutional
democracies.

[77] Palko v. Connecticut, 302 U.S. 319, 325 (1937).

[78] See Sotirios A. Barber, *The Constitution of Judicial Power* (Baltimore: Johns Hopkins
University Press, 1993), pp. 60–61, 186–87, 232–34, and 265n. Barber made a parallel
argument in *On What the Constitution Means* (Baltimore: Johns Hopkins University Press,
1984), pp. 49–51, 59–61.

[79] One could make a strong case that brutal dictators such as Adolf Hitler, Benito Mus-
solini, Josef Stalin, Gamal Abdel Nasser, Hafez al-Assad, Mu'ammar Qadafi, Saddam Hus-
sein, "Poppa Doc" Duvalier, Mao Zedong, Augusto Pinochet, and Joseph Mobutu have
been cunning, shrewd, and even quite adept at deploying some versions of rational choice.
It would be fair, however, to classify only Pinochet among these as depending much on
reason for his rule or even valuing that capacity in his subjects.

mean this response as more than a holding action: first, a commonsensical rejection of the various authoritarian models, theocratic and secular, the world has witnessed in this century; and, second, a less firm rejection of representative democracy unrestricted by constitutionalism.[80]

I do not imply that we have reached the end of history, not even the history of the state. Someday we may be able to imagine and then create a kind of political system that protects, better than does constitutional democracy, the values of human dignity and autonomy. Finality, as Disraeli once said, is not in the language of politics. My statement is only a begrudging admission that, unlike Merlin, I cannot remember the future, though I know it will be and sometimes fear what it will be.

[80] A careful reader will note the lack of literary parallelism in this sentence. I deliberately did not say "models of representative democracy" because I am not sure any exist. Constitutionalists feel more secure with such institutional arrangements as judicial review, but I am not—at least not yet—willing to argue that a political culture cannot adequately protect constitutionalism's values.

Nine

The Case against Implicit Limits
on the Constitutional Amending Process

JOHN R. VILE

THE CONSTITUTIONAL amending process has been described as "a domestication of the right to revolution"[1] and as a key that unlocks the Constitution,[2] and yet Article V of the Constitution, the amending article, contains two entrenchment clauses. The first—guaranteeing slave importation for twenty years—had a built-in termination, but the second, providing that no state would be deprived of its equal suffrage in the Senate without its consent, raises contemporary enforcement issues. Both clauses lead logically to the question of whether there are any implicit limits on the constitutional amending process.

In addressing this question, the records of the constitutional convention offer at least some guidance. The major debates on the amending process came in the closing week of deliberations. By September 10, the amending provision provided for Congress to call a convention on "the application of the Legislatures of two thirds of the States."[3] Elbridge Gerry, Alexander Hamilton, and James Madison criticized this proposal. Gerry feared that two-thirds of the states might "bind the Union to innovations that may subvert the State-Constitutions altogether." Hamilton argued that the state legislatures would "not apply for alterations but with a view to increase their own powers," and that ills would be better perceived by the national legislature. Madison objected to the

This chapter is based in part on an earlier article, "Limitations on the Constitutional Amending Process," *Constitutional Commentary* 2 (1985): 373. An expanded version of this chapter has also appeared as chapter 7 of *Contemporary Questions Surrounding the Constitutional Amending Process* (Westport, Conn.: Praeger, 1993). The author expresses appreciation to the Faculty Research Committee at Middle Tennessee State University for a research award to complete this study.

[1] Walter Dellinger, "The Legitimacy of Constitutional Change: Rethinking the Amending Process," *Harvard Law Review* 97 (1983): 431.

[2] Grover Rees III, "Throwing Away the Key: The Unconstitutionality of the Equal Rights Amendment Extension," *Texas Law Review* 58 (1980): 67.

[3] Max Farrand, ed., *The Records of the Federal Convention of 1787* (New Haven: Yale University Press, 1966), 2:557. All of the quotations in this paragraph are taken from 2:557–59.

vagueness of the convention provision, and subsequently proposed the following provision: "The Legislature of the U—S— whenever two thirds of both Houses shall deem necessary, or on the application of two thirds of the Legislatures of the several States, shall propose amendments to this Constitution, which shall be valid . . . when the same shall have been ratified by three fourths at least of the Legislatures of the several States, or by Conventions in three fourths thereof." John Rutledge, a delegate from South Carolina, almost immediately amended this proposal to include the slave importation reservation, noting that "he never could agree to give a power by which the articles relating to slaves might be altered by the States not interested in that property and prejudiced against it."

The amendment issue reemerged on September 15, when the present method of constitutional amendment was finalized. The provision requiring a constitutional convention upon the request of two-thirds of the states was adopted after Mason expressed fears that otherwise Congress would have too much control.[4] More to the point, the provision for equal suffrage in the Senate was also accepted after Roger Sherman's animadversions: "that three fourths of the States might be brought to do things fatal to particular States, as abolishing them altogether or depriving them of their equality in the Senate." Hence, he said, "The proviso in favor of the States importing slaves should be extended so as to provide that no State should be affected in its internal police, or deprived of its equality in the Senate." Madison feared that the floodgates were about to be opened. "Begin with these special provisos," he noted, "and every State will insist on them, for their boundaries, exports &c." While enough delegates shared Madison's sentiments to narrow the range of Sherman's reservations and to reject a series of amendments proposed by Sherman, the Convention adopted Morris's proposal "that no State, without its consent shall be deprived of its equal suffrage in the Senate." Madison attributed this unanimous action to "the circulating murmurs of the small States."

Elsewhere I have argued both that the existing entrenchment provision is as enforceable as any other part of the Constitution[5] and, furthermore, that, whatever doubts one might have about their desirability, new entrenchment clauses could be added to the Constitution.[6] The remedy for such clauses, were there intense opposition by the populace, would lie "outside" the Constitution, perhaps even in force of arms, rather than in an appeal to any "internal" constitutional limits on entrenchment.

[4] Ibid., 2:629–33. All of the quotations in this paragraph are taken from these pages.
[5] "Limitations on the Constitutional Amending Process," 378.
[6] Ibid., pp. 385–87.

The question of explicit restraints on the amending process leads logically to the question of whether there are any implicit limitations on Article V, a question also explored, though with different conclusions, in the contributions of Akhil Reed Amar, Mark Brandon, and Walter Murphy to this volume. The argument for such restrictions was advanced early in the nineteenth century by John C. Calhoun, vice-president under Andrew Jackson and afterward, as previously, a senator from South Carolina. As part of his general theory of nullification, Calhoun posited that states had the right, if they believed that the national government was exercising powers that had not been entrusted to it, to "nullify" the law, in effect suspending its operation until the states could adopt an amendment to grant this power to the national government. Even where states adopted such an amendment, however, Calhoun argued that states could secede in cases where such an amendment "would radically change the character of the constitution, or the nature of the system; or if the former should fail to fulfill the ends for which it was established."[7] Calhoun's arguments for secession were, of course, resoundingly rejected by the outcome of the Civil War, as were later arguments that the Thirteenth Amendment was so revolutionary as to be unconstitutional.[8]

Arguments from states' rights proponents, however, continued to be popular. These arguments were specifically applied to the amending process by Thomas Cooley, one of the most influential legal commentators of his day, in an article published in 1893. Reviewing the two entrenchment clauses within the Constitution, Cooley argued that they were not exclusive but that "there are limitations that are far more important than this, that stand unquestionably as restrictions upon the power to amend."[9] In an argument that was apparently not directed to any specific amendment, Cooley formulated four examples of unconstitutional amendments. These were an amendment that attempted to detach a certain part of the Union, an amendment that applied different taxing rules to some states, an amendment that established a nobility, or an amendment that attempted to create a monarchy.[10] Arguing that the

[7] Found in John C. Calhoun, *The Works of John C. Calhoun*, ed. Richard K. Cralle (1851–56; reprint, New York: Russell & Russell, 1968), 1:301. The quotation is from Calhoun's *Discourse on the Constitution and Government of the United States*. Calhoun's views on the amending process are analyzed in greater detail in John R. Vile, *The Constitutional Amending Process in American Political Thought* (New York: Praeger, 1992).

[8] See Sanford Levinson's contribution to this volume, Chapter 2.

[9] Thomas M. Cooley, "The Power to Amend the Federal Constitution," *Michigan Law Journal* 2 (April 1893): 117. The ensuing quotations from Cooley are taken from pp. 117–20.

[10] Lester B. Orfield lists over twenty-five differing topics that have been offered as implicit limits on the amending process. See *The Amending of the Federal Constitution* (Ann Arbor: University of Michigan, 1942), pp. 87–88, n. 12.

first fifteen amendments had all "been in the direction of further extending the democratic principles which underlie our constitution," Cooley contended that amendments "must be in harmony with the thing amended," and he distinguished that which amends a constitution from that which "overthrows or revolutionizes it." Cooley also attempted to offer a credible reason why the Founders did not include other stated restrictions on the amending process:

> If the makers of the constitution, in limiting this provision [Article V] stopped short of forbidding such changes as would be inharmonious, they did so because it was not in their thought that any such changes could for a moment be considered by congress or by the states as admissible, since in the completed instrument no place could possibly be found for them, however formal might be the process of adoption; and as foreign matter, they would just as certainly be declared inadmissible and therefore invalid without an express inhibition as with it.

Cooley proposed an analogy based on the notion of higher law. A "fruit grower" need not explicitly "forbid his servants" from placing poisons on fruit trees. "The process is forbidden by a law higher and more imperative than any he could declare." Restatement is wholly unnecessary, for "no additional force could possibly be given by re-enactment under his orders." To know the purpose of fruit growing is to know also that one does not place poisonous grafts on the trees. The same is true, presumably, of the purpose and practice of constitutionalism.

Cooley's arguments were general; he does not appear to have been concerned about any of the actual amendments that had been added to the Constitution in the tumultuous period following Appomattox. His arguments were, however, appropriated and expanded by numerous conservative commentators who subsequently hoped to persuade the courts to invalidate the Fifteenth, Eighteenth, and Nineteenth Amendments, the first the product of the Civil War and the other two the result of the Progressive Era.[11]

In a *Harvard Law Review* article challenging the national Prohibition and women's suffrage amendments, attorney William Marbury contended "that the power to 'amend' the Constitution was not intended to include the power to *destroy* it," but only to "*carry out the purpose for which it was framed.*"[12] "The power to amend the Constitution," he argued, "cannot be deemed to have been intended to confer the right

---

[11] This controversy is covered in much greater detail in Vile, *The Constitutional Amending Process*, pp. 157–82.

[12] William Marbury, "The Limitations Upon the Amending Power, *Harvard Law Review* 33 (1919): 225. Marbury is quoting from a contemporary decision, Livermore v. Waite, 102 Cal. 113, 119, 36 P. 424 (1894). For further analysis of Marbury's views, see Peter Suber, *The Paradox of Self-Amendment* (New York: Peter Lang, 1990), pp. 95–97.

upon Congress . . . to adopt any amendment . . . which would have the same tendency . . . to destroy the states, by taking from them, directly, any branch of their legislative powers."[13] Marbury further argued that Prohibition deprived each state of its equality in the Senate by opening the door to a destruction of "those functions which are essential 'to its separate and independent' existence as a state."[14] Finally, distinguishing constitutional matters from matters of ordinary legislation, Marbury argued that it was unwise to lay down conditions that might prove ultimately unsuited to the future.

A decade later, and in a similarly prestigious law journal, law professor Selden Bacon relied on an ambiguous letter sent by James Winthrop to the Massachusetts Constitutional Ratifying Convention to argue that the Bill of Rights was designed to limit the scope of future constitutional amendments.[15] While the first nine amendments protected personal rights, the Tenth Amendment addressed itself to limiting governmental powers. Moreover, by the subtle maneuver of Roger Sherman,[16] who had argued for a restriction at the Philadelphia convention limiting the scope of amendments, those powers reserved to the states and the people were those "not delegated to the United States."[17] But, asked Bacon, what power could this be other than the power of amendment? Thus viewing the Tenth Amendment as a specific limit on the amending power, Bacon concluded that only conventions had the power to ratify amendments infringing state police powers. In Bacon's paraphrase of the Tenth Amendment: "If the Federal Government wants added direct powers over the people or the individual rights of the people, it must go to the people to get them; the power to confer any such added direct powers over the people and their individual rights is reserved to the people; and the right, at the option of Congress, to get such added powers from any other source, is wiped out."[18] This argument, if accepted, would apply not only to several past amendments but also to the Child Labor Amendment proposed by Congress in 1924, which would have in effect reversed the holding of the Supreme Court in *Hammer v. Dagenhart* that regulation of child labor was beyond the scope of national power and thus reserved to the states.[19] Arguments like those of Mar-

---

[13] Marbury, "The Limitations Upon the Amending Power," p. 228.

[14] Ibid., p. 229.

[15] Selden Bacon, "How the Tenth Amendment Affected the Fifth Article of the Constitution," *Virginia Law Review* 16 (1930): 775. At this point, Bacon's analysis appears to rest on the narrowest, and therefore the most vulnerable, view of the framers' intent.

[16] Ibid., p. 778, n. 19.

[17] Ibid., p. 777.

[18] Ibid., p. 782.

[19] 247 U.S. 251 (1919). The Court had also struck down, in Bailey v. Drexel Furniture Co., 259 U.S. 20 (1922), an attempt to regulate child labor through taxation.

bury and Bacon were rejected in a series of court decisions[20] that culminated in the Court's almost complete hands-off approach to the amending process in *Coleman v. Miller*.[21]

Walter Murphy's Arguments for Implicit Constitutional Restraints on the Constitutional Amending Process

Nonetheless, many of the same arguments made earlier in this century for implicit limits on the amending process are relevant to Walter Murphy's recent attempts, including his essay in this volume, to breathe new life into the notion of implied limits on the amending process. Murphy has argued that certain provisions of the Constitution are so fundamental, and so essential to human dignity, that an amendment repealing them should be voided by the courts.[22]

Murphy offered two examples of unconstitutional amendments. The first involved restriction of the First Amendment.[23] Murphy reasoned as follows:

> **1.** Incorporation of the First Amendment into the Fourteenth means that the operative constitutional provision effectively reads: "Neither Congress nor the states, singly or together, can make a law abridging" freedom of speech, press, assembly, or religion.
>
> **2.** Constitutional amendments are law.
>
> **3.** Therefore it is outside the scope of state and legislative powers to amend the Constitution to restrict the First Amendment's protections.[24]

[20] See especially the National Prohibition Cases, 253 U.S. 350 (1920), and Leser v. Garnett, 258 U.S. 130 (1922).

[21] 397 U.S. 433 (1939). This opinion is, however, subject to a great deal of scholarly criticism. See John Vile, *Contemporary Questions Surrounding the Constitutional Amending Process*, chap. 2.

[22] In effect, Murphy is arguing for judicial recognition of implicit entrenchment provisions on Article V. Similarly, Akil Reed Amar has suggested that an amendment repealing free speech or denying to the people "certain economic and social prerequisites" would be illegal. See "Philadelphia Revisited: Amending the Constitution Outside Article V," *University of Chicago Law Review* 55 (1988): 1045. Bruce Ackerman does not believe that such rights are currently entrenched, but he favors doing so. See *We the People: Foundations* (Cambridge, Mass.: Harvard University Press, 1991), pp. 320–21.

[23] In "The Right to Privacy and Legitimate Constitutional Change," in Shlomo Slonin, ed., *The Constitutional Bases of Social and Political Change in the United States* (New York: Praeger, 1990), pp. 213–35. Murphy uses the example of the right of privacy as a right that also cannot be radically abridged under the current constitutional system.

[24] Murphy, "The Art of Constitutional Interpretation: A Preliminary Showing," in M. Harmon, ed., *Essays on the Constitution of the United States* (Port Washington, N.Y.: Kennikat, 1978), p. 151.

In a second example, Murphy imagined that an "ideology of repressive racism sweeps the country."[25] Its proponents muster the requisite majorities in Congress and in the states to ratify a constitutional amendment endorsing racial discrimination. If such an amendment were challenged in court, Murphy did "not see how the justices, as officials of a constitutional democracy, could avoid holding the amendment invalid."

Murphy outlined three arguments. The first, borrowed from the Federal Constitutional Court of West Germany, suggested that the Constitution is an entity with "an inner unity" and a commitment to "certain overarching principles and fundamental decisions to which individual provisions are subordinate."[26] In this case, he argued, "the protection of human dignity" would, as a core constitutional value, take precedence over the racist amendment. Murphy adopted a second argument from a court decision in India. He reasoned that Americans have chosen "a constitutional democracy which enshrines certain values, paramount among which is human dignity." This value is even more important than the democratic procedures by which it was intended to be secured: "By adopting and maintaining such a system of values, the American people have surrendered their authority, *under that system*, to abridge human dignity by any procedure whatever." Since this Constitution makes "no provision for destroying the old polity and creating a new one . . . its terms cannot supply legitimate procedures for such a sweeping change." Murphy further noted that "constitutional tradition establishes a legitimate process for establishing a totally new system through a convention chosen from the *entire polity*."[27] Murphy's third argument was similar to the previous two. Since "there are principles above the literal terms of the constitutional document," Murphy argued, the racist amendment would be invalid as a denial of "the right to respect and dignity," because it sought to "contradict the basic purposes of the whole constitutional system."

Despite Murphy's appealing objectives, I believe that courts should steer clear of imposing implicit limits on the substance of amendments, even in the extreme circumstances Murphy mentions. From the standpoint of constitutional interpretation and the framers' intent, the presence of two explicit limits within Article V and the constitutional convention's deliberate rejection of two others seem to argue against the

---

[25] Walter Murphy, "An Ordering of Constitutional Values," *Southern California Law Review* 53 (1980): 755. The quotations from this article are taken from pp. 755–57. All emphases are Murphy's.

[26] The material cited is quoted directly from the German court decision.

[27] This reservation suggests that Murphy's argument is more limited than it may first appear—not that certain changes simply cannot be made but rather that to make them special procedures must be utilized.

existence of still more. As Chief Justice Marshall wrote in regard to provisions in Article III: "Affirmative words are often, in their operations, negative of other objects than those affirmed; and in this case, a negative or exclusive sense must be given to them or they have no operation at all."[28]

An additional objection to judicially recognized limits on the amending process stems from what such a notion might do to the delicate balance that has been worked out during the last two hundred years between the judicial branch and the people. However one might stress the "constitutional" as opposed to the "democratic" aspects of the American government,[29] the exercise of judicial power by an unelected branch of government whose members serve for life has always been in tension with popular rule.[30] One reason that judicial review is accepted is that judgments of the courts can be reversed through the amending process. Moreover, the potential impact of the amendment process on the courts cannot be measured merely by counting those few occasions when it has been directly utilized,[31] since the possibility may have deterred court decisions in other areas as well. To empower the courts not simply to review the procedures whereby amendments were adopted but also to void amendments on the basis of their substantive content would surely threaten the notion of a government founded on the consent of the governed.[32]

Recognition of the right of the judiciary to invalidate amendments

[28] Marbury v. Madison, 5 U.S. (1 Cranch) 137, 174 (1803).

[29] The distinction is Murphy's. Murphy argues that "democracy stresses equality and popular rule" while "constitutionalism emphasizes that certain rights of the individual citizen are protected against government, even against popular government and majority rule." "An Ordering of Constitutional Values," pp. 707–8.

[30] Alexander Bickel, *The Least Dangerous Branch* (Indianapolis: Bobbs-Merrill, 1962), pp. 16–23. See also Henry Abraham, "The Judicial Function Under the Constitution: Theory and Practice," *NEWS for Teachers of Political Science* (Spring 1984): 12.

[31] The threat of using the untried convention mechanism, for example, has been linked to the passage of at least four amendments. Dwight W. Connelly, "Amending the Constitution: Is This Any Way to Call for a Constitutional Convention?" *Arizona Law Review* 22 (1980): 1016.

[32] Laurence Tribe, "A Constitution We Are Amending: In Defense of a Restrained Judicial Role," *Harvard Law Review* 97 (1983): 435–36.

In Murphy's "Consent and Constitutional Change," in James O'Reilly, ed., *Human Rights and Constitutional Law: Essays in Honour of Brian Walsh* (Dublin: Round Hall Press, 1992), he defers treating the "fear of judicial oligarchy" (p. 124; see also p. 145) but essentially argues that the virtue of government by consent is subordinate to higher constitutional notions of human dignity. For me the simple fact that both notions are embodied in the same constitution and are in potential conflict shows the danger of allowing courts to choose one or the other principle to void new amendments that may be added to the document.

might also upset the delicate balance that has been worked out among the three branches of government. There is certainly merit in the notion that while the judicial branch may interpret the Constitution, the Constitution is created by other hands, that is, by the Congress, the state legislatures, or a constitutional convention. Murphy notes the possibility, albeit arguably a fairly remote one, that the people or their agents could adopt measures that would undermine human dignity. What should also be noted, however, is that, if the judiciary took upon itself the power to void the very substance of amendments, this branch of government could itself end up undermining such dignity. Indeed, attention to American history would suggest that such dangers of judicial usurpation would be far more likely than the dangers that Murphy cites. Surely, for example, it would not have been preposterous (as Taney showed in *Dred Scott*)[33] to argue that the Constitution was adopted by whites and could not be extended to others, the Civil War Amendments to the contrary notwithstanding. As noted earlier, almost all the Progressive Era amendments were met with similar challenges.

Under the U.S. constitutional system, it is clear that the solution to a bad or unworkable amendment, the Eighteenth for example, is another one repealing it. Similarly, undesirable judicial decisions can be overturned by the courts themselves or by amendments. But what would the people or the other branches do if the courts, relying on the idea of implicit limits on the amending power, adamantly rejected all attempts at reform?

Here the role of the amending process as a "safety-valve"[34] or alternative to revolution needs to be appreciated. When popular sentiment has reached the boiling point, it is unlikely to be calmed by plugging the stopper. Even if the courts had the courage to oppose the raging tides of opinion in such contingencies—and cases such as *Dred Scott*,[35] *Plessy*,[36] *Gobitis*,[37] *Korematsu*,[38] and *Yamashita*[39] show that they have often failed in similar circumstances—there is little reason to believe they would be successful in doing anything other than sparking revolution. It is far more likely that courts accepting Murphy's invitation to judge the validity of the Constitution itself would intervene on those more problematic occasions when they could enhance their own institutional

---

[33] Scott v. Sandford, 60 U.S. (19 How.) 393 (1857).

[34] This specific analogy is found in many places. It may have been coined by Joseph Story. See Vile, *The Constitutional Amending Process*, p. 79.

[35] Scott v. Sandford, 60 U.S. (19 How.) 393 (1857).

[36] Plessy v. Ferguson, 163 U.S. 537 (1896).

[37] Minersville School District v. Gobitis, 310 U.S. 586 (1940).

[38] Korematsu v. United States, 323 U.S. 214 (1944).

[39] In Re Yamashita, 327 U.S. 1 (1946).

powers or their own view of what is best at the expense of the people and the elected branches of government.

These arguments notwithstanding, one must still meet Murphy's own positive examples and arguments. His argument against restrictions on the First Amendment has the advantage of resting on a seemingly explicit, rather than an implicit, constitutional limit, but it has problems. While an amendment may indeed be a form of law, it is unlikely to be the form referred to in the First Amendment; the two would rarely be equated in ordinary discourse. If the Founders meant no law *or* amendment, surely they would have been explicit, as they were in establishing limits in Article V.[40] Moreover, the language of the supremacy clause seems to indicate that the terms *law* and *amendment* are not used synonymously elsewhere in the Constitution.[41] Finally, Murphy's argument is inconsistent with existing constitutional interpretation under which presidents and governors can veto laws but not amendments.[42]

As to Murphy's example of a racist amendment, he first argues that unifying constitutional principles should take precedence over contrary provisions. This argument would be more compelling if one could assume that the Constitution expressed a single set of coherent principles, laid down once and for all by divine decree. Not only is the Constitution an imperfect document;[43] it is also evolutionary, with amendments and changes in interpretations designed to reflect the development of refined public opinion. In such a constitution, more recent constitutional provisions are presumptively in closer accord with the consent of

[40] Addressing a related issue, Francis H. Heller observes that "a Constitution viewed as a political document is a framework for the exercise of power in the polity. Legal rules, by contrast, purport to determine the broad range of societal relationships. When a constitution is treated as just another form of law, there results an ambiguity of thought that tends to overshadow significant functional differences." Heller, "Article V: Changing Dimensions in Constitutional Change," *University of Michigan Journal of Law Reform* 7 (1973): 71–72.

[41] The language is not conclusive, but it would appear that a proper reading would place amendments under the heading of "Constitution" rather than "the Laws of the United States." The supremacy clause, found in Article VI, reads as follows: "This Constitution, and the Laws of the United States which shall be made in Pursuance thereof; and all Treaties made, or which shall be made, under the Authority of the United States, shall be the supreme law of the Land; and the Judges in every State shall be bound thereby, any Thing in the Constitution or Laws of any State to the Contrary notwithstanding."

[42] Hawke v. Smith, No. 2, 253 U.S. 231 (1920); Hollingsworth v. Virginia, 3 U.S. (3 Dall.) 378 (1798). These precedents have been called into question by Charles L. Black, Jr., "Correspondence: On Article I, Section 7, Clause 30—and the Amendment of the Constitution," *Yale Law Journal* 87 (1978): 896.

[43] Mark A. Graber, "Our (Im)Perfect Constitution," *Review of Politics* 51 (Winter 1989): 86.

the governed than conflicting earlier provisions.[44] This is why there is no need for today's justices to ask whether blacks should be counted as three-fifths of a person or whether senators should be elected by state legislatures.

Murphy's second argument is that the nation has opted for a system in which the people "have surrendered their authority, *under that system*, to abridge human dignity by any procedure" short of "a convention chosen from the *entire polity*."[45] It is doubtful that the existing Constitution was itself written and adopted in such a convention.[46] Surely, the Constitution permitted a number of practices—including slavery and the disenfranchisement of women—that are today clearly recognized as violations of such human dignity. More important, Murphy's proposal is dangerously close to that of Calhoun's concurrent majority and could just as easily be applied—to cite some plausible historical examples—not to enhance human dignity, but as a means of protecting the South's "peculiar institution," all-white or all-male suffrage, or the election of senators by state legislatures.[47]

To turn, finally, to Murphy's contention that there are "principles above the literal terms of the constitutional document" is to enter a constitutional morass.[48] This writer accepts the notion that such natural law principles exist, but if so-called noninterpretative judicial review (based on extraconstitutional sources) is problematic and controversial, the prospect of enthroning the judiciary to rule against the Constitution is especially troubling. Not only does such a doctrine tempt the Court to assume powers it should not exercise, but judicial decisions that misinterpreted or misapplied natural law principles would be almost impossible to reverse.

Clearly, not every moral wrong has a constitutional or judicial remedy. Prudence dictates that popular rule and national union may sometimes, at least in the short term, have to take priority over the protection of a specific conception of human dignity. Ultimately, the best haven for human dignity is the cleft of a constitution, changeable by a populace that will, over time, be subject to enlightenment and improvement.

[44] This is the principle that Peter Suber identifies as the "*ex posterior* principle." See *The Paradox of Self-Amendment*, pp. 207–8.

[45] Murphy, "An Ordering of Constitutional Values," 756–57. Emphasis in original.

[46] Rhode Island did not send delegates to the constitutional convention, and delegates to the convention were appointed by state legislatures rather than elected by conventions.

[47] Murphy himself indicates that such arguments could have been plausibly raised by those seeking to restrict application of the Thirteenth and Fourteenth Amendments. See Walter Murphy, "*Slaughter-house, Civil Rights*, and Limits on Constitutional Change," *American Journal of Jurisprudence* 32 (1987): 8.

[48] Murphy, "An Ordering of Constitutional Values," p. 757.

Application of Implicit Limits to the Flag-burning Controversy

Both the strengths and weaknesses of arguments such as Murphy's—and similar reflections by Sanford Levinson,[49] Sotirios Barber,[50] and William Harris II[51]—are revealed in regard to the controversy several years ago about the constitutional legitimacy of a "flag-burning amendment." The issue was raised, of course, by the Supreme Court's rulings in *Texas v. Johnson*[52] and *United States v. Eichman*[53] voiding the application of laws designed to prohibit the burning of the American flag. With the warm encouragement of President Bush, amendments were quickly introduced in Congress to reverse these judgments. A popular version of this proposal would have provided: "The Congress and the States shall have power to prohibit the physical desecration of the flag of the United States."[54] This proposed amendment was defeated in congressional votes in 1989 and 1990.[55]

I have no hesitation in saying that a flag-burning amendment would be unwise and contrary to the wide protection typically given to free speech in America. I am equally confident, though, that if proposed and ratified according to the procedures specified in Article V of the U.S. Constitution,[56] it would have been as valid as any other part of the Constitution.

Authors of two recent articles specifically address the flag-burning

[49] Sanford Levinson, *Constitutional Faith* (Princeton: Princeton University Press, 1988).

[50] Sotirios Barber, *On What the Constitution Means* (Baltimore: Johns Hopkins University Press, 1984), p. 43.

[51] William F. Harris II, *The Interpretable Constitution* (Baltimore: Johns Hopkins University Press, 1993), chap. 4.

[52] 109 S. Ct. 2533 (1989)

[53] 110 S. Ct. 2404 (1990).

[54] Jeffrey Rosen, "Was the Flag Burning Amendment Unconstitutional?" *Yale Law Journal* 100 (1992): 1073.

[55] Ibid. For the most comprehensive treatment of the flag-burning issue, see Robert J. Goldstein, "The Great 1989–1990 Flag Flap: An Historical, Political, and Legal Analysis," *University of Miami Law Review* 45 (1990): 19–106. See also Murray Dry, "Flag Burning and the Constitution," *Supreme Court Review* (1991): 69, and Mark Tushnet, "The Flag-Burning Episode: An Essay on the Constitution," *University of Colorado Law Review* 61 (1990): 39.

[56] I reject Akhil Reed Amar's argument that the Constitution can be amended by popular referenda not specified in the Constitution. For Amar's views, see "Philadelphia Revisited," p. 1043. For critiques of Amar's view, see John R. Vile, "Legally Amending the United States Constitution: The Exclusivity of Article V's Mechanisms," *Cumberland Law Review* 21 (1990–91): 271, and David R. Dow, "When Words Mean What We Believe They Say: The Case of Article V," *Iowa Law Review* 76 (1990): 1.

amendment;[57] however, while taking different approaches, both argue that such an amendment would be unconstitutional. Eric Isaacson, whose argument is much like Murphy's, focused primarily on the language of the First Amendment, and he ultimately concluded that there was a limit not so much on the substance of amendments restricting speech as on the procedures by which they may be adopted. Jeff Rosen, whose argument on this point is somewhat reminiscent of Selden Bacon's, focused more on the issue of natural rights and on the role of the Ninth Amendment and concluded that there is an important unstated limit on the amending power.

Isaacson began from the premise that constitutional amendments are a form of "law."[58] The language of the First Amendment, however, provides that Congress "shall make no law" limiting freedom of speech. Isaacson portrayed the language of the First Amendment as unique: "It is far more restrictive than any other limitation contained in the Bill of Rights. No other provision in the Bill of Rights operates by withdrawing from Congress the *power to make any law*. Thus, the first amendment is radically different from the rest of the Bill of Rights; its only analogue may be found in the absolute disabilities to act imposed by article V."[59] For Isaacson, the language of the First Amendment was designed specifically "*to disable the Congress*,"[60] language subsequently extended through the doctrine of incorporation to state legislation as well. As such, Isaacson suggested that alteration of the First Amendment by a flag-burning exception or any other could only be made by a method of amendment that bypassed Congress and the state legislatures, that is, by amendments proposed by the people in an Article V convention and subsequently ratified by special conventions within three-fourths of the states.[61]

---

[57] Another article, James McBride, "Is Nothing Sacred? Flag Desecration, the Constitution, and the Establishment of Religion," *St. John's Law Review* 65 (1991): 322, argues on the basis of arguments advanced by Emile Durkheim that "if the [flag-burning] amendment were passed, its imposition on the Bill of Rights would introduce irreconcilable tensions into the Constitution: freedom of religion would be encroached upon by the establishment of an American civil religion, identified with the nation-state." McBride does not, however, indicate precisely whether this would be unconstitutional.

[58] Eric A. Isaacson, "The Flag Burning Issue: A Legal Analysis and Comment," *Loyola of Los Angeles Law Review* 23 (1992): 591.

[59] Isaacson "The Flag Burning Issue," p. 593. I do not see how the language of the First Amendment is any more prohibitive than that of the language restricting Congress in Article I, section 9 of the Constitution or restricting the states in Article I, section 10. The second clause of Article I, section 9, for example, says, "No Bill of Attainder or ex post facto Laws shall be passed."

[60] Isaacson, "The Flag Burning Issue," p. 595.

[61] Ibid., p. 599.

However well motivated, Isaacson's arguments are inadequate. In the first place, whatever the words of the First Amendment appear to say, the Court has not as yet interpreted these words to have the blanket meaning that Isaacson has attributed to them. Especially at the state level, laws prohibiting obscenity, libel, false advertising, perjury, fighting words, and other forms of speech continue to be upheld by the courts. Even the most liberal advocates of free speech seem to have been convinced by Holmes's example of the illegality of falsely shouting fire in a crowded theater and causing a panic.[62] As commentators have noted, at least since incorporation, "the Supreme Court's interpretation of these guarantees has been both broader [applying, for example, to executive as well as legislative actions] and narrower than a literal reading of the amendment might suggest."[63] It would therefore be inconsistent to use Isaacson's approach only in the area of constitutional amendments.

One could, of course, argue that Justice Hugo Black and other absolutists, although never commanding a majority of the Court, were nonetheless correct and that the First Amendment provision for "no law"[64] means precisely "no law." If this position is accepted, however, Isaacson would have to show that "law" not only "may" be interpreted but should be interpreted so as to include constitutional amendments.[65] For reasons suggested when criticizing Murphy's arguments on this point, however, this is a dubious argument. Despite his analysis of the purposeful nature of the language of the First Amendment,[66] Isaacson presents no direct evidence that one of the intentions of those who pressed for or ratified the First Amendment was to limit the amending process (which was already far more difficult than the normal lawmaking procedures) as opposed to the ordinary law-making process.[67] Second, Isaacson offers no reason to suggest why, if freedom of speech was of such concern, it would be any less permissible for conventions to limit this right than for legislatures. Third, the language of Article V where the amending power is specified does not refer to amendments as laws but as amendments.

---

[62] See Schenck v. United States, 249 U.S. 47 (1919).

[63] Ralph A. Rossum and G. Alan Tarr, *American Constitutional Law* 3d. ed. (New York: St. Martin's Press, 1991), p. 343.

[64] See Hugo L. Black, *A Constitutional Faith* (New York: Alfred A. Knopf, 1969), pp. 43–63. Black's authority would not on this point help Isaacson, however, because Black did not believe that the First Amendment extended protection to symbolic speech. See his dissent in Tinker v. Des Moines School District, 393 U.S. 503 (1969).

[65] Isaacson, "The Flag Burning Issue," p. 591.

[66] Ibid., pp. 593–95.

[67] Indeed, one commentator has argued that the First Amendment was designed to expand the amending power. See Amar, "Philadelphia Revisited," pp. 1058–60.

Similarly, although the language is not necessarily conclusive, the wording of the supremacy clause in Article VI of the Constitution suggests that the Constitution (and presumably the amendments that have been added to it) should be distinguished from "the Laws of the United States which shall be made in Pursuance thereof." By the same token, the provisions of the Bill of Rights are called "amendments" or "articles" rather than "laws,"[68] and it would be quite awkward, and even inaccurate, to refer to them as the first ten "laws."[69]

Surely, if the framers of the First Amendment intended to limit amendments, as well as laws, or even in addition to them, they picked some circuitous language to fulfill their purpose. As the provisions of Article V reveal, Congress has no authority "to make" any amendment. It can, of course, override a presidential veto and thus "make" a law, as it were, on its own authority; it has, however, no authority to "make" an amendment absent consent on the part of three-fourths of the states. It would seem that if it was the purpose of the First Amendment specifically to limit Article V, it should either have directly said so or at least prohibited Congress *and* the states (as it now effectively does through the doctrine of incorporation, albeit not with any specific design that Isaacson or anyone else has shown to restrict the amending process) from passing such "laws" jointly. If Isaacson is correct, by his own analysis the First Amendment would be the only one of the first ten amendments to carry such a meaning, again suggesting that the First Amendment—which was originally designated as the Third rather than First[70]— may have a more extraordinary place in American history than

[68] In proposing the Bill of Rights to the states, the first Congress used the following terminology: "*Resolved, by the Senate and House of Representatives of the United States of America, in Congress assembled*, two thirds of both houses concurring, that the following articles be proposed to the legislatures of the several states, as amendments to the Constitution of the United States, all or any of which articles, when ratified by three fourths of the said legislatures, to be valid, to all intents and purposes, as part of the said Constitution, namely—"

This language is followed by another statement, often still recorded in prefaces to the Bill of Rights, which refers to "Articles in Addition to, and Amendment of, the Constitution of the United States of America, proposed by Congress, and ratified by the Legislatures of the several States, pursuant to the Fifth Article of the original Constitution." See Philip B. Kurland and Ralph Lerner, eds., *The Founders' Constitution* (Chicago: University of Chicago Press, 1987), 5:40.

[69] When other amendments in the Constitution refer to themselves, they use the terminology of "article," "amendment," "article of amendment," or "article . . . as an amendment." See U.S. Constitution, amendments 13, 14, 15, 17, 18, 19, 20, 21, 22, 23, 24, and 26. Amendments such as the Thirteenth, Fourteenth, and Fifteenth, which have specific enforcement clauses, clearly appear to distinguish the articles of amendment from other "legislation" adopted under their authority.

[70] Akhil R. Amar, "The Bill of Rights as a Constitution," *Yale Law Journal* 100 (1991):

we have as yet come to realize. To this writer, at least, Isaacson's arguments are not convincing.

Finally, the language of Article V does not appear to designate one type of ratification for one class of amendments and a second type of ratification for others, as Isaacson seeks to do. To the contrary, this language clearly leaves the decision to Congress, specifying that amendments become valid "when ratified by the Legislatures of three fourths of the several States, or by Conventions in three fourths thereof, as the one or the other Mode of Ratification may be proposed by the Congress."

The arguments of Jeffrey Rosen against the constitutionality of the proposed flag-burning amendment are even more revolutionary than Isaacson's and would overturn many existing understandings of the workings of Article V and the amending process. Like Isaacson, Rosen ultimately concludes not that amendments restricting freedom of speech are impossible but rather that they can only be adopted by a special process and employing specific language. He bases his arguments, however, not simply on the First Amendment but on his understanding of Article V and the more elusive Ninth Amendment.

Rosen argues that the right of speech was one of the unalienable natural rights retained by the people and therefore subject, through the Ninth Amendment, to judicial protection even against the amending process. The primary obstacle to using the Ninth Amendment has been, of course, the problem of defining what particular rights it was designed to secure.[71] For Rosen, such rights can be identified by reading sources at the time of the American Founding, particularly state constitutions. Although Rosen acknowledges some difficulty in deciding which such rights were alienable—that is, which could be exchanged for some kind of societal guarantees—and which were inalienable, he included "rights of religious conscience and the right of revolution" in addition to freedom of speech in the latter category.[72] Rosen also believes that each generation has the right to add or subtract from the list of what they

---

1137–43. I raise this point to indicate that, originally the First Amendment had no special physical placement within the Bill of Rights that might have indicated that its function was significantly different from other provisions in the Bill of Rights.

[71] "The enumeration in the Constitution of certain rights shall not be construed to deny or disparage others retained by the people." U.S. Constitution, Amendment 9. See Randy Barnette, ed., *The Rights Retained by the People: The History and Meaning of the Ninth Amendment* (Fairfax, Va.: George Mason University Press, 1989). See also John H. Ely, *Democracy and Distrust: A Theory of Judicial Review* (Cambridge, Mass.: Harvard University Press, 1980), pp. 34–40.

[72] Rosen, "Was the Flag Burning Amendment Unconstitutional?" p. 1079.

consider to be natural rights, and he suggests that state constitutions are once again the place to turn for such determinations.[73]

Almost by definition, natural rights that are inalienable may not be surrendered by the people. If the people cannot surrender them, then neither can their agents, that is, their political representatives.[74] One might well agree that this would give the people the moral right to disobey unjust laws that sought to deprive them of their natural rights. Rosen, however, goes much further, arguing that such rights are "judicially enforceable" under the Ninth Amendment,[75] and that to withhold judicial protection from such rights would be to "deny or disparage" the very rights the Ninth Amendment were designed to protect.[76] Acknowledging special problems in protecting natural rights against constitutional amendments, Rosen nonetheless argues that the Court has a special responsibility to do so. Interestingly enough, though, the Court's decision would not truly be final, but, instead, would serve

> in effect [to] "remand" the amendment back to the people or to their Article V delegates and ask them if they really believe the right to be natural and retained.
>
> If the proposers and ratifiers, on remand, *are* determined to overrule the Supreme Court, they may not merely express their legislative *will* (we believe Congress should have the power to regulate flag burning); they must also provide a clear statement of their judicial *reason* (because we no longer believe the right of speech to be natural). In this way, judicial review of the substance of an amendment does not thwart popular sovereignty, but merely ensures that it is deliberately exercised as the Founders intended—within the boundaries of natural law, as defined by the people themselves.[77]

Rosen concludes that, to be accepted by the Supreme Court, an amendment would have to say "something like" the following: "Freedom of speech shall not be construed as a natural right retained by the people and protected by the First and Ninth Amendments."[78] Otherwise, by voiding amendments that fall short of expressing such sentiments, the Court "would defer to, rather than thwart, the sovereignty of the people."[79]

Again, good intentions do not a sound argument make. To begin with a minor point, Rosen seeks to ascertain the content of natural

---

[73] Ibid., p. 1082.   [74] Ibid., p. 1086.   [75] Ibid.

[76] Ibid., p. 1087. Rosen is obviously "tracking" the language of the Ninth Amendment.

[77] Ibid., p. 1088–89.

[78] Ibid., p. 1092. By Rosen's analysis, it would appear that his model amendment should also include reference to the Fourteenth Amendment.

[79] Ibid.

rights by looking at statements of the Founders and provisions in contemporary state constitutions, but it is far from clear that either supports his view that freedom of speech (particularly the kind of symbolic speech represented by flag burning) was and is recognized as such a natural right. While Rosen has a fairly convincing quotation indicating that Madison accepted free speech—albeit not necessarily symbolic speech—as a natural right, his quotation from Roger Sherman refers specifically to "writing and publishing" within restraints of "decency and freedom."[80] Moreover, Rosen appears to identify only two contemporary state constitutions—Kentucky's and Utah's—that specifically identify speech as such a right,[81] far indeed from a majority. If the courts were permitted to identify a right as natural on the basis of statements in two or more constitutions, many of which are quite prolix, it is doubtful that there would be any effective limit on its authority to overturn both laws and amendments.

There is, in Rosen's analysis, a more significant problem that has generally plagued those who have attempted to enforce the Ninth Amendment, namely, how to make a positive, judicially enforceable obligation from language that appears, like the language in that of the Tenth Amendment, which follows it, to be a simple declaration. The Bill of Rights, it will be recalled, was adopted when fears were expressed by anti-Federalists that the national government might exercise powers over speech, press, and other important rights whose protection was not specifically enumerated in the Constitution. In originally arguing against the adoption of such amendments, leading Federalists argued that a bill of rights might not only be unnecessary but could also be dangerous.[82] What if, in listing rights, the Constitution did not include a person's right to refrain from tipping a hat to a governmental official? Would such an omission indicate that governors could therefore adopt such an absurd requirement?[83] The most obvious reason to suggest that the Ninth Amendment was included in the Bill of Rights was to answer this question in the negative. The people need not worry that just because they forgot to list a right, the government therefore had the power to take it away.

Rosen seeks, however, to do more. While the Ninth Amendment is worded so as to protect rights that are *not enumerated* in the Constitu-

---

[80] Ibid., p. 1073, n. 5.   [81] Ibid., p. 1074, n. 6.

[82] Herbert Storing, *What the Anti-Federalists Were For* (Chicago: University of Chicago Press, 1981), p. 67.

[83] For indications that these were the kinds of concerns influencing those who introduced the Ninth Amendment, however, see Barnette, *The Rights Retained by the People*. I have treated the Ninth Amendment in *A Companion to the United States Constitution and Its Amendments* (Westport, Conn.: Praeger, 1993), chap. 9.

tion, Rosen attempts to interpret it to protect the right of free speech, which clearly *is so enumerated* against the possibility that such protection could be withdrawn or limited. This not only fills in the meaning of an already elusive amendment but seems to do so in direct contradiction to what the amendment says. Incidentally, if Rosen's interpretation is accurate, it would also oblige the Supreme Court to recognize and presumably enforce other unalienable natural rights, including the right of revolution—which is clearly not a legally enforceable conventional right.[84]

Another way to see the flaw in Rosen's scheme is to ask what would have happened had the Supreme Court decided differently in *Texas v. Johnson* and *U.S. v. Eichman*. The possibility that the Court could easily have done so (and, indeed, could still do so) is heightened by the 5–4 votes in these decisions and by the vigorous language used by the dissenting justices.[85] In short, a change in a single vote of a single justice would have altered the outcome. In such a case, the presumed natural right to burn the American flag would have had no national constitutional protection, and, indeed, absent a change of mind on the part of the Court itself, an amendment would have been required to afford such protection. In such a plausible case, the putative purpose of the Ninth Amendment, as envisioned by Rosen, would have been defeated, and that would have been the end of the matter.

Rosen argues, however, that, once five or more justices of the Supreme Court decided that flag burning was a right protected by the First Amendment, even an amendment could not overturn this decision, short of language specifically indicating an intent to restrict the scope of the First and Ninth Amendments. Rosen justified this stance not as a way of thwarting popular will, but as a way of giving it, as it were, a second chance. What Rosen seemingly forgot in formulating this scheme, however, is that this would not be a second chance but a third—one in which the people might well conclude that the idea of popular sovereignty had struck out.[86]

---

[84] Abraham Lincoln thus noted that "the right of revolution, is never a legal right. . . . At most, it is but a moral right, when exercised for a morally justifiable cause. When exercised without such a cause revolution is no right, but simply a wicked exercise of physical power." Quoted by James M. McPherson, *Abraham Lincoln and the Second American Revolution* (New York: Oxford University Press, 1990), p. 28. The analysis in Luther v. Borden, 7 Howard 1 (1849), suggests some of the difficulties with the view that the right of revolution may be enforced by the courts. For further analysis, see John R. Vile, "John C. Calhoun on the Guarantee Clause," *South Carolina Law Review* 40 (1989): 669.

[85] Goldstein, "The Great 1989–1990 Flag Flap," p. 98, notes, however, that dissenting opinions were more moderate in the second opinion.

[86] It is worth noting that, were a flag-burning amendment to be adopted, it would be after two clear Supreme Court decisions on the subject, making the notion of a "second chance" especially problematic.

Under existing state and national constitutions and perhaps by the principle of the Ninth Amendment itself, no act is illegal unless and until there is a law against it.[87] Thus, the people, through their representatives, make a decision about the status of certain activities when they first pass laws prohibiting them. Because of the separation of powers in both the national and state governments and the presence of bicameral legislatures at the national level and in all but one state, there is indeed a strong inertia against the passage of most legislation. In most state legislatures, there are a variety of structural and constitutional hurdles to the passage of legislation as well as the threat of executive veto.[88] There are similar and perhaps even greater obstacles to the passage of legislation in Congress.[89]

Once legislation has emerged from the state legislatures or from Congress, however, the matter of constitutionality is hardly over. Because of the acceptance of judicial review in America, such legislation may then, if it is challenged before the courts in a given case or controversy,[90] still be declared unconstitutional, as were the statutes at issue in the two flag-burning cases. This is the mechanism that already provides for the "second look" that Rosen thinks is so important.

Faced with judicial invalidation of a law, the people have three options—disobedience, acquiescence, or adoption of a constitutional amendment. This latter process is so difficult that only four decisions of the U.S. Supreme Court have been overturned in all American history.[91]

---

[87] I have not seen the Ninth Amendment explained in this fashion, but I believe this is a plausible interpretation. This would arguably make the Ninth Amendment somewhat redundant with the due process clauses of the Fifth and Fourteenth Amendments, but not significantly more so than a number of other possible interpretations.

[88] Charles Press and Kenneth VerBurg, *State and Community Governments in a Dynamic Federal System*, 3d ed. (New York: Harper Collins Publishers, 1991), pp. 266–68.

[89] A persistent criticism that has been made of American government, particularly by those who would prefer a different constitution, is that it fails to provide the same vigor and accountability as rival parliamentary models. For an examination of these and other such criticisms, see John R. Vile, *Rewriting the United States Constitution: An Examination of Proposals From Reconstruction to the Present* (New York: Praeger, 1991). For a particularly vivid description of some of the obstacles to effective and representative lawmaking in Congress, see Amar, "Philadelphia Revisited," pp. 1080–85. See also Donald Lutz's contribution to this volume, which emphasizes the extraordinary difficulty of amending the U.S. Constitution.

[90] For questions about the usefulness of this maxim of judicial restraint, see Martin H. Redish, *The Federal Courts in the Political Order: Judicial Jurisdiction and American Political Theory* (Durham, N.C.: Carolina Academic Press, 1991), pp. 87–109.

[91] The Eleventh Amendment reversed the Court's opinion in Chisholm v. Georgia, 2 U.S. 419 (1793); the Fourteenth Amendment overturned Dred Scott v. Sandford, 60 U.S. 393 (1857); the Sixteenth Amendment overturned Pollock v. Farmers' Loan & Trust Company, 158 U.S. 601 (1895); and the Twenty-sixth Amendment modified the result that would have otherwise prevailed in Oregon v. Mitchell, 400 U.S. 112 (1970).

In more than two hundred years of such history, only thirty-three amendments have been proposed by the necessary congressional majorities,[92] and, of these, only twenty-seven have subsequently been ratified by the necessary three-fourths of the states. Under Rosen's scheme, however, an amendment that attempted to limit flag desecration or alter inalienable rights should be struck down by the Court unless it says it is specifically aimed at modifying the First and Ninth Amendments, in which case it would have to go once again through the awesome amending hurdles before being valid. Not surprisingly, Rosen finds no evidence for this view in the language of Article V.

Indeed, it would be difficult to think of a parallel understanding of the amending process that has been expressed in American history without going back to the view of John C. Calhoun, whose views were outlined briefly above. By Rosen's analysis, if a majority of justices on the Supreme Court thought that there was a natural right to own slaves (and Southern defenses of slavery as a positive good for both master and slave, as well as recognitions in previous state constitutions of the rights of slaveowners, do not make this proposition appear as ludicrous as it might first appear),[93] then the Fourteenth Amendment would not have been sufficient but would have required a specific follow-up to amend the Ninth Amendment.

This illustration may further point to the whole problem with interpretations that attempt to read implicit limits into Article V. To guard against fairly unlikely scenarios, the proponents of such limits have urged the Court, as Calhoun once urged the states, effectively to usurp the sovereignty of the people as it is expressed in the amending process.[94]

It can surely be argued that the people are not always right and that popular sovereignty is no absolute guarantee of justice,[95] but the invitation to increased judicial activism ignores the already fine balance that has been worked out among the three branches of government to preserve liberty and justice. Today, charges that the judiciary is a countermajoritarian institution[96] can be cogently met by the argument that, in exercising judicial review, the Court is merely enforcing the people's will

[92] For texts of those amendments that were not ratified, see George Anastaplo, *The Constitution of 1787* (Baltimore: Johns Hopkins University Press, 1989), pp. 298–99.

[93] See, for example, Harvey Wish, ed., *Ante-Bellum: Writings of George Fitzhugh and Hinton Rowan Helper on Slavery* (New York: Capricorn Books, 1960).

[94] For identification of the amending process with popular sovereignty, see Lester Orfield, *The Amending of the Federal Constitution* (Ann Arbor: University of Michigan Press, 1942), and Max Radin, "The Intermittent Sovereign," *Yale Law Journal* 39 (1930): 514.

[95] Murphy, "Consent and Constitutional Change." See also Lawrence G. Sager, "The Incorrigible Constitution," *New York University Law Review* 65 (1990): 893.

[96] Bickel, *The Least Dangerous Branch*, p. 16.

as this will is expressed in the Constitution.[97] This claim is strained the further judges stray from the constitutional text[98] (so-called noninterpretative review).[99] Whatever difficulties judges may now face invalidating laws in the absence of clear constitutional language would be geometrically compounded if courts sought to invalidate validly ratified parts of the Constitution itself. A court seeking to invalidate an amendment adopted through Article V procedures would risk a serious backlash that might cripple all its authority. Perhaps more important, there is the distinct possibility that the courts would use their power to undermine core constitutional values. It is also possible that talk of judicially invalidated amendments will encourage a certain recklessness and lack of concern among amendment advocates, allowing them to take the same position regarding amendments that some now take in regard to laws— that is, deferring questions of wisdom and constitutionality to the courts.

If it is thus recognized that courts do not currently have the power to invalidate validly ratified amendments, it seems appropriate to consider possible remedies. As a guard against worst-case scenarios, one might propose that no amendment could be ratified by the states until first approved by two or three successive Congresses, or until states conducted hearings on the subject of ratification.[100] This, or some similar measure, would expose new amendments to increased publicity and reflection before they could be incorporated into the Constitution. Such worst-case scenarios seem far too unlikely, however, to justify such a change in an already difficult amending process.[101]

[97] In justifying judicial review, Alexander Hamilton argued that such review did not assume the superiority of the judicial branch but rather "it only supposes that the power of the people is superior to both, and that where the will of the legislature, declared in its statutes, stands in opposition to that of the people, declared in the Constitution, the judges ought to be governed by the latter rather than the former. They ought to regulate their decisions by the fundamental laws rather than by those which are not fundamental." Alexander Hamilton, James Madison, and John Jay, *The Federalist Papers*, ed. Clinton Rossiter (New York: New American Library, 1961), p. 468.

[98] As Justice White argued in Bowers v. Hardwick, 478 U.S. 186 (1986), "The Court is most vulnerable and comes nearest to illegitimacy when it deals with judge-made constitutional law having little or no cognizable roots in the language or design of the Constitution." Robert Bork approvingly quotes this comment in *The Tempting of America* (New York: Free Press, 1990), p. 119.

[99] See Eulis Simien, "It Is a Constitution We Are Expounding," *Hastings Constitutional Law Quarterly* 18 (1990): 67.

[100] Alternatively, Clement Vose has proposed that Congress conduct a three-day conference after proposing amendments to consist of delegates from the fifty states who would learn of arguments for and against the proposal. See *Constitutional Change: Amendment Politics and Supreme Court Litigation Since 1900* (Lexington, Mass.: D. C. Heath, 1972), p. 371.

[101] Writing about the electoral college, Saul Brenner argues that "the Constitution

Ultimately, then, the arguments surrounding implicit limits on Article V do not so much point to the need for future constitutional reform as they illuminate the nature and wisdom of the existing constitutional document. The Constitution—and, more specifically, the amending clause—wisely protects liberty by guarding against the transient whims of the majority, while placing its ultimate faith in the consent of the governed. To date, at least, this faith does not appear to have been misplaced.

---

should not be amended to guard against remote possibilities." Brenner, "Should the Electoral College Be Replaced by the Direct Election of the President?" *PS* 17 (Spring 1984): 247.

Ten

The "Original" Thirteenth Amendment and the Limits to Formal Constitutional Change

MARK E. BRANDON

EVEN apart from its resemblance to esoteric debates in medieval Christian theology, the notion that a constitutional amendment (even more, a constitutional provision)[1] might be unconstitutional seems almost absurd.[2] On the one hand, the very idea that an amendment, proposed and ratified according to procedures set out in what appear to be the plain words of the Constitution, could be unconstitutional seems somehow incoherent, incompatible with what we sometimes take to be our "common sense" (or with widely shared positivist preconceptions) about how constitutions work.[3] John Marshall may have put this sense best in *Marbury v. Madison*, where he held, "It cannot be presumed that any clause in the constitution is intended to be without effect."[4]

On the other hand, a constitution without authoritative limits to the power to amend, including the power to amend its explicit provisions concerning the power to amend, carries within it the possibility of its own negation. That is, a constitution, which is to some extent a device for *preserving* certain states of affairs, might become a device for *undermining* the very states of affairs it is designed in part to preserve.

Special thanks to Walter Murphy, Donald Kommers, and Judith Failer for comments on earlier drafts of this essay.

[1] Walter F. Murphy, drawing on a decision of the Federal Constitutional Court of West Germany, explores the possibility of an unconstitutional provision of an original (unamended) constitution in Murphy, "An Ordering of Constitutional Values," *Southern California Law Review* 53 (1980): 703, 755; Murphy, "*Slaughter-House, Civil Rights*, and Limits on Constitutional Change," *American Journal of Jurisprudence* 32 (1987): 1.

[2] William F. Harris II calls the notion "either a riddle, a paradox, or an incoherency." *The Interpretable Constitution* (Baltimore: Johns Hopkins University Press, 1992), p. 169.

[3] That is not to mention the possibility that the articulation and application of standards for limits to the amendability of a constitution might amount to an arrogation of institutional authority that potentially runs counter to processes of democratic decision making. For two accounts of democratic theory that address this problem, if it is a problem, see William Rehnquist, "The Notion of a Living Constitution," *Texas Law Review* 54 (1976): 693; and John Hart Ely, *Democracy and Distrust: A Theory of Judicial Review* (Cambridge: Harvard University Press, 1980).

[4] Marbury v. Madison, 5 U.S. (1 Cranch) 137, 174 (1803).

Each notion may lead to a kind of interpretive incoherence as well. Either Article V does not mean what it seems on its face to mean—that an amendment "shall be valid" when proposed and ratified according to its (Article V's) terms—or it is an alternative (super)constitution unto itself and can, without harm to itself, swallow up the rest of the Constitution on which it seems to depend for its existence. Assuming, as I do, that coherence is a fundamental goal of constitutional interpretation, the question is how to render coherent what appears patently incoherent. Less abstractly, what is a political society free to accomplish by amendment to its constitutive document(s)? Or, to be more textually attentive, what is the relationship between Article V and the rest of the Constitution? Is Article V an integral part of the larger (whole) document or is the rest of the Constitution simply riding piggyback (perhaps temporarily) on Article V?

I explore those and other questions by examining an amendment that the U.S. Congress proposed and two (perhaps three) states ratified on the eve of the Civil War. The Corwin Amendment, which I refer to in the title to this chapter as the "Original" Thirteenth Amendment, was designed to protect slavery, perhaps perpetually. That amendment presents in historical guise an opportunity to investigate whether a written constitution can successfully fix substantive limits to formal constitutional change. Are there indeed limits to the amending power? If so, what are they and where do they come from?[5] Had the Corwin Amendment been ratified, would it have been unconstitutional? (The fact that the amendment concerns what people now consider to be the easy moral question of whether slavery is a permissible practice actually permits us also to consider the relationship between constitutions and morality.)

Secession Winter and the Corwin Amendment

In the chill of the winter of 1860–61, as the second session of the Thirty-sixth Congress of the United States convened and Abraham Lincoln was preparing for his inauguration, secessionist sentiment in the Deep South was beginning to reach a fever pitch. For many Southerners, the election of a "Black Republican" as president made John C. Calhoun appear a prophet. They worried that, through patterns of immi-

---

[5] This essay does not deal directly with two other questions related to the issue. First, what are the nature and source(s) of limits, if any, to the amendability of those textual provisions (in the American Constitution, Article V and perhaps other provisions) that purport to regulate the adoption of amendments? Second, who may constitutionally decide questions about the appropriateness of amendments to a constitution (or the Constitution)?

gration and settlement, the resolution of disputes over the allocation of territories as "slave" or "free," and the imperial character of Northern capital, the North had gradually gained virtual control of the national political apparatus.[6] And Southerners consequently worried that not only were the stability and permanence of their society and institutions threatened, but also that the very character of constitutional government had been transformed into "a great national consolidated democracy" in which the national government could "claim, and practically maintain, the right to decide in the last resort, . . . the extent of its powers."[7] The fear, in sum, was that constitutional limitations had broken down. Some Southerners, wanting "the Union as it was," which was presumably to say a creature of a compact among sovereign states,[8] argued that the North had breached the compact by electing Lincoln.[9]

Although one might well argue that these Southerners misunderstood both the extent of differences between the two regions and the actual likely consequences of Lincoln's election, their fears were certainly not constructed out of whole cloth. In substance, the nation's future lay westward in the territories. Under virtually all of the plans for designating territories as slave or free,[10] the potential size of slave territories was always much smaller than that of territories in which capitalism and wage labor were to be practiced to the exclusion of slavery.[11] It was reasonable to expect that such an arrangement both would reinforce the North's advantage in population and would eventually translate into the admission of a greater number of free states than slave states. Consequently, Northern interests could gain effective control of both houses of Congress. Lincoln's election had demonstrated that they could gain control of the presidency. And although the Supreme Court was then populated with a majority of five Southerners and at least one "Copperhead" (a Northerner sympathetic to Southern interests), Northern con-

---

[6] An early articulation of this fear is present in John C. Calhoun's "Address in the Senate of the United States, on the Subject of Slavery" (March 4, 1850) (Princeton Microfiche Collection), pp. 2–4, 8.

[7] Ibid.

[8] Again, Calhoun was the most consistent and intelligent proponent of such a notion of state sovereignty. See, e.g., ibid., pp. 7, 9; and Calhoun, "Speech on the Importance of Domestic Slavery" (January 10, 1838), in Eric McKitrick, ed., *Slavery Defended: Views of the Old South* (1963), pp. 16–17.

[9] James M. McPherson, *Battle Cry of Freedom: The Civil War Era* (New York: Oxford University Press, 1988), p. 239.

[10] Note, for example, the Northwest Ordinance of 1787, the Missouri Compromise of 1820, and even Stephen Douglas's popular sovereignty, which found expression in the Kansas-Nebraska Act of 1854.

[11] This is especially true given the admission of California in 1850 and Oregon in 1859 as free states. And it was probably true despite the Supreme Court's pronouncement in Dred Scott v. Sandford, 60 U.S. (19 How.) 393 (1857).

trol of the Congress and the presidency might eventually translate into a new antislavery majority on the Court. Thus, even without new interpretations of the existing Constitution that slavery was unconstitutional,[12] a constitutional amendment prohibiting slavery in all the states was possible unless there was an enforceable substantive limitation on the nature of amendments.

Southern insecurity to one side, when Southerners began, as others had in previous years, to speak of and eventually threaten secession, many Northerners, too, miscalculated. They underestimated the intensity, popularity, and sincerity of secessionist sentiment in the South.[13] Even after South Carolina seceded on December 20, 1860, followed in rapid succession by Mississippi, Florida, Alabama, Georgia, Louisiana, and Texas during the first month of 1861, some in the North argued that the states of the Deep South were bluffing and that some sort of concession would keep them in the Union and prevent states of the Upper South from seceding.[14] On December 18, 1860, the Senate directed its Special Committee of Thirteen to investigate and report on the "agitated and distracted condition of the country, and the grievances between the slaveholding and non-slaveholding States." Although the Committee was "not . . . able to agree upon any general plan of adjustment,"[15] the House's Select Committee of Thirty-three, investigating the country's "perilous condition," recommended the adoption of certain measures to mitigate the danger of overt hostility and to preserve, or reestablish, union.

One of those measures was a proposal to amend the Constitution.[16] On March 2, 1861, absent the senators and members of Congress from the seven states of the Deep South that had seceded, an overwhelmingly Northern Congress approved a substitute resolution proposing the adoption of what would become known as the Corwin Amendment:

> *Resolved by the Senate and House of Representatives of the United States of America in Congress assembled*, That the following article be proposed to the

---

[12] Interpretations such as those of Lysander Spooner and eventually of Frederick Douglass.

[13] McPherson, *Battle Cry of Freedom*, pp. 229–31.

[14] Ibid., pp. 235, 255–57.

[15] "Report of the Committee of Thirteen" (December 31, 1860), Rep. No. 288, *Index to the Reports of the Committees of the Senate of the United States for the Second Session of the Thirty-Sixth Congress.*

[16] Ibid. As originally proposed, the amendment read as follows: "Article XII [*sic*]. No amendment of this Constitution having for its object any interference within the States with the relation between their citizens and those described in section second of the first article of the Constitution as 'all other persons,' shall originate with any State that does not recognize that relation within its own limits, or shall be valid without the assent of every one of the States composing the Union."

Legislatures of the several States as an amendment to the Constitution of the United States, which, when ratified by three-fourths of said Legislatures, shall be valid, to all intents and purposes, as part of the said Constitution, viz.:

"*Article Thirteen.*

No amendment shall be made to the Constitution which will authorize or give to Congress the power to abolish or interfere, within any State, with the domestic institutions thereof, including that of persons held to labor or service by the laws of said State."[17]

President Lincoln acknowledged the pending amendment in his First Inaugural Address and said he supported it.[18] Moreover, he chose personally to sign the resolution after Congress adopted it, the first time in our history that a president had so participated in the amendment process.[19] Three states ratified the amendment—"Ohio and Maryland through their legislatures, and Illinois through a constitutional convention"[20]—all of which would eventually find themselves on the Northern side in the Civil War. The outbreak of military conflict and the secession of four more states in the Upper South rendered moot the amendment's purpose of preserving Union by providing security to the South.

The Constitutionality of the Corwin Amendment

Suppose the Corwin Amendment had been ratified by the requisite number of states. Would it have been "constitutional"?[21] That question depends for a coherent answer on a theory of the limits to constitutional change, which in turn requires corresponding theories of interpretation, of constitutionalism, and of the American constitutional regime.

After all, the resolution of debates over the existence and extent of limits to constitutional change is not simply a function of figuring out

[17] *U.S. Statutes at Large*, vol. 12, 1859–1863, ed. G. Sawyer (1863), p. 251.

[18] Lincoln may have understood the amendment to protect slavery only where it then existed, but the amendment's plain words do not suggest such a limitation.

[19] *Journal of the House of Representatives of the United States: Being the Second Session of the Thirty-Sixth Congress*, p. 486. For an explanation of why the president's approval has been deemed, both before and after Lincoln, unnecessary, see H. Ames, *The Proposed Amendments to the Constitution of the United States During the First Century of its History* (New York: B. Franklin, 1970), pp. 196, 295–96; Hollingsworth v. Virginia, 3 U.S. (Dall.) 378 (1798).

[20] Ames, *Proposed Amendments*, p. 196.

[21] The Corwin Amendment poses the problem fairly starkly, because either that amendment is itself unconstitutional for violating some substantive account of what the Constitution means, or any subsequent amendment purporting to delegate to Congress authority over slavery is unconstitutional for violating the Corwin Amendment. Some choice is unavoidable.

what the plain and explicit words of the document that we take to be our constitution mean. Even if we were to agree that our actions are or ought to be governed by particular marks on specified pages of paper, the explicitness of the marks—combined with an assumption that we take them as signifiers both of particular meanings and, perhaps more important, of the authority and possibility of interpretation itself—typically does not provide answers, but merely poses questions.[22]

Consequently, current debates over constitutional limitations have necessarily wrestled with the constructive tensions (or irreconcilable differences) between or within more abstract categories such as parts and whole(s), procedure and substance, means and ends, and internal and external perspectives. They have also implicated arguments among positivists, natural lawyers, and others over the source(s) of political and constitutional authority (sovereignty) and over the nature and authority of law. The very structure of the debates, therefore, reflects the tension between a desire to adhere to the constitutional text and a recognition that in important ways texts are not neatly self-contained but require something "outside" themselves to give them meaning. While the former desire presupposes, at least in its strongest form, that language can tell us with some degree of certainty what to do, the latter recognition implies that constitutional categories are not determinate.[23] And as I have suggested, the debates also unavoidably rely on assumptions about the character of the Constitution or constitutionalism.

Those assumptions can come from a variety of sources, which in turn can locate their authority either in transcendental notions of morality or within the Constitution. I shall consider three types of sources that find currency among constitutional theorists. Two of those sources, natural law and platonic idealism, are largely "transcendental." One, popular sovereignty, is largely "immanent."[24] While these sources do not exhaust the range of possible sources, they do seem to mark limits that are both recognizable and oppositional.

---

[22] Hence, when Vile argues that the only limits on amendments to the Constitution are the procedural (and two substantive) limits expressed in Article V, he justifies his position in part by considering the consequences of the alternative position(s) for American constitutional government. Vile, "Limitations on the Constitutional Amending Process," *Constitutional Commentary* 2 (1985): 373. And when Taft offers a similar argument, he justifies it by exploring the theoretical implications of both the Tenth Amendment's recognition of "powers not delegated" and the nature of constitutional government. Taft, "Amendment of the Federal Constitution," *Virginia Law Review* 16 (1930): 647.

[23] Charles A. Black notes the significance of the generality and ambiguity of important provisions of the Constitution. See *Structure and Relationship in Constitutional Law* (Englewood Cliffs, N.J.: Prentice-Hall, 1969).

[24] The categories "immanence" and "transcendence" are borrowed from William F. Harris II, "Bonding Word and Polity: The Logic of American Constitutionalism," *Ameri-*

Transcendental Limits on Constitutional Possibility

Walter F. Murphy nods definitively in the direction of natural law, or more accurately its cousin, natural rights. On the issue of limits to the amending power, his theory is in important respects similar to Lysander Spooner's.[25] Murphy argues that one can "retroduce" from the Constitution, in fact from any legitimate constitution, a hierarchical ranking of constitutional values, rights, and duties. Although the structure of values in a constitutional regime is potentially complex, the foundational value, the principle that underlies the entire constitutional structure and that motivates the constitutional enterprise, is "human dignity." The hierarchy of values that grounds the constitutional text(s)—but that is itself grounded in the value of human dignity—informs the limits to "the possibility of legitimately amending the constitutional document so as to remove or materially restrict certain fundamental rights and severely cripple or even destroy the polity's structure of values."[26]

In Murphy's hands, therefore, retroduction functions both as an interpretive device and as a vehicle for confirming the basic principles of natural rights, which form the basis for the Constitution's normative theory. Hence, he can claim with some justification that his theory of natural rights is both immanent and transcendent. For him, the Constitution—including the Declaration of Independence, the Bill of Rights (especially the Ninth and Tenth Amendments), and the Preamble—becomes the positive embodiment of natural rights.[27]

In a later work, Murphy expands on his initial formulation. He argues that the plain words of Article V impose substantive limits on constitutional change, for they refer to "amendments" (that is, *modifications*), which are not equivalent to "creations of a new constitution." Conse-

---

can Political Science Review 76 (1982): 34. They refer, respectively, to the location of values within or outside the Constitution. For reasons discussed more fully below, the categories are simultaneously useful and illusory, which may in turn suggest that the very notion of the Constitution is problematic.

[25] Spooner argued that "the constitution of the United States must be made consistent throughout; and if any of its parts are irreconcilable with each other, those parts that are inconsistent with liberty, justice and right, must be thrown out for inconsistency." *The Unconstitutionality of Slavery* (1860; reprinted, New York: Burt Franklin), p. 94.

[26] Murphy, "An Ordering of Constitutional Values," pp. 703, 745, 754.

[27] Ibid., p. 757. For reasons that space will not permit me to explicate here, I suspect that Murphy's theory of natural rights is prior to the Constitution, both temporally and theoretically. Moreover, despite Murphy's ingenious interpretive claims, the theory has but a tenuous grounding in the Constitution of 1787 (or even of 1791). Consequently, I consider the theory to be transcendental.

quently, amendments must be either procedural in nature or aimed at clarifying the existing text. "Clarifications" are those substantive changes "necessary to make the Constitution intellectually coherent . . . [and to] increase the integrity of its underlying principles." Those principles are not embodied in federalism, for federalism is merely a means, albeit an important one. Principles have to do with ends, and where means and ends conflict, the former must yield to the latter. The principles of the American constitutional regime consist of three values that are closely associated, through the Declaration of Independence, with natural rights: justice, liberty, and equality.[28] To the extent that it perpetuates slavery, the Corwin Amendment modifies Murphy's retroduced values of liberty, justice, equality, and individual natural rights and hence renders the Constitution incoherent.

Despite my worry that the Declaration and the Constitution might be incompatible,[29] suppose we concede that slavery violates the principles of the Revolution and that those principles continued to hold after the constitutional founding. Do not the constitutional principles of the structure of sovereign authority, or more accurately the structure of the powers of the creatures of sovereign authority (which today we know as federalism), limit the reach of the principles of the Declaration? Murphy says no, because federalism does not rise to the level of a principle or an end. It is merely a means and is therefore always trumped by the more fundamental principles or ends of the Revolution.[30] Under Murphy's theory, individual rights always trump governmental authority. Because the Corwin Amendment is incompatible with fundamental principles of natural right, it dies.[31]

---

[28] Murphy, "*Slaughter-House*," pp. 12, 17–18. Murphy goes on to supply criteria for determining what is "in" the Constitution. Among other things, he is concerned with justifying our treating the Declaration of Independence as part of the Constitution (pp. 19–20). For reasons having to do with both the pedigree of the Declaration and its incompatibility with values readily traceable to the Constitution, I am inclined to dispute the inclusion of the Declaration in the Constitution.

[29] See n. 28, above.

[30] One might speculate whether slavery itself might have been a fundamental constitutional principle (apart from questions concerning the allocation of governmental authority). A number of Garrisonian abolitionists in the middle of the nineteenth century pressed such a claim. Although he does not speak explicitly to the issue, Murphy would probably reject the proposition that slavery could be a fundamental constitutional principle, or at least that it could be a legitimate one.

[31] Murphy offers a second criterion for determining whether an amendment to the Constitution might be unconstitutional: Does the amendment overturn certain compromises that made nationhood possible? "*Slaughter-House*," pp. 12, 17–18. It is easy to argue that slavery was such a compromise. Indeed, the U.S. Supreme Court indirectly confirmed this notion when it declared the fugitive slave clause of the Constitution "a fundamental article, without the adoption of which the Union could not have been formed." Prigg v. Pennsyl-

A second, explicitly transcendental, theory of limits to formal constitutional change is that of Sotirios Barber. It is based on an aspirational theory of the Constitution derived from the classical political theory of Plato and the moral theory of Kant. Like Murphy, Barber argues that, because "the word *amendment* ordinarily signifies incremental improvements or corrections of a larger whole,"[32] amendments must be compatible with "the Constitution's larger commitments—like democracy and the public and private attitudes conducive thereto, or human dignity, or freedom from ideological or religious impositions." Article V provides textual support for its own limited domain both by noting that amendments are valid only "as *Part* of this Constitution"[33] and by supplying explicit restrictions on permissible amendments.[34]

Barber also joins Murphy in exploiting a distinction between means and ends. Amendments are not always simply procedural in nature; moreover, procedural and substantive commitments are often difficult to distinguish. Procedural values are usually inextricably tied to substantive values,[35] and some procedural values are important enough that they "seem to be valued as ends in themselves" apart from the substantive values they might imply. Nevertheless, and perhaps inconsistently, "the means should be sacrificed to the end." "Claiming supremacy for a set of mere means would not only be irrational, it would also be unjust."[36]

Two notions seem to follow from these contentions. First, if "the

---

vania, 16 Peters 539 (1842). As I read Murphy's argument, however, the Corwin Amendment would not survive even if slavery had been fundamental to establishing nationhood. As I read him, natural right prevails in all circumstances, though Murphy has informed me that he disagrees with my interpretation of his theory.

[32] Sotirios Barber, *On What the Constitution Means* (Baltimore: Johns Hopkins University Press, 1984), p. 43.

[33] The language quoted is from Article V. The emphasis supplied is mine. Barber's argument here, as he would probably concede, demonstrates the weakness of relying exclusively on textual pegs to support one's position. His contention that this clause in Article V means that amendments must be part of (i.e., consistent with) the existing meaning of the whole document is plausible, but only in the context of corresponding theories of interpretation and the Constitution, which he later supplies. In the absence of such theories, an equally plausible interpretation of the same clause is that any amendment adopted by Article V's procedures is valid as part of the Constitution, regardless of its (the amendment's) content.

[34] Interestingly, Barber notes only one such provision of Article V: the "equal Suffrage" provision. He does not mention the provision that temporarily prohibits amendments restricting the importation of slaves or imposing some forms of direct taxation.

[35] Barber suggests that "substantive values," at least those worthy of being followed, are values that are compatible with our long-term "aspirations," as opposed to mere "immediate wants." Barber, *On What the Constitution Means*, p. 48.

[36] Ibid., pp. 43–46.

Constitution is a set of mere means," which Barber believes follows from viewing Article V as imposing only procedural limitations on the amending process, "we cannot hold it intrinsically worthy or deny the possibility of its failure." In order to hold the Constitution as worthy of being followed, therefore, we must "look upon [it] as a norm that combines the attributes of means and ends." And because it is a norm that *subordinates* means to ends, it also allows holding certain provisions of the Constitution "irrational and unjust" (and presumably, therefore, unconstitutional).[37]

Second, Barber contends that in trying to determine what the Constitution means, we must acknowledge that there is *a* (single) meaning embodied in the language of the Constitution. This meaning, he argues, is not a function of immediate wants, individual interests, or assertions of will. Nor is it simply a function of historical practices and attitudes, especially "in easy questions concerning power and in questions involving what . . . [Marshall] called 'the great principles of liberty.'" Instead, it is a function of constitutional aspiration, reason, justice, and tradition.[38] As long as we can affirm that "the ways of the Constitution constitute our best current conception of the good society—our best understanding for now" and that the Constitution continues to "serve[] the ends for which it was established," then that conception of the good society and those ends serve as substantive limitations on the amending process. Because we are not perfect, because we are willful and have wants and interests incompatible with reason, justice, and our true aspirations, the Constitution, through "relatively noncontroversial rules [and] a more or less stable structure of [governmental] offices" and through limitations on constitutional change, tries "to fortify the best in us . . . [by] restrain[ing] the worst in us."[39]

Sotirios Barber, as a constitutional theorist sitting in the twentieth century, would have little trouble arguing that slavery violates his account of the Constitution's "larger commitments," his vision of what we ought to be doing and of what is best in us as a people, and his best conception of the good society. The question, however, is how he would treat the Corwin Amendment were he sitting in the middle of the nineteenth century. Although his is fundamentally a moral theory in im-

[37] Ibid., pp. 49, 53, 54.

[38] Barber understands "tradition" not as history or past practices, but as "a theory of what we stand for as a people." What we stand for is fundamentally a moral imperative, "what we ought to have been doing and should continue to do whether we have, in fact, done it or will do it." Tradition is "a normative theory of what has always been and therefore still is best in us as a people." Ibid., pp. 84, 85. Similarly, "reason" for Barber is a transcendental category. Reasons are not rationalizations. Hence, reason is not immanent in the "logic" of a discourse; nor is it justified by reference to prevailing myths (including religion). Instead, reason is aimed at "truth itself."

[39] Ibid., pp. 34, 48, 49, 51, 57, 79.

portant respects, it possesses a historical sensibility. He writes of "our best *current* conceptions of the good society,"[40] which implicitly acknowledges a kind of moral progress rooted in historical circumstance. First, the word *our* might mitigate the pull of the platonic ideal or a moral reality insofar as it suggests the importance of *collective* conceptions of the good. Second, the word *current* seems to imply that in a historical context, people's conceptions of the good can change through time.[41]

But even this conventionalist and historicist gloss on his theory might render the amendment unconstitutional by nineteenth-century standards. For example, Barber could point to Jefferson's position on slavery.[42] He might note that many, perhaps most, of the Founders, and maybe even most Americans in the late eighteenth century, thought that slavery would die out. He might argue that the fact that the word *slavery* never appears in either the Constitution or the Corwin Amendment provides a textual indication of moral shame about the institution. He might note that Lysander Spooner, Frederick Douglass, and others were employing constitutional theories in the nineteenth century that argued that slavery was unconstitutional. He might suggest that although the cotton gin made slavery profitable in the early nineteenth century, the shortsighted self-interest that secured slavery as a historical practice could not outweigh as a constitutional matter slavery's incompatibility with Marshall's "great principles of liberty" or "the nation's highest aspirations." Even if federalism were viewed as one of the Constitution's larger commitments—that is, as a procedural value so important that it is valued as an end in itself—he might argue that federalism is inferior as a constitutional value to liberty and human dignity. As one scholar has said, people are simply not willing to die for federalism. For Barber, the Corwin Amendment neither fortifies the best nor restrains the worst in us. It would be unconstitutional.

Immanent Limits on Constitutional Possibility

Of course, one need not resort to transcendental sources for substantive limits to formal constitutional change. One might well locate such sources or standards within the Constitution. Such an enterprise would

[40] Emphasis added.

[41] Barber would recoil at the notion that his constitutional theory is conventionalist or historicist.

[42] See, e.g., Thomas Jefferson, "Answers and Observations for Demeunier's Article on the United States in the *Encyclopedia Methodique*" (1786), and *Notes on the State of Virginia* (1787), in Merrill Peterson, ed., *Thomas Jefferson: Writings* (New York: Viking, 1984), pp. 592, 298.

remain theoretical, but its method is largely interpretive. As already indicated, Murphy, perhaps even Barber, flirts with an attempt to derive his substantive constitutional theory from a method of interpretation. Murphy's retroduction is an attempt to supply such a method, under which one interprets a constitution not simply by reading isolated clauses as if one were searching for a peg on which to hang a hat, but by interpreting individual clauses in light of the "inner unity" of the whole document. "As a unit, a constitution reflects certain overarching principles and fundamental decisions to which individual provisions are subordinate."[43]

The most detailed exploration of "immanent" limits to constitutional change comes from William F. Harris II,[44] who rejects many of the transcendental tendencies of Murphy's and Barber's theories. He rejects Murphy's assumption that the essence of constitutionalism is bound up in natural rights, liberal theories of government, or notions of modern liberty and Barber's version of reason as a transcendental category. He also rejects Barber's contention that constitutionalism is fundamentally a normative or moral enterprise (or at least that it is a normative enterprise whose standards derive principally from "outside" the constitutional order). And he partly rejects the notion that substantive moral principles, even those retroduced from the constitutional document itself, operate as constraints on the amending power. For Harris, the Constitution can and may turn itself inside out. Sometimes.

Harris's constitutionalism is firmly grounded in a vision of ancient liberty, in the liberty of a political society to govern itself. For constitutionalism is essentially the choice by a society to constitute itself politically by reference to a text. The crucial problem for Harris's constitutionalism is the problem of authority: From where does a putatively constitutive text derive its authority? Harris locates the authority of the Constitution, indeed of any constitutional government, in the myth that "the people" are sovereign, that the people as a body represent "the ultimate source of constitutional authority." That myth supplies the operative limits to change under Article V.[45]

The myth of popular sovereignty supplies such limits in two ways, one substantive and the other procedural. The substantive limit, deriving from the nature of Harris's constitutionalism, asks "to what extent does the amendment cede popular sovereignty or permanently withdraw rights from the people."[46] The procedural limit refers to Article V's

---

[43] Murphy, "An Ordering of Constitutional Values," p. 755, quoting from the Southwest Case, 1 BVerfGE 14 (1951).

[44] Harris, *The Interpretable Constitution.*

[45] Ibid., pp. 241, 250–51.

[46] Two points deserve mention here. First, the notion of permanence is important, for

procedures for adopting amendments and to one other possible procedure. Harris recognizes a hierarchy of procedures, each of whose authority is linked to the extent to which it is "approximate to the whole
population."[47]

The most minor "emendations" to the Constitution could be accomplished by the least stringent procedure. More fundamental alterations
of constitutional arrangements, such as those that "implicate sovereignty" (as opposed to one or more of "the sovereign's creations") or
that accomplish what amounts to "wholesale textual alteration," would
presumably require a more authoritative pedigree, a more stringent procedure. And "categorical substantive prohibitions," including provisions that purport to be unamendable, would be unconstitutional if
"accomplished through the Article V process." Such provisions would
"violate[] the status of the Constitution as a *whole design*" unless
adopted according to the most stringent procedure available.[48] The notion of a constitution as a whole design "lies behind the assumption that
the Constitution itself may not be self-contradictory." It would also
seem to prop up claims that Article V is an integral part of the larger
constitutional structure (as opposed to being a parallel, independent
constitution) and that amendments are part of (and therefore cannot
contradict) the meaning at the core—the hierarchy of procedures—of
the Constitution. Even Article V could be amended, but only if such
amendments "ratchet" Article V closer to Article VII's procedures.[49]

The first four procedures, of course, are permutations of the possibilities provided under Article V. The fifth procedure, which in the case of
the Constitution is equivalent to an amendment's being adopted by Article VII's procedures, derives from the nature of a constitution: It is
"amendable . . . on the same terms as those by which it was given au-

---

one grounding principle of Harris's constitutionalism is (ironically) that there shall be no
orthodoxy. Hence, an "entrenching" constitutional provision may, under certain circumstances, be unconstitutional. Second, the rights that Harris refers to are apparently not the
individual rights of modern liberty, but the (collective) rights necessary for self-government. Hence, the Ninth and Tenth Amendments, in which Murphy sees evidence of the
natural (individual) rights that provide the foundation for his own constitutionalism and
for much of liberal political theory, Harris sees as the textual embodiment of a "residual
constitution-making power." Ibid., p. 253.

[47] This hierarchy, from lowest to highest, is: (1) proposal by the Congress with ratification by state legislatures; (2) proposal by the Congress with ratification by state conventions; (3) proposal by a national convention with ratification by state legislatures; (4) proposal by a national convention with ratification by state conventions; and (5) proposal and
adoption by "the same . . . [procedures] by which . . . [the Constitution] was given authority in the first place." Ibid., pp. 229–30, 235–36, 250–55.

[48] This presumably refers to Article VII's procedures.

[49] Harris, *The Interpretable Constitution*, pp. 235–36, 242–49, 259–61.

thority." Consequently, even without an explicit textual procedure for amending the document, Harris's interpretable Constitution is also "essentially" the *amendable* Constitution. And although under current liberal theories of constitutionalism the procedural and substantive standards for establishing limits to constitutional change are in tension (even conflict) with one another, Harris's constitutionalism harmonizes substance (embodied in the notion of sovereignty) and procedure (embodied in the notion of pedigree).

For Harris, the question of the constitutionality of the Corwin Amendment is an easy one, but not because slavery is immoral, illiberal, or inconsistent with modern liberty, natural rights, human dignity, or any other substantive values implicit or explicit in the Constitution. Nor, presumably, is it unconstitutional because it "retro-ratchets" sovereignty in some form, since slaves were neither part of the sovereign nor members of the political community. Rather, it is unconstitutional because it purports to be unamendable, and the polity can adopt unamendable provisions only if it complies, at a minimum, with Article VII's procedures.

On Constitutional Coherence

Under all three of the theories considered in Section II, we get happy endings, at least from the standpoint of ethical sensibilities prevailing today.[50] The possibility of perpetual slavery is detoured, either by an ingenious rationalization of the notion of sovereignty under Harris or by the better angels of our nature under Murphy and Barber. But constitutionalism is not merely about happy endings. Even if we grant the assumptions both that it is possible to give sufficient analytical content to such categories as human dignity or the good life to make them useful as moral guideposts and that constitutional inquiry is bound tightly to moral considerations, it remains the case that such moral considerations do not capture entirely the nature of the constitutional enterprise. To act constitutionally is not always to do the right thing.

Constitutions and the application of constitutional standards are not efforts to mimic, in Lockean or platonic fashion, the perfection (or imperfections) of nature or the moral reality that exists outside the cave. Nor are they, after Hobbes, necessarily efforts to ward off insurgent chaos. Instead they represent attempts, through written texts of manifold forms, to answer affirmatively Hamilton's question about the Con-

---

[50] The notion of "happy endings" is borrowed from Sanford Levinson, *Constitutional Faith* (Princeton: Princeton University Press, 1988), p. 87.

stitution of the United States: Whether it is possible to "establish[ ] good government from reflection and choice," instead of through "accident and force."[51] At bottom, then, constitutionalism is concerned with the "constitution" of political societies by reference to written texts.[52] It is the attempt to render political life comprehensible and therefore controllable through the written word. It describes and justifies a practice by which a two-dimensional blueprint ostensibly becomes realized in a three-dimensional world. It provides the foundation for the distribution of political authority in society. It need not have as its purpose or as a principal goal either a liberal theory of rights or a moral theory of decision making. It requires only that the actors in a political society justify (and perhaps envision) their actions through the arguably authoritative categories that the constitution supplies.

A constitution is a law that people, perhaps only mythically, have given to themselves. They might give it to themselves in two ways: one, by adopting it in whole or in part, that is, through initial ratification or through ratification by amendment; two, by interpreting and applying it in the ongoing life of the political society.[53] In either case, one requisite standard for comprehensibility and hence for the legitimacy of the (or *a*) constitutional enterprise is coherence.

As a standard, coherence operates along two axes, one horizontal and one vertical. Horizontally, coherence has to do with the unity, wholeness, and sensibility—in short, the meanings—of the constitutive text(s) of a political society. Vertically, coherence concerns the political society's "ethos," those values or self-understandings that both inform the construction of constitutional meanings and serve, in light of the limited flexibility of language in a given time, culture, and circumstance, as criteria for judging the acceptability of those meanings. Horizontal coherence is principally a question of principle, informed in its construction by theory. Vertical coherence is largely a pragmatic concern that is primarily informed by experience, including established practices, extra-

[51] Hamilton, *The Federalist*, No. 1 (1787).

[52] This account of constitutionalism is controversial. Walter Murphy, for example, derides it as a form of "constitutionism" that overlooks Israel, New Zealand, and Great Britain as constitutionalist societies. He also criticizes it for failing to incorporate certain substantive transcendental standards, without which Nazism, Stalinism, and Maoism become constitutionally permissible. I concede that my version of constitutionalism might exclude certain political societies—including some that are liberal with limited governments—that might claim to be constitutional and might even be attractive. I do not concede that my version necessarily sanctions Hitler or Stalin or Mao, though constitutionalism does permit a multitude of sins.

[53] The distinction between these two categories is sometimes a blurry one, for ratification requires an element of interpretation, and interpretation amounts, in effect, to a kind of ratification.

constitutional notions of morality, and even biases and predilections.[54] The correspondence of the concerns represented by the two axes goes to the legitimacy of constitutional judgment. The closer that a constitution or a constitutional judgment comes to the intersection of the two axes, the more likely it will withstand questions about and challenges to its legitimacy.[55]

The justification for coherence takes two forms, corresponding to the axes along which it operates. First, and perhaps running along the vertical axis, coherence seems inextricably tied to the notion of comprehensibility. If we are to make a world through reflection and choice, then we must make it comprehensible. We must make it understandable. And if we are to make it comprehensible, then coherence is a valuable category. Second, and tending to run along the horizontal axis, I assume that coherence is linked to the notion of standards and hence to principle. It seems clear that a polity willing to forego coherence, to forego standards, stands ready to undercut the very legitimacy of government. It undermines institutional accountability. It breeds cynicism, even despair. In short, although government can exist and society will not crumble without standards, that government will cease to be "constitutional."

But a potential challenge to horizontal coherence arises from Hume's observation: "Speculative reasonings which cost so much pain to philosophers, are often formed by the world naturally, and without reflection: As difficulties, which seem insurmountable in theory are easily got over in practice."[56] In other words, the vertical axis often subverts the force of the horizontal. In our time, though, theory's most serious challenge may come partly from within itself. For we live in an age in which visions of state-ordered harmony seem frightening, in which social and technological change seems either out of control or resistant to the application

[54] I use the term *experience* in the broadest sense. And *ethos* here is also clearly an experiential notion, although it may be given content by what we tend to think of as matters of morality, even perhaps transcendental morality. I suspect that any moral sensibilities that make their way into the consciousness of (parts of) a society are largely, if not exclusively, functions of human experience rather than divine intercession or cosmic rationality. But in any event, in order for morality, transcendental or otherwise, to play an effective and legitimate role in the construction or evaluation of ostensibly authoritative constitutional meanings, it must first make itself either manifest or covertly effective throughout a significant portion of the population. Once it becomes so manifest or effective, regardless of its initial source, it appears ultimately to be conventional in application.

[55] At the "micro" level, this correspondence is exemplified by Frederick Douglass's decision to abandon an interpretation of the Constitution that was horizontally coherent but inconsistent (vertically) with his moral sensibilities in favor of a different interpretation that was also (but differently) horizontally coherent but also consistent (vertically) with his moral sensibilities.

[56] David Hume, *A Treatise of Human Nature* (1739) ed. L. A. Selby-Biggs and P. H. Nidditch, 2d ed. (Oxford: Clarendon Press, 1978), p. 572.

of available analytic or explanatory categories, in which many intellectuals have backed themselves into "totalizing" theories from which no exit
seems possible, in which intelligent belief in external standards for behavior or practice seem implausible, impractical, or defunct.

A comprehensive defense of theory is beyond the scope of this essay,
but a partial defense might rest on a rather simplistic and unsatisfy-
ing observation: Theory and experience need each other. Disconnected
from experience, theory becomes a useless, airy nothing. And experience
becomes simply incoherent, or at the very least meaningless, without
theoretical categories of some sort to make them sensible.[57] Hence,
though they may ultimately be quixotic, the following assumptions
seem sufficiently defensible that we are justified in holding onto them.
First, both experiential and pragmatic considerations do matter for constitutionalism. Second, some form of constitutional theory is still possible in the twentieth century. And third, we can continue to use theory
to draw meaningful boundaries with practical implications in an age that
sometimes deems itself free of such illusions.

That said, one of the problems of the theories attributed to Murphy
and Barber is that although they achieve a nice *horizontal* coherence,
they may not be adequately coherent *vertically*, at least for understanding the Constitution and politics of the United States in the nineteenth
century. They seem circumstantially disembodied, insufficiently sensitive to the role of vertical coherence as a regulator of constitutional
meanings and hence of constitutional limits.[58]

But maybe Murphy and Barber are right. Maybe there are some
amendments so at odds with the existing categories of the constitutional
text or with interpreters' *perceptions* of those categories or of themselves
as a political society that the amendments simply render the text incoherent on some level and therefore virtually useless (at least on some
matters) as a constituting document. And in such cases, either we throw
out the entire document or we keep the document and throw out one or
more of the portions that render it incoherent. Plainly, Murphy and Barber would have us throw out the Corwin Amendment as incompatible with the Constitution's substantive values. The problem is that the
Corwin Amendment does not seem to have rendered the Constitution
incoherent, at least not in 1861.

---

[57] Note Einstein's suggestion to Heisenberg that "whether you can observe a thing or
not depends on the theory which you use. It is the theory which decides what can be observed." Quoted in Michael Polanyi, "Genius in Science," *Encounter* 38 (1972): 48.

[58] The presence of that defect (if it is a defect) is understandable in light of the fact that
Murphy and Barber are trying to construct substantively *principled* ways of understanding
the Constitution *in our time*, but part of the aim of this essay is to illuminate the limits to
principle, or perhaps to suggest an alternative account of principle.

The first reason, which cuts against Harris's notion of popular sovereignty, has to do with the Constitution's allocation of political authority. In nineteenth-century America, popular sovereignty (at least in the nationalist sense in which we think of it today) was as empirically empty as was the popular founding of the new constitutional order in 1789. In fact, there was a substantial body of opinion in the nineteenth century holding that the national political order was a creature, not of the people-as-sovereign, but of preexisting sovereign states. At the very least, notwithstanding Marshall's attempts to assert national governmental primacy and a version of national popular sovereignty, the Constitution was generally held out to be a document under which states retained a large degree of discretion over their internal affairs and "domestic institutions."

The second reason has to do with the status of slavery under the Constitution. Although it was possible, as Frederick Douglass and others demonstrated, to generate a horizontally coherent abolitionist reading of the Constitution, it was simply implausible under most accepted accounts of the text at the time to read the Constitution in that way. First, slaves as noncitizens were not part of the sovereign, popular or otherwise, that ratified the Constitution, either in the founding act of 1788–89 or in the continuous acts of interpretation and amendment. Second, slaves were often held to be exempt from most accounts of "the great principles of liberty" of the Declaration of Independence. Third, to speak of the Constitution of the mid-nineteenth century (without the gloss of the Declaration of Independence) as embodying human dignity or the best aspirations and traditions of the American people or even (less ambitiously) liberalism, at least on the question of slavery, seems somewhat anomalous.

Undoubtedly, there were (and are) those who viewed the Declaration of Independence as establishing for the new nation a universalistic theory of the fundamentality of the principles of individual liberty, justice, and equality. Similarly, there were (and are) those who viewed the Constitution, especially the Constitution of 1791, when the Bill of Rights was adopted, as the embodiment of that interpretation of the Declaration's principles and as necessarily implying the abolition of slavery.[59] It is equally plausible, however, as one scholar has suggested, that many Americans understood the Declaration of Independence as an articulation of principles of political self-determination and not of more radical

[59] See Don E. Fehrenbacher, *The Dred Scott Case: Its Significance in American Law and Politics* (New York: Oxford University Press, 1978), pp. 16–17. See also Winthrop Jordan, *White over Black: American Attitudes Toward the Negro, 1550–1812* (Chapel Hill: University of North Carolina Press, 1968).

and individualistic principles of modern liberty.[60] Moreover, slavery was an important part of the American system that was to be self-determined.[61] But even if we concede the libertarian and abolitionist potential of the Declaration, it is not clear that the Constitution fully (or even substantially) incorporated those principles. After the Revolution, as the new nation became threatened by economic stress and political fragmentation, the Constitution represented a tool as much for retrenchment, stabilization, and the consolidation of economic and political power as for the protection of individual liberties. If Locke was the spiritual progenitor of the Revolution, Hobbes could probably claim as convincingly to be the patriarch of American constitutional order.[62]

As Jefferson himself acknowledged, there was little dispute at the time of the founding that slavery was protected under the Constitution.[63] Whatever the state of the American mind at the time of the Founding, however, the American ethos began to change over time in more than one direction where slavery was concerned. Pulling in one direction was abolitionism, whose seeds were sown in the moral fervor of the evangelical movement, took root, and flowered in the form of secular abolitionist, manumission, and antislavery societies that retained much of the moral fervor but often little of the transcendental religious baggage of Protestant evangelicalism. Many in those movements agreed with William Lloyd Garrison that the Constitution was a "covenant with death, and an agreement with hell."[64] Others, not wishing to make such a radical break with the existing constitutional order, devised and employed clever interpretive strategies to argue the unconstitutionality of slavery

[60] Ely, *Democracy and Distrust*, pp. 77–101.

[61] David Brion-Davis, *The Problem of Slavery in the Age of Revolution: 1770–1823*, (Ithaca: Cornell University Press, 1975), p. 256.

[62] These claims are intentionally contentious and admittedly underdeveloped. The idea that the Constitution was a repudiation of the Revolution can be traced to several sources. Charles A. Beard was a proponent of the notion. See Beard, *An Economic Interpretation of the Constitution of the United States* (New York: Macmillan, 1913), pp. 19–51. Although Beard has accumulated a boatload of detractors, Gordon S. Wood seems to affirm that aspect of Beard's thesis, even if he rejects Beard's radical materialism. Wood, *The Creation of the American Republic, 1776–1787* (Chapel Hill: University of North Carolina Press, 1969). Even Forrest McDonald, who sets himself up as a critic of Beard, concedes the influence of material interest, economic consolidation, and fiscal stabilization in the constitutional founding. McDonald, *We the People: The Economic Origins of the Constitution* (Chicago: University of Chicago Press, 1958); McDonald, *E Pluribus Unum: The Formation of the American Republic, 1776–1790* (Boston: Houghton Mifflin, 1965).

[63] See T. Jefferson, "Letter to John Holmes" (April 22, 1820), "Answers and Observations for Demeunier's Article on the United States in the *Encyclopedie Methodique*" (1786), and *Notes on the State of Virginia* (1787), in *Writings*, pp. 1434, 592, 289.

[64] W. Merrill, *Against Wind and Tide: A Biography of Wm. Lloyd Garrison* (Cambridge: Harvard University Press, 1963), p. 203.

or to limit its reach in the country. For example, some incorporated accounts of natural law into constitutional interpretation.[65] Some adopted alternative, quasi-positivist attacks on the constitutionality of slavery.[66] Despite the changes, none of the antislavery interpretations of the Constitution that emerged in the 1840s and 1850s found substantial institutional support or widespread public acceptance, even as late as 1861.

If Lincoln is an accurate gauge of both Northern ethos and the outer limits of legitimate constitutional interpretation on the issue of slavery, two matters bear consideration. First, even Lincoln, who advocated the constitutional notion of perpetual union, sometimes referred to the nation as a "Confederacy,"[67] which would seem to underscore the importance of federalism for understanding the nature of the American constitutional order. Second, although he opposed slavery in general on moral grounds and opposed its extension into the territories, he had never opposed its maintenance in those jurisdictions where it already existed. In his First Inaugural Address, when he "depart[ed] from [his] general purpose not to speak of particular amendments" to state his position on the Corwin Amendment, which was then pending in Congress, he stated that he did not object to making explicit that the individual states possess control over their domestic institutions, exclusive of federal interference, that he did not object to such a provisions being made irrevocable, and that such a provision was probably unnecessary inasmuch as it was already then "implied constitutional law."[68] But even if we assume that slavery and the Constitution were incompatible in some way and that the Corwin Amendment, in protecting slavery, rendered the constitutional order more incoherent than it might otherwise have been, it would still have been difficult to contend successfully that the amendment was unconstitutional. In fact, it will rarely be possible to argue successfully that *any* amendment is unconstitutional. There are four reasons why.

First, politics is invariably tied in large part to the existence of tensions—which sometimes threaten to erupt into outright incompatibilities—among people, groups, institutions, and governments. Any con-

[65] See, e.g., Robert Cover, *Justice Accused: Antislavery and the Judicial Process* (New Haven: Yale University Press, 1975), pp. 8–30; William Nelson, "The Impact of the Antislavery Movement upon Styles of Judicial Reasoning in Nineteenth Century America," *Harvard Law Review* 87 (1974): 513; William Wiecek, *The Sources of Antislavery Constitutionalism in America, 1760–1848* (Ithaca: Cornell University Press, 1977).

[66] See, e.g., Lysander Spooner, *The Unconstitutionality of Slavery* (1860).

[67] Lincoln, "Reply to Illinois Delegation" (March 5, 1861), in *The Collected Works of Abraham Lincoln*, ed. R. Basler (New Brunswick, N.J.: Rutgers University Press, 1953), p. 275.

[68] Lincoln, "First Inaugural Address—Final Text" (March 4, 1861), in ibid., pp. 262, 270.

stitution worthy of the name will reflect those tensions to some extent, which demonstrates how fragile coherence is as a constitutional standard. Consequently, in order for an amendment to render the text incoherent, it would have to be a stark departure from a widely accepted meaning of the text to which it is attached. The Corwin Amendment was not such a radical departure.

Second, constitutional meanings are not static. The content of constitutional categories and their relation to one another change over time. Part of the reason for this goes back to the tensions between vertical and horizontal coherence. As a result, the adoption of an amendment might be evidence of a shift in what the Constitution means to certain members of the polity. If it is, an argument that the amendment renders incoherent the text as a whole is a much trickier proposition.

Third, given the relations among the Constitution's institutional actors, any expression of sentiment sufficiently strong to produce a constitutional amendment on a matter so fundamental would stand little chance of being successfully flouted by an established institution of government. Even an institution that sees its role as distinctly counter-majoritarian—as the Supreme Court has at various times in the country's history—would have difficulty withstanding the force of super-majorities strong enough to ratify an amendment. There is some chance that the Court, or some other institution, could successfully stand up to such a force, but it is surely miniscule.

Finally, substantive constitutional principle is almost always constrained by experience or practice. But in times when popular will is expressed in fairly concrete form, as it arguably is when an amendment is ratified, the constraint is a strong one. The capacity of a constitution (or more accurately, in light of considerations related to its particular allocation of political authority, the capacity of the Constitution) to enforce substantive limits on formal constitutional change is weak.

Still, one might like to hold open the theoretical possibility of challenging on substantive grounds the constitutional legitimacy of some amendments. Given that impulse, there are four related conditions pertinent to sustaining such a challenge. First, how explicitly is the value at stake embodied in the text of the Constitution? In general, though not always, the more explicit the value, the better the chance for a successful challenge. Second, what is the relation of the value at stake to other constitutional (or, because of the pull of the vertical axis, even extraconstitutional) values? The stronger the ties to *other* values, the greater the chance of a successful challenge. Third, how strongly does the amendment reflect an expression of public will? That is, by what procedure was the amendment proposed and ratified? Harris's hierarchy of procedures is pertinent here. Fourth, how recently was the amendment ratified?

This last consideration—time—cuts more than one way. On the one hand, recent ratification might indicate that public opinion on the issue remains strong, and passage of time might provide the polity an opportunity for reflection on and reconsideration of an amendment adopted in haste or in a time of political fervor. On the other hand, time can strengthen the inertial force of habit.

Under the "right" conditions, then, an institutional interpreter might be able to nullify an amendment that contradicts substantive constitutional values, once the better angels of whatever human nature there may be have spoken. But the confluence of the right conditions will probably be rare.

As for the Corwin Amendment, constitutional theory can guarantee no satisfying way out, no happy ending. Even if there had been a general textual commitment to the abolition of slavery, its pull on political society would have been weak, at least in the United States in the nineteenth century. The popular sovereign would have prevailed, not merely because it held the public sword, but also because it embodied something of the public will.[69]

---

[69] If text and theory cannot constrain, however, there is a happy counterfactual ending to oppose the unhappy one that I have proposed. Had Henry Stanton been able to gain sufficient support for his proposed amendment *abolishing* slavery, even a constitution that was arguably *proslavery* would have been little protection against the amendment's enforcement.

Eleven

Toward a Theory of Constitutional Amendment

DONALD S. LUTZ

A CONSTITUTION may be altered by means of (1) a formal amendment process; (2) periodic replacement of the entire document; (3) judicial interpretation; and (4) legislative revision. What difference does it make if we use one method rather than another? What is the relationship between these four methods? What do we learn about the constitutional system and its underlying political theory by the pattern of choice among these alternatives? These are some of the questions I shall address below.

It is true that a constitution is often used as ideological window dressing; and even in places where constitutions are taken very seriously, these documents fail to describe the full reality of an operating political system. Yet it is also true that today hardly any political system, dictatorial or democratic, fails to reflect political change in its respective constitution. Constitutions may not describe the full reality of a political system, but when carefully read they are windows into that underlying reality.

This essay is an initial attempt to use a critical, if often overlooked constitutional device—the amendment process—as a window into both the reality of political systems and the political theory or theories of constitutionalism underlying them. The method will be systematic, comparative, and, to the extent possible, empirical. We will begin with a brief overview of the theoretical assumptions that underlay the formal amendment process when it was invented; we will then identify a number of theoretical propositions concerning the amendment process and look for patterns in the use of the amendment process that can help us create empirical standards upon which to erect a theory of constitutional amendment.

Assumptions Underlying the Amendment Process

The modern written constitution, first developed in English-speaking North America, was grounded in a doctrine of popular sovereignty.[1]

[1] A good deal has been written about the role of popular sovereignty in American politi-

This belief in the people as the ultimate source of power was, from the European viewpoint, a startling innovation of either momentous or monstrous importance—depending upon whether the European was a republican or a monarchist. Even though many in Britain were skeptical at best, Americans did not regard popular sovereignty as an experimental idea, but rather one that stood at the very heart of their shared political consensus.[2] American political writing had used the language of popular sovereignty even before Locke's *Second Treatise* was published, and the early state constitutions of the 1770s contained clear and firm statements that these documents rested upon popular consent.[3]

Although the theory of popular sovereignty was well understood in America by 1776, the institutional implications of this innovative doctrine had to be worked out in constitutions adopted over the next decade. Gradually it was realized that a doctrine of popular sovereignty required that constitutions be written by a popularly selected body other than the legislature, which Americans labeled a convention, and then ratified through a process that elicited popular consent—ideally in a referendum. This double implication was established in the process used to frame and adopt the 1780 Massachusetts and 1784 New Hampshire constitutions, although the referendum portion of the process did not become standard until the nineteenth century. Americans moved quickly to the conclusion that if a constitution rested upon popular consent, then the people could also replace it with a new one. John Locke had argued that the people could replace government, but only when those entrusted with the powers of government had first disqualified themselves by endangering the happiness of the community to such a degree that civil society could be said to have reverted to a state of nature.[4] The Americans went well beyond Locke, and his chief interpreter,

---

cal thought. See, for example, Edmund S. Morgan, *Inventing the People: The Rise of Popular Sovereignty in England and America* (New York: W. W. Norton, 1988); and Willi Paul Adams, *The First American Constitutions* (Chapel Hill: University of North Carolina Press, 1980), especially chap. 6.

[2] Donald S. Lutz, *The Origins of American Constitutionalism* (Baton Rouge: Louisiana State University Press, 1988), especially chap. 7.

[3] This position is developed further in Donald S. Lutz, *Popular Consent and Popular Control: Whig Political Theory in the Early State Constitutions* (Baton Rouge: Louisiana State University Press, 1980), pp. 218–25.

[4] This is the interpretation argued by Adams in *The First American Constitutions*, p. 139. However, most political theorists probably interpret Locke as saying that the constitution may be changed when those in power have put *themselves* in a state of nature vis-à-vis civil society. Under this interpretation, civil society has not ended, since the social compact is still operative—i.e., the people continue to give their consent to be bound in the selection of government by the majority. Since those in government no longer follow majority will, they have implicitly withdrawn their consent and moved outside the civil

William Blackstone, by institutionalizing constitutional change while still in civil society, which is to say whenever they wanted. It is of considerable importance that they included not only the replacement of a constitution, but also its formal amendment.

The first new state constitution in 1776, that of New Jersey, contained an implicit notion of amendment, but the 1776 Pennsylvania document contained the first explicit amendment process—one that used a convention process and bypassed the legislature.[5] By 1780 almost half the states had an amendment procedure, and the principle that the fundamental law could be altered piecemeal by popular will was firmly in place.

In addition to popular sovereignty, the amendment process was based on three other premises central to the American consensus in the 1770s—an imperfect but educable human nature, the efficacy of a deliberative process, and the distinction between normal legislation and constitutional matters. The first premise held that humans are fallible, but capable of learning through experience.[6] Americans had long considered each governmental institution and practice to be in the nature of an experiment. Since fallibility was part of human nature, provision had to be made for altering institutions after experience revealed their flaws and unintended consequences. Thus the amendment process was predicated not only on the need to adapt to changing circumstances, but also on the need to compensate for the limits of human understanding and virtue.

A belief in the efficacy of a deliberative process was also part of the general American constitutional perspective. A constitution was viewed not as a means to arrive at collective decisions in the most efficient way possible, but to arrive at the best possible decisions in pursuit of the common good under a condition of popular sovereignty. The common good is a more difficult standard to approximate than the good of one class or a part of the population, and the condition of popular sovereignty, even if operationalized as a system of representation, requires the involvement of many more people than forms of government based on other principles. This in turn requires a slow, deliberative process for any

---

society into a state of nature. This is closer to the interpretation used by Americans during the Founding era.

[5] While this was the first explicit amendment process in a state constitution, the first explicit use of an amendment process anywhere was in William Penn's 1678 Frame of Government, which undoubtedly explains why the 1776 Pennsylvania Constitution was first among the postindependence state documents. See John R. Vile, *The Constitutional Amending Process in American Political Thought* (New York: Praeger, 1992), pp. 11–12.

[6] For the phrasing and theoretical importance of this assumption, I am indebted to Vincent Ostrom, *The Political Theory of a Compound Republic: Designing the American Experiment.*

political decision, and the more important the decision, the more deliberative the process should be.

Constitutional matters were considered more important in 1789 America than normal legislation, which led to a more highly deliberative process that distinguished constitutional and normal legislative matters. The codification of the distinction in constitutional articles of ratification and amendment resulted in American constitutions being viewed as a higher law that should limit and direct the content of normal legislation.

In sum, the amendment process invented by the Americans was a public, formal, highly deliberative decision-making process that distinguished between constitutional matters and normal legislation, and returned to roughly the same level of popular sovereignty as that used in the adoption of the constitution. The assumptions underlying the amendment idea require that the procedure be neither too easy nor too difficult. A process that is too easy does not provide enough distinction between constitutional matters and normal legislation, thereby violating the assumption of the need for a high level of deliberation and debasing popular sovereignty. One that is too difficult, on the other hand, interferes with the needed rectification of mistakes, thereby violating the assumption of human fallibility and preventing effective recourse to popular sovereignty when necessary.

The literature on constitutions at one time made a distinction between major and minor constitutional alterations by calling the former "revisions" and the latter "amendments." The distinction turned out in practice to be conceptually slippery, impossible to operationalize, and therefore generally useless.[7] It would be more helpful to use "amendment" as a description of the *formal* process developed by the Americans, and "revision" to describe processes that instead use the legislature or judiciary. Unless we maintain the distinction between formal amendment and revision, we will lose the ability to distinguish competing constitutional theories.

The innovation of an amendment process, like the innovation of a written constitution, has diffused throughout the world to the point where only 5 of the existing 142 national constitutions lack a provision for an amending process.[8] However, the diffusion of written constitu-

[7] On this point, see Albert L. Sturm, *Thirty Years of State Constitution-Making: 1938–1968* (New York: National Municipal League, 1970), p. 18. See also Chapter 2 in this volume, by Sanford Levinson, who notes the presence of this distinction in some state constitutions in the United States and its use at least by the California Supreme Court to strike down some efforts at change by popular referendum on the grounds that they are "revisions" rather than mere "amendments."

[8] Henc van Maarseveen and Ger van der Tang, *Written Constitutions: A Computerized Comparative Study* (Dobbs Ferry, N.Y.: Oceana Publications, 1978), p. 80.

tions and the amendment idea do not necessarily indicate widespread acceptance of the principles that underlie the American innovation. In most countries with a written constitution, popular sovereignty and the use of a constitution as a higher law are not operative political principles. Any comparative study of the amendment process must therefore first distinguish true constitutional systems from those that use a constitution as window dressing, and then go on to recognize that among the former there are variations in the amendment process that rest on assumptions at odds with those in the American version. Indeed, it is the efficiency with which study of the amending process reveals such theoretical differences that draws us to it.

At the same time, a comparative study of amendment processes allows us to delve more deeply into the theory of constitutional amendment as a principle of constitutional design. For example, we might ask the following questions: What difference does it make when constitutions are formally amended through a political process that does not effectively distinguish constitutional matters from normal legislation? Why might we still want to draw a distinction between formal amendment and revision by normal politics as carefully and as strongly as possible?

One important answer to the question is that the three prominent methods of constitutional alteration other than complete replacement—formal amendment, legislative revision, and judicial interpretation—reflect, in the order listed, a declining commitment to popular sovereignty; and the level of commitment to popular sovereignty may be a key attitude for defining the nature of the political system. However, it is not always possible to tell when popular sovereignty has been abandoned for an elitist alternative. For example, some constitutions by design, and others by accident, leave so much room for interpretation that what some call amendment-through-interpretation is actually specification in the face of ambiguity. That is, those who write constitutions often purposely leave considerable room for interpretation. Formal constitutional provisions may not always define a single-peaked preference—that is, one clear choice that dominates all alternatives—but, rather, a range of acceptable possibilities, all of which may be understood as undergirded by popular sovereignty. As long as interpretation does not move outside a range of possibilities defined by a normal language interpretation of the constitutional provision, even if the operation of the political system is significantly changed as a consequence, there has not really been an amendment but rather a specification of a choice within a range of possibilities. Thus, rather than focusing only upon whether the operation of a political system is changed, we should also consider the range of possibilities permitted by a constitutional provision.

With these considerations and assumptions as background, it is possible to begin the generation of testable propositions that can be used in the construction of a theory of amendment.

Basic Assumptions and Propositions

Every theory has to begin with a number of assumptions. We have seen how the original American version rested on the assumptions of popular sovereignty, an imperfect but educable human nature, the efficacy of a highly deliberative decision-making process, and the distinction between normal and constitutional law. While these help define the working assumptions of one theory of amendment, albeit the original one, they do not provide a complete basis for describing even the contemporary American theory, let alone a general theory of amendment. We turn now to developing a theory that includes the American version but also accounts for, and provides the basis for analyzing, any version of constitutional amendment.

Our first working assumption has to do with the expected change that is faced by any political system.

> *ASSUMPTION 1*: Every political system needs to be altered over time as a result of some combination of: (1) changes in the environment within which the political system operates (including economics, technology, and demographics); (2) changes in the value system distributed across the population; (3) unwanted or unexpected institutional effects; and (4) the cumulative effect of decisions made by the legislature, executive, and judiciary.

A second assumption concerns the nature of a constitution.

> *ASSUMPTION 2*: In political systems that are constitutional, in which constitutions are taken seriously as limiting government and legitimating the decision-making process they describe, important alterations in the operation of the political system need to be reflected in the constitution.

If these two assumptions are used as premises in a deductive process, they imply a conclusion that stands as a further assumption.

> *ASSUMPTION 3*: All constitutions require regular, periodic alteration, whether through amendment, revision, or replacement.

Revision, as noted earlier, refers to alterations in a constitution through judicial interpretation or legislative action. However, we are initially more concerned with the use of a formal amendment process, and this requires that we develop several concepts for use in our propositions. The first concept is that of amendment rate.

"Amendment rate" does not refer to the number of amendments a constitution has. Rather it refers to the average number of amendments passed per year since the constitution came into effect. Many constitutional scholars criticize constitutions that are much amended.[9] However, constitutionalism and the logic of popular sovereignty are based on more than simplicity and tidiness. Any people who believe in constitutionalism will amend their constitution when needed, as opposed to using extraconstitutional means. Thus, a reasonable amendment rate will indicate that the people living under it take their constitution seriously. Furthermore, the older the constitution is, under conditions of popular sovereignty, the more successful it has been, but also the larger the number of amendments it is likely to have. However, it is the *rate* of amendment that is important, not the total number of amendments.

In sum, a successful constitutional system would seem to be best defined by a constitution of considerable age that has a total number of amendments, which, when divided by the age of the constitution in years, represents a reasonable amendment rate—one that is to be expected in the face of inevitable change. A less than successful constitutional system would seem to be defined by a very high rate of constitutional replacement, an exceptionally high rate of amendment, or an exceptionally low amendment rate.

This raises the question of what constitutes a "reasonable" rate of amendment as opposed to one that is too high or too low. Since we will use a systematic study of actual amendment rates, we hope to illuminate this question empirically rather than in an a priori manner. This means we must initially use a symbolic stand-in for our propositions. Futhermore, since a reasonable rate is likely to be a range of rates rather than a single one, the symbol will represent a range with an upper and a lower boundary such that anything above this reasonable rate is probably too high, and anything below the range too low. We shall use <#> to symbolically represent this reasonable range of amendment rates.

The first proposition is frequently found in the literature, but it has never been systematically verified, or its effect measured.

PROPOSITION 1: The longer a constitution, the higher its amendment rate, and the shorter a constitution, the lower its amendment rate.

[9] For an overview of the standard criticisms about the shortcomings of state constitutions in this and other respects, see Sturm, *Thirty Years of State Constitution-Making*, especially pp. 1–17.

Commentators frequently note that the more provisions a constitution has, the more targets there are for amendment, and the more likely the constitution will be targeted because it deals with too many details that are subject to change. While on the one hand this seems intuitively correct, the data that are used usually raise the question of which comes first—the high amendment rate or the long constitution? This is because a constitution's length is usually given as of a particular year, and not in terms of its original length. So for example, the Alabama Constitution of 1901 had reached the stupendous length of 174,000 words by 1991 and had an extemely high amendment rate of 8.07 per year. Was the constitution long because it had a high amendment rate, or did it have a high amendment rate because it was long to begin with? We will answer this question in the next section using data from American state constitutions. For now it is sufficient to note that the question turns out to be an important one to resolve because the empirical relationship is so strong and consistent that in order to test every other proposition it will be necessary to control for the length of a constitution.

Our second proposition is also a common one in the literature, although it too has never before been systematically tested.

PROPOSITION 2: The more difficult the amendment process, the lower the amendment rate, and the easier the amendment process, the higher the amendment rate.

As obvious as this proposition is, it cannot be tested until one shifts from the number of amendments in a constitution to its amendment rate, and until one develops an index for measuring the degree of difficulty associated with an amendment process. Such an index is presented in the next section as part of what is needed to develop a way of predicting the likely consequences of using one amendment process versus another. Until these consequences can be predicted with some degree of reliability, we cannot sensibly evaluate competing forms of formal amendment in terms of their being too easy or too difficult.

The literature on American state constitutions generally argues that these documents are much longer than the national Constitution because they must deal with more governmental functions. For example, if a constitution deals with matters such as education, criminal law, local government, and finances, it is bound to be more detailed, longer, and thus have a higher amendment rate. From this we can generalize to the following proposition.

PROPOSITION 3: The more governmental functions dealt with in a constitution, the longer it will be, and the higher rate of amendment it will have.

The concept of popular sovereignty was originally developed to justify the replacement of one government by another, and therefore the complete replacement of a constitution is perfectly in accord with the concept. During the bicentennial of the U.S. Constitution much was made of the document's age—usually to the positive. Our concern here is not to praise or blame either high or low rates of constitutional replacement, but to develop a general theory that will help us understand why a constitution may be altered by replacement instead of by amendment or revision, and what difference it makes. Whether for good or for ill, some political systems replace their constitutions with great regularity while others rarely replace theirs.

It would seem that constitutions are usually replaced for one of three reasons. An abrupt change in regime may leave the values, institutions, and/or implications of the old constitution seriously at odds with those of the people now in charge. Or even without the specific demarcation denoted by the notion of regime change, a society might simply come to feel that the constitution written years before has simply not kept up with a host of important, albeit incremental, changes through time. Finally, the old constitution may have been changed so many times that it is no longer clear what lies under the encrustations, and clarity demands a new beginning. Once again we make use of our "reasonable" rate of amendment.

PROPOSITION 4: The further the amendment rate is from the mean of <#>, either higher or lower, the greater the probability that the entire constitution will be replaced, and thus the shorter its duration. Conversely, the closer an amendment rate is to the mean of <#>, the lower the probability that the entire constitution will be replaced, and thus the longer its duration.

A low rate of amendment in the face of needed change may lead to the development of some extraconstitutional means of revision, most likely judicial interpretation, to supplement the formal amendment process. We can now, on the basis of earlier discussion, generate a string of propositions that will prove useful in a discussion at the end of this essay on theories of constitutional construction.

PROPOSITION 5: A low amendment rate associated with a long average constitutional duration strongly implies the use of some alternative means of revision to supplement the formal amendment process.

PROPOSITION 6: In the absence of a high rate of constitutional replacement, the lower the rate of formal amendment, the more likely the process of revision is dominated by a judicial body.

PROPOSITION 7: The higher the formal amendment rate, (a) the less likely the constitution is being viewed as a higher law; (b) the less likely a distinction is being drawn between constitutional matters and normal legislation; (c) the more likely the constitution is being viewed as a code; and (d) the more likely the formal amendment process is dominated by the legislature.

PROPOSITION 8: The more important the role of the judiciary in constitutional revision, the less likely the judiciary is to use theories of strict construction.

PROPOSITION 9: Reasonable rates of formal amendment and replacement tend to be associated with a belief in popular sovereignty.

After testing Propositions 1 through 4 using data from the American state constitutions, we shall seek further verification by examining the amendment process in nations where constitutionalism is taken seriously and does not serve merely as window dressing. The American state documents are examined first because data on them are readily available and easily comparable and because the similarities in their amendment processes reduce the number of variables that must be taken into account. Moreover, together they constitute about half of human experience with serious constitutionalism.

Amendment Patterns in American State Constitutions, 1776–1991

The data in Table 1 provide a state-by-state breakdown on some of the constitutional characteristics that the literature has deemed important, such as a constitution's length, date of adoption, number of years in effect, and frequency of replacement. We will begin with a consideration of length.

Albert Sturm, one of the most able students of state constitutions, summarizes the literature as seeing state constitutions burdened with (1) the effects of continuous expansion of state functions and responsibilities and the consequent growth of governmental machinery; (2) the primary responsibility for responding to the increasing pressure of major problems associated with rapid urbanization, technological development, population growth and mobility, economic change and development, and the fair treatment of minority groups; (3) the pressure of special interests for constitutional status; and (4) continuing popular distrust of state legislatures resulting from past abuses, which result in detailed restrictions on governmental activity. All of these factors contribute to the length of state constitutions, and it is argued that not only do these pressures lead to many amendments, and thus greater length, but that greater length itself leads to the accelerated need for amendment simply by providing so many targets for change.[10] Thus, the length becomes a surrogate measure for all of these other pressures to amend, and is a key causal variable.

Table 1 shows that the average amendment rate is much higher for the state constitutions than it is for the national Constitution. Between 1789 and 1991, the U.S. Constitution was amended 26 times for a rate of 0.13 (26 amendments divided by 202 years equals 0.13 amendments per year). As of 1991, the fifty state constitutions had been in effect for an average of 95 years, and had been amended a total of 5,845 times, or an average of 117 amendments per state. This produces an average amendment rate of 1.23 for the states (117 amendments per state divided by the 95 years the average state constitution had been in effect). The state rate of amendment (1.23) is thus about 9.5 times the national rate (0.13).

The data from Table 1 allow us to begin our analysis of the propositions developed earlier. Proposition 1 hypothesized a positive relationship between the length of a constitution and its amendment rate. The longer a constitution is when it is adopted, the higher its amendment rate should be. Table 2 summarizes the findings, which strongly support Proposition 1. Furthermore, the relationship holds whether we use the original or the current length, which includes the results of the amendments.

The average length of state constitutions increases from about 18,300 words as originally written to about 28,300 as amended by 1991. Not only is Proposition 1 supported, but there is good reason, when these propositions are being tested with foreign national constitutions, for using either the original length or the amended length. The relationship

[10] Much of the data on state constitution making has been taken from, or calculated on the basis of data in, Sturm, *Thirty Years of State Constitution-Making*; Albert L. Sturm, "The Development of American State Constitutions," *Publius* 12 (1982): 90; H. W. Stanley and R. G. Niemi, *Vital Statistics on American Politics*, 3d ed. (Washington, D.C.: C.Q. Press, 1992); James Q. Dealey, *Growth of American State Constitutions* (New York: Da Capo Press, 1972); Walter F. Dodd, *The Revision and Amendment of State Constitutions* (New York: Da Capo Press, 1970); Daniel J. Elazar, *American Federalism: A View from the States*, 2d ed. (New York: Thomas Y. Crowell Co., 1972); Fletcher M. Green, *Constitutional Development in the South Atlantic States, 1776–1860* (New York: Da Capo Press, 1971); and Ellis Paxson Oberholtzer, *The Referendum in America* (New York: Da Capo Press, 1971). Cross-national constitutional data have been taken from the constitutions themselves, and from commentary on these constitutions, found primarily in Albert P. Blaustein and Gisbert H. Flanz, *Constitutions of the Countries of the World*, 19 vols. (Dobbs Ferry, N.Y.: Oceana Publications, 1987 and supplements).

TABLE 1
Basic Data on American Constitutions, 1991

State	No. of Consts.	Average Dura- tion	Current Const. Since	No. of Yrs. in Effect	Ori- ginal Length in Words	No. of Times Amended	Amend- ment Rate
Alabama	6	29	1901	90	65,400	726	8.07
Alaska	1	32	1959	32	11,800	22	0.69
Arizona	1	79	1912	79	28,900	109	1.38
Arkansas	5	31	1874	117	24,100	76	0.65
California	2	72	1879	112	21,400	471	4.21
Colorado	1	115	1876	115	22,000	115	1.00
Connecticut	4	54	1965	26	8,800	25	0.96
Delaware	3	72	1897	94	19,000	119	1.27
Florida	6	25	1969	22	18,900	53	2.41
Georgia	10	21	1983	8	26,000	24	3.00
Hawaii	1	32	1959	32	16,800	82	2.56
Idaho	1	101	1890	101	18,800	107	1.06
Illinois	4	43	1971	20	12,900	6	0.30
Indiana	2	88	1851	140	9,100	38	0.27
Iowa	2	73	1857	134	9,700	48	0.36
Kansas	1	130	1861	130	10,200	87	0.67
Kentucky	4	50	1891	100	21,800	29	0.29
Louisiana	11	16	1975	16	47,300	27	1.69
Maine	1	171	1820	171	10,100	157	0.92
Maryland	4	54	1867	124	25,200	200	1.61
Massachusetts	1	211	1780	211	11,600	116	0.55
Michigan	4	39	1964	27	18,600	16	0.59
Minnesota	1	133	1858	133	8,500	112	0.84
Mississippi	4	44	1890	101	20,100	102	1.01
Missouri	4	43	1945	46	39,300	74	1.61
Montana	2	51	1973	18	11,600	15	0.83
Nebraska	2	63	1875	116	16,100	189	1.63
Nevada	1	127	1864	127	14,100	108	0.85
New Hampshire	2	108	1784	207	8,000	142	0.69
New Jersey	3	72	1948	43	16,400	39	0.91
New Mexico	1	79	1912	79	22,000	120	1.52
New York	4	54	1895	96	26,800	207	2.16
North Carolina	3	72	1971	20	10,300	27	1.35
North Dakota	1	102	1889	102	18,100	125	1.23
Ohio	2	95	1851	140	14,200	145	1.04
Oklahoma	1	84	1907	84	58,200	133	1.58
Oregon	1	132	1859	132	11,200	188	1.42
Pennsylvania	5	43	1968	23	20,800	19	0.83

TABLE 1 (*cont.*)

State	No. of Consts.	Average Dura-tion	Current Const. Since	No. of Yrs. in Effect	Ori-ginal Length in Words	No. of Times Amended	Amend-ment Rate
Rhode Island	2	108	1843	148	7,400	53	0.36
South Carolina	7	31	1896	95	21,900	463	4.87
South Dakota	1	102	1889	102	21,300	97	0.95
Tennessee	3	65	1870	121	11,100	32	0.26
Texas	5	29	1876	115	28,600	326	2.83
Utah	1	95	1896	95	13,900	77	0.81
Vermont	3	71	1793	198	5,200	50	0.25
Virginia	6	36	1971	20	18,100	20	1.00
Washington	1	102	1889	102	16,300	86	0.84
West Virginia	2	64	1872	119	15,900	62	0.52
Wisconsin	1	143	1848	143	11,400	124	0.87
Wyoming	1	101	1890	101	20,800	57	0.56
Mean:	2.9	77	1896	95	18,300	117	1.23
U.S. Constitution:	1	202	1789	202	4,300	26	0.13

Source: Data on the number of constitutions, the year the current constitution went into effect, and the number of times the constitution has been amended are taken from H. W. Stanley and R. G. Niemi, *Vital Statistics on American Politics* (Washington, D.C.: C.Q. Press, 1992), pp. 13–14. All other data have been determined by the author.

TABLE 2

The Length of a U.S. State Constitution and Its Amendment Rate as of 1991

Length in words	5,000–10,000	10,000–15,000	15,000–20,000	20,000–25,000	25,000–30,000	Over
Amendment rate [a]	0.53 (7)	0.83 (13)	1.28 (11)	1.61 (10)	2.20 (5)	2.99 (4)
Amendment rate [b]	0.52 (6)	0.76 (9)	1.06 (6)	1.43 (11)	1.64 (7)	2.20 (11)

[a] The amendment rate using the length of the constitution when it was adopted. The number of constitutions in each category is indicated below the amendment rate in parentheses.

[b] The amendment rate using the length of the Constitution as of 1991, which includes all amendments. The U.S. Constitution has approximately 7,300 words when the amendments are included, as opposed to the approximately 4,300 it had originally.

TABLE 3
State Amendments by Category, 1970–79

Category Topic	Total Proposed	Total Adopted	Percent Adopted	Percent of All Amendments
Bill of Rights	75	60	80%	4.3%
Suffrage and Elections	125	90	72	6.4
Legislative branch	205	114	56	8.1
Executive branch	145	102	70	7.3
Judicial branch	131	106	81	7.5
Local government	98	66	67	4.7
Taxation and Finance	308	198	64	14.1
State and local debt	122	60	49	4.3
State functions	182	127	70	9.0
Amendment and revision	53	37	70	2.6
General revision proposals	24	9	38	0.6
Miscellaneous proposals	53	43	81	3.1
Local amendments	559	394	70	28.0
TOTALS	2,080	1,406	68	

Source: Based on a table from Albert L. Sturm, "The Development of American State Constitutions," Publius: The Journal of Federalism 12 (Winter 1982): 90.

between size and amendment rate is the strongest and most consistent one found in the analysis of state data.

State constitutions, on average, are significantly longer than the U.S. Constitution. Can we account for this difference? Proposition 3 suggests that the wider range of governmental functions at the state level results in significantly longer documents, and thus, in line with Proposition 1, produces a higher amendment rate, which makes them longer still.

Table 3 uses data from a recent decade to show the relative importance of different amendment categories. Amendments dealing with local governmental structure (4.7 percent), local finances (an indeterminate part of 4.3 percent), or local issues (28 percent) make up at least one-third of all amendments and pertain to a topic, local government, that is excluded from national constitutional concern. Without amendments for local matters, the average state amendment rate would fall from 1.23 to about 0.8—a reduction in the ratio to around six times the national rate.

Amendments dealing with state debt and new state functions are also outside the range of national concern, and if these were excluded the state amendment rate would fall to about 0.67, which is five times the national rate.

The national Constitution deals with suffrage and election matters in two brief sentences that leave these matters to the states. However, nine of the twenty-six amendments to the U.S. Constitution deal with elections or suffrage, and therefore this category cannot be considered a special burden of the state.

Additions and changes to rights, and amendments dealing with the operation of the legislative, executive, and judicial branches, are not special burdens of state constitutions either. However, despite the Sixteenth Amendment in the U.S. Constitution, the matter of taxation and finance is to a certain extent a special state burden that adds to its amendment rate. Most of these amendments deal with what might be termed control of the cash flow. The strong inclinations at the state level to (1) limit the taxing power, (2) control the methods of raising money through other means such as bonds, and (3) prevent corruption by instituting an ever more refined system of financial checks and cross-accountability flow from a source completely missing at the national level. As a conservative estimate, we could consider about half of these amendments to be so motivated, which would reduce the state amendment rate to about 0.58, or four and a half times the national rate.

Finally, the method of amending and revising constitutions is itself the subject of amendment at the state level, though never, thus far, at the national level. If we exclude these from the count as well, we end up with an adjusted state amendment rate of about 0.54. This figure is still about four times the national amendment rate, but by eliminating the amendments that flow from concerns that are peculiar to state constitutions we now have a figure that we can compare to the national rate of 0.13 using what amounts to the same base. In other words, the difference between 0.13 and 0.54 represents what we might term the "surplus rate," which still needs to be explained. However, an interesting question, one that seems never to be asked, is whether a state rate of amendment four times the national rate is too high, or a national amendment rate one-fourth that of the state average is too low.

The answer depends in part on your attitude toward judicial interpretation. Propositions 5 and 6 suggest that if you have reasons to prefer judicial interpretation as a means of modifying a constitution over a formal amendment process, then the amendment rate for the national document is not too low. However, if you have reasons to prefer a formal amendment process, such as an attachment to popular sovereignty, then the answer may well be that the amendment rate of the U.S. Constitution is too low and the amendment rates of the states within <#> is to be preferred.

Propositions 5 and 6 assume a low rate of amendment coupled with constitutional longevity. Proposition 4, on the other hand, posits a general relationship between the rate of amendment and constitutional longevity. Table 4 provides an initial look at this relationship.

A majority of states have had only one or two constitutions in their respective histories. Three would seem to be an optimal number with respect to minimizing amendments, but even those states that have had four constitutions have an amendment rate that is below average. However, beyond four constitutions there is a marked and consistent trend toward a very high amendment rate. Why this should occur at five constitutions and not at, say, three is not obvious.

Of course, Table 4 may be measuring the difference between old and new states, since a new state cannot have been around long enough to have six, seven, or eleven constitutions. To correct for this possibility, we can divide the number of constitutions a state has had into the number of years it has been a state. The result, which we can term the rate of replacement, indicates the average duration of a state's constitution, and is a measure of constitutional activity that controls for a state's age. Table 5 shows the results and, together with Table 4, suggests that a high amendment rate is associated with a high replacement rate.

However, Proposition 4 predicts that the rate at which constitutions are replaced will increase as the amendment rate moves up *or* down with respect to <#>. In Tables 4 and 5 the amendment rate was the dependent variable. However, if we make it the independent variable instead, we can see if the bi-directional effect occurs, and thus directly test Proposition 4.

Table 6 shows the average duration of the state constitutions grouped according to amendment rate. The lower the average duration, the higher the replacement rate. Proposition 4 predicts that the replacement rate will be highest, and thus the average duration lowest, as the amendment rate moves above or below <#>, which is yet to be defined. Table 6 supports Proposition 4 by showing that the average duration of a state's constitution declines as the amendment rate goes above 1.00 and as it goes below 0.76. What this means is that for American state constitutions, an amendment rate between 0.76 and 1.00 is associated with the longest-lived constitutions, and thus with the lowest rate of constitutional replacement. This range, then, will be defined as <#>.

There are thirteen constitutions with amendment rates within <#> as we have just defined it: Connecticut (0.96), Colorado (1.00), Maine (0.92), Minnesota (0.84), Montana (0.83), Nevada (0.85), New Jersey (0.91), Pennsylvania (0.83), South Dakota (0.95), Utah (0.81), Virginia (1.00), Washington (0.84), and Wisconsin (0.87). The average of these rates is 0.89, which we will use to define # within <#>.

Everything discussed to this point has dealt with characteristics of entire constitutions. Another possible source of variance, according to the

TABLE 4
Number of Constitutions and the Amendment Rate

Number of constitutions a state has had	1	2	3	4	5	6	7–11
Amendment rate	1.08	1.10	0.81	1.07	1.44	3.82	3.19
Number of constitutions in category	19	9	5	8	3	3	3

TABLE 5
Average Duration of Constitutions and Amendment Rate 1776–1991

Average duration of constitutions[a] (in years)	1–25	26–50	51–75	76–100	101–25	126–50	151+
Amendment rate	2.37	1.95	1.26	1.10	0.93	0.84	0.64
Number of constitutions in category	3	13	13	6	8	5	2

[a] The number of years since a state's first constitution was adopted divided by the number of constitutions it has had since then.

TABLE 6
Amendment Rate and Average Duration of a Constitution

Amendment rate	0–0.5	0.51–0.75	0.76–1.00	1.01–1.25	1.26–1.50	1.51–1.75	1.76–2.00	2.0+
Average duration (in years)	71 (7)	90 (8)	100 (13)	86 (4)	79 (4)	57 (6)	40 (0)	38 (8)

literature, is the nature of the amendment process itself. We turn now to this topic as a means of testing Proposition 2, and for developing an index with which to measure the difficulty of a given amendment procedure. We will then be ready to look at the constitutions of other nations.

Amendment Patterns and the Characteristics of the Amendment Process

In the American states the method of ratifying an amendment can essentially be held constant: Every state but one now uses a popular referendum for approval. However, amendments may be initiated by the state's legislature, an initiative referendum, a constitutional convention, or a commission. It is generally held that the more difficult the process of initiation, the fewer amendments proposed and thus the fewer amendments passed. Similarly, many believe that the initiative, by making the process of proposing an amendment too easy, has led to a flood of proposals that are then more readily adopted by the electorate that initiated them. Another widely held belief is that the stricter or more arduous the process a legislature must use to propose an amendment, the fewer amendments proposed.

As Table 7 shows, during the period 1970–79, relatively few amendments were proposed by other than a legislature. One-third of the states use popular initiative as a method of proposing amendments, and yet even in these states the legislative method was greatly preferred. The popular initiative has received a lot of attention, especially in California, but in fact it has thus far had a minimal impact.

What has been the relative success of these competing modes of proposing constitutions? Table 8 shows that the relatively few amendments proposed through popular initiative have a success rate roughly half that of the two prominent alternatives. The popular initiative is in fact more difficult to use than legislative initiative, and it results in proposals that are less well considered. Ironically, the easier method to use, legislative proposal, tends to produce a more well-considered amendment proposal—one that is more likely to be acceptable, and thus accepted.

The popular initiative has not produced a flood of proposed amendments, and it is not a method with a higher rate of success. Popular initiative is a more difficult method, and has a lower success rate. But what about the varying methods for legislative initiation? States vary in how large a majority is needed in a legislature for a proposal to be put on the ballot, and some states require that the majority be sustained in two consecutive sessions. Table 9 summarizes what we find in this regard.

TABLE 7
Method of Initiation and State Amendment Rate 1970–79

Method of Initiating Amendment	Proposed by Legislature	Popular Initiative	Special Convention
Amendment rate	1.24	1.38	1.26
Percentage of amendments using this method	91.5%	2.2%	6.3%
Number of constitutions in category	50	17	5

Source: Based on data from Albert L. Sturm, "The Development of American State Constitutions," Publius 12 (Winter 1982): 78–79. Total of all methods will exceed fifty since many states specify the possibility of more than one method of initiating amendments. The initiative method adds about five amendments a year nationwide beyond what we would expect using only the legislative proposal method.

TABLE 8
Success Rate of Various Methods for Proposing Amendments in the Fifty States, 1776–1979

	All Methods	Legislature	Initiative	Convention
Proposed	7,563	6,637	566	360
Adopted	4,704	4,268	182	254
Success rate	62%	64%	32%	71%

TABLE 9
Comparative Effect of Majority Size on Amendment Rate

Required legislative majority	50% + 1	50% + 1 Twice	60%	67%	75%	67% Twice
Ratio of difficulty to simple majority	1.00	1.04	1.26	1.62	1.83	3.56
Number of constitutions in category	11	6	9	19	1	4

In this table we have normed the decline in the amendment rate produced by each type of legislative majority against that of the least difficult method. That is, since simple majority rule by the legislature results
in the highest amendment rate, we ask what difference it makes to use a
more difficult method for initiating amendments. The data indicate that
in the American states, when the method of initiation is stiffened to require majority legislative approval twice, the amendment rate for that
state's constitution goes down by 4 percent, which is the same as making
the difficulty of amendment 4 percent higher. That is indicated here by
the Index of Difficulty rising to 1.04. A requirement for a three-fifths
legislative majority (60 percent) reduces a state's amendment rate by 26
percent compared to the amendment rate of states using a simple majority requirement, which is reflected here in an increase in the Index of
Difficulty to 1.26.

Even though the data are drawn from the entire universe under study
(American state constitutions), the number of cases (states) is too small
to generate undying confidence in the results we obtain. Nevertheless,
in the absence of better data, and keeping this major caveat in mind, we
can reach the following conclusions from Table 9.

1. Generally speaking, the larger the legislative majority required for initiation, the fewer amendments proposed and the lower the amendment rate.

2. Requiring a legislature to pass a proposal twice does not significantly
increase the difficulty of the amendment process if the decision rule is one-
half plus one.

3. The most effective way to increase the difficulty of amendment at the
initiation stage is to require the approval of two consecutive legislatures using
a two-thirds majority each time.

One can also use the variance in the degree of difficulty between alternative legislative majorities to establish the core of an Index of Difficulty, an initial attempt at which is presented in Table 10, for any
amendment process. The index identifies more than seventy possible actions that could in some combination be used to initiate and approve a
constitutional amendment; together, they cover the combinations of
virtually every amendment process in the world. The index scores assigned to all but a few of these more than seventy possibilities in the
index are derived from data on American states. Each score is a number
that represents a ratio of difficulty normed to a simple majority approval
in two legislative houses, as used in Table 9.

For example, approval by a simple majority in one house is assumed
to be one-half as difficult as similar approval in two houses and therefore
assigned an index score one-half of 1.00, or 0.50. To illustrate another
example, we know from Table 8 that amendment proposals made by

popular initiative have almost exactly one-half the success rate of those initiated by the legislature in American states. Since nineteen states use a two-thirds majority, and seventeen use a simple majority, the minimum score for a popular initiative must be one-half of the weighted scores for the method used in all fifty states. This combined weighted score for legislative initiative in all fifty states turns out to be almost exactly 1.50, and thus the index score for the easiest popular initiative must be twice as difficult, or 3.00. Index scores for larger numbers of voters required for popular initiative (identified in the index as voter "petitions") are assigned estimated increments of difficulty. As a final example, we know from state data that since 1776 64 percent of all amendment proposals made by a state legislature have been approved. We also know from state data that the approval rate is almost identical since the nearly universal adoption of popular referenda as the means of approval replaced approval by state legislatures. We can thus say that a popular referendum used as the means for approving a proposed amendment is about as difficult as having the state legislature approve it. As just noted, the average degree of difficulty for state legislative action, weighted for the relative frequency of using one type of majority versus another, is 1.50. We thus assign a weight of 1.50 to approval by popular referendum using the most usual means—one-half plus one of those voting—and add estimated increments for larger majorities.

The index score assiged to a given amendment process is generated by adding together the numbers assigned by the index to every step required by that process.

How the index works can be illustrated by using it with the amendment process described in Article V of the U.S. Constitution. There is more than one path to amendment, and each must be evaluated. A two-thirds vote by Congress, since it requires two houses to initiate the process, is worth 1.60; whereas initiation by two-thirds of the state legislatures is worth 2.25. The latter path leads to a national convention, which uses majority rule in advancing a proposal, thus adding 0.75—under the assumption that the special initiating body is elected. The first path still totals 1.60, and the other now totals 3.00. Ratification by three-fourths of the states through either their legislatures or elected conventions adds 3.50. The path beginning with Congress now totals 5.10, while the path beginning with the state legislatures and using a national convention totals 6.50. Even though the second path has never been successful, and one can see more clearly now why it hasn't, it is still a valid option. For the total amendment process we can use the lower figure unless or until the more difficult procedure is ever used, indicate the range of difficulty by using 5.10–6.50, or average the two paths together to obtain a composite index score of 5.80. Thus far we have

TABLE 10

An Index for Estimating the Relative Difficulty of an
Amendment Process

Constitutional Requirement	Increment
Initiation Requires	
Action by an executive	Add 0.25
Action by a special appointed body	Add 0.50
Action by a special elected body	Add 0.75
Action by a Unicameral Legislature	
Legislative approval by a majority of ½ + 1	Add 0.50
Legislative approval *twice* using ½ + 1	Add 0.50
Legislative approval by an absolute majority	Add 0.65
Legislative approval *twice* by absolute majority	Add 0.65
Legislative approval by a ⅗ majority	Add 0.65
Legislative approval *twice* by ⅗ majority	Add 0.65
Legislative approval by a ⅔ majority	Add 0.80
Legislative approval by a ¾ majority	Add 0.90
Legislative approval *twice* by ⅔ majority	Add 1.75
If an election is required between two votes	Add 0.25
Action by a Bicameral Legislature	
Legislative approval by a majority of ½ + 1	Add 1.00
Legislative approval *twice* using ½ + 1	Add 1.00
Legislative approval by an absolute majority	Add 1.25
Legislative approval *twice* by absolute majority	Add 1.25
Legislative approval by a ⅗ majority	Add 1.25
Legislative approval *twice* by ⅗ majority	Add 1.25
Legislative approval by a ⅔ majority	Add 1.60
Legislative approval by a ¾ majority	Add 1.80
Legislative approval *twice* by a ⅔ majority	Add 3.55
If an election is required between two votes	Add 0.50
A petition of 0–250,000 voters	Add 3.00
A petition by 250,000–500,000 voters	Add 3.50
A petition by more than 500,000 voters	Add 4.00
Multiple state legislatures, ½ + 1	Add 2.00
Multiple state conventions, ½ + 1	Add 2.00
Multiple state legislatures or conventions, ⅔	Add 3.00
Multiple state legislatures or conventions, ¾	Add 3.50
Approval Requires	
Action by an executive	Add 0.50
Approval by a special body, ⅓ or less	Add 0.25
Approval by a special body, ½ + 1	Add 0.50
Approval by a special body, absolute majority	Add 0.65
Approval by a special body, ⅗ majority	Add 0.65
Approval by a special body, ⅔ majority	Add 0.80

TABLE 10 (*cont.*)

Constitutional Requirement	Increment
Approval requires (cont.)	
Approval by a special body, ¾ majority	Add 0.90
If any of the above acts a second time	Add 0.50
Action by a Unicameral Legislature	
Legislative approval, ⅓ majority or less	Add 0.25
Legislative approval, ½ + 1	Add 0.50
Legislative approval *twice* by ½ + 1	Add 0.50
Legislative approval, absolute majority	Add 0.65
Legislative approval *twice* by absolute majority	Add 0.65
Legislative approval, ⅗ majority	Add 0.65
Legislative approval *twice* by ⅗ majority	Add 0.65
Legislative Approval, ⅔ majority	Add 0.80
Legislative approval, ¾ majority	Add 0.90
If an election is required between two votes	Add 0.25
Legislative approval *twice* by ⅔ majority	Add 1.75
Action by a Bicameral Legislature	
Legislative approval, ⅓ majority or less	Add 0.50
Legislative approval, ½ + 1	Add 1.00
Legislative approval, absolute majority	Add 1.25
Legislative approval *twice* by absolute majority	Add 1.25
Legislative approval, ⅗ majority	Add 1.25
Legislative approval *twice* by ⅗ majority	Add 1.25
Legislative approval, ⅔ majority	Add 1.60
Legislative approval, ¾ majority	Add 1.80
Legislative approval *twice* by ⅔ majority	Add 3.55
If an election is required between two votes	Add 0.50
A popular referendum, ½ + 1	Add 1.50
A popular referendum, absolute majority	Add 1.75
A popular referendum, ⅗ or more	Add 2.00
Multiple state legislatures, ½ + 1	Add 2.00
Multiple state conventions, ½ + 1	Add 2.00
Multiple state legislatures or conventions, ⅔	Add 3.00
Multiple state legislatures or conventions, ¾	Add 3.50
Majority of voters *and* majority of states	Add 3.75
Unanimous approval by state governments	Add 4.00

tended to use a weighted score that reflects the actual use of one method versus another, and since the 6.50 path has never been used, a weighted composite score would be 5.10, which is what we will use here.

If we perform the same calculation for the American states, we find that the average index score is 2.92, with very little variance. The highest state score is 3.60 (Delaware), and twenty-six states are tied for the lowest score at 2.75. Another sixteen states have a score of 3.10. Thus, while we were able to detect variance between select subsets of states (see Table 9), in general the range of variance is modest compared with that found in the constitutions of other nations.

We have reached a point where we can now begin to test our propositions using data from the constitutions of other nations. Because there are fewer nations that take constitutionalism seriously than there are American states, and because data are not available for some of these nations, the total set of international constitutions that can be used to test our propositions is not very large. The results using cross-national data can thus be viewed as highly suggestive, though not empirically conclusive.

Cross-National Amendment Patterns

The first thing to be noticed in Table 11 is that the U.S. Constitution has the second most difficult amendment process. This implies, if Propositions 2 and 4 are correct, that the amendment rate for the U.S. Constitution is too low, because its amendment procedure is too difficult, while the average amendment rate for the U.S. state constitutions is not too high.

Table 12 shows the same basic relationship between the length of a constitution and its amendment rate that we found with the American constitutions (see Table 2).

Table 13 shows a linear relationship between the Index of Difficulty and the rate of amendment that is entirely in line with our expectations. The more difficult the amendment process, the lower the amendment rate.

Finally, the curvilinear relationship we found between the amendment rate and average duration of American state constitutions also seems to hold for national constitutions (compare Table 6 with Table 14); although now <#> seems to be somewhat higher—between 1.00 and 1.25 rather than between 0.76 and 1.00. There is a moderate range of amendment rate, which tends to be associated with constitutional longevity.

TABLE 11
Basic Data on Selected National Constitutions

Country	Amendment Rate	Index of Difficulty	Length in Words	Age of Const.[a]	Number of Consts.	Since
Argentina	1.04	2.10	10,600	139	3	1819
Australia	0.09	4.70	11,500	91	1	1901
Austria	7.00	0.80	36,000	63	1	1929
Cameroon	1.29	2.30	4,200	20	2	1961
Columbia	1.73	2.75	25,100	106	7	1811
Costa Rica	1.70	3.20	15,100	33	7	1844
Denmark	0.07	3.90	6,000	39	1	1953
Finland	0.71	2.30	18,300	73	1	1919
France	0.12	3.00	6,500	24	6	1789
Germany	0.97	4.60	22,400	43	1	1949
Greece	0.89	3.25	22,100	17	9	1844
Iceland	0.16	3.00	3,800	48	1	1944
India	1.49	4.10	95,000	42	1	1950
Ireland	0.55	3.00	16,000	55	1	1937
Italy	0.24	4.15	11,300	46	2	1861
Kenya	2.72	1.75	31,500	28	1	1964
Japan	0.00	3.25	5,400	47	1	1945
Luxembourg	1.80	1.80	4,700	124	1	1868
Malaysia	5.18	1.60	91,400	35	1	1957
Mexico	2.94	2.55	40,600	75	6	1814
Nigeria	0.00[b]	4.60	47,200	5	5	1960
Norway	1.14	3.60	6,500	178	1	1814
Papua New Guinea	1.75	2.10	53,700	17	1	1975
Spain	0.08	4.60	8,700	24	9	1812
Sweden	4.72	1.00	40,800	18	2	1809
Switzerland	0.78	4.75	13,300	119	4	1798
United States	0.13	5.10	7,400	203	1	1789
Venezuela	0.04	4.75	20,500	29	25	1811
Western Samoa	0.95	4.10	22,500	30	1	1962
Yugoslavia	0.75	5.60	72,100	14	4	1946
Averages	1.48	3.26	24,000	59		
American states	1.24	2.92	28,200	95	3 per gen. ed.	

[a] The age of a constitution in years, as of 1992.

[b] Data are for the most recent civilian constitution. The military constitution of 1984 revised the 1979 document by adding 206 amendments.

TABLE 12
Length of Constitution and Amendment Rate of Selected
National Constitutions

Length in words	0–10,000	10,000–20,000	20,000–30,000	Over 30,000
Amendment rate	0.53 (9)	0.73 (7)	1.30 (5)	2.95 (9)

TABLE 13
The Amendment Rate and the Degree of Difficulty in Amending
National Constitutions

Index of difficulty	0.0–1.0	1.0–2.0	2.0–3.0	3.0–4.0	4.0–5.0	5.0 +
Amendment rate	5.86 (2)	2.48 (3)	1.32 (9)	0.76 (5)	0.53 (9)	0.45 (2)

TABLE 14
The Amendment Rate and Average Duration of Selected National Constitutions

Amendment rate	0.00–0.50	0.51–1.00	1.01–1.50	1.51–2.00	2.00–2.50	2.51–3.00	3.01+
Average duration	56 (10)	49 (7)	95 (4)	70 (4)	— (0)	52 (2)	37 (3)

The difficulty of the amendment process and the length of a constitution are key factors affecting a constitution's amendment rate, and thus the probability it will be replaced. A high rate of constitutional replacement is apparently associated with rates of amendment that are either too high or too low. There would seem to be a "healthy" pattern where a constitution is amended at a regular but moderate rate to keep up with change. Such a constitution will start out relatively short, and although it may over time end up having a good number of amendments, it will also be an old constitution that is still relatively short. Aside from brevity, a moderately difficult amendment process is also important. If the Index of Difficulty proves useful for measuring the difficulty of an amendment process, and thus the likely amendment rate the amendment process will produce, it should be possible to design for an inherently moderate amendment rate with more confidence.

TABLE 15

National Constitutions Grouped according to Their General Amendment Strategy

	Legislative Complexity Plus a Referendum	Legislative Complexity Plus State Approval	Legislative Complexity Only	Parliamentary Supremacy
	Australia	Germany	Argentina	Austria
	Denmark	India	Columbia	Cameroon
	Ireland	Mexico	Costa Rica	Kenya
	Italy	Nigeria	Finland	Malaysia
	Japan	Venezuela	France	Papua New Guinea
	Spain	Yugoslavia	Greece	Sweden
	Switzerland	United States	Iceland	
	Western Samoa		Luxembourg	
			Norway	
Average length	11,800	43,600	12,500	42,900
Average amendment rate	0.35	0.90	1.03	3.78
Average index score	4.06	4.47	2.72	1.59

To return to our initial topic, the difficulty of the amendment process may be related to a commitment to (1) popular sovereignty, (2) a deliberative process, and/or (3) the distinction between normal legislation and constitutional matters. We can examine these relationships by grouping our thirty national constitutions according to which one of four general amendment strategies is used.

Working from right to left in Table 15, the first strategy can be labeled "Parliamentary Supremacy." This amendment strategy is consistent with the general Westminster form of government in which Parliament is the dominant player in all aspects of politics. This strategy does not utilize any of the three assumptions just listed. A second strategy is to use legislative complexity—some combination of extraordinary majority, multiple votes, intervening elections, delay, procedural checkpoints—as a means of making the amendment process more deliberative, which also draws a distinction between normal legislation and constitutional matters.

Although the Index of Difficulty rises, on average, about 75 percent as a result of this complexity, and the amendment rate falls almost 75 percent, the process is still dominated by the legislature such that we cannot say popular sovereignty is reflected institutionally.

The third strategy adds to legislative complexity the basic requirement that some majority of constituent governments also approve the amendment. This strategy thereby uses an even more complex decisionmaking process, which emphasizes the deliberative process and the distinction between constitutional and normal legislative matters much more than does the Legislative Complexity strategy. In addition, there is implicit an assumption of popular sovereignty, although the people are treated as grouped into substates with these state governments as a stand-in for the people. This strategy seems to reflect a rather weak commitment to popular sovereignty. However, federal systems usually need to combine a commitment to popular sovereignty with one to a highly deliberative process that protects minorities within the population, and ratification by constituent governments serves both ends. This dual need is exemplified in the Swiss amendment process, which requires ratification by both a majority of its states and a majority in a referendum. Australia, another federal system, requires a referendum that produces a majority of votes in a majority of the states. Federal systems that use ratification by constituent governments for the amendment process are committed to popular sovereignty, but their federal structure requires them to both express popular will through state mediation and provide the extra dose of procedural complexity that federal systems almost by definition require—or else they would not be federal systems to begin with. It is perhaps most correct to say that the State Approval strategy of constitutional amendment institutionally reflects an indirect popular sovereignty rather than a weak one. In any case, the State Approval strategy has an average Index of Difficulty score that is 65 percent higher than that for the Legislative Complexity strategy, and an amendment rate that is about 15 percent lower.

The fourth strategy is to add a referendum to the approval of constituent states, or in place of such state approval. This, the most difficult amendment ratification strategy, institutionalizes the most direct form of popular sovereignty, and also emphasizes the deliberative process and the distinction between constitutional and normal legislative matters. The Index of Difficulty score falls off slightly, about 10 percent, while the amendment rate falls off another 60 percent.

Table 15 also shows that countries that use a referendum form of amendment, as well as those that use solely a complex legislative form, have, on average, much shorter constitutions. These are framework constitutions that define the basic institutions and the decision-making process that connects the institutions. Except for that of the United States, and that of Germany, the nations in the other two categories use a code-of-law form of constitution, which contains many details about preferred policy outcomes and places in their documents what amounts to a basic code of law. These constitutions tend naturally to be much longer. A code-of-law form of constitution implies a reduced distinction between normal legislation and constitutional matters, as what in other systems would be "normal legislation" is put into the document. We can conclude that in general the State Approval strategy is aimed less at enhancing this distinction via a more difficult amendment process than it is in enhancing the deliberative process to protect minorities. Again, the U.S. document seems to be an exception in the State Approval category.

A number of interesting inferences can be based on Table 15. First, a short frame-of-government document using legislative complexity, without assuming popular sovereignty, can achieve about the same rate of amendment as a document based upon popular sovereignty that uses a much more difficult process but has the greater length of a code form. One can relax the level of difficulty and greatly reduce the rate of amendment simply by shortening the length of the constitution.

Second, the U.S. Constitution is unusually, and probably excessively, difficult to amend. The United States should move either to the strategy of using a referendum, in which case its amendment rate may well triple, or else reduce the number of states required for amendment ratification to two-thirds (from three-fourths), which would also roughly triple the amendment rate.

Third, we have already determined that the amendment rate is highly correlated with the degree of difficulty. We can now see that different amendment strategies, which reflect different combinations of assumptions about constitutionalism, have definite levels of difficulty associated with them. That is, institutions have clear, and in this case predictable, consequences for the political process.

Finally, both the length of a constitution and the difficulty of amendment may be related to the relative presence of an attitude that views the constitution as a higher law rather than as a receptacle for normal legislation. Certainly it seems to be the case that a low amendment rate can either reflect a reliance upon judicial or legislative revision, or else encourage such reliance in the face of needed change. It is not out of the question that the inordinate difficulties facing those who wish to amend the U.S. Constitution led to an unusually (and some would undoubtedly say "inordinately") heavy reliance on innovative judicial interpretation.

The theory of constitutional amendment advanced in this essay has posited a connection between the four methods of constitutional alteration. Propositions 1 through 4 developed the concept of amendment rate in such a way that we were able to show an empirical relationship between the formal amendment of a constitution and its complete replacement. Propositions 5 through 9 used amendment rate to relate these two methods of alteration to the other two—judicial and legislative revision. We have now reached a point where we can systematically include these last two methods in the overall theory. Toward that end it is worth considering briefly Propositions 5 through 9 in the light of our findings on the amendment process in national constitutions.

> PROPOSITION 5: A low amendment rate, associated with a long average constitutional duration, strongly implies the use of some alternative means of revision to supplement the formal amendment process.

The countries that have an amendment rate below <#> (defined as 1.00–1.50 for national constitutions), and also have a constitution older than the international average of fifty-nine years (with no interludes of military government) include Australia, Finland, Norway, Switzerland, and the United States.[11] The proposition implies that these countries either have found an alternative means, such as judicial revision in the United States, or that they are under strong pressure to find another means.[12]

> PROPOSITION 6: In the absence of a high rate of constitutional replacement, the lower the rate of formal amendment, the more likely the process of revision is dominated by a judicial body.

In the absence of further research, we have only indirect evidence for this proposition. Table 15 shows that the lower the rate of amendment,

---

[11] Of those other constitutions with an amendment rate well below <#>, Ireland's will reach fifty-nine years of age in 1996, Iceland's in 2003, Japan's in 2004, Italy's in 2005, Germany's in 2008, Denmark's in 2012, and France's in 2017, assuming none of them is replaced before then.

[12] It is beyond the scope of this effort to systematically test the tendency in these countries to develop an alternate means of constitutional alteration, but Australia provides an interesting example. Australia has one of the most difficult amendment processes in the world: Proposed amendments must first be passed by both houses of Parliament, or by one house twice, and then ratified, in most cases, by both a majority of voters nationwide and a majority of voters in at least four of Australia's six states. Certain amendments, dealing with state representation in the national Parliament and the redrawing of state boundaries, require majority approval in all six states. Australians also have a High Court that resolutely refuses to become involved in innovative constitutional interpretation. The result is rather widespread dissatisfaction among Australians with their constitution, but a continuing inability to revise or replace it. See Cheryl Saunders, "Constitutional Amendment—the Australian Experience," paper prepared for delivery at the 1992 Annual Meeting of the American Political Science Association, September 3–6, 1992.

the further we get from legislative dominance. Executive revision is not a part of normal constitutional theory, so we are left with the judiciary.

PROPOSITION 7: The higher the formal amendment rate, (a) the less likely the constitution is being viewed as a higher law; (b) the less likely a distinction is being drawn between constitutional matters and normal legislation; (c) the more likely the constitution is being viewed as a code; and (d) the more likely the formal amendment process is dominated by the legislature.

Our discussion of Table 15 has supported all parts of this proposition, although only parts (b) and (d) have direct empirical support.

PROPOSITION 8: The more important the role of the judiciary in constitutional revision, the less likely the judiciary is to use the theories of "strict construction."

In the absence of further research, Proposition 8 is a prediction to be tested. To aid that research, the next section will develop a clearer definition of "strict construction."

PROPOSITION 9: Reasonable rates of formal amendment and replacement tend to be associated with a belief in popular sovereignty.

We now have enough evidence to reject this proposition in its strict sense. The pattern of amendment rates for national constitutions suggests the range of 1.00–1.50 for <#>, our "reasonable" range. The constitutions in the Parliamentary Sovereignty group are much higher than this range (one standard deviation from the mean of this group runs from 1.75 to 5.18), and the Referendum group is too low (0.08–0.78). The constitutions with an amendment rate within <#> are evenly divided between the State Approval (0.75–1.49) and Complex Legislative (0.89–1.80) groups, which means that about half use an institutionally indirect version of popular sovereignty, and half use institutions that imply legislative rather than popular sovereignty. Even if we relax the definition of <#> by 0.25 in either direction, we take in as many additional constitutions from each category. Proposition 9 is rejected, which implies that the assumption of popular sovereignty is not necessary for designing a useful, effective amendment process.

In our effort to develop a theory of constitutional amendment, Propositions 5 through 8 together indicate the need to develop a systematic overview of the operational attitudes toward a constitution if we are to explain the relationship between the four means of constitutional change. The relative presence of these modes of thought is the last major link in our theory of amendment.

"Pure" Modes of Constitutional Construction and Their Relation to the Amending Process

Those who interpret a constitution are said to put a construction on the words, and thus judicial interpretation is often construed by the legal community as "constitutional construction." Since judicial interpretation and legislative revision are prominent alternatives to the formal amendment process, it will be useful to lay out the major contending modes of constitutional construction that appear in various constitutional systems. We are interested in the extent to which a mode of constitutional construction leaves room for a formal amendment process.

What follows is a description of modes of construction as they have been abstracted from Chester James Antieu's characterization of the answers given in various countries to the question of how they should interpret their respective constitutions.[13] This list cannot be found in Antieu's work, since he blithely mixes the different theories together. However, a careful reading allows us to unravel and describe a number of distinct positions. These theories of constitutional construction are purified in the sense that they will be distinguished from one another as much as possible. However, like Antieu, judges are likely to blend or mix principles from two or more without realizing the logical contradictions into which they have wandered. The following list, while logically defensible, is intended primarily as a heuristic device for understanding some of the possible theoretical relationships between approaches to constitutional construction and the formal amendment process.

1. Strict Construction—Historical

Emphasis is placed on the intent of those who wrote the constitution—signified by careful attention to the historical records pertaining to the writing and adoption of the document as the basis for interpretation. Words are to be read as much as possible with the meaning they had at the time of the constitution's writing and adoption. The constitution tends to be interpreted as a higher law that negates any legislation or judicial interpretation that is inconsistent with original intent. Put another way, a constitutional provision should not be interpreted in such a way as to defeat the evident purpose for which the framers wrote it. Constitutional content may be altered only through formal amendment

[13] Chester James Antieu, *Constitutional Construction* (Dobbs Ferry, N.Y.: Oceana Publications, 1982). Use was also made of Edward McWhinney, *Judicial Review in the English-Speaking World* (Toronto: University of Toronto Press, 1956).

processes that recur to a process of constitutional legitimation equivalent to that used to ratify original intent. One would expect the formal amendment rate to be high in a political system where this mode of construction is used.

2. Strict Construction—Textual

Emphasis is placed on the natural and currently accepted meaning of words as found in a standard dictionary; attention is paid to the logic implied by a strict adherence to the rules of grammar; and different sections of the constitution are read together, although the constitution is not usually construed as a coherent, theoretical whole. Little if any attention is paid to original intent, or to the possible impact of one reading versus another. Indeed, it is this mode of construction that leads some courts to reach decisions that seem pedantic and contrary to common sense—such as reversing a case on the basis of a technicality that seems to be required by constitutional language. If the meaning of a constitutional passage has been altered over time by a shift in ordinary language, this is considered a valid alteration, and if such a new meaning is not acceptable, the formal amending process must be used to undo the alteration caused by the shift in the ordinary use of the language. Since changes in the use of language can be considered random in their impact with respect to the need for constitutional change, and since such a mode of constitutional construction would seem to preclude much judicial interpretation, the rate of formal amendment for a political system using this mode of construction would probably be quite high.

3. Legalistic Construction

Emphasis is placed on the range of meaning that can be sustained by a reading of a constitutional provision using judicial precedent as determinative. Rather than seeing any provision as having a singular, exclusive, or "single-peaked" meaning, each provision is viewed as allowing a range of possible behavior that falls within the limits defined by the statement. The range of meaning, and thus the allowable limits upon the behavior it defines, is summarized in the set of legal precedents brought to bear. Thus, the meaning of a provision is subject to expansion or contraction depending upon the set of precedents deemed relevant. Constitutional purpose is contained in these precedents rather than in the "mischief" that this provision was designed to remedy.

There is less room for a supreme court to maneuver with this mode of construction than with the teleological mode, although they are somewhat related, since over time judicial precedent will tend to define what looks functionally equivalent to basic principles. As with the teleological mode, pressures for formal amendment will not be strong, since adjustments in constitutional meaning can be gradually updated through evolving precedent to meet changing circumstances. Since there is less room for a court to maneuver than in the teleological mode, the rate of formal amendment will tend to be somewhat higher than in that mode.

4. Teleological Construction

Emphasis is placed on construing every constitutional provision in conformity with the basic principles or fundamental purposes contained in the basic law. Rather than viewing a constitutional provision in isolation, its meaning is viewed in the context of the entire document, which is viewed as a theoretically coherent whole and as evolving in its implications. Thus, there is a "progressive construction" as the basic principles of a constitution are applied to new circumstances that were not foreseen by those writing the document. Careful attention is paid to basic principles that undergird and inform the entire document. Interpreters rely upon "reasonable intent," the spirit of the law, not upon a strict rendering of the words. That is, constitutions are not to be interpreted according to the words used in particular clauses, but rather the whole constitution is to be examined in order to determine the meaning of any part. Such an approach requires relatively infrequent amendment since only shifts in the underlying, basic principles require an alteration in the constitution. Otherwise, the Supreme Court and/or legislature may engage in broad interpretation of constitutional provisions as long as such interpretations are generally seen as being in conformity with the constitution's basic principles.

5. Judicial or "Natural Law" Construction

Emphasis is placed upon what is reasonable to civilized people, with members of the court standing in as the conscience of those people. Such an approach is often typified by an interest in the decisions reached by supreme courts in other countries, but this mode of construction is just as often characterized by a judicial activism that is fueled by domestically conditioned value systems. "Natural law" can have a religious basis, such as fundamentalist Christianity, Islam, or Judaism; but it can also be secularly grounded in rationalism, humanism, or social science, for example. Secular versions will tend to be more cosmopolitan and internationalist in the implications drawn from the constitution, while religious versions will tend to be more particularistic and culture-bound in constitutional construction. Since this mode of constitutional construction provides the widest leeway for judicial activism, formal constitutional amendment in political systems using this mode will tend to be very low.

6. Political or Social Construction

Emphasis is placed on the balancing of competing values, interests, factions, classes, social needs, or institutions, with an eye on the impact upon political society. Any form of extraneous evidence may be brought to bear, especially empirical data, scholarly works, or opinions (both legal and nonlegal) bearing on the probable relative costs, benefits, and incentives of the decision on the parties involved. Typically, the court will ask if reason or fairness demands that one side prevail even though the other party also has a constitutionally sustainable case. Such construction is often invited by constitutional provisions that contain language such as "may not unduly infringe upon," or "may, within reasonable limits." Such a mode of construction is usually associated with a constitution that has many such vague statements. Because the judiciary is virtually invited to determine the constitution's meaning, the rate of formal amendment for this mode of constitutional construction is quite low.

7. Statutory Construction

Emphasis is placed upon finding a singular, literal meaning for a constitutional provision that is congruent with the purpose of a provision in terms of what it was intended to accomplish. There is little or no attempt to determine the logical imperatives of a theory that might make sense of the entire constitution when considered as a whole with related parts. With this mode of construction the constitutional provision tends to be read as equivalent to a normal statute, and thus not as a higher law. As with a statute, constitutional provisions are interpreted in view of the purpose to be accomplished by its enactment. Even so, with the proclivity for narrow construction comes the need to frequently alter provisions that do not address or resolve new issues, and there is a tendency for the legislature to frequently amend the constitution through normal legislation. Common law countries using the Westminster model are especially prone to this mode of construction, since that model begins with an assumption of parliamentary sovereignty. There is little need for a formal amendment procedure beyond specifying the legislature's role in constitutional revision, although some countries using the Westminster model have a separate amendment procedure anyway.

These modes of constitutional construction have been presented in a rather "pure" form. Most judicial systems are probably a blend, since adherents of two or more modes would be contending for supremacy, although this is yet to be determined empirically. In any case, these modes have been roughly rank-ordered according to their predicted rate of formal amendment—from highest to lowest. This rank ordering must still be empirically tested, as well as the modes' relative rates of formal amendment, but for now we will predict the following *ranges* of formal amendment rates, using as a basis for our estimates the amendment patterns discovered earlier.

	Range	*Mean*
1. Strict construction—historical	1.75–2.75	2.25
2. Strict construction—textual	1.50–2.50	2.00
3. Legalistic construction	0.75–1.75	1.25
4. Teleological construction	0.50–1.50	1.00
5. Judicial or natural law construction	0.00–1.00	0.50
6. Political or social construction	0.00–0.50	0.25
7. Statutory construction	3.00–4.50	3.75

These overly precise predictions suggest that once we determine the theory or theories of constitutional construction in use in a given country, the pattern will be to sort into four distinguishable categories. Those countries where we find a statutory form of construction dominant on the court and among those prominent in other major political bodies will exhibit a very high rate of formal amendment. We have used here the amendment rate we determined empirically from our examination of national constitutions. The lowest rates of amendment will be associated with constitutions where judicial (natural law) or political (social) construction is used, and it will be difficult to distinguish the two in their effects.

Countries where legalistic or teleological construction predominates will have moderate amendment rates, and it will be difficult to distingish the effects of these two modes. Finally, countries where some form of strict construction is used will tend to have an amendment rate significantly higher than the legalistic-teleological combination, but recognizably lower than that associated with statutory construction. Again, it will be difficult to distinguish the effects of the different forms of strict construction.

From this abstraction of the modes of construction we can derive several more propositions to be tested later as part of a theory of amendment.

PROPOSITION 10: The stricter the mode of construction tied to the words of a constitution, the higher the rate of formal amendment, and vice versa.

This proposition is self-explanatory from the previous discussion.

PROPOSITION 11: A relatively difficult amendment process will tend to be associated with a broad theory of judicial construction, one in which the court has few if any restrictions on how it justifies its decisions, and an easy amendment process will be associated with a narrow theory of construction.

This says nothing more than that, in the face of the inevitable need to adjust to change, the more difficult the formal amendment process, the more need there is for judicial activism in this regard, and thus the more likely that broad theories of construction will be used by the constitutional court (i.e., the less it will tend toward strict construction). A relatively easy amendment process, on the other hand, will relieve these pressures, and the constitutional court is likely to use more restrictive theories of construction. If a constitution can be altered by legislative action, the court is likely to take itself completely out of the amendment process.

PROPOSITION 12: Courts will usually develop internally competing theories of construction that are contiguous.

That is, if a theory of strict construction is used, it will tend to be in conflict with another theory of strict construction rather than with a social or natural law construction. Likewise, social and natural law theories of construction will be in competition with each other rather than with theories of strict construction. We can expect a similar competition between legalistic and teleological theories of construction. The use of the statutory construction mode tends to preclude the use of any of the others.

These twelve propositions form the core of a theory of constitutional amendment that has analytic coherence, empirical import, and normative implications. We could add other propositions by formalizing some of the points that have been repeatedly made, such as: "The statutory construction mode tends to be associated with political systems based on parliamentary sovereignty"; or "The rate of amendment may be manipulated by adjusting the length of a document and the difficulty of its amending process, separately or together"; or "Frame-of-government constitutions tend, on average, to be less than one-third as long as code-of-law documents." However, the general parameters of the theory are now clear, as is the direction for future research.

Twelve

The Politics of Constitutional Revision in Eastern Europe

STEPHEN HOLMES AND CASS R. SUNSTEIN

A CONSTITUTION, among other things, is a document that is unusually difficult to change. Constitutionalism hinges upon a distinction between the procedures governing ordinary legislation and the more onerous procedural hurdles that must be overcome in order to recast the ground rules of political life. To understand the amending power and its limits, therefore, is to understand the balance of rigidity and flexibility, of permanence and adaptability, that lies at the heart of constitutional government. To institutionalize a constitutional system, as post-Communist drafters from Tirana to Tallinn are now attempting to do, means, among other things, to establish clear rules for, and restraints upon, future constitutional change.

A seemingly simple, albeit important, practical question raised by all such attempts is what amending formula should be adopted by these particular countries during this particular phase of their dramatic economic, political, and social transformations. The amending power is not a legal technicality but may, in turn, color the political process as a whole. The answer that we propose and defend in this chapter can be stated succinctly: The procedure for constitutional modification best adapted to Eastern Europe today sets relatively lax conditions for amendment, keeps unamendable provisions to a minimal core of basic rights and institutions, and usually allows the process to be monopolized by parliament, without any obligatory recourse to popular referenda.

This arrangement, or so we will argue, should make possible necessary but legally channeled readjustments to swiftly changing circumstances without undermining the already weak legitimacy of democratically accountable assemblies. We urge this approach with some ambivalence. Under better conditions, a sharp split between constitutional law and ordinary law would be preferable.[1] But the peculiar conditions of Eastern Europe do not make this a sensible solution.

[1] See John Rawls, *Political Liberalism* (New York: Columbia University Press, 1993), for an account of why this might be so.

Some Theoretical Issues

Before turning to recent experiences with constitutional revision in Eastern Europe and defending our recommendation, we introduce a few analytical points. An amending formula, first of all, provides a way for framers to share some of their authority over the constitution with subsequent generations. Because of this relationship to the initial framing power, the amending power trenches upon core issues of democracy and sovereignty. Constitutional revision raises the question of the source of law or "popular sovereignty" in its most institutionally concrete form.[2] If all political agency must be authorized by the constitution, whence comes the authority to remake the constitution? If the amending power is conceived as wholly subordinate to the constitution, it presents an obvious anomaly.

This anomaly is strikingly expressed in an abortive attempt by French constitutional theorists to classify the authority to revise the constitution. Following usage established by Abbé Sieyes in the late eighteenth century, French constitutionalists distinguish between the framing power—*le pouvoir constituant*—and the three established branches of government—*les pouvoirs constitués*. The amending power does not fit comfortably into either category. It inhabits a twilight zone between authorizing and authorized powers. To classify it, therefore, French constitutionalists resort to farfetched terms, such as *le pouvoir constituant institué* and *le pouvoir constituant derivé*.[3] They might as well have confessed their embarrassment and called it *le pouvoir constituant constitué*. Strangely enough, there is something to this oxymoron. The amending power is simultaneously framing and framed, licensing and licensed, original and derived, superior and inferior to the constitution. This acrobatic both/and pattern alerts us to the undertheorized dilemma posed by the constitutionally regulated power to revise constitutional regulations of power.

Whence comes such a metapower, since it obviously cannot derive wholly from the constitution itself? The traditional democratic answer has been "the people." It is almost as if the electorate, through its residual right to initiate and ratify constitutional amendments, retains some of its original authority to choose the nature of the political regime, to lay down the ground rules of subsequent decision making, and to establish the limits and legitimate aims of government action.[4] As Bruce Ack-

---

[2] See especially the essays by Bruce Ackerman and Akhil Reed Amar in this volume.

[3] Georges Burdeau, Francis Hamon, and Michel Troper, *Droit Constitutionnel*, 23rd ed. (Paris: Librairie Générale de Droit et de Jurisprudence, 1993), p. 356.

[4] On sovereignty and constitutionalism in the American context, see Samuel Beer, *To Make A Nation* (Cambridge, Mass.: Harvard University Press, 1993).

erman and others have argued, democracy would be incomplete if the citizenry could act only through periodic elections and public discussions of concrete policy alternatives conducted through a free press.[5] To this must be added the right to change or not to change fundamental value commitments and the rules of the game. Political legitimacy in liberal systems ultimately depends upon the option to bring about change, used or held in reserve.

The legitimacy of a liberal constitution has a similar foundation, paradoxically, in its own liability to revision. It is accepted, or deserves to be accepted, partly because it could be changed.[6] Constitutional government, in its American variant at least, cannot dispense with the concept of supraconstitutional sovereignty or authority *over* the constitution. This is an especially good pattern to imitate, we suggest, when social turbulence makes it advisable to design liberal-democratic constitutions in a way that holds open a legal path to ongoing constitutional transformation. Indeed, the American idea should be taken much further—and in a way that reforms that idea fundamentally—under conditions in which uncertainty and factionalism make it risky to attempt a sharp distinction between constitutional politics and ordinary politics.

A theory of the amending power must probe the difficult relationship between constitutional limits on power and the limbo-inhabiting power to revise these limits. By so doing, it can help us answer some old and fundamental questions. What is the connection between democracy and liberalism, for instance, or between collective self-rule and limited government? Is there some sort of contradiction or deep tension here? Is the genuine democrat logically committed to being an antiliberal? Is the true liberal bound to be fearful of and hostile to democracy? Does constitutional rigidity thwart the popular will? The amending power draws attention to these questions in several stark ways. For instance, the procedural obstacles to easy constitutional amendment form the core of the countermajoritarian dilemma. Why should a majority, in a democratic country, be prevented from doing whatever it wants?

One answer might be that "democracy" cannot be reduced to majoritarian decision making. We might adopt a conception of democracy that contains certain preconditions that operate as constraints on majoritarian rule. The right to free speech, for example, is part of the basis for democracy. Constitutional protection of free speech is hardly inconsistent with democratic principles. The same may well be true of the right

---

[5] See Bruce Ackerman, *We the People* (Cambridge, Mass.: Harvard University Press, 1991).

[6] For Eastern Europe, as we will argue below, the crucial implication of this principle is that the more difficult it is to amend a constitution, the less plausible it becomes to infer "consent" from a failure to amend it.

to vote, the right to religious liberty, and the right to private property. Many liberal rights are best understood as preconditions for a well-functioning democracy, and not as antidemocratic at all. We can see constitutions as precommitment strategies, designed to safeguard goals that would predictably be compromised by agents of the people, or by the people themselves. The alleged paradox of liberal democracy has been greatly overstated; democracy and liberalism are mutually reinforcing creeds.

But there are at least potential tensions between liberal and democratic goals. It is for this reason that a stringent amending formula, of the sort that many observers recommend for Eastern Europe, might seem to suggest a bias for liberalism *against* democracy. The very existence of an amending formula, on the other hand, might suggest a bias *for* democratic procedure over moral substance. The neutrality of democratic proceduralism should not be neglected here; supermajoritarianism, just like majority rule, implies that decisions are legitimated by their source, not by their content. The amending power, as it exists in some Western liberal-democratic constitutions, implies that the basic framework of political life *can* be wholly changed, as long as a proper procedural benediction is secured.

Amendability suggests, to put it crudely, that basic rights are ultimately at the mercy of interest-group politics, if some arbitrary electoral threshold is surpassed and amenders play by the book. Is this a correct way of understanding liberal democracy? Does Article V of the U.S. Constitution imply the triumph of procedure over substance, formal rules over moral norms? Are there no fundamental rights beyond the reach of politics? Are there no goods that are protected absolutely, rather than depending on a percentage of votes?

This question can be reformulated in practical terms. Does the political system of a specific country, say the United States or Germany, admit judicial review of procedurally correct constitutional amendments? The United States does not, on the ground that the constitution-remaking power is superior to the power of judicial review;[7] but Germany does, on the ground that an amendment, even if passed in the formally correct manner, may be inconsistent with the core or fundamental features of the constitution. Germany entrenches certain rights in the sense that it places them beyond not only politics, but even the kind of revision represented by constitutional amendment.

The form taken by the amending power, in other words, sheds light

---

[7] Though see especially Walter Murphy's contribution to this volume, which vigorously argues in favor of the opposite view, seemingly endorsed also, at least in part, by Mark Brandon and Akhil Reed Amar in their essays. John Vile makes the case against such review.

on the variety of theories underlying different liberal democracies. It helps us identify the broad norms and basic commitments behind the constitutional fine print. It helps explain how various framers conceived the relationship between procedure and substance, for instance, or the distinction between the core and the periphery of the constitutional order. In the American case, the amending power builds upon a democratic conception of popular sovereignty, of the authorizing democratic will that stands above the constitution and is able to change it in toto. This idea fits well with the self-conscious American revision of the English understanding of sovereignty. The German Constitution, while gesturing in the direction of popular sovereignty, declares many provisions unamendable, allowing the unelected court effectively to block certain attempts by the elected branches to change the constitution.

One final point before turning directly to more narrowly regional concerns. Every functioning liberal democracy depends on a variety of techniques for introducing flexibility into the constitutional framework.[8] The two usual methods are, first, amendment and, second, judicial interpretation in the light of evolving circumstances and social norms. There are intriguing interaction or mutual compensation effects of constitutional amendment and constitutional interpretation, and these can help us understand better the relationship between the judiciary and the political branches. Both parliaments and courts can actually benefit from a stringent amending procedure. If amendments are relatively difficult, the legislature has a ready alibi for failure to give in to the electorate, and the court, in turn, will gain in prestige because it can pose as the guardian of the ark of the covenant. (Consider, as testing cases, the American experiences over school prayer, school desegregation, poll taxes, abortion, and flag burning.) As circumstances change over time, flexible interpretation also diminishes the pressure for frequent amendment. Consider, for example, the American experience during the New Deal, in which flexible interpretive practices enabled the Constitution to be accommodated to new social needs and norms.[9]

The free availability of amendment may have a range of diverse effects on the courts. If it is easy to amend the Constitution, the stakes of constitutional decision are lowered, for an erroneous or unpopular judicial decision can be overridden.[10] Moreover, the availability of the amendment option may embolden the court, since the judges will know that

[8] See Donald Lutz's essay in this volume for a thorough canvass of such techniques.

[9] Bruce Ackerman treats the New Deal as a structural amendment to the Constitution (see *We the People*); but we think it is more accurate to see the New Deal as a product of reasonable interpretive practices.

[10] Within the United States, probably the best example of this phenomenon is the use of the initiative and referendum process of constitutional amendment.

mistaken decisions can be corrected. For Eastern Europe, it is especially important to keep in mind the following point: Stringent amending formulas will allow parliaments faced with large social problems to deflect social disapprobation and to escape democratic accountability in difficult times.

Eastern Europe

How are these somewhat abstruse theoretical issues reflected in the constitutional politics now under way in Eastern Europe? When the Communist system collapsed in Albania, Bulgaria, Czechoslovakia, Estonia, Hungary, Latvia, Lithuania, Poland, Romania, Russia, and Ukraine, one of the first acts of the wobbly new regimes was a solemnly enacted constitutional amendment.[11] Throughout the region, the unstitching of the hammer and sickle from uniforms and banners was accompanied by the deletion of the clause that appeared in every Soviet-era constitution stipulating the leading role of the Communist party. And this was only the beginning. The dénouement of the Polish Round Table talks in 1989, for instance, was the amendment of the 1952 Constitution to bring it into line with the compromises stuck between Solidarity and the party. Similar attempts to codify a swiftly changing balance of social forces occurred throughout the region. And it was not inappropriate that the greatest political transformation of this century was decorated by, or embodied in, constitutional amendments. Communist-era constitutions were repeatedly amended, of course.[12] But to found a new regime through the strategic use of the amending power, which was never the purpose of earlier modifications, represents a *wholly non-Bolshevik* method for reacting to and promoting social change. The old order was not overthrown but simply negotiated and codified away.[13] Such a beginning was meant by the actors involved to register or symbolize a commitment to a nonrevolutionary form of political change. The rule of law had begun. There was to be no more rumbling of tanks. Future transformations would come seriatim, could not be wholly planned in advance, and would be legal, public, and nonviolent.

[11] It is interesting that in Germany, the Western democracy most convulsed by the collapse of communism, constitutional amendments (concerning the right of asylum and the role of the army) have also become the stuff of newspaper headlines and heated parliamentary debates.

[12] The theory behind the amendment of Communist constitutions may have been this: "When events overtake the Constitution, the latter . . . is to be amended or replaced; the constitution is not to restrain social change." W. E. Butler, *Soviet Law* (London: Butterworths, 1988), p. 144.

[13] Andras Sajo, "States of Post-Communism," *East European Reporter* (May–June 1992): 39.

However peaceful, these dramatic acts of constitutional revocation and revision were not meant to be modest. They had important symbolic and expressive functions; they also registered the ambition of would-be democratic peoples to take their destinies into their own hands, to master the unprecedented changes coursing over them, to make basic choices about where they want to go as separate peoples, now that the great colonizing power had collapsed. Given the massiveness and nearly total unexpectedness of the change in question, no observer would suggest that modifying constitutions will allow the inhabitants of the former Muscovite empire to seize political control of their own lives. But the story of the amending power in Eastern Europe is partly a story of the uphill battle of now unsupervised peoples to do just that. This is why the amending power is also a subject for comparative politics, not for constitutional theory alone.

Consider, as a first although admittedly untypical example, the Russian Federation. Ruslan Khasbulatov, before he was deposed by Boris Yeltsin from his position as Speaker of the Russian Supreme Soviet, had several constitutional lawyers on his staff whose job was to tell him when his legislative proposals conflicted with the constitution. When Khasbulatov learned of a possible conflict, he did not abandon his legislative proposal, of course, but with breathtaking nonchalance initiated the procedure whereby the constitution itself could be changed. Put succinctly, constitutional amendments have been used in contemporary Russia (by Yeltsin as well as by Khasbulatov) as just another technique for outmaneuvering one's political enemies of the moment. Or, in Jon Elster's words, the constitution is viewed as an instrument of action instead of a framework for action.[14] The idea that constitutional revision represents some kind of "higher track of lawmaking,"[15] different from and superior to the elbowing and intrigues of ordinary political life, is dramatically belied by recent Russian experience. And while Russia lies on one extreme of the spectrum, the subordination of constitutional revision to everyday political antics and aims is a trend observable everywhere in the region.[16] It follows that the conception of constitutions as precommitment strategies—however helpful it may be for analyzing some constitutional processes and for conceiving of constitutionalism in general—is descriptively inaccurate for Eastern Europe.

[14] Jon Elster, "Constitutionalism in Eastern Europe: An Introduction," *University of Chicago Law Review* 58 (1991): 470.

[15] See Ackerman, *We the People*, describing the American experience in this way.

[16] We do not deny that high principle plays a role in constitutional politics in Eastern Europe. For example, the elaborate catalogue of protected rights—building on Western examples and international human rights documents—tends to undermine the view that strategy and partisanship can explain everything. See the discussion in Cass R. Sunstein, "Something Old, Something New," *East European Constitutional Review*

The Politics of Constitutional Change

Politicians and publics socialized to autocracy, it is sometimes said, cannot be expected to treat legal texts as in any way sacred. And it is undoubtedly true that the lack of a firm constitutional tradition helps contribute to the absence of a clear split between constitutional and nonconstitutional processes. Under communism, of course, the constitution did not furnish reliable brakes on the behavior of political actors. But the concept of a constitutional culture, purportedly missing from the region for historical reasons, not only promotes unnecessary pessimism. It is also deeply unclear. (Was there such a culture in Weimar Germany? Is there one in India today?) We think that a different approach, emphasizing present problems rather than the unfavorable legacies of the past, will be more helpful.

Why, in Eastern Europe today, does the "higher track" of constitutional politics collapse so easily into the "lower track" of ordinary politics? First of all, no myth of the framers has had a chance to arise. Indeed, many of the political actors of today were personally involved in striking the constitutional bargains of yesterday. Moreover, most of those bargains were negotiated in spectacular ignorance about the subsequent course of events. The powers of presidency in both Poland and Hungary, for instance, were designed with false assumptions about the eventual occupant of this office. Why should Lech Walesa respect limits that were created to hamstring General Wojciech Jaruzelski? Why should Arpad Goncz, a member of the liberal opposition, keep within his constitutionally assigned powers, since he knows that these restrictions were originally contrived *by his own party* to limit the options of Imre Pozsgay?

It is especially hard to respect deals that *we ourselves* originally struck for strategic reasons, to protect our hides or to outmaneuver opponents who have now completely disappeared from the scene. But these are the myopic bargains before which constitutional piety, as advocated by some legalistic observers, would demand that East European politicians now humbly kneel down. The personal involvement of current movers and shakers in earlier constitution-making processes, the remarkable speed at which the political landscape has been changing, and a limited capacity for foresight on all sides have just as much to do with the absence of sacralized constitutions in Eastern Europe as does the lack of an

---

(1992): 18. With the new constitutions, as with new laws, there is a mixture of principled argument and strategic behavior. Our point is that, in general, there is no sharp split between constitution making and the ordinary processes of politics.

inherited constitutional culture. It is largely the current situation, not custom, that prevents politicians from seeing disregard for the constitutional text as a wholly inadmissible derogation of duty.

Legislative chambers in Eastern Europe, it should also be said, have everywhere been doubling as constituent assemblies. The time and attention they have been able to devote to constitutional considerations have therefore been quite limited. Even more important, the *weak legitimacy and internal fragmentation of elected parliaments* is a regional pattern. The "forum" parties, once united by opposition to the old regime, are splintering. What is missing is effective representation and powerful parties capable of attracting large national constituencies, at least as much as a penchant to worship the constitutional text. Parliaments whose popular legitimacy is weak and that are fragmented into dozens of "taxi parties" or "couch parties" involved in constantly shifting alliances (making it difficult to cobble together stable and internally coherent coalition governments) will naturally have a hard time creating a constitutional framework that earns general respect.

All of this is hardly surprising. Moreover, it has certain advantages. Social, economic, and political turbulence is going to continue in these countries for years, and even decades. So what is the optimal balance of constitutional rigidity and flexibility in such circumstances? Is it realistic to try to establish *definitive* arrangements under such fluid conditions? Might not rigid constitutions produce greater unpredictability than flexible ones? In these countries, political actors not only routinely miscalculate their future interests, but political groupings repeatedly undergo kaleidoscopic realignments, transfers of loyalty, and transformations of identity. They dissolve and reform, disappearing and reappearing in unpredictable ways. A parliamentary fraction may strike a sensible bargain today, but its bargaining partner may also vanish tomorrow. All striving for institutional permanence here is bound to fail. Where public pressure for change is likely to mount, easily accessible legal pathways to change (i.e., the chance to readjust to unexpected events and altered circumstances), must be built into the constitutional order itself. Some tolerance for some procedural irregularities in the process of constitutional revision, moreover, is to be expected, and should not necessarily be roundly condemned, especially because technical legalisms have little democratic legitimacy even in the eyes of democratic Western electorates.[17]

---

[17] A good example is De Gaulle's 1962 introduction of a presidential system into France by means of a procedurally unconstitutional referendum; the amendment was at first decried by constitutional lawyers, but their protests were useless since the decision was accepted by the public. For Eastern Europe, consider the last-minute rule change that allowed the Polish Sejm to pass a major constitutional amendment in August 1992. For

In general, no group of framers, given the universally acknowledged proneness of all actors to commit colossal blunders in turbulent circumstances, can plausibly monopolize authority over the constitutional framework, refusing to share this authority with subsequent generations, or even with the successor representative assembly. Amateurish drafting guarantees that numerous mistakes will become visible with benefit of hindsight. The personal domination of the drafting process by a tiny number of powerful deputies and their backroom constitutional experts means that some clauses will be smuggled into the constitution without anyone noticing, only to be discovered, to the consternation of some later on. A stringent amendment procedure, patented in the West, whereby constitutional provisions are cemented into the system, implies *deference* toward the decisions of the framers. Because such deference cannot be conjured magically out of the East European air, given who the framers are and the purposes they visibly pursue, a lax amending formula, one that will not saddle successors with the schemes and follies of predecessors, is unusually desirable.

Western observers have been tempted to condemn easy paths to constitutional modification in Eastern Europe, however, and to denounce more generally the "confusion" between constitutional politics and ordinary politics characteristic of every post-Communist society. This reaction is understandable. Good institutional arrangements should certainly be entrenched if they can offer firm protection to democratic liberty and even to the preconditions for economic prosperity. A large and distinctive advantage of a firm constitution is that it promotes a high degree of stability in a way that can be facilitative rather than constraining to political arrangements. Especially in the current circumstances in Eastern Europe, it may seem particularly important to produce a stable constitution now, and in that process to inaugurate the sharpest of splits between constitutional law and ordinary law. When circumstances are changing so rapidly, in a context threatening to market arrangements and democratic processes, it may appear indispensable to use constitutionalism in order to provide a firm backdrop for private and public arrangements. Above all, confusion may seem unacceptable. It may matter less what the rules are than that there are rules.

There is something to be said for this view, and we will try to describe arrangements that can accommodate some of the relevant concerns. But

---

background, see Louisa Vinton, "Poland's 'Little Constitution' Clarifies Walesa's Powers," *RL/RFE Reports* 1, no. 35 (September 4, 1992): 19; and Wiktor Osiatynski, *East European Constitutional Review* 1, no. 3, p. 13. Walesa, it is true, signed this amendment only after the constitutional court ruled that the rule change was itself constitutional.

the view is far too simple. What looks like confusion from a high-altitude Western perspective may have its own rationale on the ground. Not only does social turbulence demand a good deal of flexibility and "ad hockery," but *the very creation of a constitutional culture in post-Communist societies depends upon a willingness to mix constitutional politics and ordinary politics.* Perhaps the most fundamental part of any constitution is the elemental choice of regime type. Soviet-style constitutions did not explicitly forbid amendments that would transform the Communist system into a capitalist one. But we may safely infer that such a prohibition, the flip side of the elemental "choice" of socialism, was implicit and understood by all. To change a communist constitution into a liberal-democratic one required something more drastic than modification, revision, or amendment. It required the wholesale destruction of the old and the creation, from ground zero, of the new. It required a *constitutional revolution*, or new founding. Because the basic "choice of regime" is involved, as we already suggested, the legal transformations under way in Eastern Europe must be seen as constitutional revolutions rather than incremental constitutional revisions.[18]

More precisely, they are constitutional revolutions *cloaked* as constitutional revisions. Most striking, from this perspective, is the discordance of content and form. A wholesale constitutional replacement was presented to domestic publics and the world at large as an act of constitutional tinkering. One of the most revolutionary changes of modern times was symbolically de-revolutionized. A total rupture with the past, all aspects of society being reformed simultaneously, was packaged as a piecemeal reform. This was unrealistic, of course. As Vaclav Havel said, commenting upon the Czecho-Slovak partition, "States do not begin and end in a constitutional fashion."[19] But the aspiring liberal democracies of Eastern Europe have all *pretended* to begin and end in this way. The clause about the leading role of the party was revoked, presidencies created, constitutional courts put in place, bills of rights enacted, and so forth—all by sitting or newly elected legislatures. It probably had to happen in this manner, of course, since there was no pathway to change that seemed more promising than this. But the packaging of political revolution as mere constitutional revision, as a procedurally correct exercise of the amending power (used but never taken seriously before), provides an important clue to current conditions in the region.

[18] See chapter 2 of this volume, by Sanford Levinson, for a discussion of the difference between "amendment," "revision," and "revolution."

[19] "Havel—Constitutional Purism a Waste of Time for CSFR," October 3, 1992, LEXIS, (Nexis), CTK National News Wire.

Chicken Little

In every Eastern European country, including Poland, the basic choice of regime fell out of the sky. The transition from communism to a rudimentary form of democratic capitalism may have been anticipated by scattered opposition elites; it may have been accompanied by mass euphoria; but it was *not* achieved by mass mobilization, and thus cannot, even now, be viewed realistically as an expression of the national will. What occurred in 1989 was not only a revolution; it was also an unexpected act of decolonization. The Soviet patron went home. A large part of the revolution was precisely this exodus of what seemed like an occupying military force. Western observers have received the downfall of communism as a vindication of democratic liberty, of religious and political freedom, and of a certain conception of appropriate economic arrangements. Undoubtedly much of this is true. But we cannot overstate the extent to which the developments of 1989 represented a repudiation of the mere fact of foreign domination from the Soviets—in some ways a repudiation that was independent of the particular form that the domination took.

Because the die was cast by Moscow, the new regimes established across the region are just as much the product of the actions (i.e., nonactions) of the Red Army as were the Communist regimes established in 1948. The constitutional about-face, the basic choice of a liberal-democratic regime, was not really prepared domestically, but instead thrust on the satellite states from abroad, by the unilaterally withdrawn threat of a Russian crackdown. Some latitude for fine-tuning was left to national forces. But this does not alter the overwhelming *heteronomy* of the "revolutions" of 1989—a point that bears directly (as we will soon see) on the selection of amendment procedures.

This heteronomy also helps explain the historical anomaly of revolution-by-constitutional-tinkering. Wholly new political arrangements have been institutionalized throughout the region on the basis of a string of constitutional amendments passed by weakly legitimate parliaments, assemblies that are, in turn, fragmented into a chaos of small parties. The disproportion between means and ends could not be more striking. How could such a massive change be introduced by such a feeble institution deploying such feeble measures? The answer lies in the power vacuum left in the wake of Moscow's unexpected collapse. Power is relative, and the power of parliaments in Eastern Europe, however small, usually looms large in societies where all rival centers of power are (for the time being)[20] even weaker. These parliaments, in any case, were

---

[20] The parliaments of Eastern Europe can govern as long as no rival institutions emerge

suddenly charged with a monumental task for which they were monumentally ill prepared. Their members were and are inexperienced in governance and they do not enjoy high public prestige. Their relative power, as a result, may be difficult to sustain. The absence of a historically anchored constitutional tradition is only one problem among many. Even if agreements between mutually suspicious and opportunist deputies, prone to conspiracy thinking and vulnerable to blackmail, could be hammered out, there is no way these assemblies could simply impose (*octroyer*) a constitution upon a passive citizenry and expect it to last or be obeyed.

These various considerations converge on a single conclusion: *Constitution making in Eastern Europe must be a long, drawn-out political act*. Only in this way can a revolution delivered on a platter be transformed into a basic choice of regime made, or rather *achieved*, by the countries themselves. The fundamental choice of liberal democracy, one that fell out of the sky, must now be brought down to earth and worked out politically, by trial and error, by consultation and debate, if it is to gain the public support it needs. This can be achieved best by vesting the parliament with full authority to frame a new constitution and with a flexible capacity for constitutional amendment (we offer details below).

To be sure, this *parliamentization* of constitution making has many drawbacks: false starts, half steps and missteps, interim arrangements based on myopic bargains, legislative deadlocks, interest-group pressures, the short-term stalling of economic reform, technically botched or amateurish constitutional provisions, and so forth. But this "collapse" of constitutional politics into ordinary politics has two great advantages that outweigh all the obvious disadvantages. First, it provides an opportunity for the political nation to be introduced, over time, to the large questions of constitutional government (presidentialism versus parliamentarism, proportional representation versus single-member districts, unicameralism versus bicameralism, legislative supremacy versus judicial review, and so forth) *while* such issues are being seriously debated. And, second, it provides a chance for opposition elites, trained in clandestine nonacquiescence and witness bearing (and therefore inclined to irony and "principled stands"), to learn the arts of public coalition formation and governance. And it achieves this constitutional education for both officials and citizens without under-

---

capable of aggregating still diffuse and uncoordinated discontent. If the Polish church, say, decided to tap into the resentments of the employees of the mammoth and uncompetitive state-owned enterprises, the problems of governance in the country would be markedly increased.

mining, as easy recourse to popular referenda might do, the still feeble legitimacy of representative institutions. (Note also that a significant risk of referenda, under current conditions, is that very few people will vote.)

Parliamentary fumbling, or trial and error, in the constitutional arena appears more desirable than deplorable when viewed from this perspective. To expect that societies that are so disorganized socially could establish a "higher track" of constitution making *outside* the parliament, moreover, is as unrealistic as to expect that the representative assembly will stay its hand and bypass the fundamental controversies dividing society. Neither the mobilized masses nor a commission of experts could do the job in question. Furthermore, to hand over the constitution modifying process to a special convention, separate from parliament, and operating in the pure legal air above the political fray, may seem plausible to visiting law professors; but it would be quixotic in the conditions in Eastern Europe today. Because the most fundamental questions—such as, What sort of regime do we want?—have not been answered by the citizenry, and since no organized forum for national political debate is about to develop outside of the assembly, ordinary parliamentary politics is necessarily *about* constitutional questions. In today's circumstances, constitutional choices are partisan choices and institutional arrangements are necessarily experimental. The rules of the game cannot be clearly distinguished from the content of the game. (This is all the more true since political scientists have little predictive knowledge to offer about the political consequences of competing constitutional arrangements.)

As a result, we should not expect constitution drafting and modification in Eastern Europe to be untainted by political interests. Indeed, it would be futile to attempt to separate the currently inseparable, assigning the "lower track" of ordinary politics to one assembly and the "higher track" of constitutional politics to another. There is no choice but to accept the drawbacks of a highly politicized, and that means parliamentarized, process. Such an arrangement guarantees that everyday politics is part of an ongoing constitutional crisis. But tolerance for crisis, without resort to mass violence, seems much greater in Eastern Europe than most observers have predicted. The politicization of constitution making in Eastern Europe, in any case, is not fundamentally the result of confusion or a cultural deficit or a failure to understand the Western distinction between politics and law, or the difference between the instruments of action and the framework of action. It is the result of a need for public legitimation, difficult to achieve, of a constitutional revolution that was delivered unexpectedly from abroad.

Survey of the Amending Procedures in Eastern Europe

We now briefly describe amending procedures in existing Eastern European constitutions, actual or in draft.[21] Our central contrast is between Bulgaria and Romania, on the one hand, and Poland and Hungary, on the other.

The Hungarian Parliament and the Polish Sejm enjoy a great deal of free authority to amend the constitution. Their power in this regard is both exclusive and unlimited by subject matter. The two assemblies are subject only to two procedural constraints, supermajorities of two-thirds and attendance requirements.

The Bulgarian and the Romanian assemblies are far more limited in their authority. First, the Bulgarian National Assembly and the Bulgarian Parliament both face subject-matter restrictions.[22] The Romanian Parliament must also rely on a referendum. Its amending power is not exclusive, sufficient, or necessary. In this respect it is the weakest parliament in Eastern Europe. While the Bulgarian National Assembly is granted the power to amend the Constitution on its own, and while the National Assembly cannot be bypassed by other bodies, its amending procedure is extremely cumbersome. Thus the National Assembly faces attendance and supermajority requirements. In order for amendment to proceed, a proposal must garner a three-fourths vote from all the members of the Assembly—the most stringent supermajoritarian requirement in Eastern Europe. Moreover, at least one month must pass between initiation and the first vote for ratification. Finally, the Bulgarian formula requires three different ballots on the three different days.[23] While the Romanian Parliament is the weakest amending power, the Bulgarian National Assembly is the most tightly bound.

We choose these four countries to make an analytical point. Constitutionalists tend to favor a system of deep entrenchment of constitutional provisions (i.e., a stringent amending formula) and recourse to popular referenda. This may be desirable in Western democracies, but it is inappropriate, we argue, in Eastern Europe. The amending formula should be relatively lax, and it should be virtually monopolized by parliament, with no recourse to referenda.

The countries chosen for comparison illustrate this point. Bulgaria's constitution is legally more fully entrenched than any other in Eastern

---

[21] For help with this section, we are most grateful to Christian Lucky, whose excellent memorandum we have adapted for our purposes.

[22] Romanian Constitution, Art. 148; Bulgarian Constitution, Art. 158.

[23] Art. 155(1).

Europe, and Romania's gives popular referenda the greatest role. By comparison, Poland and Hungary have established relatively lax conditions for constitutional amendment and have kept the amending power in the hands of the established powers. (The Hungarian Constitution begins with a "declaration of temporariness," while Poland is operating at present under a document known as "the interim constitution.") From a Western perspective, therefore, Bulgaria and Romania should be seen as having made greater strides toward establishing *sacralized constitutionalism* than Poland and Hungary. But this is not an adequate account. Stopgap constitutionalism—embodied in the Polish and Hungarian systems—is the most effective kind in Eastern Europe because, among other reasons, important choices can be tolerated more easily by losers if these choices are perceived as temporary and up for further consideration at a later date. The "deep entrenchment" of constitutional provisions, on the other hand, and the availability of referenda in southeastern Europe, result from the dominance of ex-Communists, eager to "lock in" their privileges, over the constitution-drafting process there. Given the atomization of these societies, "going to the people" is not especially democratic. The "plebiscitary legitimacy" gained via referenda can be easily manipulated by political elites. In Eastern Europe, in any case, the harder it is to amend a constitution and the greater role granted to popular referenda and extraparliamentary authorities, the less constitutionalism matters as a political force.

Why should the least liberal leadership in the region have been the first to create liberal constitutional frameworks? The reason seems to be that old-regime elites, fighting a rear-guard action, have both a greater opportunity and a greater incentive to implement new constitutions than do post-Communist elites. They have a greater opportunity because Communist-dominated parliaments (which double, as noted, as constituent assemblies) can be more easily disciplined than can parliaments in countries such as Hungary and Poland, where political life has become highly pluralistic and old-regime leaders have been largely driven from the scene. And they have a greater incentive because they have the most to gain by presenting themselves as the "fathers" of a liberal political order, and the most to lose if a new constitution permits confiscation of ill-gotten gains and the prosecution of officials for crimes committed under the old system.

So much for the contrast between two different general conceptions of the appropriate amending formula; we are now prepared to offer more details. Several constitutions prohibit the amendment of certain provisions altogether. At least three documents contain explicit and absolute restrictions on the scope of the amending power: the Constitution of Romania, the draft constitution of Ukraine, and the Constitution of the Czech Republic. Article 148(1) of the Romanian Constitution expressly prohibits any amendments that attempt to alter "the national, unitary and indivisible character of the Romanian State, *the Republican form of government*, territorial integrity, independence of the judiciary, [and] political pluralism." The same approach appears in Article 257 of the draft constitution of Ukraine, which provides that "no amendments or additions to the Constitution may be introduced which are . . . *aimed at altering the rule of the Constitution.*" The Czech Constitution says, "An amendment to the *essential requirements for a democratic legal state shall be inadmissible.*"[24] Other provisions placed beyond the reach of formal revision include those addressing "fundamental rights and freedoms"[25] and those protecting "human rights."[26]

The Bulgarian Constitution takes a different approach. Rather than prohibiting the revision of the protected provisions altogether, Bulgaria, as noted, offers an amending institution that is cumbersome and time-consuming: the amending convention. Among the new Eastern European constitutions, only the Bulgarian Constitution provides for an amending convention, called by the National Assembly upon a two-thirds vote of all its members.[27] Moreover, the Constitution entrenches provisions that establish the form of state structure and government, preserve the inviolability of human rights, and define the territory of the republic.[28]

Many of the Eastern European documents ban amendments during states of war and states of emergency. The Romanian Constitution is representative of this type of restriction: "The Constitution shall not be revised during a state of siege or emergency or at wartime." Similarly, the draft constitution of Lithuania prohibits amendment during "a state of emergency or martial law"[29] and the Constitution of Estonia prevents revision "during a state of emergency or a state of war."[30] The Russian constitution is less restrictive by prohibiting amendment when the president is unable to perform his duties,[31] while the Ukrainian draft constitution presents an ambiguous circumspection of the amending power by restricting formal revision "under conditions of an extraordinary crisis."[32]

[24] Art. 9(2).
[25] Romanian Constitution, Art. 148(2). The official language of Romania is also protected from revision.
[26] Ukrainian draft constitution, Art. 257. The Czech Constitution does not prohibit the amendment of provisions that protect human rights or fundamental freedoms.
[27] Art. 160.
[28] Constitution of the Republic of Bulgaria, chap. 9, Art. 158.
[29] Art. 154.
[30] Art. 161.
[31] Russian constitution, Art. 92(3).   [32] Art. 257.

The Eastern European documents allow for different agents of change. Under the Albanian draft constitution, the Albanian People's Assembly enjoys the greatest amending power in Eastern Europe. Article 78(2) mandates that the People's Assembly "approves and amends the Constitution." This is done "when the majority of the deputies present have voted for [the laws and other acts]." No other institution in Eastern Europe has the unilateral power to enact an amendment with an ordinary legislative plurality.[33]

Other institutions of constitutional revision in Eastern Europe have the power of amendment. Article 24(3) of the Hungarian Constitution says that "for the amendment of the Constitution . . . the affirmative votes of two-thirds of the Members of Parliament are required." The Hungarian Parliament's control is exclusive because no other institution has a claim to participate in the amending procedure. The Parliament's amending power is sufficient for change because it may unilaterally revise the constitution of its own accord. Finally, its amending power is necessary to effectuate change because no amendment can be enacted without its approval. The Polish Sejm has similar power. Article 106 of the "Little Constitution" says, "The Constitution may be amended only by a law passed by the Sejm of the Republic of Poland by a majority of at least two-thirds of the votes requiring the presence of at least half the total number of Deputies." The Constitution of the Czech Republic also falls into this category. Article 39(4) holds that "in order to adopt a constitutional act . . . three-fifths of all deputies and three-fifths of all senators present must give their approval."

Some institutions are granted sufficient power to enact an amendment, and also maintain the authority to block all amendment proposals, yet do not hold exclusive power over the amending procedure. Consider the Assembly of the Republic of Macedonia. Pursuant to Articles 68, 130, and 131 of the Macedonian Constitution, the Assembly can both initiate and ratify an amendment. Like the Polish Sejm and the Hungarian Parliament, the Macedonian Assembly alone may ratify an amendment proposal;[34] but unlike these institutions, the Macedonian Assembly must share access to certain steps of the amending procedure with other institutions. Article 130 provides that an amendment proposal may be initiated by the president, the government, by 30 representatives, or by the petition of 150,000 Macedonian citizens.

The next category of constitutions is that in which the assembly's power to amend the constitution is sufficient, but neither exclusive nor

---

[33] The revisionary power of the People's Assembly extends even further than this. According to Article 78(2), the People's Assembly "decides on the conformity of the laws with the Constitution and interprets them."

[34] Art. 69 and 131.

necessary. The draft constitution of Ukraine offers the clearest example. Article 256 of the Ukrainian draft allows the National Assembly the power both to initiate and to ratify an amendment. But the same article provides for a method of amendment based on popular petition and referendum. "Amendments and additions to the Constitution may be introduced . . . by written petition containing the signatures of no less than two million electors." Such an initiative "shall be approved by an all-Ukrainian referendum."[35]

We can therefore identify four different systems for the allocation of amending powers among political institutions.[36] First, some constitutions grant the assembly exclusive power over the amending process. Among this group are the Hungarian Parliament, the Polish Sejm, and the Czech Parliament. Second, some constitutions grant to the assembly both the necessary and the sufficient power to amend the constitution, but also grant other institutions the right of access to the amendment process. Third, the Romanian Constitution gives no institution the power to amend any part of the Constitution unilaterally. Finally, some constitutions give the assembly power to enact amendments, but do not make that power exclusive. In most instances, these constitutions allow direct popular participation, with the right of petition and referendum being granted to the citizenry. Ukraine, Slovakia, and Latvia are of this variety. In some of these cases, direct popular participation is at some point dependent upon the president or the assembly for approval. The Croatian and the Slovenian constitutions are examples; in still other cases, there are amending provinces. Within each province some institution has exclusive, necessary and sufficient power to effectuate change in that province. The Russian constitution, the Bulgarian Constitution, the Lithuanian Constitution, and the Estonian draft constitution are among these.

There are also different procedural requirements in the various constitutions and drafts. The Albanian draft constitution gives the People's Assembly the power to determine its own amending procedure. No procedural hurdles hamper the Assembly's power to revise the constitution beyond normal legislative procedures. Next to the Albanian, the Polish Constitution is the most flexible in Eastern Europe. The Polish Sejm has only two procedural requirements placed upon it. First, a constitutional revision requires a two-thirds plurality; second, at least half the members of the Sejm must vote to enact an amendment.[37] The Hungarian Constitution is slightly more difficult to amend. Like the Polish, the Hun-

---

[35] Art. 256.

[36] See also the detailed taxonomy developed by Donald Lutz in his contribution to this volume.

[37] Art. 106.

garian Constitution may be revised with a two-thirds plurality of Parliament. But in the Hungarian case, all the members of Parliament must cast a vote on an amendment proposal.[38]

Supermajority requirements and turnout requirements are common in Eastern Europe. Every constitution here surveyed, except the Albanian, requires some supermajority for constitutional revision.

Some constitutions place absolute time constraints on the amending procedure. Under the Bulgarian Constitution, an amendment proposal must sit for one month before the National Assembly can act on it. Article 163 of the Estonian Constitution requires the amendment proposal to be read three times. Between each reading one month must pass. Along similar lines, Lithuania, Latvia, and Bulgaria require the assembly to vote on the amendment proposal more than once. The Latvian Constitution also requires that three ballots be taken.

A final procedural hurdle is the plurality required to pass a referendum. In almost all countries that use the referendum, a regular majority is sufficient. The Lithuanian Constitution, however, requires that three-fourths of the electorate approve of an amendment proposal before it is passed (Article 156). Ukraine is the only country that uses an absolute figure—one million—as the plurality requirement.

What Is to Be Done?

From the previous section, it should be clear that the amending formula reflects two basic choices: (1) is the procedure difficult or easy? and (2) is the procedure dominated by the established powers, or is a popular referendum involved? We argue, against the grain of most contemporary constitutional theory, for a lax procedure dominated by the assembly.

We begin by noting a reasonable fear—that under our proposal, the amending power will be overused, thus endangering stability and perhaps democracy itself. In the circumstances of Eastern Europe, the fear seems unrealistic. First, in highly fragmented parliaments, even a simple majority for amendment will be difficult to muster. Second, most East European politicians seem to recognize that imperfect or unimproved constitutional provisions are not wholly dysfunctional. Textual ambiguity provides useful room for maneuver. It is unlikely that there will be ready resort to constitutional change even if such change is relatively easy to bring about as a matter of technical law.

Our basic argument runs into the teeth of the old cliché: A "balance must be struck" between rigidity and flexibility in constitutional en-

---

[38] Art. 24(3).

trenchment. The reasoning behind this proverbial balancing approach can be easily stated. On the one hand, if a constitution is too difficult to amend, if it is excessively rigid, it is liable to break. An overly rigid constitution, based on a stringent amending formula, invites extraconstitutional solutions (or free-floating interpretation, which poses dangers of its own). On the other hand, if a constitution is too easy to amend, it will invite the constitutionalization of political life, or the collapse of constitutional politics into ordinary politics. A lax amending procedure, especially when monopolized by the assembly, will encourage legislators to attempt to outmaneuver their opponents of the moment by changing the rules of the game while in midstream. It will also make basic rights vulnerable to political winds and eliminate the kinds of stability and facilitation that are provided by agreement on basic institutional arrangements.

We believe that, in this context, we should abandon this balanced approach. More specifically, we urge a general presumption in favor of flexible amending procedures dominated by the established powers, especially the legislature. Let constitutional politics collapse into ordinary politics—for this "collapse" is not only inevitable but, under current circumstances in Eastern Europe, desirable. Let the constitutional process drag on, for several years, one pro tempore arrangement replacing another. The needs of the transition from state socialism, after all, are not the same as the needs of an established or incipient liberal democracy building on existing understandings and traditions (like the young United States[39] or, in quite a different way, postwar Germany). So why

---

[39] As the countries of the former East bloc struggle to establish constitutional democracies in difficult circumstances today, we should ask ourselves again how the United States managed to launch a stable liberal-republican regime at the end of the eighteenth century. The endurance of the Constitution written at Philadelphia in 1787 was not foreordained. The members of the Constituent Assembly in Paris in 1791, whose ideals were not radically discrepant from those of the American Founders, produced a respectable, if not perfect, liberal constitution that spattered to a swift and miserable end. Why did the Americans succeed and the French fail? There are many reasons, of course, stemming from the vastly different political, religious, economic, demographic, and military situations of the two countries. (While the French were saddled with Louis XVI, moreover, the United States was favored with George Washington.) But one additional reason deserves to be pointed out. Unlike their French contemporaries, the American Founders devised their Constitution *after a period of frustration with the weakness of the central government.* They aimed, therefore, not only to prevent tyranny, but also to create an energetic government with the capacity to govern, to rule effectively, and to "promote the general Welfare." This devotion to governmental effectiveness, this passion for state building, was virtually absent at the Paris Constituent Assembly. Framed in response to the unpredictable arbitrariness of monarchical rule, the French Constitution of 1791 proved so constricting that, when the first crisis struck, authorities were driven to slough it off and govern extraconstitutionally. By contrast, the desire simultaneously to limit and reinforce the state resulted, in the American case, in a stable constitutional regime that was neither tyrannical nor weak.

should the framework established for the former be bequeathed to those who will be grappling with the latter? Anyway, there is nothing particularly healthy about *la rage de vouloir conclure*.[40] The postponement of permanence is not always foot dragging, but may also be the sage acknowledgment of an ongoing social earthquake, where foundation builders must trim their ambitions to create immortal works. The entrenchment gained by a stringent amending formula, moreover, will adversely affect the political process by raising the stakes of constitutional choice, increasing the perceived benefits of confrontation. Losers face the possibility of total frustration, which makes them less likely to accept compromise and more likely to risk deadlock. If no side sees a chance to entrench its partisan advantage permanently, by contrast, all parties may slowly develop a taste for concession making.

The assumption underlying this recommendation is the following. *The central task of the states of Eastern Europe today is the creation of legitimate democratic authority.* The fundamental challenge is less to restrict abusive authority—though this is also important—than to create accountable authority.[41] The collapse of Sovietism left East European societies with virtually no institutions to build upon. (What role does the Solidarity trade union now play in constructing Polish democracy?) Institution building, therefore, must not be forgotten in the race to prevent future abuses of power. Any arrangement that obstructs the creation of democratic authority, or undermines it once it has been created, is to be shunned.

Some commentators have deplored the fact that the new constitutions and constitutional drafts embody bargains among parliamentary forces rather than high-minded legal principles. But this squeamishness about public bargaining is precisely one of the forces that must be overcome in order to consolidate the transition to constitutional democracy.

We do urge that Eastern European countries should experiment with different approaches for entrenching provisions. It would not make sense to offer a blueprint here, but our preferred approach is an innovation in constitutional practice: a three-tiered system of amendability.[42] Under this approach, most of the Constitution would be easily amendable. But some provisions would not be amendable at all (as in the Ger-

---

[40] Albert Hirschman, *Journeys Toward Progress: Studies of Economic Policymaking in Latin America* (New York: Norton, 1973), pp. 313–16.

[41] Constitutional lawyers tend to be poor political advisers in today's circumstances because *constitutional law assumes the preexistence of the political authority that needs to be limited.* Like many economists, most of them are professionally biased against constitutional techniques for state building or reinforcing the governing capacities of public authorities.

[42] We are grateful to Andras Sajo for helpful discussion.

man Constitution), or could be changed only by a strong majority that has favored revision on two or more occasions. Still other provisions would be amendable with some difficulty, but without the severe obstacles facing the most entrenched provisions.

Under this approach, we suggest that two sets of rights should be most strongly entrenched. First, a specified list of individual rights should be made immune to revision. This list should include, first and foremost, rights that are indispensable to democratic legitimacy. We therefore suggest that freedom of speech, the right to vote, religious liberty, and freedom from discrimination on grounds of race, religion, ethnicity, and sex should be especially protected against politics, including constitutional politics. The category of entrenched rights should also include rights against abuse of the criminal justice system—including the basic right to fair hearing.

Second, we suggest that some of the broad outlines of the institutional arrangements might be safeguarded against too easy change. Thus, for example, the political process might be prevented from overcoming the judgment that there will be one president, or that there will be three separated powers within a system of checks and balances. So, too, the provisions that guarantee basic democratic arrangements—the right to free speech, democratic elections, the right to vote—should be made immune to constitutional revision.

By contrast, the social and economic rights that one finds spelled out in a number of actual and proposed Eastern European constitutions should be easily amendable, especially if they are considered fit for judicial enforcement and not simply aspirational goals. Consider, for example, the fact that the Hungarian Constitution protects not merely the right to equal pay for equal work, but also the right to an income conforming with the quantity and quality of work performed. What would it mean for the Hungarian Constitutional Court to take these provisions seriously? Similarly, the Slovak draft includes the right to a standard of living commensurate to each citizen's potential and that of society as a whole, as well as the right to just pay. One also finds in some constitutions such rights as food, shelter, and even recreation complementing more traditional rights of private property, free speech, and the like. We think that these former guarantees should be amendable through ordinary legislative processes.

So much for the basic issue of entrenchment. Who should be allowed to bring about constitutional change? From what we have said thus far, it follows that most issues of constitutional revision should be decided by the parliament. Those who disagree, and wish for a more "populist" process, should answer the following question: What message is conveyed to the citizenry if popular referenda are given a central role in the amending process? Our answer is that such a provision implies that the voice of the people is not adequately expressed through the representative process. *In other words, referenda implicitly erode the legitimacy of democratically elected assemblies by expressing the seemingly reasonable belief that the most important choices should not be left up to politicians.* But this principle is less democratic than it first sounds. Since the parliaments in question have little enough legitimacy as it is, reliance on referenda may be the straw that breaks the camel's back.

A parliament that did not deal directly with the major choices facing society, leaving them instead to special constitutional conventions and then to the courts, could not pretend tò a position of leadership in the nation. In its first stages, at least, democracy should be parliament- and not court-centered, and it should avoid ready resort to popular referenda. Any system that preempts the right of parliament to make the most vital decisions will ultimately damage the prospects of both democracy and limited government.

Does the Czecho-Slovak "divorce," engineered by politicians in Prague and Bratislava and supported by less than 40 percent of the electorate, provide an important counterexample to this thesis? Would a popular referendum, bypassing the federal and state parliaments, have been more democratic and led to a more satisfactory (as well as more legitimate) outcome? We doubt it. The reason is that liberal democracy must assign responsibility to officials to make decisions, and hold them accountable if the decisions turn out badly. Seen in this light, referenda seem as undemocratic as imperative mandates and immediate recall. Ultimately, the feasibility of the union would have depended upon the ability of the federal legislature to govern the country as a whole and to maintain authority over the two state assemblies. This is not a task that could have been fulfilled by an extraparliamentary appeal. If a government cannot govern, referenda will not help. Hence the failure to save the union registered a political incapacity that would probably have trivialized the federal government in a relatively short time.

There are additional problems with using referenda as the mode for constitutional change. In Eastern Europe, the political process is generally in poor repute; a referendum might well attract very few voters. This would be a disaster for political legitimacy. Moreover, popular opinion is unstable and highly subject to short-term swings based on manipulative politics.[43] At least if it works even moderately well, representative processes can have an important and salutary filtering effect.

[43] There is an extensive literature debating the relationship between democracy and the initiative and referendum found in many of the western states in the United States. See, e.g., Thomas E. Cronin, *Direct Democracy: The Politics of Initiative, Referendum, and Recall* (Cambridge, Mass.: Harvard University Press, 1989); Lynn A. Baker, "Direct Democ-

We summarize here all the arguments about the need to provide for constant readjustments and "updating" in the fluid circumstances of Eastern Europe. Certainty and predictability cannot be produced by constitutional rigidity. On the contrary, rigid constitutions invite extra-constitutional solutions that cannot, in principle, be foreseen. The more difficult it is to amend a constitution, moreover, the less plausible it becomes to infer "consent" from the failure to amend it. That is acceptable in certain conditions—like those of the contemporary United States—but it is a terrible fault in circumstances where the principal need is to create both public confidence in representative institutions and political accountability of elected officials.

The Role of the Constitutional Court

Constitutional lawyers have played a much greater role than political scientists in the drafting processes in Eastern Europe. This may be unfortunate. Many of these constitutional lawyers seem to believe that judicial review, whereby the court casts itself in the role of "guardian of the constitution," is the central institution of liberal democracy. In established democratic systems, this conceit is harmless enough. But it has some destructive consequences in Eastern Europe. If a constitutional court can successfully convince the citizenry of a new democracy that *it alone* defends the deepest interests of the people, then it will have helped erode further the feeble legitimacy of the representative assembly. This is harmful to the liberal cause the judges aim to help.

The parliaments of Eastern Europe are bound to be amateurish operations, torn by unseemly scandals and sectarian rifts, for some years to come. The problems they face are formidable and they have a very limited capacity to "deliver the goods" (for instance, capitalist wages combined with socialist benefits). Incompetent and parochial deputies have quickly gained the contempt of intellectuals, who have ceased worrying about a lapse back into communism and thus feel wholly free to express their discontent with the fledgling democracy. Moreover, the live broadcast of assembly sessions means that the public has become far more aware than it might otherwise have been of absenteeism, proxy voting, cronyism, clientalism, place hunting, and subgroup feuding. It is not surprising, then, that newspapers are full of brilliant political satire.

racy and Discrimination: A Public Choice Perspective," *Chicago-Kent Law Review* 67 (1992): 707; Julian N. Eule, "Judicial Review of Direct Democracy," *Yale Law Journal* 99 (1990): 1503; Hans A. Linde, "When Initiative Lawmaking Is Not 'Republican Government': The Campaign Against Homosexuality," *Oregon Law Review* 72 (1993): 19.

This is a sign of normalization *unless* it begins to reflect a tilt toward antiparliamentarianism in general.

To this should be added the legacies of Sovietism. (So we are not wholly opposed to "cultural" considerations.) From a Marxist perspective, *public bargaining about rival interests is immoral.* As a result, the new parliaments of Eastern Europe must struggle to overcome a public perception that their modi operandi themselves are illegitimate. Curiously enough, there is an unholy alliance here between the culture of communism and the culture of human-rights lawyers, much involved in the constitution-making process. The latter, too, believe that there is no room for bargaining when the important things are at stake. Their success at getting their position accepted in Eastern Europe probably has something to do with the general bias against public bargaining characteristic of all post-Communist societies. The relatively high prestige of constitutional courts in the region (which advocates of a stringent amending formula unwisely hope to increase still further) may derive at least in part from the strange resemblance between this unelected body of people who make decisions in secret (without public bargaining) and the old Politburo (which also claimed to speak with the "higher voice" of the people).

Overconfidence in the judiciary and overemphasis on the bill of rights are especially problematic given the poor quality of the sitting judges and the embryonic condition of legal education. (We put to one side the case of Hungary, whose constitutional court has already established itself as one of the most authoritative in the world.) But a court-centered democracy is unlikely to last in any case. The greater power and prestige granted to the constitutional court, the more diminished may be the power and prestige of parliament, and the more difficult it may be to create legitimate and accountable authority through elections, especially in countries with a history of compulsory voting in fake elections. And if a military or presidential coup occurs, the only force capable of protecting the constitutional order will be the parliament. It will be unfortunate, in this event, if the constitutional drafters will have helped feed growing public disgust with politicians in general and the constitutional court will have contributed to a lowering of the assembly's already-damaged prestige.

We do not contend that a constitutional court is a bad idea, or that it cannot accomplish considerable good. On the contrary, we believe that such a court can help bring about the transition to democracy and constitutionalism. We mean only to suggest that the court is merely a part of the picture, and a secondary part at that. The point bears on the topic of constitutional amendment. If the court will play a secondary role, it cannot be counted on to furnish the sorts of creative interpretation (found in, say, Germany and the United States) that serve to keep the founding document consistent with changing circumstances and values. And if constitutional interpretation cannot accomplish this function, it becomes all the more important to allow relatively easy resort to constitutional amendment.

Concluding Points

Central authority, including the bureaucratic capacities (from bankruptcy courts to land-survey offices) presupposed by successful marketization, has to be created in the internally disorganized countries of Eastern Europe. On what basis will this authority be constructed? Using a loose Weberian typology, we may distinguish among various forms of legitimacy. Consent to political decisions can be attained by charismatic leadership, appeal to traditional religious values, a playing of the nationalist card, palpable success at economic reform, *or by democratic elections.* Democratic legitimacy, as we explained above, rests paradoxically on the possibility of change, on the foreseeable opportunity to "throw the rascals out." This may seem to be a great deal under Western conditions. But its value in Eastern Europe ought not to be overestimated. Put differently, *democratic legitimacy* is inherently weak because it is *purely procedural,* based on majoritarianism or the counting of votes. It carries with it a host of substantive commitments; but it contains no substantive message that might appeal more directly and morally or emotionally to the concerns of the electorate, especially an inexperienced electorate looking for meaning and perhaps for a savior. Czech voters, for instance, seem to care less about Klaus's democratic credentials (the origins of his authority) than about the success or failure of his economic reforms (the effects of his policies). This is a typical pattern; it even plays a role in the West.

The relative weakness of the democratic form of political legitimacy is also important in Eastern Europe because of the *antipower ethos* natural in countries emerging from totalitarian rule. Branislaw Geremek speaks for many when he says that the primary challenge today is "to hold the line against creeping overpoliticization."[44] This antipolitical syndrome—this antipathy to institutionalized forms of power, including democratic entities—is part and parcel of a general skepticism about the capacity of organized entities to bring about desirable change. It is exacerbated by the sudden importance given, in the throes of transforma-

[44] Branislaw Geremek, "Civil Society Then and Now," *Journal of Democracy* 3, no. 2 (April 1992): 6; while puffing "civil society," Geremek also admits that "a real danger is presented by the fall in interest in politics, by retreatism from public life" (p. 11).

tion, to the legal and economics professions. Some economists believe that a "free market" can be established in post-Communist societies simply by handing the keys to the factories over to private individuals while keeping the state at bay. Similarly, some constitutional lawyers believe that the central function of constitutionalism is to *prevent tyranny*, including especially *the tyranny of the majority* (i.e., oppression by democratically elected officials, accountable to a majority of the voters). As a result, they want to increase the power of constitutional courts and decrease the power of parliaments. As a general prescription, this is probably a strategic mistake, which will have the consequence of making a relapse into autocracy more rather than less likely.

A constitution is not simply a device for preventing tyranny. It has several other functions as well. For instance, constitutions do not only limit power and prevent tyranny; they also construct and guide power and prevent anarchy. More comprehensively, liberal constitutions are designed to help solve a whole range of political problems: tyranny, corruption, anarchy, immobilism, collective action problems, absence of deliberation, myopia, lack of accountability, instability, and the stupidity of politicians.[45] Constitutions are multifunctional. It is a radical oversimplification to identify the constitutional function exclusively with the prevention of tyranny.

The identification is also excessively negative. The positive or facilitative dimensions of constitutionalism must also be taken into account, especially in countries shattered by a wholesale disintegration of state authority and involved in impromptu state building while trying to avoid scapegoating and campaigns for ethnic homogenization. A constitution can be an instrument of government. It can establish rules that help put democracy into effect. It can create an institutional framework that, if it functions properly, makes decision making more thoughtful and mistakes easier to learn from. It can prevent power wielders from invoking secrecy and shutting themselves off, as they naturally would do, from criticisms, counterarguments, and fresh ideas. At the same time, it can mobilize collective resources for solving collective problems.

This positive vision of constitutionalism is rare among constitutional specialists in Eastern Europe. Advocates of *negative constitutionalism* dominate the discussion and make it difficult to see the advantages for governmental effectiveness to be gained from constitutional channeling of sovereign power. This is unfortunate. If constitutions are designed with a primarily negative purpose, to prevent tyranny, they will probably lead to political deadlock, and thus invite tyranny. If the government

---

[45] As the last item shows, constitutionalism will always be as much an ideal standard or unattainable goal as a political reality.

cannot govern, if it cannot pass its reform program, for example, public pressure will mount to throw the hampering constitution off and govern extraconstitutionally. In short, the challenge of constitutional drafting in Eastern Europe is positive as well as negative. Theorists should therefore place greater emphasis than they have hitherto done on *positive constitutionalism*. The task is to create a limited government that is nevertheless fully capable of governing.

Constitutional lawyers and economists tend to share an unfriendly attitude toward state power. Many of them concur that the state is a dangerous force and, more specifically, that "civil society" in Eastern Europe will grow only if the government is crippled or limited to a bare minimum. They also introduce a sophisticated, Tocquevillean worry about the "tyranny of the majority" to the ongoing debate. But this literary touch is not necessarily helpful.

The fact is that political decision-making authority will eventually emerge in Eastern Europe. The questions are: on what basis and within which constraints? The danger is that nondemocratic forms of legitimacy will eclipse democratic ones. Charisma, nationalism, traditional Catholic or Orthodox Christianity, excessively efficacious marketization—all of these are, in principle, potentially nondemocratic sources of governmental legitimacy. Would-be rulers who control these sources of legitimacy can, if social strains mount sufficiently, outmaneuver rulers who simply win the most votes. Qualitative legitimacy will throw quantitative legitimacy into the shade. Hence, the basic problem in post-Communist societies is not to hamstring the autocratic state or to avoid the tyranny of the majority. On the contrary, *the crucial task is to create government that is simultaneously accountable and effective*. More specifically, the challenge is to create a parliamentary system that is capable of governing effectively and of integrating the more substantive or qualitative forms of legitimacy within itself (shutting down all rival claimants). If this does not occur, then the democratic principle itself will be discredited and authority will drift away from electorally accountable officials toward unaccountable ones.

This observation bears directly on the question of constitutional amendment. A stringent amending formula, we might say, registers what is under current circumstances an unwise attempt to codify a dual democratic legitimacy. The entrenched constitution is familiarly said to embody *the higher voice of the people*, a voice that can trump the elected legislature. In Eastern Europe, this would be a myth; it would amount in practice (at least in part) to the superiority of the unelected constitutional court over the parliament. Seen from the assembly's viewpoint, it could promote collective irresponsibility. Deputies have readily available an alibi for failure: We cannot do this or that because such actions are forbidden by the constitution as interpreted by the courts. That is a questionable arrangement, given the current weakness of public confidence in state institutions, and not only for the reasons given above, but also because judges are notoriously less able to communicate with citizens than are politicians. The total superiority of a constitutional court over the parliament, in a situation where government as a whole is viewed as an establishment game having little relevance to the lives of most people, will simply exacerbate the problem of public alienation, making the creation and consolidation of democratic authority all the more difficult.

There is no clear evidence, incidentally, that constitutions based on low political bargains, rather than high legal principles, are particularly unstable. Such an "ignoble" source may be a great asset. To the extent that constitutions are publicly acknowledged as codified bargains, there will be less temptation to mythologize the constitutional framework and treat it unrealistically as the word of God (or "We the People").[46] The rational reason for a subsequent generation to respect the terms of the constitutional settlement, in any case, has less to do with the source than with the content of the constitution. If a constitution does not help current citizens to solve their problems and achieve their aims, it will and should have little appeal, no matter how great the supermajority that originally ratified it. The appropriateness of treating a constitution as "sacred" surely depends on what the constitution contains. (This simple point is ignored by those who complain about the "culturally backward" flippancy with which most East European politicians treat their constitutions.) Thus, respect for the constitution must be based on the public perception that the constitution is (still at least generally) good.

Moreover, it is possible to give a measure of stability to the system without relying on myths about the vox populi. All that a democratic electorate needs to know to resist every whimsical impulse to "improve" the constitution is (1) that *all* rules, including the alternatives proposed, have defects and deplorable side effects, and (2) the costs of change are likely to outweigh the benefits. If the rules of the game are functioning fairly well, this is all that needs to be said to prevent endless tampering with the constitutional framework. No appeal need be made to a "higher track of lawmaking," implicit in the constitution, reserved to the "higher self" of the nation, and riding high above the lowly politics of ordinary lawmaking. Such an appeal also carries the risk of unjustified ancestor worship.

[46] This mythologizing is one source of the overlegitimation of constitutional courts. It may be that the great need in Eastern Europe, whatever may be the case elsewhere, is not so much for "constitutional faith" (see Sanford Levinson, *Constitutional Faith* [Princeton: Princeton University Press, 1988]) as for "parliamentary" or, even more to the point, "political" faith.

Finally, the complete subordination of ordinary politics to the constitution, treated as a sacred framework that cannot be changed and that governs in the last resort, is possible only under very specific historical conditions. Court-centered democracy worked wonderfully well in West Germany, a country that became *a political dependency* and was democratized on that basis alone. Many important choices were simply "off the agenda" for the politicians of the early Federal Republic. Because politics itself was strictly limited by postwar Germany's international situation, it was possible to develop a strict political style that strictly subordinated the legislature to the constitutional court, and that virtually eliminates the idea of popular sovereignty or of a democratic power over the constitution. Attempts to transplant this arrangement from Germany to Eastern Europe, however tempting, are destined to fail. Such borrowing might function well if Poland or Hungary were semi-sovereign dependencies of the Western powers, as Germany was after 1945. But this is not going to occur. As a result, the German model, however popular among constitutional lawyers, should be treated with a great deal of caution.

The reasons are simple but fundamental. The elementary principles of liberalism, while powerful and politically successful, have certain inherent limitations. For instance, the principles of equality before the law and majority rule, while they depend on the preexistence of specific territorial borders, cannot justify any given territorial borders. Liberal principles cannot fully answer an absolutely fundamental question within a system of territorially organized states: Who belongs to the political community and is entitled to share in decision-making power or in the benefits distributed by the state? To the extent that the amending power assumes the existence of a sovereign people authorizing the constitutional settlement and capable of reshaping it, it too presupposes a pre-given answer to the question of membership. This means that liberal constitutionalism depends upon at least some basic decisions that it cannot justify. Put differently, liberalism constructs the palace of constitutional democracy from the second floor up.

Another lacuna in the justificatory arsenal of liberalism concerns property. Liberal principles can perfectly well justify a *system* of private ownership, on the grounds that it benefits all citizens, including nonowners. But liberalism cannot easily justify the particular assignment of first property rights. As a result, liberal property systems function best, and are perceived as most legitimate, when the origins of ownership are shrouded in obscurity. This was the case in every Western democracy. It is not the case in Eastern Europe today.

Indeed, one of the strongest arguments against any attempt to raise East European constitutions far above the political fray lies here. The basic issues with which contemporary politicians in Eastern Europe must

grapple concern territorial boundaries, the question of political membership, the assignment of first property rights and the sudden redistri-
bution of social wealth (including *nomenklatura* privatization), settling
scores or closing the books on the past. These problems, faced by no
Western democracy today, cannot be easily resolved by invoking liberal
principles. And they cannot be addressed judicially, by a nonaccountable
body of knowledgeable men and women. They will also not be imposed
by a conquering army and accepted by a defeated and morally chastened
people. They can be resolved only politically. Crucial decisions must be
made with all the messiness of parliamentary bargaining and ad hoc
compromise, carried out to some extent under the public eye. Only in
this way can decisions be reached that have a chance to win durable public consent. It is futile and even illegitimate to attempt at the outset to
entrench certain answers in a constitutional framework immunized
against change. Attempts to depoliticize or juridify constitution making
are unreasonable in societies where the future is so open and the choices
so basic and so large.

Thirteen

Midrash: Amendment through the Molding of Meaning

NOAM J. ZOHAR

Amendment and Revelation

It is sometimes asserted that the need for change and adaptation in legal systems stems from the fallibility of their human authors and the inevitable imperfections of their handiwork.[1] But even a system like the Jewish Halakha—which views itself as based on divine revelation—cannot remain forever unchanged. In principle, this should pose no theoretical problem: After all, such a system may well provide for the establishment of specific norms by nondivine authorities, functionally akin to positive lawmaking by legislatures. Hence, just as in the modern state specific laws can be changed or repealed without affecting the underlying constitution, so (arguably) can some details of Jewish law be altered without impinging upon the divine "constitution." "Deeper" changes, however—the like of which would (in a system based on human authority) necessitate an amendment procedure—would appear to pose a serious problem. How can anyone purport to "amend" divine revelation?

In this essay I shall try to illustrate and explain how the sages of classical Judaism conceived and implemented a mode of effectively amending scriptural law. This mode, known as Midrash, involves an assertion of radical control over the meaning of the revealed text. I shall argue that halakhic Midrash is functionally equivalent to constitutional amendment, while noting important differences in their manners of operation and conceptual underpinnings. First, though, we need some clarification of the key distinction between mere legal change and constitutional amendment, and of how this distinction might apply to the halakhic system.

The notion of "constitutional amendment" involves two terms. The first sets it apart from legal change outside the ambit of the constitution, that is, truly *extra*constitutional change. One must, therefore, identify

---

[1] Thus the title of this volume and the emphasis of Sanford Levinson's introductory discussion.

what counts as a constitution, including, presumably, any provisions for amendment. The second distinguishes certain changes in the constitution from mere shifts in the way it is applied or interpreted.[2] Thus, when looking for a similar phenomenon in a system of divinely revealed law, we must first consider what part of that system can properly be considered a "constitution"; and second, what, if anything, might come under the heading of "amendment."

The first issue, isolating a "constitution," arises simply because revealed law—unlike, say, a monarchic legal system constituted by divine right—involves not only God's authority, but also the direct expression of that authority in a specific set of laws. Thus the basic premises and institutional arrangements—the stuff of a constitution—are promulgated simultaneously with detailed legislation based on those premises and enforceable by those institutions, seemingly ruling out any further legislation.[3] God has spoken: All that remains is to obey.

This leads directly to the second problem: If the Law is invested with God's authority, how can it ever be amended? It would appear that the only avenue for amendment must be some new revelation, wherein God Himself would announce laws supplanting His previous decrees.[4] If such a possibility is granted, no complicated doctrine would be needed to account for it; all we should require would be an effective "principle of recognition," whereby valid new revelations could be identified.

The Jewish tradition of religious law rules out, however, any divine intervention subsequent to the initial revelation. A classic talmudic story relates Rabbi Eliezer's attempt to have his legal teachings prevail against the majority in the rabbis' asssembly, by calling on various miraculous signs and, finally, on a voice from heaven:

> Then Rabbi Eliezer appealed to heaven, and a heavenly voice said: "What have you against Rabbi Eliezer? The law is as he says." Rabbi Joshua, however, replied: "It is written in Scripture, 'it [i.e., the Torah] is not in heaven!' (Deuteronomy 30:12)." What does this mean? Rabbi Yirmiya explained: "The Torah has been given on Mount Sinai, so we no longer pay attention to

---

[2] This distinction between interpretation and amendment is, of course, the core of Sanford Levinson's contribution to this volume (See Chapter 2).

[3] This indeed seems to be a consistent assumption in biblical Israel. In sharp contrast to other monarchs in the ancient Near East, the Israelite king was not a promulgator of laws. See M. Noth, *The Laws in the Pentateuch* (London: SCM Press, 1984), p. 14.

[4] Regarding divine amendments reported expressly in the Bible, see David Daube, "Jehovah the Good," *S'vara* 1, no. 1 (1990): 17–23. Many more changes, however, are, as it were, "unadmitted." See M. Fishbane, *Biblical Interpretation in Ancient Israel* (Oxford: Clarendon Press, 1985), and Michael Walzer, "The Legal Codes of Ancient Israel," *Yale Journal of Law and the Humanities* 4 (1992): 335–49.

heavenly voices; for on Mount Sinai You have already written into the Torah to decide according to the majority."

[Some years later] Rabbi Nathan met Elijah, the prophet,[5] and asked him: "What did the Holy One, blessed be He, do at that moment?" Elijah replied: "God smiled and said: 'My children have won against me, my children have won.'"[6] (Baba Metzia, 59b)

Note that Rabbi Joshua raises no doubt as to the authenticity of the heavenly voice. Indeed, the very force of his retort lies in its being a protest against God's illicit response to the request for divine intervention. And the Talmud, by adding that God smilingly accepted this rebuke from His "children," suggests that God happily acquiesced in His exclusion from any determination of the law beyond the initial revelation.[7] This would seem to preclude any amendments to scriptural law, leaving room only for interpretation. Whether this is done by judges deciding individual cases or by legal scholars seeking to formulate principles for existing or future decisions, such interpretation is by definition undertaken with fidelity to the given Law. Traditional interpretations might be questioned and sometimes overturned;[8] with respect to the initially received Law, however, not only amendment but even the repeal of specific laws seems impossible.

Admittedly, the Sages did hold that they were permitted—and sometimes even required—to override biblical law in the light of various exigencies, in order to meet "the needs of the hour."[9] The measures legitimized in such terms might be truly temporary, but might equally be proclaimed for a long duration—perhaps indefinitely. But even then, the rationale is more like that of emergency executive powers than like

[5] Elijah, who, according to the Bible, ascended to heaven alive, is portrayed in Jewish legend as a perennial contact between heaven and earth.

[6] Translation adapted from that offered in Walter Kaufmann, *Critique of Religion and Philosophy* (New York: Harper, 1958), p. 239.

[7] This doctrine has further talmudic support (see, e.g., T.B. Temura 16a), but, as is evident even from the story mentioned in the text, it was not universally shared among the Sages. For a historical analysis, see Ephriam E. Urbach, "Matay Paska ha-Nevu'a" ("When did Prophecy Cease?"), in *The World of the Sages* (Hebrew)(Jerusalem: Magnes Press, 1988), pp. 9–49. In medieval writing, the doctrine was most consistently emphasized by Maimonides; see *Maimonides' Introduction to the Talmud*, trans. Z. Lampel (New York: Judaica Press, 1987), pp. 58–63. (This translation should not, however, be heavily relied on, because it was made from an obsolete Hebrew version instead of from the original Arabic, which is extant in Maimonides' own handwriting.)

[8] On this kind of legal innovation, see Joel Roth, *The Halackhic Process: A Systematic Analysis.* (New York: Jewish Theological Seminary, 1986), pp. 352ff.

[9] See T.B. Sanhedrin, and the systematic exposition by Hanina Ben Manahem, *Judicial Deviation in Talmudic Law: Governed by Men, not by Rules* (New York: Harwood, 1991).

that of constitutional amendment. The authoritative law itself is never changed but merely suspended, implying continued discomfort—at least on the cognitive level.

In terms of the mandated behavior, changes justified in this manner are very like amendments, and their examination is surely relevant to our present pursuit.[10] The actual incidence of such cases is, however, naturally not very high; and they do not constitute the main bulk of rabbinic amendments of biblical law, most of which are achieved by means of halakhic Midrash.

Midrash: Amendment or Interpretation?

Understanding of this entire issue in Jewish law is confounded by the fact that Midrash usually has the external trappings of interpretation; we are faced with myriad legal pronouncements, which—by their formal appearances, at least—claim the authority of Scripture. Moreover, numerous rulings and renditions found in the midrashic collections are indeed nothing more than straightforward legal interpretation. However, many rabbinic implementations of scriptural law severely stretch the notion of "interpretation," to the point that it becomes implausible to view them as mere applications of existing law. Without a conceptual framework for distinguishing among the various types of rabbinic legal commentary on Scripture, progress cannot be made toward defining some segment of the Halakha as a "constitution," nor toward an examination of its mode of amendment.

Assuming that midrashic literature is for many readers unfamiliar, I shall begin with two brief examples. These have been chosen as samples of the more radical sort of halakhic Midrash, that which involves redefinition rather than plausible interpretation. Having thus illustrated the nature of the phenomenon, I shall proceed to describe two rival accounts of it in medieval teaching. A Maimonidean perspective will then serve to define that part of the Halakha that is akin to a constitution. However, parting company with Maimonides, I will analyze the manner in which this part itself can undergo fundamental changes amounting to amendments, as illustrated in our two examples. Drawing directly on some reflections of the Sages regarding the nature of the midrashic enterprise, I shall finally offer a rationale for halakhic amendment in terms of human control of scriptural meaning.

[10] See, for a very preliminary discussion of such suspensions, Sanford Levinson, "On the Notion of Amendment," *S'vara* 1, no. 1 (1990): 25–31.

Two Examples

The Monarch's Military and Economic Power

Biblical law places severe limitations on the economic and military power of the state. It enjoins the king not to accumulate many horses or much gold and silver—two main elements of military power:

> Only he shall not multiply horses to himself
> - - - neither shall he greatly multiply to himself
> silver and gold. (Deuteronomy 17:16–17)[11]

The point of these prohibitions is to preserve reliance on God, preventing what is perceived as the hubris of self-sufficiency.[12] This is clearly revealed in the prophetic denunciation of acquiring horses:

> Ha!
> Those who go down to Egypt for help
> and rely on upon horses!
> They have put their trust in abundance of chariots,
> In vast numbers of riders,
> And they have not turned to the Holy One of Israel,
> They have not sought the Lord. (Isaiah 31:1)

Similarly, when Gideon has an army of thirty-two thousand, God demands that their number be greatly reduced before they may go to battle with divine blessing: "The Lord said to Gideon: 'You have too many troops with you for me to deliver Midian into their hands; Israel might claim for themselves the glory due to me, thinking, "Our own hand has brought us victory'" (Judges 7:2). Most of the army is encouraged to leave, but ten thousand remain; God declares this number also to be too great, and is satisfied only when Gideon remains with a mere three hundred soldiers (7:3–8). In the military lore of modern Israel, this story is told as a model of guerrilla tactics: Against a numerically superior army,

---

[11] Generally, I have quoted the new Jewish Publication Society (JPS) translation (Philadelphia, 1978). The present quotation, however, is from the older 1916 JPS translation, which by virtue of its literal rendition makes it possible to follow the Midrash.

[12] The third prohibition in the same paragraph, forbidding the king from taking many wives, is equally designed to limit his political options, since diplomatic marriages were a major tool of forging alliances. The nature of such marriages, and of the inroads they entailed against the purist cultural isolationism preached by the prophets, is reflected in the critical stories about Solomon (1 Kings 3–11, especially 10:14–11:4); indeed, these stories and the set of prohibitions in Deuteronomy share a common perspective. See generally M. Weinfield, *Deuteronomy and the Deuteronomic School* (Oxford: Clarendon Press, 1972), especially p. 281, n. 3.

a small mobile force—capable of surprise attack—is to be preferred. But this secular Midrash is contrary both to the original sense of the story and to the humbling purpose of the law in Deuteronomy.

Rabbinic Midrash radically changes this law, by introducing a distinction between the military and financial power of the state on the one hand, and the king's personal holdings on the other hand:

> *Only he shall not multiply horses to himself:* One might think that he also may not multiply horses for his chariots and for his horsemen; therefore the verse says, to himself—to himself he may not multiply them, but he may multiply them for his chariots and his horsemen.

> neither shall he greatly multiply to himself silver and gold: One might think that he may not multiply them even for the purpose of maintaining an army; therefore the verse says, to himself—for himself he may not multiply them, but he may multiply them to maintain the army. (Sifre Deuteronomy 158–59)[13]

The biblical concern over amassing power is first explicitly spelled out, then rejected; it is only personal aggrandizement that remains prohibited.

Is this an instance of legal interpretation? The rabbinic comment has the logical form of a qualification: Yes, horses and gold and silver are prohibited, but only in certain circumstances—or rather, only when they are accumulated for particular purposes. Moreover, the qualification is grounded in a specific word, the Hebrew *lo* ("to himself") tagged onto the verb denoting the prohibited accumulation. Yet even disregarding the unequivocal evidence from the wider biblical context, the midrashic "interpretation" here is patently forced.

The language of the Hebrew original is totally unremarkable, warranting no restrictive application whatsoever. In terms of semantics, the extra word *lo* could hardly have been omitted, since (unlike the English *accumulate*) the Hebrew verb standing apart has a primary transitive sense, that is, causing others to have (or to be) many (the old translation, quoted above, conveys this with its literal *multiply*). And in terms of usage, the identification of state resources as the king's own was entirely natural in the Sages' day no less than in the biblical setting.

Because there is some subjective element in any judgment of meaning, I suppose that someone might nevertheless insist that the Midrash here constitutes a plausible interpretation. Anyone who studies the midrashic corpus,[14] however, will become quickly convinced that forced or

---

[13] From the translation by R. Hammer, *Sifre: A Tannaitic Commentary on the Book of Deuteronomy* (New Haven: Yale University Press, 1986), pp. 192–93.

[14] Two central works have been translated into English. There is a good Hebrew-

arbitrary renditions are extremely common—a fact acknowledged not only by modern critical scholarship, but also by medieval commentators as well as by the Sages themselves (see below, "Rabbinic Amendment: The Molding of Meaning"). For the sake of the present discussion, let us illustrate this by citing one more example.

Crop Gathering in the Seventh Year

Biblical law expressly prohibits garnering any crops in the sanctified Seventh Year: Its yield is to be consumed directly from the field, sharing with the landless, with domestic animals, and with wild beasts alike:

> Six years you may sow your field and six years may you prune your vineyard and gather in the yield. But in the seventh year the land shall have a sabbath of complete rest, a sabbath of the Lord: you shall not sow your field or prune your vineyard. You shall not reap the aftergrowth of your harvest or gather the grapes of your untrimmed vines; it shall be a year of complete rest for the land. But you may eat whatever the land during its sabbath will produce— you, your male and female slaves, the hired and bound laborers who live with you, and the cattle and the beasts in your land may eat all its yield. (Leviticus 25:3–7)

The midrashic rendition of this law dismantles the verses' syntax in a striking (though not uncharacteristic) manner:

> *The cattle and the beasts*—What does this come to teach us? If the beast which is not kept by you may eat, surely the cattle, which is kept by you, may eat!—If it had read so [mentioning the beasts alone], I would have thought that one may gather in for the cattle to eat without a [time] limit. The verse thus mentions cattle and beast together: as long as the beast [can] eat in the field, the cattle [may] eat at home; once it has become unavailable to the beast in the field, one must make it unavailable to the beast at home. (Sifra B'har Perek 1:8)[15]

Scripture's unambiguous demand for a year of classless sharing is canceled: One may gather the crop into storage, effectively barring access to the landless and the beasts alike. The initial prohibition is replaced by a much milder demand. An identical midrashic move is applied to the verse that expresses (concerning the parallel law of the jubilee year [Le-

---

English edition of the Mekhilta—*The Midrash on Exodus* (Mekilta de-Rabbi Ishmael), trans. J. Z. Lauterbach (Philadelphia: Jewish Publication Society, 1961)—and a more recent, superb English edition of the *Sifre on Deuteronomy* (see n. 13, above).

[15] This section, as well as the following citation from Sifra, is my own translation.

viticus 1:12]) the explicit demand of eating "direct from the field": "*You may only eat the growth direct from the field*—As long as you [can] eat from the field, you [may] eat at home; once it has become unavailable in the field, make it unavailable at home" (Sifra B'har Perek 3:3).

One must merely *remove* from storage those reserves remaining after the expiration of a certain phase, defined as "as long as it [some of the crop] is still available in the field." Examination of cognate passages reveals the full scope of this extension; it refers not to the yield of one's individual field, but to that of an entire region: As long as any specimen of some kind of crop is yet ripening and becoming available to the beasts somewhere, the stores everywhere may be maintained.[16]

Answering the Kara'ite Challenge: Two Medieval Theories

Some of the clearest Rabbinic accounts of such radical reinterpretations were formulated in response to the early medieval challenge of the Kara'ite movement. The Kara'ites, not unlike latter-day Protestants, denied the validity of rabbinic Midrash and demanded faithfulness to the ostensibly plain meaning of the biblical text.

A classic statement of the rabbinic account is found in the Epistle of R. Sherira Ga'on.[17] According to him, the primary authority for the rabbinic version of the Law lies not in its scriptural derivation, but rather directly in revelation—to which he ascribes an enormously expanded scope. R. Sherira's redescription of revelation draws on the traditional notion of a "double Torah": the "written Torah," which is canonized Scripture, and the "oral Torah," which refers to the body of rabbinic teachings.[18] This traditional concept of "double Torah" is taken to signify a two-pronged revelation: Along with the core text, a vast complementary body of (oral) instruction was also revealed, equally invested with God's authority.

[16] See Sifra B'har Perek 3:5, and Mishnah Shevi'it 9:2–5, where the definition of "the same crop" is also extended to include, minimally, different varieties of the same plant—if not whole classes of produce lumped together. On other rabbinic innovations in the laws pertaining to the Seventh Year, see Zvi M. Zohar, "The Consumption of Sabbatical Year Produce in Biblical and Rabbinic Literature," in Harvey E. Goldberg, ed., *Judaism Viewed from Within and from Without: Anthropological Studies* (Albany: State University of New York Press, 1987), pp. 75–103.

[17] Rav Sherira's Epistle was published in English as *The Iggeres of Rav Sherira Gaon*, trans. and ann. N. D. Ravinowich (Jerusalem, 1988); cf. in particular pp. 20, 40.

[18] The notion of "oral Torah" should not be confused with the Greek idea of an "unwritten law." The Greek term denotes a natural or divine Law that is independent of, and superior to, the "written law"—i.e., the positive law enacted by human legislators—and can serve to criticize it. The rabbinic "oral Torah," in contrast, is complementary to Scripture; it is said to have been conveyed orally at first, but even when put into writing, it did not become "written" in the canonical sense reserved for Scripture.

R. Sherira's approach makes it possible to see the midrashic commentaries as a pious endeavor aimed at harmonization, rather than as an attempt to ground legal conclusions in dubious "interpretations" of the biblical text. Having received two bodies of revealed law, the Sages strove to bring them into line with each other. Once one is prepared to accept the "oral Torah" as revealed divine Law in its own right, the motivation for such an effort at harmonization seems quite understandable; though the purpose of the often contrary wording of the "written Torah" then remains something of a (divine) mystery.

Needless to say, this view offers us little help in our quest for a segment of Halakha that could be deemed a constitution, much less for any possibility of amending the divine Law. Indeed, R. Sherira's system appears to rule out not only constitutional amendment, but even routine legal change: All details of (talmudic) Halakha are embedded in the "double revelation," frozen in holy stasis.

Whatever the value of R. Sherira's view in terms of Jewish dogmatics, however, it is patently unhistorical; in fact, rabbinic law shows much evidence of development and adaptation. And as a hermeneutic approach, it involves a rather strained reading of the midrashic literature, which is occupied through and through with relating laws to the biblical text. It is not enough to posit an (understandable) motive to harmonize; the method of producing the desired harmony—the very substance of Midrash—must itself be understood. But instead of explaining what the Sages had thought they were doing with Scripture, R. Sherira argues, in effect, that their enterprise of relating legal teachings (and legal arguments) to the text is nothing but a chimera: The entire body of detailed laws was revealed independently.

As we will presently see, this image is not consistent with several statements made by the Sages themselves regarding their activity. An alternative position, closer at once to the Sages' own approach[19] and to the conceptual aims in this essay, was developed in Maimonides' polemic against R. Sherira's teachings.

Maimonides readily concedes that important parts of Jewish law are indeed fashioned by human hands. He emphasizes, however, that this by no means detracts from the authority of the laws involved, for the Sages' mandate to determine continually the details of Torah law was itself established by God. Maimonides distinguishes between a (rather minimal) core revelation that can never be disputed or changed and the remainder of the law, which is rightly traced to rabbinic implementation, and is subject to constant reevaluation.

Because nothing in the received revelation may ever be disputed,

[19] For a critical discussion of this approach, and of the relation of Midrash to the laws it argues for, see David Weiss Halivni, *Midrash, Mishnah, and Gemara: The Jewish Predilection for Justified Law* (Cambridge, Mass.: Harvard University Press, 1986).

Maimonides offers a striking retrospective criterion for determining its scope: Any law about which we find record of (legitimate) disagreement is proven not to have been part of the core revelation! It is worth noting that the criterion is meant to work one way only: Unanimous acceptance is no proof of divine origin.

This Maimonidean view facilitates a plausible answer to the first of our conceptual questions. The core revelation functions like a constitution, setting the parameters for rabbinic legislation. Legal change is easily accounted for with respect to most of the halakhic corpus. The authority of the core "constitution" is, however, held to be absolute: Any change or amendment of the revealed Torah is expressly ruled out—even if authored by God Himself.

Rabbinic Amendment: The Molding of Meaning

In depicting this revealed core ("constitution"), no part of which may be expressly repealed or changed, Maimonides here deemphasizes the manner in which this core itself can be altered.[20] But when describing the Sages' mode of deriving law from Scripture, he does not employ a verb denoting "interpretation" (if indeed there is any verb that means this unambiguously in premodern Hebrew). He merely refers explicitly to the midrashic mode of exposition—which frequently involves the phenomenon illustrated in our examples: namely, the very free license that rabbinic explication takes with respect to the plain meaning of biblical law. Elsewhere, Maimonides himself candidly points to discrepancies between some laws' plain meaning in the biblical text (which reflects God's initial legislative intent) on the one hand, and those laws' halakhic rendition, on the other hand.[21]

In fact, many of the Sages themselves were quite conscious of these discrepancies, talking of them with a sense of achievement rather than discomfort. In an oft-quoted legend, R. Yehudah (in the name of Rav) tells of a visit paid by Moses to the academy of Rabbi 'Akiva, the great hero of bold midrashic innovations:

> When Moses climbed the mountain he found the Holy One, blessed be He, sitting there and fashioning little crowns for the letters. Then he said to Him: Lord of the world, for whose sake are you doing that? He replied: there is a man who will come to be after many generations, called 'Akiva ben Joseph; he

[20] In fact, Maimonides' application of this criterion is somewhat doctrinaire; several laws that he lists as harking back to Sinai can be shown to have been the subject of early disputes.

[21] See Moses Maimonides, *Guide of the Perplexed*, trans. S. Pines (Chicago: University of Chicago Press, 1963), pt. 3, sec. 41, pp. 558, 567.

will one day derive heaps and heaps of doctrines concerning every little hook. Then he said before Him: Lord of the world, show him to me. He replied: turn around. Then he turned around and sat behind the eighth row, but he did not understand their conversation and was dismayed. When 'Akiva came to a point about which his students asked him how he knew, he replied to them that this was a doctrine given to Moses on Sinai. Then Moses was calmed— (T.B., Menahot 29b)[22]

The very sanctification of the text became a fountainhead for great creativity. Not one word of the divine Torah could be changed, but the meaning of its words was radically subject to rabbinic determination. Should such radical reinterpretation be classified as "amendment"? Before attempting to answer, let us see one further reflection of the way the Sages viewed the nature of their enterprise; the text is presented as an answer to a person denying the authority of the Mishnah:

> Both Scripture and Mishnah are the words of God. What, then, is the difference between Scripture and Mishnah? This can be learned from the parable of a king who had two dear servants. He gave to each a measure of wheat and a bundle of flax. So what did the clever one do? He took the flax and wove it into a cloth, and he took the wheat and made it into flower; he sieved and milled it, kneaded it and baked it. Then he arranged it on the table, spread the cloth over it and put it aside to await the king's arrival. As for the foolish one, he did nothing at all. Eventually the king came into his house and said to them, "My sons, bring me what I gave you." The one brought out the bread upon the table, with the cloth spread over it; and the other brought out the wheat in a basket, with the bundle of flax on top of it. Oh, the shame of it! Oh, the disgrace! Now, you must admit which of them would be the more favored—he who brought out the table with the bread upon it!
>
> Thus when the Holy One, blessed be He, gave the Torah to Israel, what he gave them was wheat to be made into flower, and flax to be made into cloth. (*Seder Eliyyahu Zuta*, chap. 2)[23]

The metaphor is quite striking: That which was received from God was given as *raw material*, to be worked and made into something useful. The opposite attitude, that of slavishly preserving the divine gift of Torah in its original form, is explicitly caricatured.

This framework facilitates an intelligible account of the working of Midrash, such as depicted above in our two examples. Rendering the

---

[22] The translation here mostly follows Walter Kaufmann, who quotes this passage in a discussion of "Judaism and Truth" in *Critique of Religion and Philosophy* (New York: Harper, 1958), pp. 193–94. The word I give here as *derive* was rendered by Kaufmann "present"; the original is a verb constructed from "d.r.sh.," the same root as for Midrash.

[23] Translation adapted from that offered by Zohar, "The Consumption of Sabbatical Year Produce," p. 103, n. 2.

word *lo* ("to himself") as embodying a far-reaching qualification, sub-
verting in effect the plain intent of the biblical law, is not meant to pose
as a plausible "interpretation." Rather, by infusing this word with an
artificial significance, the Sages are recasting the entire passage, making
wheat into bread and flax into cloth: transforming utopian vision into
realistic law.

I do not mean to imply that this was the only theological model by
which the authors of Midrash understood their own enterprise. There is
no reason to assume that one uniform understanding was shared by all
of the Sages; other sources can support a view like that of R. Sherira.
Indeed, the first of the two texts cited here (the story of Moses on the
mountain) might suggest an alternative model, that of deciphering a
code: R. 'Akiva's midrashic expositions astonished Moses, but had they
not been foreseen by God?

Yet the image of treating the text as raw material seems best suited for
making sense of the numerous instances of Midrash represented by our
second example, which involves not mere alteration in the meaning of
words but outright violence to syntactic strings. "You may eat from the
field" is rendered, in effect, "*You may eat* [from stores at home, *as long
as* some produce is available] *from the field.*" The phrase "from the field"
is commandeered into a sort of symbolic service, made to stand for a
time span. In the previous example, the Sages redefined a crucial word,
and were thus able to elegantly alter the meaning of the passage and the
scope of the law. Here their work is textually less elegant; this emphasizes more clearly the drastic legal shift achieved.

If the term *interpretation* is reserved for renditions constrained by the
text's plain meaning, then Midrash is surely not interpretation; however,
even *amendment* seems too mild a term for describing the midrashic
freedom celebrated by the Sages. In (modern) constitutional amendment, alteration of a legal norm involves changing the constitution's
text; in order to override the text's authority, a formal procedure is required for an appeal to the sovereign people.[24] In rabbinic Judaism,
however, there is no authority that can override the absolute commitment to the initial revelation. The text is eternally fixed; but its meaning
is ultimately fluid. Paradoxically, the very supreme authority carried by
the revealed "constitution" seems to make the control of its (legally
binding) meaning into a vehicle for radical change.[25]

[24] Such an alteration is thus formally recognized as more fundamental than ordinary
legal change, which, leaving the constitution intact, remains bound to its authority.

[25] That rabbinic "interpretation" is unconstrained by the language of Scripture does not
necessarily imply that there were no other constraints. These could be substantial, such as
notions about God's character, entailing constraints on what might be attributed to Him
(I owe this point to Jeff Stout), or social, that is, the limits of what the community will
accept; see Mishna Horayot 1:3, 5.

Appendix

Amending Provisions of Selected New Constitutions in Eastern Europe

Albania

Albania has no special procedure for amendment. A constitutional amendment is enacted as any other piece of legislation.

Bulgaria

§153: The National Assembly shall be free to amend all provisions of the Constitution except those within the prerogatives of the Grand National Assembly.

§154: 1. The initiative to introduce a constitutional amendment bill shall belong to one-fourth of the members of the National Assembly and to the president.

2. An amendment bill shall be debated by the National Assembly not earlier than one month and not later than three months from the date on which it is introduced.

§155 1. A constitutional amendment shall require a majority of three-fourths of the votes of all members of the National Assembly in three ballots on three different days.

2. A bill that has received less than three-fourths but more than two-thirds of the votes of all members shall be eligible for reintroduction after not fewer than two months and not more than five months. To be passed at this new reading, the bill shall require a majority of two-thirds of the votes of all members.

§158: Only a Grand National Assembly is able:

—to adopt a new constitution
—change the territory of Bulgaria
—change the form of state structure
—amend §5 (2) and (4) (relating to the direct application of the Constitution and the application of international agreements)
—amend §57 (1) and (3) (irrevocability of human rights)
—amend Chapter 9 (pertaining to the method of amendment)

This Appendix was compiled by Christian Lucky.

§160(1): A two-thirds vote is required in the Assembly to call a Grand National Assembly.

§162: At the Grand National Assembly, a two-thirds majority vote is required on three different days for any proposal to be effected.

§162(1): A Grand Assembly can only resolve the constitutional amendment bills for which it was elected.

Croatia

§87: The Chamber of Representatives may call a referendum on a proposal for the amendment of the Constitution, a bill or on any other issue falling within its competence.

The president of the republic may, on the proposal of the government and with the countersignature of the president of the government call a referendum on a proposal for the amendment of the Constitution.

In such a referendum a decision is made by the majority of the voters who voted provided that the majority of the total number of electors have taken part in the referendum. Decisions made at referenda are binding.

§136: The right to propose an amendment of the Constitution of the republic belongs to at least one-fifth of the representatives of the Chamber of Representatives, the president, and the government.

§138: A decision to amend the Constitution on the basis of a prior opinion of the Chamber of Counties is made by the Chamber of Representatives by a two-thirds majority vote of all representatives.

Hungary

The Hungarian Constitution has no special method outlined for constitutional amendment, save that under §24(3), the affirmative votes of two-thirds of the members of Parliament are required.

Poland

§160: Amendments are made by a joint resolution of the Sejm and Senate passed by a majority of two-thirds of votes.

§161: Appears to give the president final power to ratify an amendment proposal that has passed the Sejm and Senate.

§161(1): Appears to require that a national referendum take place on any proposed amendment endorsed by five hundred thousand citizens.

The referendum comes after the proposal has passed the Sejm and the Senate and before the proposal goes to the president for signature. That is, there can be no referendum unless a proposal has passed the Sejm and the Senate. If the referendum fails, then the proposal is dead. If it passes, then the president is compelled to sign it.

Romania

§146(1): Revision of the Constitution may be initiated by the president on proposal of the government, by at least one-fourth of the number of deputies or senators, as well as by at least five hundred thousand citizens with the right to vote.

§146(2): The citizens who initiate the revision of the Constitution must belong to at least half the number of the counties in the country and in each respective county or in the city of Bucharest at least twenty thousand signatures must be recorded in support of this initiative.

§147(1): The draft proposal [of an amendment] must be adopted by the Chamber of Deputies and the Senate, by a majority of at least two-thirds of the members of each chamber.

§147(3): The revision shall be final after approval by a referendum held within thirty days from the date of passing the draft of the proposed revision.

Limitations on Amendment

§148(1): The provisions of this Constitution with regard to the national, independent, unitary, and indivisible character of the Romanian state, the republican form of government, territorial integrity, independence of the judiciary, political pluralism, and official language shall not be subject to revision.

§148(2): No revision shall be made if it results in the suppression of the citizens' fundamental rights and freedoms, or the safeguards thereof.

§148(3): The Constitution may not be revised during a state of emergency or war.

Russia (Constitution Ratified in December 1993)

§92.3: When the president is unable to perform his duties, the acting president of the Russian Federation does not have the right to submit proposals on amendments to the constitution.

§134: Provides for the initiation of constitutional amendments by the president of the Russian Federation, the Federation Council, the State Duma, the government of the Russian Federation, legislative (representative) organs of subjects of the Russian Federation, and also by a group composed of at least one-fifth of the members of the Federation Council or deputies of the State Duma.

§136: States that amendments to Chapters 3–8 of the constitution are adopted if approved by a majority of at least three-fourths of the total number of members of the Federation Council and at least two-thirds of the total number of deputies of the State Duma, and come into force after they have been approved by the organs of legislative power of at least two-thirds of the subjects of the Russian Federation.

§135: By contrast, stipulates that revisions of Chapters 1, 2, and 9 (outlining basic rights and amending procedures) of the constitution must first be supported by a vote of three-fifths of the total number of members of the Federation Council and deputies of the State Duma. In this case, in accordance with federal constitutional law, a Constitutional Assembly will be convened. This Constitutional Assembly either confirms the immutability of the constitution or elaborates a draft of a new constitution, which is adopted by the Constitutional Assembly by a vote of two-thirds of the total number of its members or is submitted to a nationwide vote. If a nationwide vote is held, the constitution is considered adopted if votes for it are cast by more than one-half of voters casting their votes, provided that more than one-half of voters have cast their votes.

§66.5: States that the status of a territorial subject of the Russian Federation can be changed only with the consent of that subject, whether it be a kray, oblast, city of federal significance, autonomous oblast, or autonomous okrug.

Slovenia

§168: Allows initiation of amendments by no fewer than twenty deputies of the National Assembly, by the government, or by thirty thousand voters.

§169–170: Ratification may be by a two-thirds majority of all deputies voting or by a national referendum, if demanded by thirty deputies.

Ukraine

§256: Allows initiation of amendments either by one-third of the members of each house or by petition of two million electors, with ratification by either two-thirds of the members of each house or by an all-Ukrainian referendum.

§257: No amendments to the Constitution may be introduced that are directed against the independence and territorial integrity of the Ukraine; that are aimed at altering the rule of the Constitution, restricting defined forms of property, or limiting human rights; or that are added under the condition of an emergency.

Contributors

BRUCE ACKERMAN is the Sterling Professor of Law and Political Science at Yale University

AKHIL REED AMAR is the Southmayd Professor of Law at the Yale Law School

MARK E. BRANDON is Professor of Political Science at the University of Oklahoma

DAVID R. DOW is Professor of Law at the University of Houston Law Center

STEPHEN M. GRIFFIN is Professor of Law at the Tulane University School of Law

STEPHEN HOLMES is Professor of Political Science and Law at the University of Chicago

SANFORD LEVINSON is the W. St. John Garwood and W. St. John Garwood Jr. Regents Chair in Law at the University of Texas Law School

DONALD S. LUTZ is Professor of Political Science at the University of Houston

WALTER F. MURPHY is the Edward S. Corwin Professor of Politics at Princeton University

FREDERICK SCHAUER is Frank Stanton Professor of the First Amendment at the John F. Kennedy School of Government at Harvard University

CASS R. SUNSTEIN is the Karl N. Llewellyn Professor of Jurisprudence at the University of Chicago Law School

JOHN R. VILE is Chair, Department of Political Science, Middle Tennessee State University

NOAM J. ZOHAR is a member of the faculty of the Bar-Illan University in Israel and a fellow of the Shalom Hartman Institute of Jewish Philosophy in Jerusalem

Index

Ackerman, Bruce, 7, 33–35, 51, 118, 119, 125–27, 130, 131–36, 141, 147, 156n.27, 276–77, 279n.9
Akiva, Rabbi, 142–43, 316, 318
Albania, constitution of, 292, 293
Amar, Akhil Reed, 9, 24n.40, 29, 30, 69n.3, 72n.4, 73, 118, 119, 123–25, 126, 127, 130, 131, 137, 138, 140, 141, 147, 156n.27, 193, 202n.56
"amendment rate," 243–74 passim
Antieu, Chester James, 268
Appleby, Joyce, 58
Article V. *See* United States Constitution
Articles of Confederation, 69, 93–96, 131, 154n.30, 166, 169n.21
Australia: constitution of, 261, 266

Bacon, Selden, 195
Balkin, Jack, 33
Barber, Sotirios, 189, 202, 223–25, 226, 228, 231
Beard, Charles, 233n.62
Becker, Carl Lotus, 165
Bell, John, 132
Berns, Walter F., 181n.59
Bickel, Alexander, 118–19, 129
Blackstone, William, 94, 95, 239
Bolling v. Sharpe, 172
Bork, Robert, 14, 23n.34, 35–36, 83
Brandon, Mark, 9, 10, 193
Breckenridge, John, 132
Brest, Paul, 118n.7
British constitution, 8–9, 155
Brown v. Board of Education, 169
Bulgaria: constitution of, 289–91, 293, 294
Burke, Edmund, 168

Calhoun, John C., 193, 201, 211, 216
Canada: constitution of, 164, 168, 182n.60
Cardozo, Benjamin Nathan, 189
Carroll, Daniel, 97, 99
Civil War (American), 45, 47, 70, 126, 183
Coleman v. Miller, 196

commerce: power of U.S. Congress to regulate, 7–8, 31
Committee on the Constitution System, 38
Constitutional Convention of 1787, 3, 68, 139, 191
constitutional convention under Article V of U.S. Constitution, 6
constitutionalism, 39–43, 178–80, 187, 226, 229, 275, 302–3
Cooley, Thomas M., 193–94
Corwin Amendment, 216, 218–19, 222, 224–25, 228, 231, 234–36
countermajoritarian dilemma, 118, 126, 129–30, 211–12, 277
Czech Republic: constitution of, 291, 292, 293

Dahl, Robert A., 173
Davis, Jefferson, 48, 113, 167
Declaration of Independence, 89, 96n.18, 101, 166, 180, 181, 221, 222, 232–33
DeGaulle, Charles, 283n.17
Dellinger, Walter, 147, 159n.32
Dillon v. Gloss, 6
Douglas, Stephen A., 132, 133
Douglass, Frederick, 30–31, 225, 230n.55, 232
Dred Scott v. Sandford, 126, 133, 169, 199
dualist democracy, 65–66, 84–85, 303–4

Eastland, James O., 186
Elster, Jon, 281
Equal Rights Amendment, 5, 30
Estonia: constitution of, 291, 293, 294
extension of time for ratification of proposed amendments, 5

Federal Farmer, 102
Federalist, The: No. 1, 110; No. 39, 140; No. 40, 178; No. 43, 128, 141; No. 49, 4, 43; No. 78, 97n.23; No. 84, 27; No. 85, 128–41
Finer, Herman, 176–77
Finn, John E., 183
flag-burning amendment to U.S. Constitution (proposed), 202

formalism, 84–86
France: constitution of, 180, 261
Frankfurter, Felix, 15, 185
Freundel, Barry, 20n.25
Fundamental Constitutions of 1669, 3–4

Garrison, William Lloyd, 233
Geremek, Branislaw, 301
Germany: constitution of, 17, 170, 176, 177, 184, 261, 178, 179, 296–97, 305
Gerry, Elbridge, 191
Gibbons v. Ogden, 169
Ginsburg, Ruth Bader, 30n.54
Godel, Kurt, 10
Golak Nath's Case, 168, 176n.40, 178n.49
Goncz, Arpad, 282
Graham, Howard Jay, 32n.63
Greenawalt, Kent, 156
Griffin, Stephen, 4, 7
Grimes, Alan P., 112
Gunther, Gerald, 147

Halakha (Jewish law), 8, 20n.25, 307, 310–18
Hamilton, Alexander, 27, 19, 95n.16, 97n.23, 128, 139, 141, 191, 228
Hammer v. Dagenhart, 172n.29, 195
Hans v. Louisiana, 172n.29
Harper v. Virginia Board of Elections, 31–32
Harris, William P., 16, 21, 168–69, 202, 226–28, 232
Hart, H.L.A., 146, 149–51
Hatch, Orrin G., 15n.5
Havel, Vaclav, 285
Hawking, Stephen W., 171
Heller, Francis H., 200
Henry, Patrick, 102–3, 105, 107, 141
Hoar, Roger Sherman, 109–10
Hobbes, Thomas, 233
Holmes, Oliver Wendell, Jr., 13–14, 166, 172
Holmes, Stephen, 10–11, 34, 40n.14
Home Building & Loan Association v. Blaisdell, 24
Hughes, Charles Evans, 24
Hume, David, 230
Hungary: constitution of, 289–90, 292, 293, 294, 297

index of difficulty of amendment, 256–60, 262–64

"interpretation" (distinguished from "amendment"), 14–18, 21, 24, 33, 259n.32, 241, 279, 308, 311–13, 317–18
Iredell, James, 27
Ireland: constitution of, 180, 261
Isaacson, Eric, 203–6
Israel: constitution of, 8–9
Italy: constitution of, 176, 261

Jaruzelski, Woyciech, 282
Jefferson, Thomas, 24, 42, 90, 91, 92, 101–2, 121n.19, 129, 181, 185, 225, 233
Johnson, Andrew, 48, 75–77, 80, 81

Kant, Immanuel, 167
Kara'ites, 314
Kelsen, Hans, 146, 149, 152, 155–56, 157
Khasbulatov, Ruslan, 281
Kohl, Helmut, 17

Latvia: constitution of, 293, 294
Levinson, Sanford, 37, 147, 202
Lincoln, Abraham, 31, 48, 75, 81, 132, 133, 134, 169–70, 209n.84, 216–17, 219, 234
Lithuania: constitution of, 291, 293
"living Constitution," 13
Lochner v. New York, 82, 83
Locke, John, 3, 101, 137–38, 233, 238
Lutz, Donald, 10, 121n.18

Macedonia: constitution of, 292–93
Madison, James, 4, 16, 17, 21, 22, 29, 43, 65, 70, 94–95, 97, 99, 106, 114, 128, 137, 138, 139, 140, 166, 178, 191–92, 208
Maimonides, Moses, 310, 315–16
Marbury, William, 194–95
Marbury v. Madison, 23, 126, 169, 216
March, James G., 179n.52
Marshall, John, 21–24, 167, 181n.59, 198, 215, 232
Maryland: constitution of, 96–97
Mason, George, 3, 101, 192
McBride, James, 203n.57
McCarthy, Joseph, 186
McCulloch v. Maryland, 21–24, 32, 34, 126, 169, 181n.59
McPherson, James, 47, 167
Merlin the Magician, 171, 190

Midrash, 307, 310–15, 317–18
Moses, 316–17
Mundt, Karl, 186
Murphy, Walter, 9, 10, 19, 121–22, 193, 196–210, 221–22, 226, 228, 229n.52, 231

"nested opposition," 33
New Deal, 34, 51, 54, 67, 68, 69, 70, 75, 79–82, 126, 134, 279n.9
Nixon, Richard, 186
Norway: constitution of, 176, 261

Olsen, Johan P., 179n.51

Pendleton, Edmund, 105, 107
Planned Parenthood v. Casey, 83
Poland: constitution of, 289–90, 292, 293–94
popular sovereignty, 81–113 passim, 119–22, 124, 125, 132, 136, 187–88, 207, 211, 220, 226–27, 232, 237–41, 243, 246, 251, 263–64, 267, 270, 279
Pozsgay, Imre, 282

Queen v. Keegstra, 184

Ramsay, David, 100
Randolph, John, 172
R.A.V. v. St. Paul, 185
Raven v. Deukmejian, 20, 177
Rawls, John, 180, 184
Reagan, Ronald, 68, 82–84
Reconstruction (following U.S. civil war), 48, 67, 68, 69, 73–74, 76–77, 79, 132–33, 183
Rehnquist, William, 13, 14, 29
rescision by a state of its ratification of a proposed amendment, 5
"revision" (as distinguished from "amendment"), 19–20, 176–77, 240
Roane, Spencer, 22
Roe v. Wade, 83
Romania: constitution of, 289–91, 293
Roosevelt, Franklin D., 51–53, 54, 70, 80, 81, 134–35, 174
Rosen, Jeffrey, 203, 206–11
Rosenau, Pauline Marie, 171
Rousseau, Jean-Jacques, 124n.31
rule of recognition, 149–52, 154, 155, 156
Russia: constitution of, 291, 293
Rutledge, John, 139, 192

Scalia, Antonin, 83, 185
Schauer, Frederick, 28n.47, 31n.61
Seward, William, 133
Sherira, Rabbi, 314–15, 318
Sherman, Roger, 139, 192, 195, 208
slavery, 46, 192, 217–18, 224–25, 232–34
Slovakia: constitution of, 297
Spooner, Lysander, 221, 225
Stafford, Jo, 164
state constitutions (within United States), 45, 246–60
Stevens, Wallace: "Crude Foyer," 142
Sturm, Albert, 246
Suber, Peter, 17n.13, 22n.31
Sunstein, Cass, 10–11, 34
Sutherland, George, 24
Swayne, Noah, 183

Tammelo, Ilman, 152
Texas v. Johnson, 202, 209
Tocqueville, Alexis de, 41
Torah, 121, 143
Tribe, Laurence, 147
Trudeau, Pierre, 164

Ukraine: constitution of, 291–92, 293, 294
United States Constitution
—Article I, 117
—Article V, 5–7, 9–10, 21, 36, 71–74, 90–92, 105, 112, 114, 117–18, 122, 127–29, 136–44 passim, 146–47, 168, 175, 191–93, 200, 205, 216, 221–22, 225–27, 257
—Article VII, 95–97, 103, 109, 114, 131, 227
—Bill of Rights, 27, 56, 208
—First Amendment, 27–23, 107, 175n.40, 187, 196–97, 203–5
—Fifth Amendment, 172
—Ninth Amendment, 106–7, 181n.59, 206–10, 221, 227n.46
—Tenth Amendment, 29, 106–7, 208, 221, 226n.46
—Thirteenth Amendment, 19, 30–31, 75, 183, 193
—Fourteenth Amendment, 32, 75–76, 77–78, 183
—Fifteenth Amendment, 31–32, 183, 194
—Sixteenth Amendment, 60
—Seventeenth Amendment, 50, 60
—Eighteenth Amendment, 194

—Nineteenth Amendment, 31–32, 194
—Twenty-fourth Amendment, 32
—Twenty-seventh Amendment, 5–6, 25
United States v. Eichman, 202, 209

Vattel, Emmerich de, 94
Vile, John, 9, 10, 147, 220n.22
Virginia Delcaration of Rights, 99, 101

Walesa, Lech, 282, 284n.17
Walter, Francis, 186
Washington, George, 3, 5, 65, 140, 295n.39
Webster, Noah, 41, 163, 170, 189

welfare state, 55, 68
White, C. A., 19
White, James Boyd, 22–23, 25, 32, 34
Willkie, Wendell, 168
Wilson, James, 27, 98, 103, 105, 107, 110, 113
Winston, David, 143
Winthrop, James, 195
Wittgenstein, Ludwig, 143
Wood, Gordon, 107, 233n.62

Yeltsin, Boris, 281

Zohar, Noam, 8